Python Simplified with Generative AI

Hands-on Python development with GenAI tools
integrating data science and web interfaces

Duc T. Haba

Ashley R. Haba

Evan M. Haba

bpb

www.bpbonline.com

First Edition 2025

Copyright © BPB Publications, India

ISBN: 978-93-6589-933-7

LIMITS OF LIABILITY AND DISCLAIMER OF WARRANTY

To View Complete
BPB Publications Catalogue
Scan the QR Code:

Dedicated to

How can you measure the depth of a mom's love? It's in the quiet moments that shape our lives. Like a snowy day in Nebraska, with a mom at the wheel of an old Ford Pinto, driving her son to college through a storm. There's no tragedy, no great epiphany.
Just a mom and her son, inching forward, mile by mile, through the swirling snow. That kind of love carries you, even when the road is hard to see. Thank you, Mom, Phuong Kim, for every mile, every moment, ands every unspoken act of care.
I love you. This book is for you.

- Duc T. Haba

To those who challenge themselves.
Your greatest gift is your perspective; stay creative and curious.

- Ashley R. Haba

My father (Bao) is my inspiration to my work, I started my journey with computer science because I wanted to be like him. Thank you for all your support, I love you. This book is for you.

- Evan M. Haba

About the Authors

- From a researcher at Xerox PARC, Oracle, RRKidz, and Cognizant to becoming a founder of mobile and AI startups, **Duc T. Haba** is a world-class AI thought leader and Chief AI Officer. With 30+ years in software, a Marquis Who's Who Honoree in 2024, an AI book author (two published books), and an AI lecturer and teacher, Duc is well-known in the Silicon Valley as a technology entrepreneurial veteran featured on Apple News in Feb. 2025.

- **Ashley R. Haba** is a senior communication major at Santa Clara University with the goal of learning something new each day. She is minoring in creative writing and has a love for poetry and short-form fiction. Moreover, she enjoys knitting, weightlifting, and trying new foods. With a penchant for writing, Ashley has written over a hundred flash fiction stories and poems centered around mental health and overcoming trauma. Currently, she is working on a series of linked stories and can be found writing plenty of flash fiction pieces.

- **Evan M. Haba** is currently attending his second year at the University of San Francisco, majoring in computer science. He really enjoys swimming and is on his school's water polo club team. Moreover, he loves working on projects with GenAI, and has recently participated in a DEPLOY/24 hackathon where he used GenAI as a part of his projects.

About the Reviewer

Ghaith M. Alomari is an experienced data professional, and IT specialist with a strong background in cloud computing, data science, and automation. He specializes in SQL, Python, Power BI, ML, and cloud-based data solutions. Moreover, he is adept at leveraging tools such as AWS, Snowflake, and Apache NiFi to build efficient data pipelines. His expertise extends to DevOps, DataOps, and infrastructure automation, focusing on ETL processes, business intelligence solutions, and machine learning.

Passionate about optimizing data workflows and automating repetitive tasks, Ghaith continuously explores cutting-edge technologies in machine learning, AI-driven analytics, and cloud infrastructure. As an avid reader, he stays up to date with the latest trends in data, DevOps, and analytics, and he actively engages in technical discussions on data governance, security, and AI-driven business intelligence.

Acknowledgements

We extend our heartfelt gratitude to our family and friends, who patiently endured our odd writing hours and absentminded moments during conversations while our thoughts wandered to what we just wrote and what could be written next. Your support and understanding meant the world to us.

A special thank you to BPB Publications for believing in this project and providing the platform to bring it to life. We are deeply grateful for the insights and encouragement from our editor and the dedicated BPB staff assigned to this book. Your guidance and expertise were invaluable.

We could not have written this book without each of you. Thank you.

Preface

This book bridges the gap between traditional education and the practical challenges students encounter today. Instead of relying on conventional programming guides, it combines hands-on learning with modern Generative AI tools like GPT-4o and Copilot. Written by college students alongside an experienced AI expert, it focuses on meeting the needs of a generation that thrives on creativity, quick access to information, and learning through practical experience.

This book takes a fresh approach to learning by prioritizing exploration and creativity, much like the way Gen Z engages with games, apps, and hands-on activities. Instead of starting with technical details like algorithms and syntax, it introduces coding through interactive, practical projects in Python Jupyter Notebooks. These projects are relatable and grounded in everyday experiences, making the process intuitive and enjoyable.

It is designed specifically for college students who find conventional programming textbooks intimidating. It offers a flexible and personalized learning method, demonstrating how GenAI tools can support your studies. You'll explore Python fundamentals through practical projects while building confidence in your programming skills. The hands-on approach fosters creativity and curiosity, making applying what you have learned to other areas like science, history, or communication easier.

By the end of this book, you will acquire practical skills beyond just understanding Python code. You will learn how to confidently write and debug Python programs using Jupyter Notebooks, working through projects that reflect real-world applications. Throughout this journey, you will also gain a deeper understanding of how to integrate Generative AI tools, such as GPT-4 and Copilot, into your workflow. These tools will serve as collaborators, enhancing your learning and problem-solving abilities.

You will enhance your creative thinking abilities and tackle coding challenges with curiosity and resourcefulness. In addition to coding, the book provides you with transferable skills applicable to various fields. These skills include breaking down complex problems, experimenting with solutions, and adapting tools to meet your needs. Whether you apply these skills in science, history, communication, or other areas, you will gain a strong foundation for learning in an AI world.

Chapter 1: Introduction to GenAI - This chapter is your introduction to Generative AI, focusing on getting started with ChatGPT-4. You will learn what makes GenAI unique, how it works, and the practical ways it can assist you in solving problems, creating content, and exploring new ideas. The chapter provides a step-by-step guide on setting up and accessing GPT-4, ensuring you can start using it immediately. You will also gain insights into prompt engineering—crafting inputs that guide the AI to deliver precise and valuable results. By the end, you will understand how to navigate and use GPT-4 effectively, making it a valuable part of your learning and work process.

Chapter 2: Jupyter Notebook - In this chapter, you will learn about the practical uses of Python Jupyter Notebooks, specifically in the Google Colab environment. The focus will be on combining live code with text, visuals, and interactive widgets, creating a versatile space for data analysis and experimentation tasks. Instead of diving into Python programming immediately, this chapter prioritizes understanding the features of Jupyter Notebooks. You will also explore tools like GPT-4o to help generate and analyze code. Through practical examples, you will develop the skills to explore the tool's capabilities and tailor it to your needs, laying a solid groundwork for more advanced learning in subsequent sections.

Chapter 3: Dissect The Calculator App - This chapter looks at how Generative AI, such as ChatGPT-4o, can enhance your learning of Python programming through a practical project in Jupyter Notebooks. Using a Python-based calculator app as an example, it shows how to break down and understand the code with the support of GenAI's analytical tools. You will follow a clear, step-by-step guide for building the app, using AI to clarify concepts, explain the logic behind the code, and offer suggestions for improvements. Whether you are a beginner or just seeking a new way to learn, this chapter provides a practical approach that combines GenAI assistance with programming, helping you better understand complex concepts and build your confidence in coding.

Chapter 4: Sorting on My Mind - This chapter offers a detailed look at sorting algorithms using Python Jupyter Notebooks and GPT-4o for an interactive learning experience. Sorting is an essential topic in computer science, and it is crucial to understand how different algorithms work for programming and data processing. You will study various algorithms, from bubble sort to quick sort, and implement them in Python to understand their logic and uses. With the help of GPT-4o, you will receive explanations, answers to questions, and code suggestions in real time, providing a personalized learning experience. This hands-on method is designed for learners of all levels to enhance their understanding of sorting algorithms and improve their Python programming skills in an engaging and supportive setting.

Chapter 5: Pandas, the Data Tamer - This chapter covers the Pandas library in Python, which is essential for data manipulation and analysis. It also discusses using Generative AI tools like GPT-4o to write Python Pandas code. This chapter suits learners of all levels and focuses on practical applications. You will learn about Pandas' main features, including working with dataframes and series, cleaning and visualizing data, and applying advanced data manipulation techniques. With the help of Generative AI, the chapter provides straightforward explanations, code examples, and answers your questions to help you understand these concepts better. By engaging in hands-on practice using Jupyter Notebooks, you will develop the skills to work with real-world data and improve your data analysis abilities.

Chapter 6: Decipher CNN App - This chapter covers the steps to create an image classification app using **Convolutional Neural Networks** (**CNNs**) with Fast.ai. You will gain hands-on experience in organizing projects, preparing image data, and training CNNs while receiving real-time assistance to help clarify concepts and answer questions related to coding. By the end of the chapter, you will understand how CNNs detect image patterns, apply these methods to real-world situations, and use AI tools to support your learning. This practical approach involves working with Python, Fast.ai, and AI assistance to make image classification more accessible.

Chapter 7: Gradio and Hugging Face Deployment - This chapter introduces the practical integration of Hugging Face, Gradio, and ChatGPT-4 within Python Jupyter Notebooks, focusing on building and deploying interactive AI applications. You will learn to access and implement advanced Hugging Face models, such as those for natural language processing, and connect them to user-friendly Gradio interfaces for web-based interaction. Along the way, ChatGPT-4o serves as a coding assistant, helping to explain concepts, debug code, and guide you through challenges. By the end of this chapter, you will have the skills to set up a working AI web application, gaining hands-on experience in deploying AI models while improving your understanding of the technology and its real-world applications.

Chapter 8: Fairness and Bias - Chapter 8 explores the critical issues of AI fairness and ethics, using ChatGPT-4o as both a learning tool and a case study. It delves into how biases can arise in AI and GenAI systems, from biased training data to technical decisions, and examines their real-world impacts, such as algorithmic discrimination. Readers will gain practical insights into recognizing and questioning potential biases in AI outputs, learn about current efforts to create fairer AI systems and understand their role as users in advocating for ethical AI practices. By the end of the chapter, you will be equipped to critically evaluate AI and GenAI technologies, make informed decisions in using them, and contribute to a future where AI aligns more closely with human values.

Chapter 9: Your Turn to Be a Code Walker - The last chapter focuses on helping readers determine if a career in programming and computer science is a good fit for their skills, interests, and goals. It looks at the changing role of GPT-4o in programming. It provides a straightforward overview of the field, including the various job opportunities, the importance of problem-solving and teamwork, and the impact of AI-assisted coding. Readers will learn about the necessary skills and mindset for programming, how to use GenAI as a helpful tool, and the overall job landscape in the technology sector. By the end of the chapter, readers will better understand the challenges and benefits associated with pursuing a career in programming, allowing them to make informed choices about their future.

Code Bundle and Coloured Images

Please follow the link to download the
Code Bundle and the *Coloured Images* of the book:

https://rebrand.ly/966to2y

The code bundle for the book is also hosted on GitHub at
https://github.com/bpbpublications/Python-Simplified-with-Generative-AI.
In case there's an update to the code, it will be updated on the existing GitHub repository.

We have code bundles from our rich catalogue of books and videos available at
https://github.com/bpbpublications. Check them out!

Errata

We take immense pride in our work at BPB Publications and follow best practices to ensure the accuracy of our content to provide with an indulging reading experience to our subscribers. Our readers are our mirrors, and we use their inputs to reflect and improve upon human errors, if any, that may have occurred during the publishing processes involved. To let us maintain the quality and help us reach out to any readers who might be having difficulties due to any unforeseen errors, please write to us at :

errata@bpbonline.com

Your support, suggestions and feedbacks are highly appreciated by the BPB Publications' Family.

Did you know that BPB offers eBook versions of every book published, with PDF and ePub files available? You can upgrade to the eBook version at www.bpbonline. com and as a print book customer, you are entitled to a discount on the eBook copy. Get in touch with us at :

business@bpbonline.com for more details.

At **www.bpbonline.com**, you can also read a collection of free technical articles, sign up for a range of free newsletters, and receive exclusive discounts and offers on BPB books and eBooks.

Piracy

If you come across any illegal copies of our works in any form on the internet, we would be grateful if you would provide us with the location address or website name. Please contact us at **business@bpbonline.com** with a link to the material.

If you are interested in becoming an author

If there is a topic that you have expertise in, and you are interested in either writing or contributing to a book, please visit **www.bpbonline.com**. We have worked with thousands of developers and tech professionals, just like you, to help them share their insights with the global tech community. You can make a general application, apply for a specific hot topic that we are recruiting an author for, or submit your own idea.

Reviews

Please leave a review. Once you have read and used this book, why not leave a review on the site that you purchased it from? Potential readers can then see and use your unbiased opinion to make purchase decisions. We at BPB can understand what you think about our products, and our authors can see your feedback on their book. Thank you!

For more information about BPB, please visit **www.bpbonline.com**.

Join our book's Discord space

Join the book's Discord Workspace for Latest updates, Offers, Tech happenings around the world, New Release and Sessions with the Authors:

https://discord.bpbonline.com

Table of Contents

CHAPTER 1
Introduction to GenAI

Introduction

Before discussing Python and GenAI and all of their many complexities, we would want to inform the readers that this introductory chapter is beginner friendly. We will go about this chapter methodically and structure the content in a way that is easy to follow and understand. This chapter will focus on introducing the use of GenAI, familiarizing ourselves with how it can be used and how to use it most effectively. At times, pictures will be provided so that you can follow along with what is being done to get hands-on experience completing the tasks. At other times, summaries will be provided with opinions or thoughts on the researched material from GenAI.

Let us get started, shall we?

Structure

In this chapter, we will cover the following topics:

- Understanding GenAI
- Using GenAI to understand GenAI
- Understanding Python
- Prompt engineering

- GenAI limitation
- Security and privacy

Objectives

In this chapter, we are focusing on a few key things. By the end, you will know how to access GenAI, specifically GPT-4, and set up Python on your computer. These tools are the foundation for everything we do, so it is essential to get comfortable with them now. Along the way, we will introduce the basics of Python and show how we will use it to tackle practical projects throughout this book.

We will also take time to understand what GenAI is and how to use it effectively. This chapter includes recognizing its strengths and limitations and learning how to craft prompts that get the best results. By the end of this chapter, you will be ready to use GenAI as a tool to support your learning and problem-solving.

Let us jump in and start exploring GenAI.

Understanding GenAI

GenAI, or Generative AI, stands for Generative Artificial Intelligence. GenAI refers to a set of technologies that are capable of creating original content based on patterns and information that they learn from extensive datasets. In other words, they are able to create new things from existing information, whether that be text, images, music, videos, or code. A few key characteristics of GenAI are:

- **Learning from data:** GenAI systems are trained on large amounts of data, using methods like deep learning- which is an AI that uses layered neural networks to analyze different data forms, then learning from these patterns- to recognize complex patterns and understand structures within the data.

- **Content creation:** Unlike traditional AI that focuses on processing and analyzing data, GenAI actively creates new content, which can range from composing music to drafting articles, and from creating virtual environments to designing graphical content.

- **Adaptability:** These models can adapt to various styles, genres, and requirements, making them incredibly versatile tools in creative industries.

- **Automation and efficiency:** GenAI can significantly speed up content creation processes, automate repetitive creative tasks, and assist in generating ideas and prototypes.

In this chapter, we will use terms like Generative AI and GenAI interchangeably, both being used to reference Generative Artificial Intelligence. We will use the GenAI platform ChatGPT-4 in this textbook.

Note: GenAI is NOT the same as just regular AI. GenAI and regular AI differ primarily in their outputs and functions. Regular AI interprets and processes data to make decisions or predictions, used for things, such as identifying spam emails or recommending products. GenAI creates new content, drawing from learned data patterns. It generates text, images, music, or code that mimic the input data's style but are original creations. The picture below was created using ChatGPT!

We asked GenAI DALL-E 3 to generate an image that shows the difference between GenAI and traditional AI.

Figure 1.1: ChatGPT interpretation of the difference between AI and GenAI

Figure 1.1 is a striking image. On the right, you will see an elegant, colorful depiction of a woman surrounded by swirling, smoky hues. On the left, there is a contrasting black-and-white image of a woman augmented with mechanical gears.

Now that we have a solid understanding of what GenAI is, let us go over how to access and use the platform.

Importance of GenAI

GenAI is becoming increasingly popular, and its importance is evident across various sectors. The following are a handful of reasons as to why GenAI is considered important, highlighting how it can be used in today's world:

Innovation in content creation: GenAI tools like DALL-E, GPT (like ChatGPT), Gemini, and others are transforming content creation by enabling the rapid production of original content, ranging from art and music to complex written material and interactive media. This not only speeds up the creative process, but also democratizes content creation, allowing more individuals and organizations to produce high-quality content without extensive resources.

- **Automation and efficiency:** GenAI enhances productivity and efficiency. For instance, it can automate repetitive tasks such as data entry, content moderation, and even coding, which allows human workers to focus on more complex and strategic topics.

- **Personalization:** AI can analyze vast amounts of data to generate personalized content for users, such as targeted advertisements, personalized shopping experiences, or customized news feeds. This level of personalization improves user engagement and satisfaction.

- **Educational tool:** In education, GenAI can create customized learning materials that adapt to the skill level and learning pace of students individually. AI tutors can provide additional support and guidance, offering explanations, generating practice problems, and even assessing student work.

- **Healthcare advances:** In healthcare, generative models are used to synthesize medical data, create personalized medicine, and generate training materials for various medical conditions. These models can help in understanding disease patterns, drug discovery, and providing virtual assistance to patients and healthcare providers.

- **Enhancing research and development:** GenAI can accelerate R&D cycles in scientific fields by generating hypotheses, designing experiments, and analyzing data much faster than traditional methods. This is crucial in fields like pharmacology, environmental science, and materials engineering.

- **Entertainment and media:** In the media and entertainment industries, GenAI is used to generate realistic special effects, create new forms of interactive media, and even script and plot stories.

Overall, the importance of GenAI lies in its vast potential to impact various aspects of life, improving efficiency, fostering creativity, and offering solutions that were previously impossible or economically unfeasible. Now that we understand possible uses, we can take a look at how to access ChatGPT-4.

Accessing ChatGPT-4

In this section, we will go over how to access ChatGPT-4, which is the platform we will be using throughout this textbook. This includes the following five-step process with figures to walk you through the accessing and downloading of ChatGPT-4:

1. Start by bringing up a browser and typing **https://chat.openai.com/** into the search bar. You can also just search ChatGPT and pick the option that brings you to that link. The following figure showcases the searching of search engine for ChatGPT:

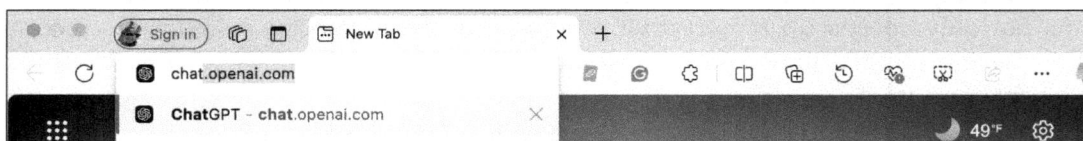

Figure 1.2: Searching in search engine for ChatGPT

Figure 1.2 shows the web browser search for ChatGPT website.

The following figure showcases the ChatGPT website:

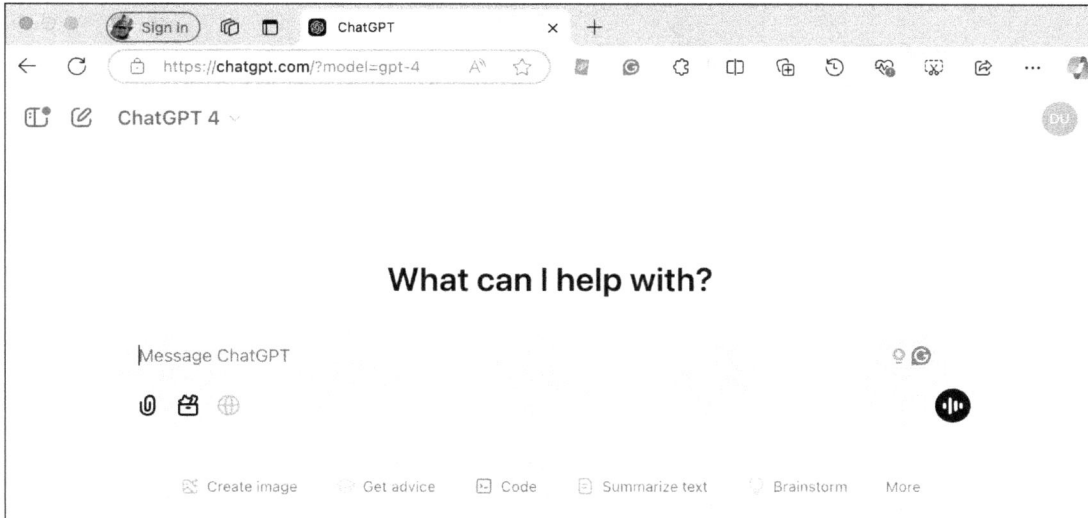

Figure 1.3: *ChatGPT website*

Figure 1.3 shows the ChatGPT website as of November 2024.

Let us now make sure we have the right version.

To ensure that you have the correct version of ChatGPT, look at the upper middle left-hand side of your screen. You should see a button that reads *ChatGPT 4*. Click on that. The following figure shows what the screen should look like after clicking:

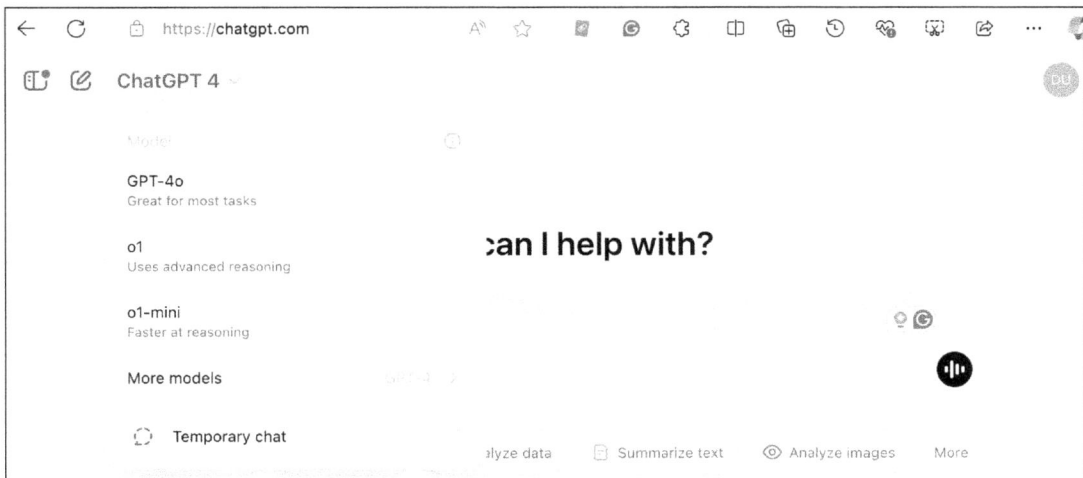

Figure 1.4: *Hovering options on ChatGPT website*

Figure 1.4 shows the options for ChatGPT models as of November 2024.

Right now, you must be using version 4 of ChatGPT, which is great for everyday tasks, however, to learn Python we will need to purchase ChatGPT 4o.

Click **Upgrade to Plus** under the ChatGPT-4 option. If you do not already have an account, this will bring you to a screen on which you are able to create an account. Go ahead and use whichever email you would like your account to be linked to and create your account. Make sure you are signed in. The following figure shows the **Create an account** screen:

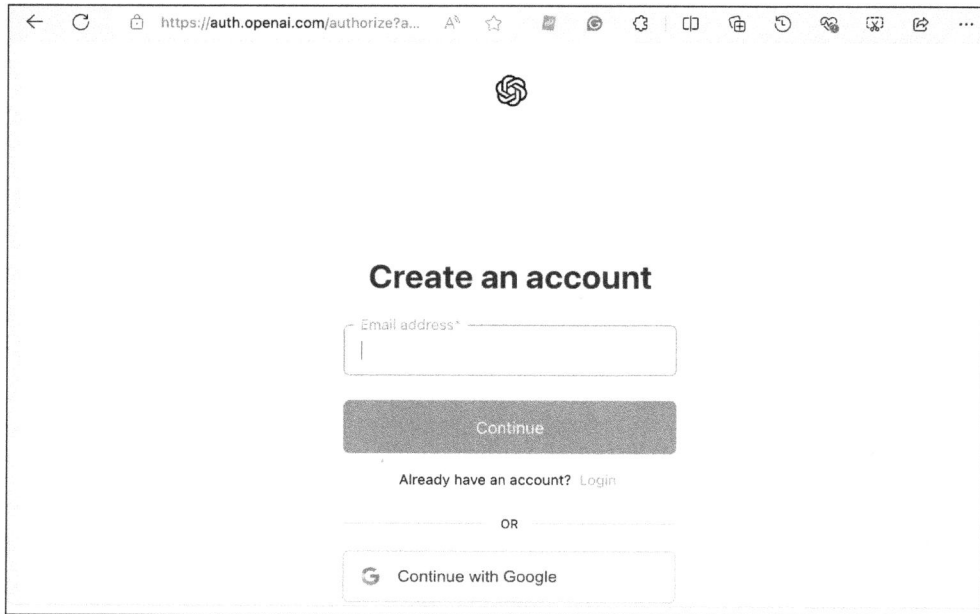

Figure 1.5: *ChatGPT account creation page*

Figure 1.5 shows the ChatGPT account creation page as of November 2024.

Once you sign in, navigate to that upper left-hand corner mentioned in *step 2*. If you already have an account, this will bring you to a screen where you can see the plan options. The following figure shows the plan options:

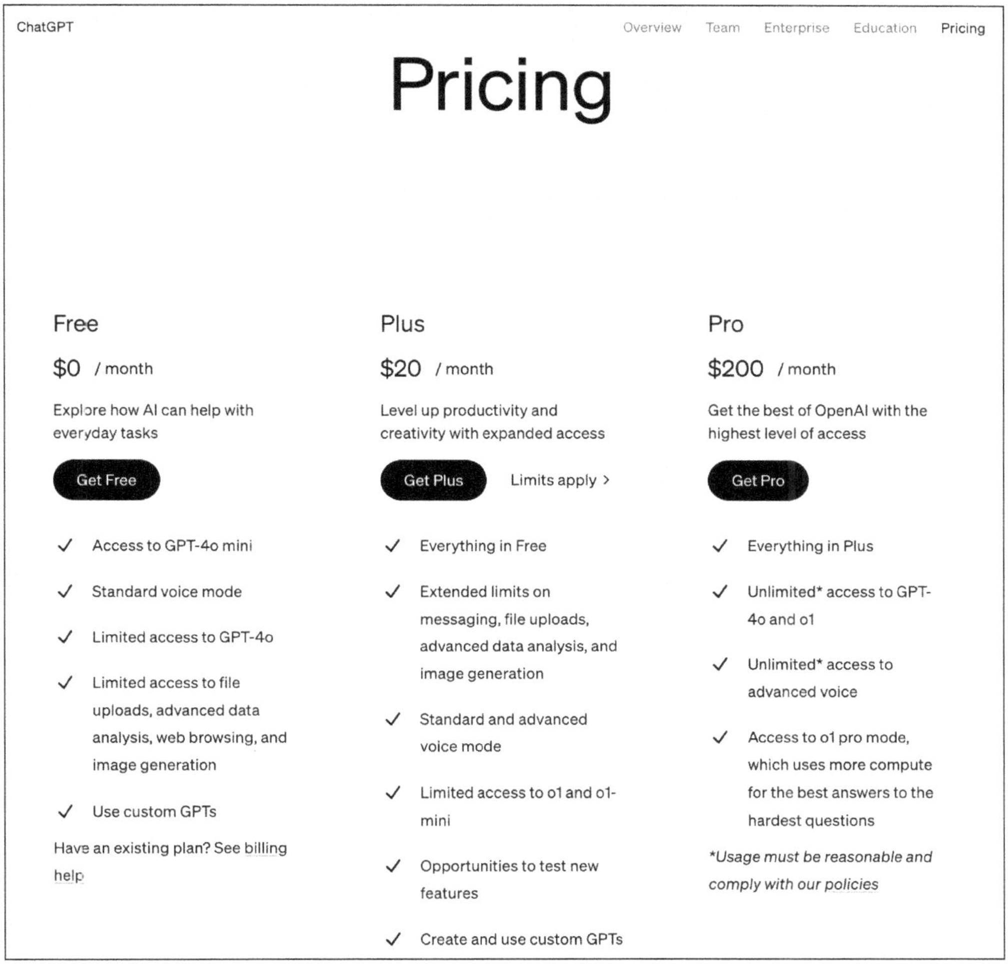

Figure 1.6: *ChatGPT plan options*

Figure 1.6 shows the ChatGPT pricing plan options as of November 2024.

We want to upgrade to Plus, so let us choose that option.

Click on **Get Plus**. This will bring you to a payment screen where you can input your email linked to the account, the payment method, and the billing address. Go ahead and put in your information to pay, then when you are done, press **Subscribe** to submit your payment.

Reload the site or research for ChatGPT so that the information updates. Navigate your cursor to the upper middle-left again and ensure that you are using *ChatGPT 4o* or the newest version of ChatGPT, not *ChatGPT 4 mini*.

The following figure showcases what your screen should look like now:

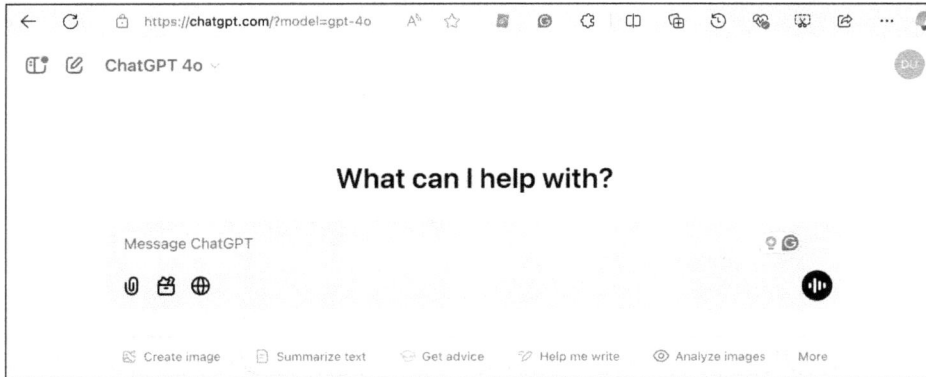

Figure 1.7: *ChatGPT, version 4o, as seen in the upper left corner*

Figure 1.7 shows the ChatGPT 4o paid version as of November 2024.

It is important to note that ChatGPT 4o will look the same on every device, whether that be a laptop, an iPhone, a tablet, or a desktop computer. As it is accessed online, go to your preferred browser and search for the website. Alternatively, there is a ChatGPT app that you can download if you prefer to have the website in app form.

The following figure showcases how the ChatGPT app looks in the Apple app store website:

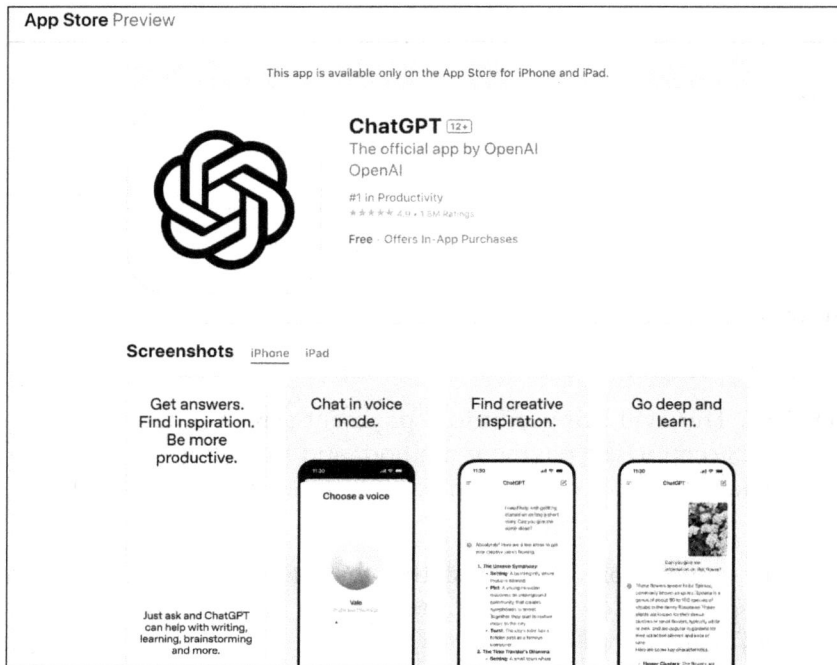

Figure 1.8: *ChatGPT app on the Apple app store*

Just a quick heads-up: there are a lot of ChatGPT apps on the Apple Store with similar names and black-and-white swirl icons. Make sure to choose the one shown in *Figure 1.8*. The developer is OpenAI.

The following figure showcases ChatGPT on the Google Play website:

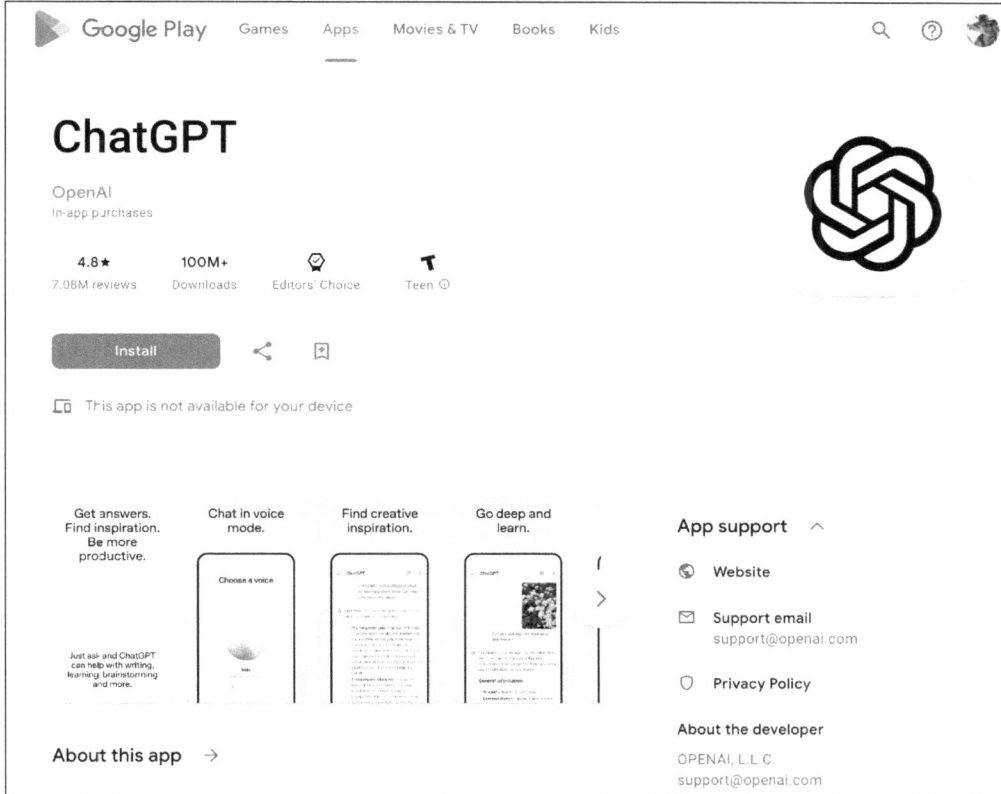

Figure 1.9: *ChatGPT app on Google Play*

A friendly reminder: there are plenty of ChatGPT apps on Google Play with similar names and black-and-white swirl icons. Be sure to choose the one shown in *Figure 1.9*. The developer is OpenAI.

Feel free to use whichever form of the site that's most comfortable. Regardless of if you choose to use the online website or the downloadable app, you will have access to the same content and same abilities. Now we can use GenAI and have its full potential at our fingertips. Now what? In particular, the two topics are as follows:

- Using GenAI to understand GenAI
- Application

Let us begin with understanding GenAI.

Using GenAI to understand GenAI

Before collaborating on this book, we had barely ever used GenAI. We had heard about it from friends using it mainly for their assignments and was not sure if it was something that would be helpful to us. We were unaware of its uses and how it could make a difference in our academic experiences. Needless to say, we had a lot of questions.

We can start off by familiarizing ourselves with ChatGPT-4o. We started by asking it plainly, **What is GenAI?**.

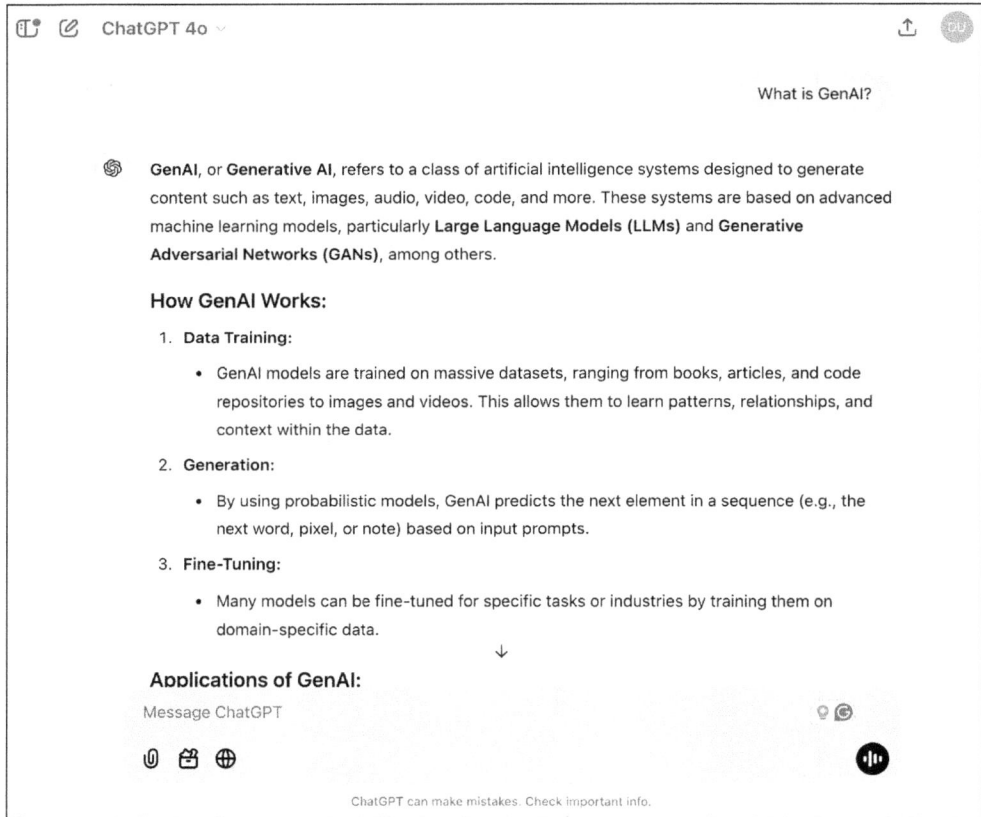

Figure 1.10: ChatGPT's response to "What is GenAI?"

In *Figure 1.10*, a few of the terms were unfamiliar, so to experiment with GenAI, let us ask the **artificial intelligence** (**AI**) to summarize what GenAI is in 50 words or less. This will present us with a concise response. The following figure shows GenAI's response to being asked to summarize in 50 words or less:

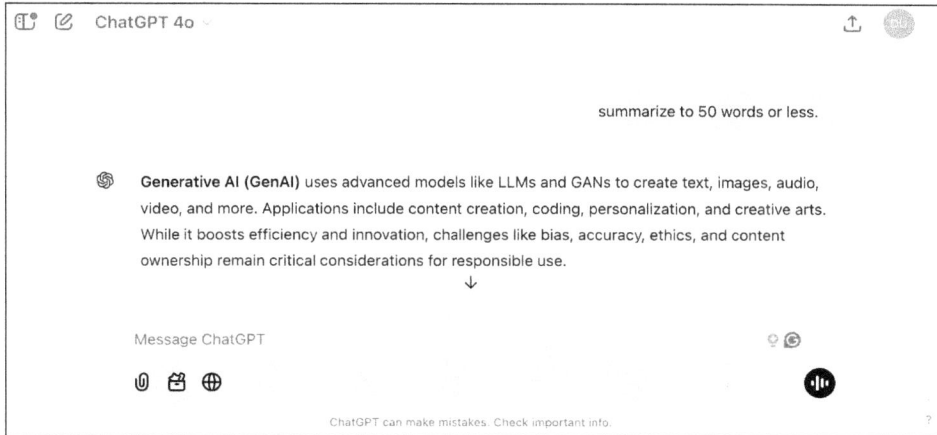

Figure 1.11: *ChatGPT's response 50 words*

Figure 1.11 shows ChatGPT's response to **Summarize what GenAI is in 50 words or less**.

Next, let us ask it to explain what GenAI is to an elementary school student so we can see it in simple language. The following figure shows the GenAI's response:

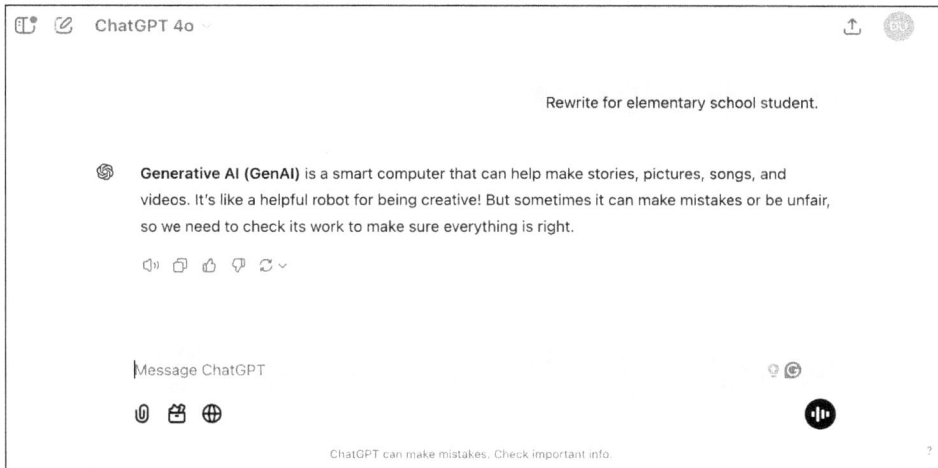

Figure 1.12: *Kid version*

Figure 1.12 shows ChatGPT's response to summarize what GenAI is to an elementary school student. It uses terms like robot, smart computer, stories, and pictures, making it easier for kids to understand and relate to.

Having access to such quick summarizing is extremely useful. Continuing to prompt the website with more questions is beneficial if feeling stuck or needing a word defined, making it easy for any questions to be answered concisely. OK, now you try. Access ChatGPT-4 and give it a go. Really, it is pretty cool.

Application

Ask ChatGPT-4 some questions. Start by asking yourself, *What is GenAI?* So you can see for yourself how it works. Continue to ask any questions you may have, and experiment with which topics you ask about. Here are some that we found interesting:

- Explain GenAI to a 5-year-old.
- Follow up by asking *Can you expand on that?* or *Can you explain more?* You will see how ChatGPT-4 knows you are still talking about your previous statement and will put it in the same context. Is that not cool?
- Why would a college student need to use GenAI?
- Write me lyrics to a song about GenAI.
- Why should a programmer use GenAI?
- If GenAI were a person, what color would their hair be?

These are just some examples, however, feel free to ask anything. If it tells you something interesting, feel free to explore that idea and ask it to expand on existing questions.

Now that we have some experience and feel comfortable using and navigating ChatGPT-4, let us take a look at another big objective of this chapter: learning about what Python is.

Understanding Python

Python is an incredibly popular programming language, often recognized for its clear syntax and readability. It is commonly used among beginners and experienced developers alike, and its versatility allows it to be applied across various domains such as web development, data analysis, and AI. Due to its ease of use, Python is going to be our language of choice when learning how to code in the upcoming chapters. While we will not be exploring the complexities of Python and how to code with it specifically in this chapter, let us take a look at some of the characteristics of this language. In particular, the two topics are as follows:

- Characteristics of Python
- Application

Let us kick off with the characteristics of Python.

Characteristics of Python

The following are some of the characteristics of Python:

- **Easy to learn:** Python is straightforward, and its commands are similar to English, making it easy to pick up and understand. This lets developers focus on solving problems rather than struggling with complex syntax and the order of stringing code together.

- **Interpreted language:** Python code is run one line at a time, which makes it easier to find and fix errors because you can see exactly where things go wrong.

- **Dynamic typing:** You do not have to specify the type of data a variable will hold in Python; the language figures it out while the program is running. This flexibility is convenient but can lead to unexpected errors in larger programs.

- **Lots of ready-to-use code:** Python has a big collection of pre-written code that helps with many common programming tasks, like working with files, managing system operations, or dealing with internet data.

- **Open source and community-driven:** Python is free to use and share, even for business purposes, because it is open source. It is supported by a large community of users who contribute to its development and offer support through forums and other resources.

- **Works everywhere:** Python programs can run on any system that has a Python interpreter, such as Windows, Mac OS, and Unix systems. This makes Python very portable.

Python is highly flexible and user-friendly, making it a good choice for many different types of programming projects. Utilizing ChatGPT to answer more specific questions about Python proved useful. Let us ask for tips for learning Python as a beginner.

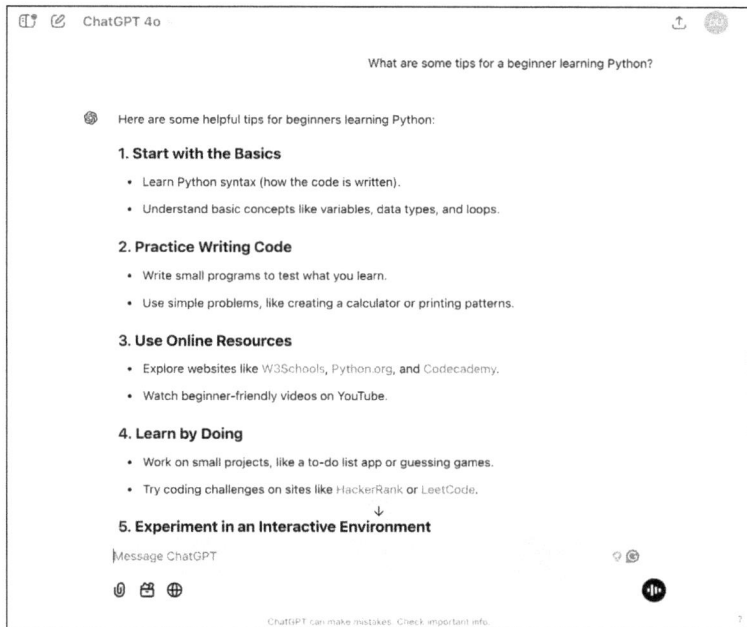

Figure 1.13: *Tips for beginner Python coder*

Figure 1.13 show ChatGPT responding to **What are some tips for a beginner learning Python**? There are ten tips in total.

The following key points were brought up:

- **Understanding and practicing the basics:** Ensure that you practice regularly to familiarize yourself with basic syntax and structures.

- **Work on projects and utilize online resources:** Keep your creativity flowing by working on small projects, and make sure to utilize online resources for help with any questions. Small projects that can integrate into your everyday life, such as a simple program that can function as a to-do list to keep you organized, help to demonstrate practical application.

- **Understand debugging and join a community:** Learn how to read error messages so that you know how to fix and troubleshoot mistakes as you go. The development of these problem-solving skills is critical to the learning process. Join a community of Python coders who can help in providing motivation and guidance through specific questions.

Remember to keep these things in mind as you start your coding journey. Throughout this learning process, we encourage you to utilize ChatGPT when you have any questions about understanding Python.

Application

Let us try utilizing ChatGPT to better understand the different ways we can use Python. This will not only increase our understanding of how Python is used but also help us get comfortable with prompting ChatGPT. Try to prompt ChatGPT to answer the following:

- What types of video games use Python in their code?
- What type of jobs use Python?
- What other coding languages are there?
- How long does it take to learn Python?

Note: Python was released in February 1991 by Guido van Rossum, who named the coding language Python after being inspired by Monty Python's Flying Circus.

If you have any questions, it is good to get in the habit of using ChatGPT for further, personalized clarification. Pairing customized help with learning Python can help to clarify questions that might arise throughout your learning experience. One element that can make your experience with using ChatGPT 4 smooth is knowing how to create prompts that are clear and direct. This next section will help in clarifying the differences between a clear and unclear prompt.

Prompt engineering

Prompt engineering is the practice of designing and refining inputs to get the best possible outputs from AI models. This has become significantly more important due to the rise of

Large Language Models, like the GPT series from OpenAI, which respond based on the inputs they receive. When we prompt ChatGPT, we have to remember that while machine learning is incredibly smart, they are not human. We need to be sure to craft intentional messages that are precise and provide enough context so that the AI is able to understand how to best answer our questions. As we will use ChatGPT as a personal helper in our journey to learning Python, we have to become very good at properly guiding our AI assistant to best provide us with help. Let us discuss some of the key elements of prompt engineering. We will go over:

- The key aspects of prompt engineering
- Importance in AI interactions
- Applications of prompt engineering

Now, let us discuss each of these.

Key aspects of prompt engineering

The following are the key aspects of prompt engineering:

- **Precision:** Crafting prompts that are clear and precise in their request to reduce ambiguity in the model's responses.

- **Contextualization:** Providing the right amount of context within a prompt to guide the model in generating relevant and accurate responses.

- **Adaptation:** Modifying prompts based on the observed performance of the AI to improve its outputs, which involves an iterative process of testing and tweaking.

- **Instruction giving:** Instruct the model explicitly about the desired format, detail, or structure of the output, which can greatly affect the outcome.

Importance in AI interactions

The following are the important aspects of AI interaction:

- **Optimization:** Well-crafted prompts result in more accurate, relevant, and useful outputs, optimizing the interaction between humans and AI.

- **Efficiency:** Effective prompts can reduce the need for follow-up questions or corrections, making interactions more efficient.

- **Task suitability:** Through prompt engineering, models can be guided to perform tasks due to their general knowledge and reasoning capabilities.

We can also take a look at a few applications of proper prompt engineering and how we can utilize this to help us in our jobs and everyday lives.

Applications of prompt engineering

The following are a few examples of AI application:

- **Content creation:** In generating written content, artistic concepts, or programming code, prompt engineering helps specify and refine the output.

- **Data analysis:** When querying models for data insights, effective prompts ensure that the analysis is aligned with the user's needs.

- **Education and training:** In educational settings, prompts can be engineered to create customized learning experiences that cater to the student's level and learning goals.

Now that we have some background as to why prompt engineering is an important part of our learning process, we can do some practice with crafting good questions. Let us say we want to ask ChatGPT for the best cake recipe to make for a birthday party. We could say *What is the best cake recipe?* Let us see what ChatGPT responds with. The following figure shows GenAI's response.

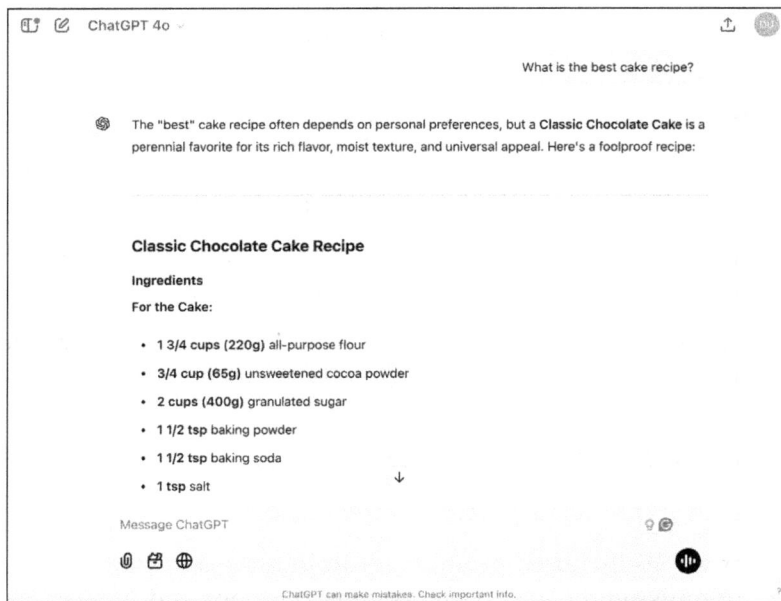

Figure 1.14: Best cake recipe

Figure 1.14 shows ChatGPT response to **What is the best cake recipe?** It starts by listing the ingredients, then provides step-by-step cooking instructions, and even includes some pro tips at the end.

Let us say that the friend is allergic to chocolate. We can ask again, prompting the AI in a slightly different way to get a better catered response. The following figure shows GenAI's response to *What is the best cake recipe for someone allergic to chocolate?*:

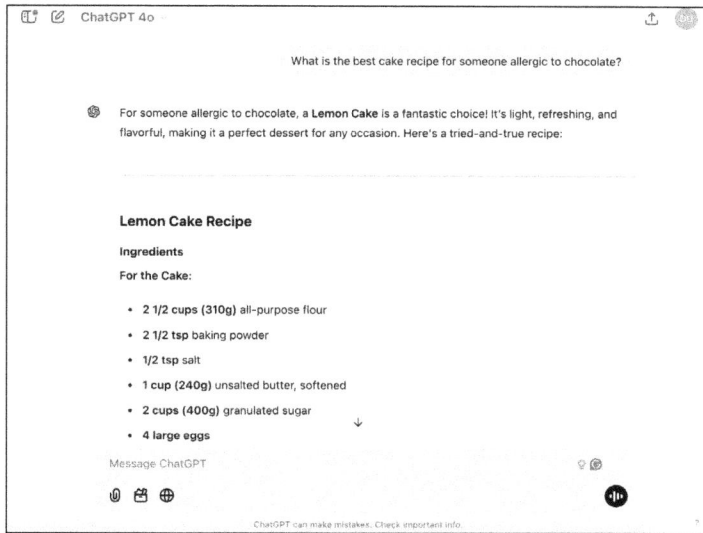

Figure 1.15: *Best allergic to chocolate cake recipe*

Figure 1.15 shows ChatGPT's response to the question, *What is the best cake recipe for someone allergic to chocolate?* Same as before, ChatGPT listed ingredients, step-by-step cooking instructions, and pro tips.

Better, but lemon is a bit boring for a birthday party. Let us try one more time. The next figure shows GenAI's response to being asked *What is the best cake recipe that isn't chocolate and for a birthday party?*.

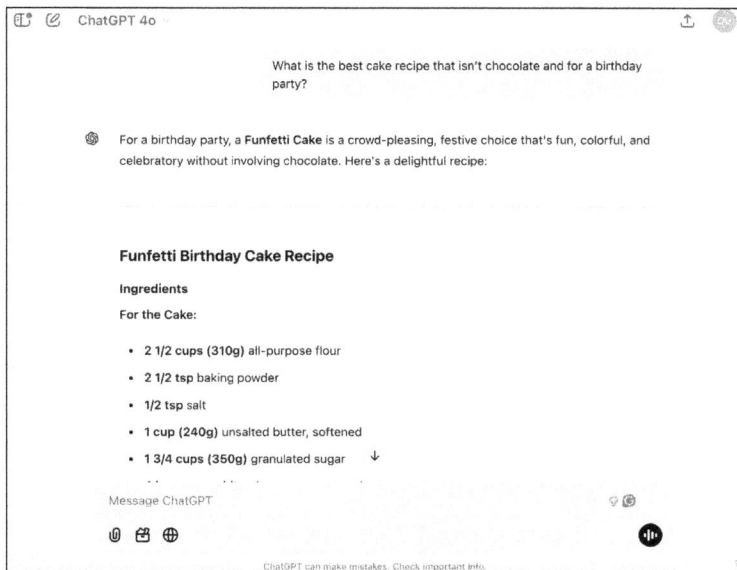

Figure 1.16: *Party birthday cake*

Figure 1.16 shows ChatGPT's response to *What is the best cake recipe that isn't chocolate and for a birthday party?* along with ingredients, step-by-step cooking instructions, and pro tips for the Funfetti cake.

Through this process, we can see how prompting the AI correctly can help a person get better, more accurate responses to a question. The ability to craft clear prompts helps to ensure that the information received is relevant and helpful to the original question. Being better equipped with new knowledge of how to properly engineer prompts let us go about this in a different way. Instead of asking a long series of questions, we can simply ask, *What is the best birthday cake that is fun, not chocolate, and has an interesting flavor?*. Let us see what ChatGPT responded with.

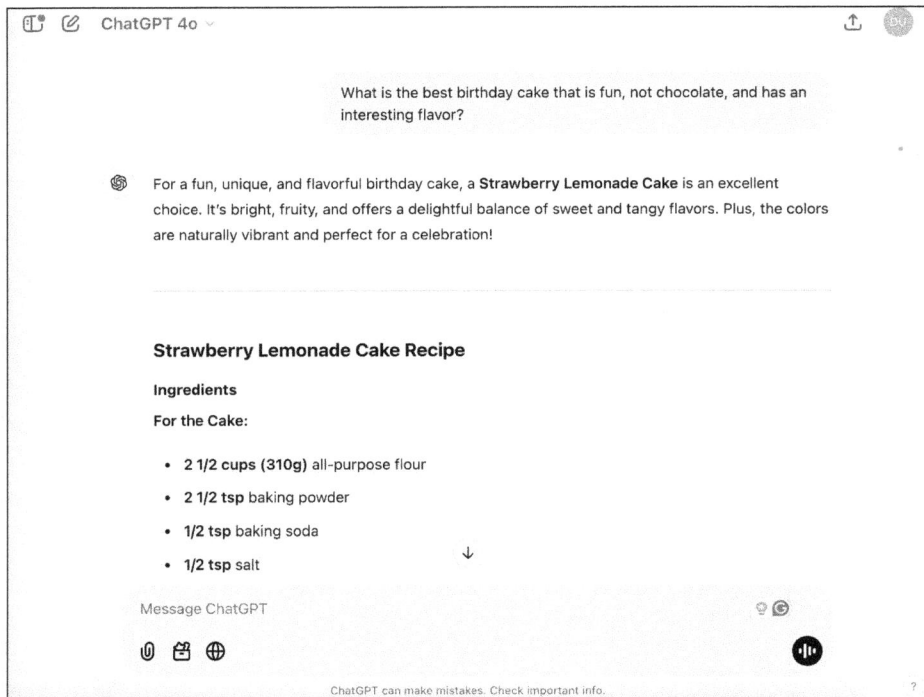

ChatGPT 4o ⌄

What is the best birthday cake that is fun, not chocolate, and has an interesting flavor?

For a fun, unique, and flavorful birthday cake, a **Strawberry Lemonade Cake** is an excellent choice. It's bright, fruity, and offers a delightful balance of sweet and tangy flavors. Plus, the colors are naturally vibrant and perfect for a celebration!

Strawberry Lemonade Cake Recipe

Ingredients

For the Cake:

- **2 1/2 cups (310g)** all-purpose flour
- **2 1/2 tsp** baking powder
- **1/2 tsp** baking soda
- **1/2 tsp** salt

Message ChatGPT

ChatGPT can make mistakes. Check important info.

Figure 1.17: Interesting flavor cake

Figure 1.17 shows ChatGPT's response to *What is the best birthday cake that is fun, not chocolate, and has an interesting flavor?* along with the ingredients, step-by-step cooking instructions, and pro tips for the Strawberry Lemonade cake.

By simply changing the questions' wording and giving a bit of thought to what you needed to ask, the response was much more precise.

Although it takes a few moments to draft a question with the proper wording, the results are much more streamlined and appropriate to what we need. Make sure to practice this a couple of times to get the hang of it!

We have discussed the ways in which ChatGPT and GenAI are positive and can be used in many different instances, however, are there any instances where GenAI should not be used. The limits and navigation are explored in the next section, taking a look at some of the things that it should not be used for.

GenAI limitations

GenAI limitation refers to the various constraints and different challenges that AI systems have when being tasked to do something. Let us take a look at a few common categories that GenAI struggles with. We will go over the following:

- Understanding content and context
- Data dependency
- Creativity and innovation
- Security and privacy
- Ethical decision making

Let us start with the topic of understanding content creation.

Understanding content and context

While AI can process and respond to questions based on data, it often has a hard time understanding deeper, implicit contexts, especially complex human interactions or abstract ideas. This still poses a challenge to AI systems because although these systems are extremely good at identifying patterns in data, they operate at a surface level of processing inputs and producing outputs based on those patterns. GenAI has trouble recognizing some of the more subtle cues that we humans can have in our writing, communication, and interactions with one another, leading to inaccuracies or details being missed.

AI also struggles with understanding context, or it needs extra prompting to provide context to a question so that the answer is most relevant to your topic. Contexts can change quickly and are influenced by current events, cultural shifts, or new information. This makes it hard for AI systems to adapt to these fast-paced changes without being updated or retrained to look for specific details. There is a certain nuance to human language that is hard for AI to pick up on, such as sarcasm. Elements like this are often misinterpreted by AI systems due to their lack of ability to contextualize these cues.

Data dependency

The way AI works to create concise answers is by analyzing patterns and information from incredibly large data sources. These sources are human created, which means that they are heavily dependent on data from us, and there is a chance that the AI will tell us false information. All the information that we put online can be used and considered when

AI is finding and searching for the best response to our questions, and sometimes, it pulls from sources that are not very trustworthy or accurate. AI can make mistakes because humans can make mistakes.

Creativity and innovation

Although AI can simulate creative processes by recombining existing information into new formations, true originality and the ability to innovate from scratch are still traits that it does not possess. As it draws from human-created sources, all creative works done by AI are linked back to original works created by humans. Think heavily inspired by, or as if the AI is creating a new, remixed version of something creative that already exists online. While they are not able to create the new content themselves, they are able to mimic the ways in which humans create and draw inspiration from outside sources.

The following figure shows GenAI's response when being prompted to generate a picture of the limitations of GenAI:

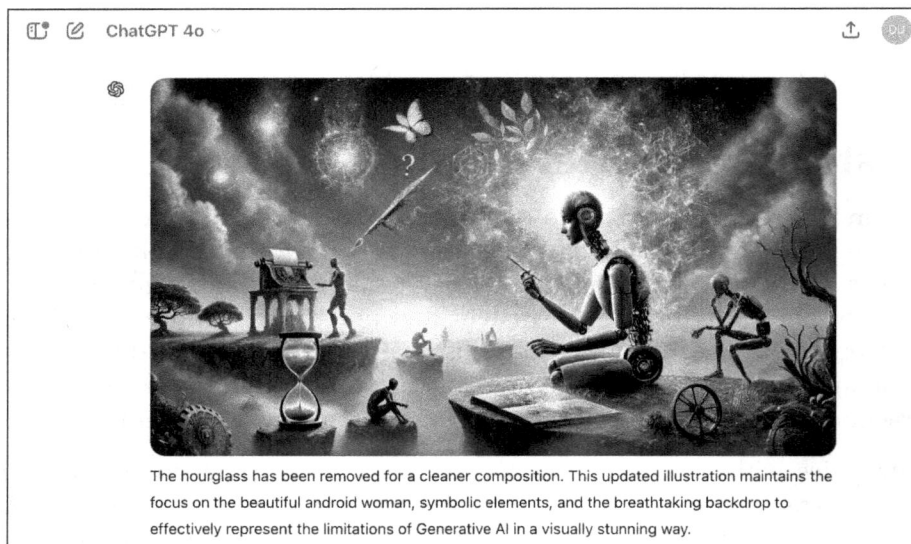

The hourglass has been removed for a cleaner composition. This updated illustration maintains the focus on the beautiful android woman, symbolic elements, and the breathtaking backdrop to effectively represent the limitations of Generative AI in a visually stunning way.

Figure 1.18: Limitations of GenAI

Figure 1.18 shows ChatGPT's response to **Please generate a picture which shows the limitations of GenAI**.

While these issues are constantly being improved upon, certain limitations pose a more serious issue. For example, GenAI runs into problems when considering factors such as security, privacy, and ethical decision-making. Let us discuss these issues of security and privacy and ethical decision-making.

Security and privacy

Concerns around security and privacy are always important, and it is becoming more evident now that these AI technologies are becoming more present in our everyday lives. Several elements that we need to consider when looking at these risks are:

- **Data breaches**: AI systems often require access to large amounts of data to learn and make decisions. This data can include sensitive personal information, which, if not properly secured, could be vulnerable to breaches. A data breach in an AI system can lead to exposure of personal details, financial information, and other confidential data.

- **Surveillance and monitoring**: AI technologies, such as facial recognition and location tracking, are powerful tools for surveillance. While they can serve beneficial purposes like enhancing security, they also raise significant privacy concerns. Unregulated or excessive surveillance can lead to a loss of privacy and is seen as intrusive.

- **Manipulation and control**: AI can be used to create convincing fake audio and video, manipulate public opinion, and influence political scenarios. This manipulation can be a profound threat to personal privacy and security, affecting individuals' ability to control their own data and the truthfulness of the information they receive.

- **Lack of transparency**: Many AI systems operate where the decision-making process is not transparent. This lack of transparency can make it difficult for users to understand how their data is being used and to contest decisions made by AI, which can lead to privacy infringements.

Ethical decision making

When thinking about the ways in which AI technologies should function, something that is brought up is how AI should go about decision-making in an ethical way. Although, generally, there is a consensus about what is right versus wrong, each situation calls for a unique responding course of action. Furthermore, when making decisions, AI may draw from ethical wrongdoings from content that it finds online from others. Later in the book, we will cover this in more detail, but for now, here is a brief overview of certain issues AI runs into when making ethical decisions:

- **Bias and discrimination:** The data used to train AI systems can include biased information or reflect historical inequalities. This can lead to AI systems perpetuating these biases, affecting decisions in areas like hiring, lending, and law enforcement. While not a direct privacy issue, biased data can lead to privacy violations by unfairly targeting certain groups.

- **Moral dilemmas:** AI systems may face situations where they need to make decisions that have moral implications. For example, autonomous vehicles may need to make split-second decisions in scenarios where harm is unavoidable, such as deciding between two potential accidents. Programming an AI to handle such moral dilemmas in a way that aligns with human ethical standards is extremely difficult.

- **Accountability and responsibility:** When an AI system makes a decision that leads to negative outcomes, determining who is responsible—the designer, the user, or the AI itself—is complicated. This is particularly relevant in fields like healthcare, autonomous driving, and law enforcement. Ensuring accountability in AI decisions is a major ethical challenge.

Now that we have gone over the possible limitations, let us wrap up this chapter with a brief overview of what we have learned and covered so far.

Conclusion

In this chapter, we learned what GenAI is, how to access it, and ways to properly utilize all of its helpful functions. We discussed what Python is and how it will be used in our upcoming chapters. Lastly, we learned about common limitations of GenAI to better understand its function and place within our learning experience.

Feel free to come back to this chapter at any time if you need a refresher on the introduction of your future practice with AI. The next chapter will go in-depth about the fundamentals of coding and how to best get started on your coding journey so that it goes smoothly.

Join our book's Discord space

Join the book's Discord Workspace for Latest updates, Offers, Tech happenings around the world, New Release and Sessions with the Authors:

https://discord.bpbonline.com

CHAPTER 2
Jupyter Notebook

Introduction

This chapter is designed to be your friendly guide, unveiling the powerful features of one of the most popular tools in data science, programming, and education. Jupyter Notebooks, with their unique blend of code, visuals, and narrative, offer an interactive canvas for beginners and seasoned professionals.

Whether you are analyzing data, teaching complex concepts, or just experimenting with Python, Jupyter Notebooks provides a flexible and user-friendly environment. So, buckle up and get ready to unlock the full potential of Python Jupyter Notebooks, where coding meets creativity in the most inspiring way!

This chapter aims to introduce and explain the usage of Jupyter Notebook, with a focus on using the Google Collab environment. We will explore the process of learning about Jupyter Notebook using GenAI. It is important to note that the list of features presented is incomplete, but it covers a significant portion of the tool. We encourage readers to explore features independently and deeply dive into them. Our objective is to hold off on teaching Python coding until later chapters. Furthermore, we plan to copy the code generated by GenAI, specifically, GPT-4/Copilot, to the Jupyter Notebook to observe its functionality and then use that experience to draw connections between code and explanation.

Structure

This chapter will contain the following topics:

- Understanding Jupyter Notebook
- Access to Jupyter Notebook
- Installing Jupyter Notebook with pip
- Code and text cell
- Special Google Collab features

Objectives

In this chapter, we set specific objectives to enhance your understanding and proficiency using Python Jupyter Notebooks and Google Colab. Firstly, we aimed to introduce the fundamental concepts and architecture of Jupyter Notebooks, giving you a strong foundation in how they function and can be utilized in various programming and data analysis tasks. Secondly, we explored the additional features and benefits of using Google Colab, emphasizing its ability to provide free access to computational resources like GPUs and TPUs, which are essential for high-performance computing tasks, particularly in machine learning.

Another key objective was to guide you through the practical steps of accessing and setting up these platforms, ensuring you can confidently navigate and use Jupyter Notebooks and Google Colab for your projects. We also illustrated how to integrate these tools with other services, such as Google Drive, to enhance your workflow and facilitate collaboration.

Finally, we encouraged a spirit of independent exploration, empowering you to explore deeper into the functionalities and experiment with advanced features at your own pace. By achieving these objectives, we hope to have provided you with the tools and knowledge to fully leverage Jupyter Notebooks and Google Colab in your educational or professional endeavors.

Understanding Jupyter Notebook

Jupyter Notebook introduces the fascinating world of Python, a dynamic and versatile tool that has transformed how data scientists, researchers, and educators work with code and data. This section explores the essence of Jupyter Notebooks, exploring its interactive environment where code, visual output, and descriptive text coexist in a single document. As we unravel the features that make Jupyter Notebooks an indispensable asset across various fields, you will gain insights into its user-friendly interface, support for multiple programming languages, and robust data visualization and collaborative projects capabilities.

Whether you are a seasoned programmer or a newcomer to coding, understanding how to use Jupyter Notebooks effectively will enhance your analytical skills and broaden your toolkit for tackling complex data challenges.

Jupyter Notebook is an open-source application that is celebrated for its versatility and accessibility. This openness has inspired a variety of platforms that offer Jupyter Notebook environments, many of which are free with optional paid upgrades. Popular choices include Google Colab, Kaggle Notebook, Amazon SageMaker, and Microsoft Azure AI. These platforms enhance the Jupyter experience, providing unique features tailored to different needs, from cloud-based collaboration to advanced machine learning tools.

The following figure is an example of the Jupyter Notebook interface on Google Colab, showcasing its clean, interactive design, which makes coding and data exploration intuitive and efficient:

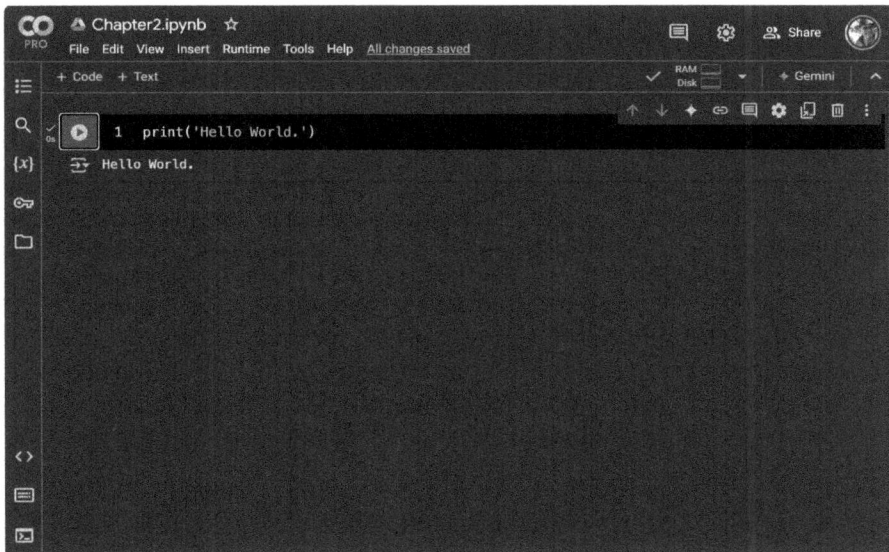

Figure 2.1: *Screenshot of Jupyter Notebook on Google Colab*

Figure 2.1 shows a typical Jupyter Notebook on Google Colab in dark mode.

We will explore the critical features of Python Jupyter Notebooks that make it a premier tool for coding and data analysis. Each feature contributes to the Notebook's adaptability and efficacy in various tasks, from simple computations to complex scientific research. We will look at the interactive coding environment that facilitates experimental development and debugging, the support for rich media and multiple programming languages that enhance its versatility, and its powerful collaboration and sharing tools that streamline group projects and educational efforts.

Following this, subsequent sections will provide a comprehensive breakdown of each feature, illustrating how they can maximize productivity and innovation in your work.

These features include interactive coding, extensive libraries, and extensions, ease of sharing, support for multiple programming languages, rich media support, and Python Jupyter Notebooks compared to other Python IDEs.

To better understand Jupyter Notebooks, here are the six topics we will cover:

- Interactive coding
- Extensive libraries and extensions
- Ease of sharing
- Multiple programming languages
- Rich media support
- Notebook and other Python IDEs

Let us start with interactive coding.

Interactive coding

Interactive coding is one of the standout features of Python Jupyter Notebooks, allowing users to execute code in discrete, manageable blocks known as **cells**. This modularity provides a unique advantage: immediate feedback and results from each piece of code, facilitating quick iterations and adjustments without rerunning entire scripts.

This real-time interaction speeds up the development and debugging processes and enhances learning, making it easier to understand the effects of code changes as they happen. Users can experiment with different parameters or methods and see the outcomes instantly, making Jupyter Notebooks an ideal environment for exploratory data analysis, model testing, and educational demonstrations where step-by-step execution and result observation are crucial.

Additionally, to enhance Jupyter Notebooks' interactiveness, they offer many add-ons or extensions to cater to your needs, such as exporting pure Python code (**.py** file), auto-linking to your GitHub account, and saving files to your Google Drive directory.

The interactivity of the Jupyter Notebook makes it a perfect starting point for beginners. There is no need for a complicated setup, and there is no waiting for code to compile; everything happens instantly. Whether it is a successful output, an error, or a bug, the feedback is immediate, creating a learning experience that feels responsive and engaging.

This immediacy reduces the friction of experimentation, allowing learners to dive into coding with curiosity and focus on the fun of trying something new.

Extensive libraries and extensions

Python Jupyter Notebooks are enriched by an extensive array of libraries and extensions that amplify their functionality and utility across various domains. These libraries and extensions integrate with the core Jupyter environment to provide additional tools for data visualization, machine learning, and even real-time user collaboration.

For example, libraries like Matplotlib and Seaborn can be used within notebooks for sophisticated data visualizations. At the same time, extensions like Jupyter Widgets enhance interactivity, allowing for user inputs and dynamic visual updates within the notebook.

Other extensions, such as the Nbextensions, provide customizable usability improvements, from auto-completion features to code folding, which streamline the coding process and enhance productivity.

Python boasts an impressive ecosystem, with over 450,000 libraries available to extend its functionality. These libraries cover nearly every imaginable field, making Python a powerhouse for developers, researchers, and data scientists.

The top five categories of libraries include:

- **Data analysis and visualization**: Libraries like Pandas, Matplotlib, and Seaborn provide data manipulation and visualization tools.

- **Machine learning and AI**: Powerhouses like TensorFlow, PyTorch, and Scikit-learn dominate the world of AI and predictive modeling.

- **Web development**: Frameworks like Django and Flask simplify building robust and scalable web applications.

- **Scientific computing**: NumPy and SciPy make complex mathematical and scientific computations more approachable.

- **Automation and scripting:** Libraries like Selenium and BeautifulSoup help automate repetitive tasks and scrape web data efficiently.

This extensive collection of libraries would not be possible without the vibrant Python community, which includes over 8.5 million contributors worldwide. These users constantly innovate, maintain, and improve Python libraries, ensuring they stay relevant and powerful for evolving needs.

This ecosystem of add-ons broadens Jupyter Notebooks' capabilities and tailors the experience to meet specific user needs and preferences, making it a versatile platform for novice and expert users.

Ease of sharing

The ease of sharing is a fundamental aspect of Python Jupyter Notebooks, making it incredibly straightforward to distribute work and collaborate. Notebooks can be shared as files directly, which retain the code, outputs, and narrative text in a single package, or they can be exported into various formats such as HTML, PDF, and slides for presentations, ensuring that the content is accessible even to those without Jupyter.

This versatility supports multiple use cases, from academic instructors sharing lecture materials to data scientists distributing detailed reports with interactive elements. Additionally, Jupyter Notebooks are compatible with version control systems like Git, enhancing their shareability and facilitating collaborative projects where changes and contributions can be tracked and merged systematically.

Python Jupyter Notebook makes collaboration with friends and colleagues effortless. Unlike traditional IDEs, there is no need to worry about everyone having the same coding environment or setup. Jupyter Notebooks are platform-independent and work across web browsers and desktop OS.

Best of all, they are free to use, with no additional costs or licenses required. This flexibility ensures that teams can focus on coding and sharing ideas without the hassle of technical barriers, making collaboration more accessible and enjoyable.

This sharing fosters a collaborative environment where ideas and findings can be easily exchanged and built upon globally.

Multiple programming languages

Python Jupyter Notebooks offer robust support for multiple programming languages, making them a versatile tool for diverse users. While predominantly associated with Python, Jupyter Notebooks also support languages such as R, Julia, and Scala, thanks to the underlying Jupyter kernel architecture.

Each kernel acts as a separate execution environment tailored to a specific language, allowing users to select the one that best fits their project's needs. This multi-language support enables cross-disciplinary teams to work within the same notebook environment, integrating different programming languages for complex analyses that require varied data processing or modeling approaches.

We take a closer look at Jupyter Notebook, which is incredibly versatile and supports a wide range of programming languages through its kernel system. While Python is the most popular, several other languages are also widely used and supported. Here are the top five languages, along with their approximate daily usage and contributor statistics:

- **Python:**
  - o **Daily access**: Over five million users
  - o **Contributors**: 8.5 million
  - o Python remains the backbone of Jupyter, driving its popularity in data science, AI, and general programming tasks.
- **R:**
  - o **Daily access**: Approximately 800,000 users
  - o **Contributors**: 500,000

- o Known for its statistical and data visualization capabilities, R is a favorite among statisticians and data analysts.

- **Julia:**
  - o **Daily access**: Around 150,000 users
  - o **Contributors**: 30,000
  - o Julia's high performance for numerical computing makes it a strong contender in scientific research and machine learning.

- **Scala:**
  - o **Daily access**: Nearly 100,000 users
  - o **Contributors**: 20,000
  - o Widely used in big data and distributed computing, Scala integrates well with platforms like Apache Spark.

- **JavaScript:**
  - o **Daily access**: About 75,000 users
  - o **Contributors**: 15,000
  - o JavaScript support extends Jupyter's capabilities to web development, enabling interactive data visualizations with tools like *D3.js*.

These numbers highlight the vibrant, multilingual community around Jupyter Notebook, ensuring continuous development and support for users across various domains.

For educational purposes, this allows instructors to teach concepts in a language familiar to students or demonstrate how the same problem can be tackled in different languages, enhancing learning and understanding.

Rich media support

Python Jupyter Notebooks excel in their ability to support rich media, a feature that significantly enhances the presentation and comprehensibility of data. Users can integrate various forms of media, such as images, videos, and interactive visualizations, directly into their notebooks.

This multimedia capability is further complemented by support for HTML, LaTeX, and Markdown, which allows for creating richly formatted textual content alongside the code. Such integrations are crucial for creating comprehensive narratives that explain complex data or models in a visually engaging manner. This feature is precious in educational settings, where visual aids can help clarify concepts, and in data science, where interactive plots and custom visualizations play a critical role in data exploration and presentation.

One of the most powerful yet often overlooked features of Jupyter Notebook is allowing documentation to be integrated directly alongside the source code. This feature eliminates the need for separate documentation files, addressing a common and costly problem in programming, from college projects to enterprise-level development.

In the world of software, the absence of proper documentation is a well-known issue that can lead to staggering costs. For example, an application might take a year to develop, costing millions of dollars. However, maintaining or extending that application can become two to three times more expensive without comprehensive documentation. Poorly documented code creates confusion, slows new developers' onboarding, and increases the likelihood of errors, ultimately driving up the cost of ownership.

Jupyter Notebook solves this by enabling coders to combine executable code, explanatory text, visuals, and multimedia into a single, interactive document. This integration makes it easier to understand and share work and ensures that documentation evolves alongside the code, saving both time and money in the long run.

Incorporating these diverse media types ensures that Jupyter Notebooks are not just coding tools but powerful storytelling devices in data-driven research and communication.

Notebook and other Python IDEs

Python Jupyter Notebook stands out from other Python **Integrated Development Environments (IDEs)** like PyCharm or Visual Studio Code primarily due to its exceptional interactivity and suitability for exploratory analysis. Imagine you are a detective with a magnifying glass, examining clues individually to solve a mystery. In Jupyter Notebook, each piece of your code can be run separately in little chunks called **cells**. This is like checking each clue independently. So, if you run a piece of code that does not work as expected, you do not have to redo everything from scratch—just tweak that little part.

For example, if you were trying to find out the most popular ice cream flavor among your friends, you could write a bit of code to ask each friend about their favorite flavor and store these answers. If something goes wrong while asking or storing the answers, you can fix that part without repeatedly asking everyone. Other IDEs, while powerful for building big apps, typically require you to rerun the whole script, which can take a lot more time and might mix up your investigation.

Jupiter's way of handling things promotes tinkering and playing with your code, testing out different ideas quickly, just like how you might try out different puzzle pieces to see where they fit. This makes it incredibly excellent for exploring data, trying new things, and learning by doing. It is more complex in other environments where you might have to keep running the whole program repeatedly. Plus, you can see the results under your code, adding pictures or even interactive graphs that help you understand what's happening at a glance.

From both technical and cost perspectives, Python Jupyter Notebook is a more practical option than traditional Python IDEs. While many IDEs require paid licenses, Jupyter Notebook is entirely free, eliminating any financial barriers to entry. Additionally, IDEs often tie you to a single laptop or desktop due to installation requirements, whereas Jupyter Notebook only needs an internet connection and a browser. This flexibility allows you to work from virtually anywhere, whether it is your favorite bakery, an internet café, or even halfway across the globe.

Sharing your work is also significantly easier with Jupyter Notebook. You can effortlessly collaborate with friends or colleagues worldwide by sharing your notebook files or linking to cloud-based platforms like Google Colab. This advantage is especially valuable in regions or businesses where purchasing and installing new IDE software can be prohibitively expensive or restricted by local regulations. Jupyter Notebook breaks down these barriers, providing a cost-effective and universally accessible tool for coding and collaboration.

That is why Jupyter Notebook is like a super-smart playground for curious minds diving into data.

Access to Jupyter Notebook

Learning Python Jupyter Notebooks begins with accessing and setting up properly—a first step that guides the way for all the innovative work you will accomplish using this powerful tool. In this section, we will guide you through installing Jupyter Notebooks, setting up the environment on your machine, and navigating the initial steps to create and manage your notebooks.

Additionally, we will explore how to access notebooks via cloud services, which can enhance your flexibility and collaboration capabilities. By the end of this section, you will be well-equipped to explore your projects with Jupyter, leveraging its full potential to enhance your coding and data analysis endeavors.

When selecting an online platform for Python Jupyter Notebooks, several top contenders stand out: Google Colab, Microsoft Azure Notebooks, IBM Watson Studio, Databricks Community Edition, and Kaggle Kernels. Each offers unique functionalities tailored to specific needs, ranging from machine learning to data analytics, with varying resource availability and community support.

Now we will take a deeper look into what makes each platform unique, explaining the benefits and drawbacks. In particular, we will cover:

- Google Colab
- Accessing Google Colab
- IBM Watson Studio
- Databricks Community Edition
- Kaggle Kernels
- Installing Jupyter Notebook with pip

Let us start learning about Google Colab.

Google Colab

Google Colab provides a user-friendly environment with free access to GPUs and TPUs, which is ideal for machine learning projects requiring substantial computational power. The platform integrates with Google Drive for easy data management and collaboration. However, the dependence on Google's infrastructure means that users might experience slower performance during peak times and limited customization of the underlying hardware.

On the positive side, Google Colab has become one of the most popular platforms for Jupyter Notebook users, offering an experience for coding, data analysis, and machine learning. Designed to make powerful tools accessible to everyone, it combines the flexibility of Jupyter Notebook with the scalability and convenience of Google's cloud infrastructure. Whether you are a beginner experimenting with Python or a seasoned data scientist building machine learning models, Google Colab offers unique advantages that set it apart.

The top three benefits for Google Colab are as follows:

- **Free access to powerful hardware:** Google Colab provides free access to GPUs and TPUs, enabling users to run computationally intensive tasks like machine learning and deep learning without requiring expensive hardware. This feature makes it an excellent choice for students, researchers, and developers on resource-heavy projects.

- **Zero setup and cloud-based convenience:** There is no need to install or configure anything. Log in with your Google account, and you are ready to code. Being cloud-based, Colab allows you to access your work from anywhere using any device with a browser.

- **Effortless collaboration and sharing:** Integrated with Google Drive, Google Colab makes sharing notebooks as easy as sharing a document. Real-time collaboration allows multiple users to edit and run code simultaneously, fostering teamwork and learning.

In summary, Google Colab stands out as a versatile and user-friendly platform for Jupyter Notebook users. It combines the power of free hardware, cloud-based accessibility, and collaboration. Whether exploring Python, analyzing data, or building complex machine learning models, Google Colab simplifies the process, making it invaluable for learners and professionals.

Accessing Google Colab

Each option has its pros and cons; however, the remainder of this chapter will focus solely on installing Google Colab and Jupyter Notebooks. Signing up and accessing Google Colab is straightforward and integrates with your existing Google account.

The following step-by-step process will guide you along the way of installing Google Colab.

The first step is open your web browser and go to the Google Colab website by typing **https://colab.research.google.com** in the address bar. First, you need to sign in to Google. If you do not have a Gmail account, you can sign up for a free one. Once on the Google Colab page, press the new notebook button on the bottom left of the panel, as shown in the following figure:

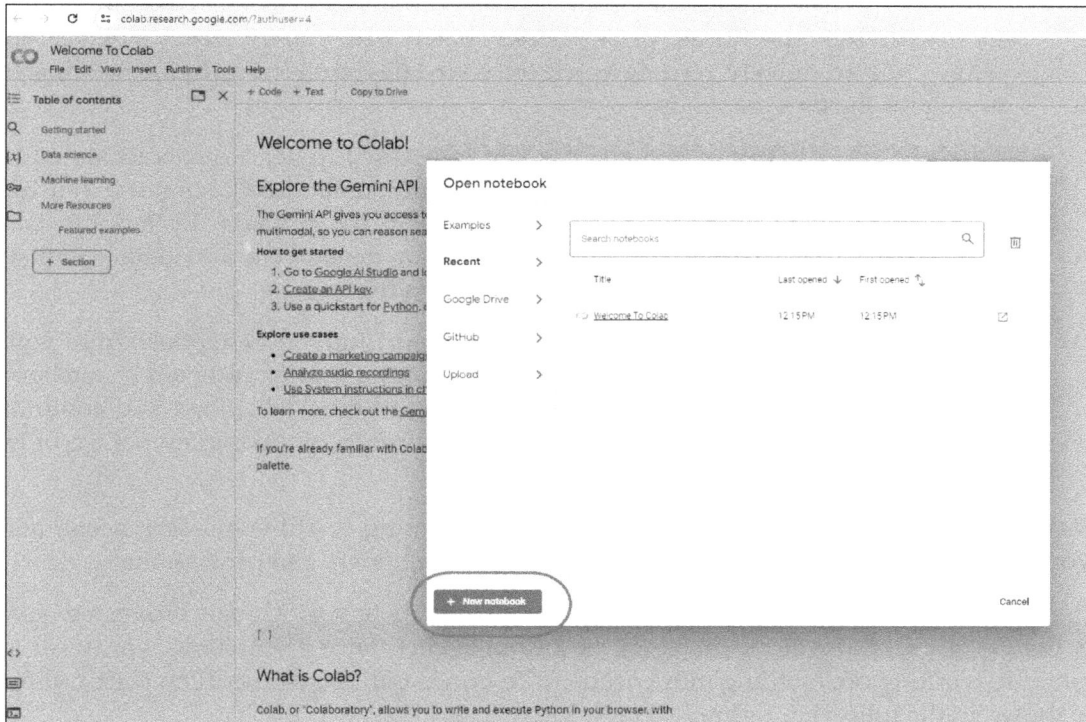

Figure 2.2: *Adding Google Colab to your Google Drive using the new notebook button*

Figure 2.2 shows an option to create a new notebook. When you create a new notebook in Google Colab, the platform automatically instantiates a new server instance. This process means you are starting with a fresh environment. Any previously installed Python libraries, configurations, or work from earlier sessions will no longer be available. While this ensures a clean slate for your new project, it also requires reinstalling any necessary dependencies and reconfiguring your environment for each session. This fresh start can be an advantage for quick prototyping and ensures no leftover settings interfere with your new work.

As shown in *Figure 2.2*, Google Colab provides other options for accessing and managing your notebooks, whether starting fresh, revisiting recent work, or importing files. Here is a quick guide to the available choices.

- **Example:** The **Example** section offers a curated list of sample notebooks designed to help you start with Google Colab. These examples are beginner-friendly tutorials that walk you through key features like running Python code, visualizing data, and leveraging machine learning tools. We highly recommend these resources for new users as they provide a practical, hands-on introduction to using Colab effectively.

- **Recent:** The **Recent** section displays a list of Jupyter Notebooks you have recently opened. These notebooks can originate from various sources, such as your Google Drive, GitHub repositories, or notebooks shared with you by others. This feature allows you to quickly resume work on your latest projects without needing to search for the files manually.

- **GitHub:** The **GitHub** option enables you to access Jupyter Notebooks stored in your GitHub repositories or those shared by friends and collaborators. You can easily browse and open notebooks directly from the platform by linking your GitHub account, streamlining the workflow for developers and data scientists who frequently use version control and collaborative coding.

- **Upload:** The **Upload** feature allows you to import Jupyter Notebooks from your local machine. Whether you have been working offline or received a notebook file via email or other means, this option lets you quickly upload and continue your work on Google Colab's cloud-based environment, taking advantage of its powerful features.

Each option ensures flexibility and convenience, catering to different user needs and workflows, making Google Colab a versatile tool for beginners and professionals.

The alternative way to start Google Colab is to go directly to your Google Drive, navigate to the Google Collaboratory directory, and double-click on the Notebook you wish to continue working on. Nothing more needs to be done, and you are ready to start coding, as shown in the following figure:

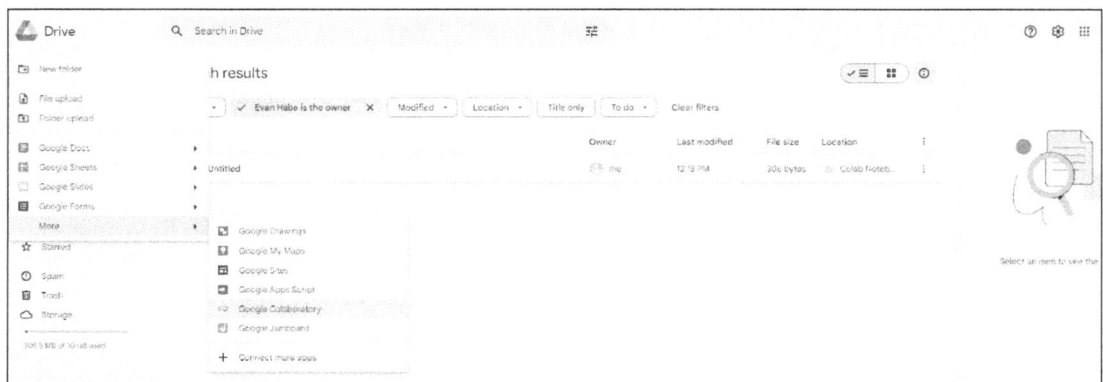

Figure 2.3: Starting a new Colaboratory in Google Drive

Figure 2.3 illustrates a method for starting Google Colab without remembering the starting URL. By double-clicking on the Notebook on your Google Drive, the system will launch your browsers, load your Notebook, and engage with Google Colab.

Microsoft Azure Notebooks

Microsoft Azure Notebooks offers a tightly integrated experience with other Azure services, making it an excellent choice for users already within the Microsoft ecosystem. It supports a variety of languages and has good scalability options. On the downside, it can have a steeper learning curve if you are unfamiliar with Azure, and the cost can increase significantly as usage scales.

The top three benefits of using Microsoft Azure Jupyter Notebooks are as follows:

- **Enterprise-grade scalability:** With Azure, you can effortlessly scale your notebooks, leveraging powerful virtual machines, GPUs, and advanced cloud computing resources. This option makes handling everything from small experiments to large-scale machine-learning pipelines easy.

- **Seamless integration with Azure services:** Azure Notebooks integrates with other Azure tools, such as Azure Machine Learning, Azure Data Lake, and Azure Blob Storage. This integration streamlines workflows by connecting notebooks to storage, data pipelines, and deployment tools within a unified platform.

- **Collaboration and security:** Azure offers robust collaboration tools and enterprise-grade security features. Teams can share and edit notebooks securely, with features like role-based access control, encryption, and compliance with global standards, ensuring sensitive data remains protected.

In conclusion, Microsoft Azure Jupyter Notebooks provide a powerful and flexible environment for data science and machine learning, backed by the scalability and security of the Azure ecosystem. Whether you are working individually or as part of a team, its integration with Azure services and robust collaboration tools makes it an excellent choice for handling complex projects quickly and confidently.

IBM Watson Studio

IBM Watson Studio is robust in features, supporting Jupyter Notebooks and other data science tools. It suits enterprises requiring strong integration with AI and machine learning models. The platform offers powerful collaboration tools. However, the interface can be complex for beginners, and the platform's advanced features may come at a higher cost than more straightforward notebook services.

The top three benefits of IBM Watson Studio for Jupyter Notebooks are as follows:

- **AI-Powered insights and tools:** IBM Watson Studio integrates Jupyter Notebooks with advanced AI and machine learning capabilities. This option allows users to quickly build, train, and deploy models using pre-built AI tools, **automated machine learning (AutoML)**, and Watson's natural language processing features.

- **Enterprise-grade collaboration and security:** Designed for teams, Watson Studio provides secure collaboration features, including version control, role-based access, and compliance with industry standards. It protects sensitive data while enabling teamwork across departments and locations.

- **Scalable and integrated cloud environment:** Watson Studio offers a scalable cloud infrastructure, allowing users to efficiently manage resources for small experiments or large-scale machine learning projects. It integrates with IBM Cloud services, providing access to powerful tools like IBM DataStage, IBM SPSS, and data lake storage solutions.

In conclusion, IBM Watson Studio enhances Jupyter Notebooks by combining the power of AI-driven tools, enterprise-grade collaboration, and scalable cloud infrastructure. It is an ideal platform for professionals and teams seeking a secure and efficient environment to build, deploy, and easily manage machine learning projects.

Databricks Community Edition

Databricks Community Edition offers users a slice of its comprehensive data science and engineering environment with the added benefit of community support and resources. It is powerful in handling big data scenarios. While it provides free access, the functionalities are limited compared to the full version, and the environment can be less intuitive for those unfamiliar with Spark or big data platforms.

The top three benefits of Databricks Community Edition with Jupyter Notebook are as follows:

- **Big data and Spark integration:** Databricks Community Edition brings the power of Apache Spark directly into Jupyter Notebook, allowing users to process and analyze massive datasets quickly. This integration makes it a top choice for big data analytics and machine learning workflows.

- **Free access to clusters:** With the Community Edition, users can access Databricks clusters at no cost. This option enables the execution of distributed computing tasks without requiring expensive hardware, making it an excellent resource for students, researchers, and developers.

- **Collaborative workspace:** Databricks offers an intuitive, collaborative workspace where multiple users can share and work on notebooks in real-time. This feature fosters teamwork and makes it easy to manage projects across teams while maintaining version control and a streamlined workflow.

In conclusion, Databricks Community Edition with Jupyter Notebook combines the power of big data processing, free access to Spark clusters, and a collaborative workspace, making it a versatile platform for data science and machine learning. Its ability to handle large-scale datasets and support teamwork ensures it is an excellent choice for professionals, students, and researchers aiming to build impactful projects in a cost-effective and efficient environment.

Kaggle Kernels

Kaggle Kernels fosters a community-focused environment where users can engage directly with various datasets and participate in competitions. This platform is excellent for those looking to improve their data science skills or contribute to collaborative projects. The main limitation is that it is less suited for private or commercial projects due to the public nature of the workspaces and a focus primarily on competition-related tasks.

The top three benefits of Kaggle Kernels with Jupyter Notebook are as follows:

- **Preloaded datasets and libraries:** Kaggle Kernels have access to an extensive library of datasets and preinstalled Python and R libraries, saving time on setup. This feature lets users jump straight into analysis, making it ideal for competitions, projects, or exploring data-driven insights.

- **Cloud-based and free:** Kaggle Kernels operate entirely in the cloud, eliminating the need for local installations or high-performance hardware. It is free to use, ensuring that anyone with an internet connection can work on advanced data science and machine learning tasks without cost barriers.

- **Collaborative learning environment:** Kaggle provides a community-driven platform where users can share, fork, and collaborate on notebooks. This feature fosters a supportive learning environment, enabling users to learn from others' work, improve their skills, and contribute to the community.

In conclusion, Kaggle Kernels with Jupyter Notebook combines accessibility, convenience, and collaboration into a single platform. With preloaded datasets, cloud-based functionality, and a vibrant community, it is an excellent choice for beginners and experts to experiment, learn, and succeed in data science and machine learning.

When all else fails, the surest and most controlled method is to install Jupyter Notebook locally. The following section will walk you through the process step by step.

Installing Jupyter Notebook with pip

First, make sure that you have Python installed. Python 3.10 or higher is recommended, and you can check if it is installed by opening the Terminal and typing:

```
Terminal> python3 --version
```

If Python is not installed, you can download and install it from the official Python website.

Once Python is installed, follow these steps to install Jupyter Notebook:

1. **Open the Terminal:** You can find the Terminal in your applications under utilities or search for it using spotlight.

2. **Update pip:** Ensure your version of pip is up to date by running:

```
Terminal> python3 -m pip install --upgrade pip
```

3. Install Jupyter Notebook: Now, use pip to install Jupyter:

```
Terminal> python3 -m pip install notebook
```

4. **Launch Jupyter Notebook:** Once installed, run the following command in the Terminal to start Jupyter Notebook:

```
Terminal> Jupiter notebook
```

This will open Jupyter Notebook in your default web browser.

The top three benefits of installing Jupyter Notebook with pip on your local laptop or desktop are as follows:

- **Complete control and customization:** Installing Jupyter Notebook locally on your laptop allows you to customize your environment to fit your needs. You can install any Python libraries, configure settings, and even add extensions to enhance functionality, giving you complete control over your development environment.

- **Offline accessibility:** A local installation means you can work on your projects anytime, even without an internet connection. This feature is particularly useful for areas with limited connectivity or where cloud platforms are unavailable or impractical.

- **Data privacy and security:** By running Jupyter Notebook locally, your data and projects remain on your device, providing a more secure option for working with sensitive or confidential information compared to cloud-based solutions.

In conclusion, installing Jupyter Notebook locally with pip offers unmatched flexibility, offline accessibility, and enhanced data security. It is an excellent choice for users who want complete control over their development environment, needs to work without relying on an internet connection or prioritize data privacy. A local setup empowers you to tailor Jupyter Notebook to your needs while keeping your projects secure and easily accessible.

We have completed the big section of *Understanding Jupyter Notebook*. The following section explains the features and functions of the Jupyter Notebook, starting with the code and text cell.

Code and text cell

In Google Colab, you work within a notebook containing two main cell types: code and text. These cells are the building blocks of a notebook, allowing you to separate your programming from your documentation, which can include explanations or instructions. This setup facilitates a clean, instructional, or collaborative environment where the code context is easily understood, making it ideal for educational purposes, data analysis projects, and more. Getting acquainted with these cells is a main part of learning Jupyter Notebooks, we will explore each thoroughly.

Jupyter Notebook provides flexibility when working with code and text cells, making it a powerful tool for experimentation, documentation, and structured workflows. Code cells are not bound by sequential execution, allowing you to run them in any order. Unlike traditional scripts that execute from top to bottom, Jupyter Notebook lets you focus on specific parts of your code without re-running everything. You can also insert new code cells anywhere within the notebook, not just at the bottom, allowing you to reorganize or expand your work as your project evolves.

Text cells, on the other hand, are perfect for adding documentation, notes, and explanations to enhance the clarity of your notebook. Supporting Markdown allows for formatted text, headings, lists, and even images, enabling you to present your code clearly and professionally. Like code cells, you can add, rearrange, or delete text cells at any position within the notebook. This feature makes annotating your work easy or provides insights without interrupting the overall flow.

By blending code and text cells, Jupyter Notebook creates an interactive environment that is both functional and informative. Whether learning, collaborating, or presenting, this flexibility allows you to adapt your notebook to suit your needs.

Using GTP4o as an assistant, let us begin learning and writing Python code. You can post any coding question and ask GPT4o to write and explain the code.

Code cells

Code cells are where you write and execute your Python code. When you type code into a code cell and run it (using the play button beside the cell or pressing *Ctrl+Enter* on Windows laptop and *Command+Enter* on Apple MacBook), Google Colab executes the code and displays the output immediately below it. This interactive execution allows for real-time data processing and analysis, making it easy to test and refine your code incrementally.

In Python, the foundational elements such as variables, lists, if statements, and loops allow you to build complex and efficient programs, which we will cover in detail in the next chapter.

The **Print** statement in Python is used to send output to the screen. It lets you see the values of variables, messages, or any information you want to show. You just put what you want to see inside the parentheses of **print()**, and Python will display it for you. For example, **print("Hello, world!")** will show **Hello, world!** on the screen. It is like telling Python, **Hey, show this to me!**

Variables store information that can be referenced and manipulated in your code, essentially named containers for data.

An example of variables definition can be found in the following *Figure 2.4*:

```
CO        ▲ Chapter2.ipynb  ☆                              ▤   ⚙   ⧉ Share   🌐
PRO       File  Edit  View  Insert  Runtime  Tools  Help  All changes saved

   + Code  + Text                                    ✓  RAM ▭  ▼  | ◆ Gemini  ^
                                                        Disk ▭

                                                    ↑  ↓  ◆  ⊖  ▤  ⚙  ⬜  🗑  ⋮
  ▶      1  # from GPT4o:
         2  # Write Python example of assigning values to varibles and print them
{x}      3  name = "Ada Loveace"   # A string
         4  age = 28               # An integer
         5  height = 1.7           # A floating point
         6
         7  # Printing variables
         8  print(name, "is", age, "years old and", height, "meters tall.")

      ⌑ Ada Loveace is 28 years old and 1.7 meters tall.

  [ ]    1  Start coding or generate with AI.
```

Figure 2.4: Jupyter Notebook Python variables, string, int, and float

In *Figure 2.4*, line #2 is the prompt we write in GPT4o. We then copied and pasted the code into our Jupyter Notebook. Notice that you may see different Python code results when you type the same prompt into GPT4o, but the concept remains the same.

Line #3 assigns **Ada Lovelace** to the variable **name**, which is a string variable. Notice the quote characters around the string. Line #4 assigns **age** to be **28**, which is an integer variable, and line #5 assigns **height** to be **1.7**, which is a float variable.

Lastly, line #8 prints out the result below the code cell of: **Ada Lovelace is 28 years old and 1.7 meters tall**

To add a new code cell, click the + **Code** button located in the upper left corner of *Figure 2.4*. This action will insert a new code cell just below your current cursor position or active cell. For keyboard shortcuts, on a Windows laptop, use the *ALT+A* key combination, and on an Apple MacBook, use the *Option + A* key combination.

For the next example, we ask GPT4o to write code for Python type **list**. Lists are a data structure in Python that allows you to store a sequence of items under a single variable name. These items can be of different types, including numbers, strings, or even other lists.

An example list statement is in *Figure 2.5*:

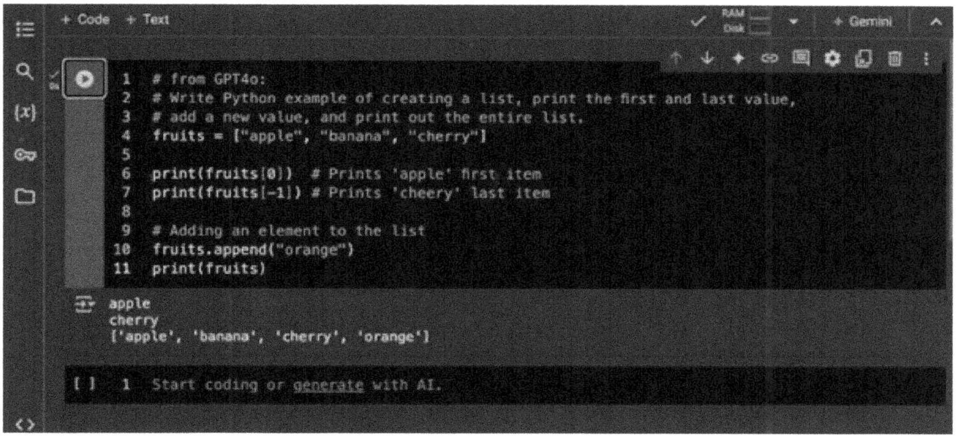

Figure 2.5: Jupyter Notebook Python list

In *Figure 2.5*, line #2 and #3 is a prompt we used in asking GPT4o to write the Python code for a **list** example. As usual, we copied the pasted the code into our Jupyter Notebook. Once again, when you type the same prompt to GTP4o, the generated Python code may be different from what you see here. In other words, you may not see the **fruits** list but maybe a **people** name list.

Line #4 defines a **list** type of **string** variable. The variable name is **fruits** and the values are **apple**, **banana**, and **cherry**.

Line #6 prints the first list value, index zero. The output is **apple**, and line #7 prints the last list value, index -1. The output is **cherry**.

Line #10 appends **orange** to the **fruits** list, and line 11 prints the entire list. The output is: **['apple', 'banana', 'cherry', 'orange']**.

The next example of using code cell is condition statement. The **if** statements, a form of conditional logic, enable your program to execute particular code only when specific conditions are met, making your scripts more innovative and adaptable.

An example **if** statement can be found in the following *Figure 2.6*:

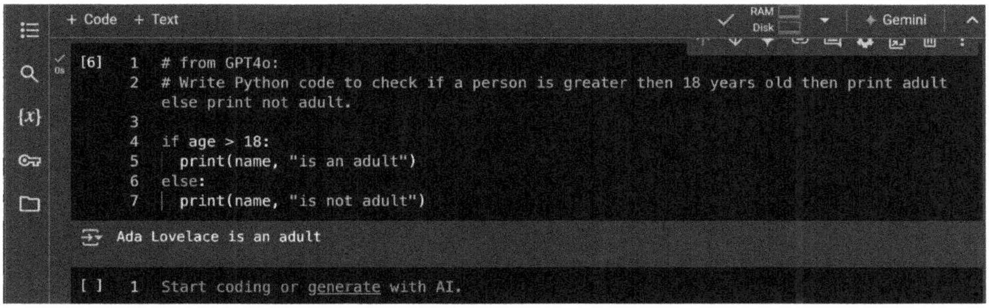

Figure 2.6: Jupyter Notebook, Python if/else statement

In *Figure 2.6*, line #2 is the prompt for GPT4o asking for example of Python if and else statement. We then copied and pasted the code to our Notebook. When you do the same, you might see slightly different code output.

Line #4 through line #7 are the **if else** construct. Notice the age and name variable were defined earlier in a separate code cell. That code cell is *Figure 2.4*, line #3 and #4. The output is: **Ada Lovelace is an adult.**

Other than greater than, **>**, there are other testing conditions, such as less than, **<**, equal, **==**, greater than and equal, **>=**, less than and equal, **<=**, and the **is** condition. You should use GPT4o to learn about these conditions. In addition, you should learn about nested **if,** **elif**, and **else** statements. The next chapter, Chapter 3, *Dissect the Calculator App*, will cover these in detail.

The last example of using code cell is looping. Loops (such as **for** and **while** loops) provide a way to repeatedly execute a block of code for every item in a list or until a particular condition changes. This is invaluable for tasks that require repetition, such as processing items in a list or generating sequences of numbers. Together, these elements form the building blocks of Python programming, allowing you to create robust and dynamic solutions in your Jupyter Notebook code cells.

An example of a Loop code structure is in *Figure 2.7*:

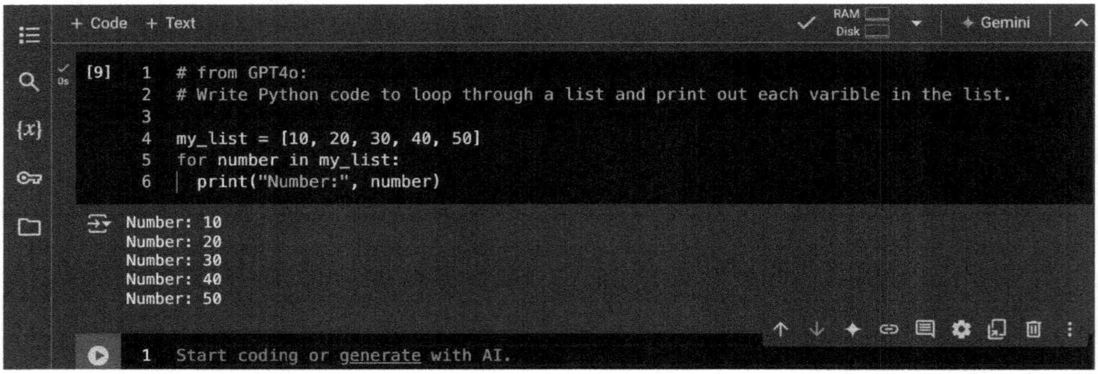

Figure 2.7: Jupyter Notebook, Python loops

In *Figure 2.7*, line #2 is the prompt we used to ask GPT4o to write a Python example code for demonstrating looping. As with other examples, GPT4o not only writes the code but also gives a full explanation of it. However, we only copy the code to our Jupyter Notebook. We should copy the GPT4o explanation of the code in our text cell. Thus, our Jupyter Notebook can have a complete code and description for later review.

Line #4, define a list of integers named **my_list** with values 10, 20, 30, 40 and 50. Line #5 and #6 are the for loop and printing each value in the **my_list**.

Our examples of the Python Jupyter Notebook code cells conclude. Next, we will examine the text cell.

Text cells

Text cells, on the other hand, are used for adding narratives, explanations, formulas, or instructions to your notebook. These cells support Markdown, a lightweight markup language that allows you to add formatting elements like headers, bold, italics, hyperlinks, bullet lists, and more. You can also incorporate LaTeX for mathematical equations, enhancing your notebook's readability and educational value.

Text cells use Markdown, a lightweight markup language that enables you to add formatting using plain text. It is simpler than HTML but powerful enough to handle most formatting needs. You can incorporate mathematical notation directly into text cells using LaTeX syntax, particularly useful in academic, scientific, and technical documentation. Besides text, you can embed images, videos, and hyperlinks, which makes the notebook more interactive and informative.

When you enter text into a text cell in a Google Colab Jupyter Notebook, the interface is designed to provide a clear and intuitive editing experience. By default, the screen is split vertically during text editing. On the left side, you can write Markdown code using simple syntax to format your text, create headings, add lists, or include images. On the right side, you can see a real-time preview of how your content will appear once rendered. This split view allows you to experiment with formatting and adjust your content instantly, achieving the desired look without switching back and forth between editing and display modes.

For added convenience, Google Colab allows you to customize keyboard shortcuts for common actions, including adding a new text cell. This option can significantly speed up your workflow, especially when working on larger notebooks that require frequent annotation or documentation. By default, you can use *CTRL+M* on Windows or *Option+M* on a MacBook to insert a new text cell directly. These shortcuts make it easy to structure your notebook as you work, keeping your notes and explanations organized alongside your code.

The following figure shows the basic Markdown formatting:

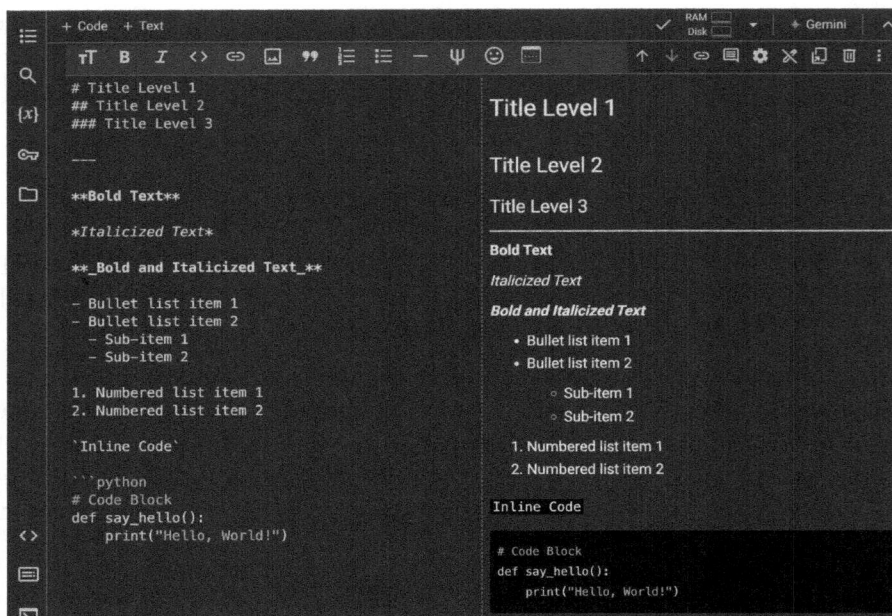

Figure 2.8: Jupyter Notebook Markdown

In line with the previous code cell examples, we are using GPT-4o to assist with our coding. We crafted the following prompt for GPT-4o and then copied the output into our Jupyter Notebook. The example is show in *Figure 2.8*. When you do this, you see that, along with the code, GPT-4o gives the full explanation of markup language and how each markup works.

In *Figure 2.8*, the markup code appears on the left, while the preview displays on the right. Along with the *CTRL+M* on Windows or *Option+M* on Apple, you can click on the + **Text** button on the upper left of the screen, next to the + **Code** button.

The Markdown language used in Jupyter Notebooks, including Google Colab, is designed to be simple and intuitive, making it easy to format text and enhance the presentation of your notebooks as in *Figure 2.8*. For example, you can use # to create a title or main heading, ## for a subheading, and ### for a smaller sub-subheading. A horizontal line can be added with ---, and you can style text with * for italics and ** for bold. Bullet lists are created with -, while numbered lists use numbers followed by a period, like 1. There are a few others explained in *Figure 2.8*.

One of the best aspects of using Markdown in Google Colab is that you do not need to memorize these commands. The interface includes a toolbar at the top of the text cell editor with icons that make formatting accessible even for beginners. For instance, clicking the B icon will automatically insert the syntax for bold text, and the *image* icon lets you insert images without typing the Markdown manually. These icons provide a visual way to apply formatting, making it easy to learn Markdown syntax as you go.

This combination of straightforward syntax and user-friendly tools allows you to create well-organized and visually appealing notebooks with minimal effort. Whether you are documenting your code, creating tutorials, or presenting results, Markdown's simplicity and Colab's built-in support ensure that formatting is quick and accessible.

The next example of the text cell is using LaTeX for mathematical equations.

Using LaTeX in Jupyter Notebook offers a powerful way to display mathematical and scientific notation with precision and clarity. Its syntax allows you to create beautifully formatted equations, symbols, and expressions that are easy to read and professional in appearance. Whether you are explaining complex formulas, documenting scientific research, or visualizing mathematical concepts, LaTeX ensures your work is presented clearly and accurately. Integrated directly into text cells, it streamlines the process of combining narrative with technical notation, making it an essential tool for educators, researchers, and students. This is shown in the following figure:

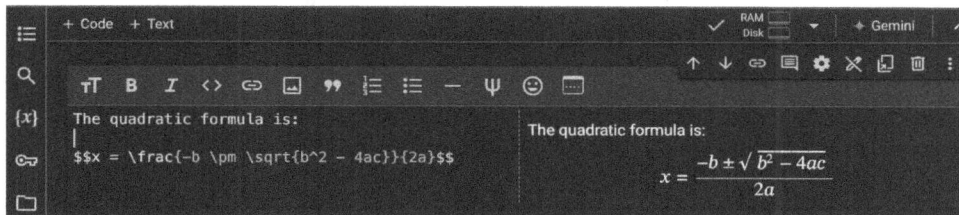

Figure 2.9: *Jupyter Notebook, LaTeX, quadratic formular*

We used GPT-4o once again to help us learn about LaTeX. The prompt we provided was: *Write an example of using LaTeX for mathematical equations.* The response from GPT-4o included a comprehensive explanation of LaTeX and its usage, along with several examples. We selected the quadratic formula and included it in *Figure 2.9.*

The LaTeX syntax is not complicated to learn. However, are you glad you have GPT-4 to help or even write it for you?

Here are a few more LaTeX examples in the text and accompanying code cells:

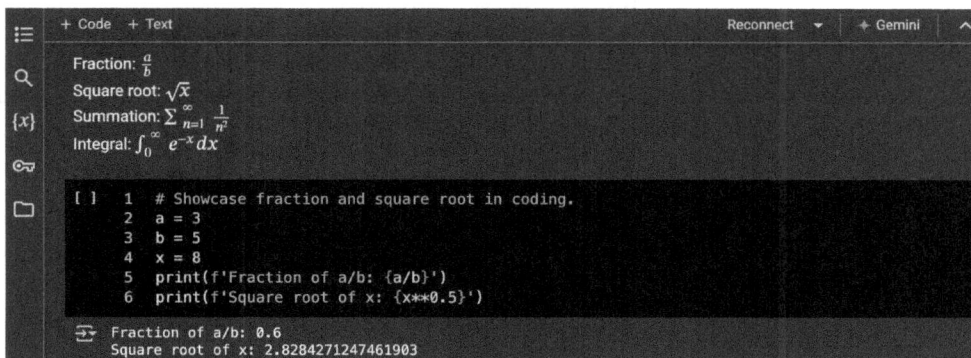

Figure 2.10: *Jupyter Notebook, complex equations*

Figure 2.10 showcases a new set of LaTeX examples, generated using GPT-4o, to demonstrate how mathematical and scientific notations are beautifully rendered in Jupyter Notebooks. This figure includes a range of examples, from simple fractions and square root notations to more advanced expressions like summation and integral equations. The LaTeX markup that generates these expressions is hidden by default in the preview mode, providing a clean and professional appearance. However, you can easily view and edit the underlying LaTeX code by clicking on the text cell. Doing so will return the split-screen view of the code and preview, similar to what was illustrated earlier in *Figure 2.9*.

To enhance the understanding of how LaTeX works with functional code, we have added a code cell directly below the text cell in the same screenshot. This image allows you to see both the LaTeX-rendered formulas and the corresponding Python calculations side by side. The Python code calculates a fraction **a/b** and the square root of **x**, bridging the gap between theoretical notation and practical computation. This layout emphasizes the flexibility of Jupyter Notebooks, where text, equations, and code seamlessly combine to create an interactive and educational workspace.

In conclusion, text does not have to be used only in text cells. The purpose of Jupyter Notebook code cells is to execute code, but you can effectively use markup syntax through Python comments to enhance readability and maintainability.

Using markup language and LaTeX in Jupyter Notebook text cells offers a range of benefits that enhance your notebook's overall usability and presentation. Markdown provides a simple and intuitive way to format text, allowing you to create headings, bullet points, numbered lists, and emphasize text with bold or italic styles. These additions make organizing and annotating your work easy, ensuring clarity for personal reference and collaborative projects. Markdown transforms your notebook into a cohesive and interactive document by combining narrative, instructions, and notes with code.

LaTeX, on the other hand, extends text cells' capabilities by enabling precise representation of mathematical and scientific notation. Complex equations, fractions, square roots, integrals, and summations can be displayed cleanly and professionally, making it invaluable for educators, researchers, and students. Integrating LaTeX within text cells allows seamless blending of technical content with explanatory text, bridging the gap between theory and practice.

Together, Markdown and LaTeX empower users to create functional, visually appealing, and highly informative notebooks. They provide an effective means of documenting workflows, sharing insights, and presenting polished reports.

Along with using text cells for documentation, in-line code comments are crucial for annotating your code to provide explanations, denote sections, and offer insights that are not immediately apparent from the code itself. Single-line comments, denoted by a **#**, allow you to briefly explain what a particular line of code is doing, making your code easier to understand for others or yourself when you revisit it later.

For more extensive explanations, multiline comments using triple quotes (""") can be employed to cover detailed descriptions over several lines without interrupting the code execution flow. Although these multiline strings are technically not comments, they serve a similar purpose in practical use by allowing large blocks of text to be ignored by the Python interpreter.

This capability to incorporate comments directly alongside code fosters more precise communication within teams and aids in documenting complex algorithms directly within the execution environment.

The following figure is an example of comment markups:

```
:≡        + Code   + Text                                          Reconnect   ▾   + Gemini   ∧

Q       [ ]  1   # This is a single line comment, as you see throughout previous examples
             2
{x}          3   """
             4   This is a multiline comment.
             5   Using inline comments along with the text cell with markup langauge and LaTex
☞            6   notation is the best way to document your code.
             7
             8   These comments are ignored by the Python interpreter, but they will be exported
▢            9   with the pure python (.py) files.
            10   The documentation from the text cell will not be exported in the .py files.
            11   """
            12   def are_you_happy():
            13       print("I am tickled pink.")
            14       return True                # always return happy == True
```

Figure 2.11: Jupyter Notebook inline comments

In *Figure 2.11*, line #1 is the single line comment, starting with "**#**" character. Lines 3 to 11 are the multiline comments block, starting and ending with tripple qoute. Lines 12 to 14 are a fun function of asking **are_you_happy()**.

In summary, having explored the essential components of Google Colab, such as code and text cells, which facilitate the integration of executable code with rich explanatory text, we now focus on some of the specialized features that make Google Colab a practical tool for data scientists and researchers.

These features include accessing accessible GPUs and TPUs, real-time collaboration options, and direct integration with Google Drive.

Special Google Collab features

Google Colab stands out as a premier platform for data science and machine learning, offering several unique features that significantly enhance its users' usability and functionality. Its most notable offerings are free access to **Graphics Processing Units (GPUs)** and **Tensor Processing Units (TPUs)** for intensive computations.

Google Colab offers many advanced features for free, making it an accessible and powerful tool for users of all levels. Unlike other platforms, there is no need to sign any additional contracts, and these free features are not limited to a trial period—they remain available indefinitely. This feature allows students, researchers, and developers to explore and build projects without worrying about hidden costs or time restrictions.

Google offers a paid upgrade to Colab Pro for those with more demanding computational needs. This plan provides access to more powerful GPUs and longer runtimes, enabling users to tackle resource-intensive tasks such as training large-scale machine learning models. However, there is often no need to upgrade unless you are working on projects requiring significant computational resources—such as training **Large Language Models (LLMs)** like Stable Diffusion 3.5-Large or other complex deep learning models. The free version of Google Colab is sufficient for most small to medium-sized projects, data analysis, and experimentation.

These real-time collaboration capabilities mirror the interaction of Google Docs and robust integration with Google Drive for convenient data management and storage. These features collectively make Google Colab an invaluable tool for researchers, educators, and data scientists, efficiently facilitating advanced computational tasks and collaborative projects.

The top three Google Colab features are as follows:

- Free access to GPUs and TPUs
- Real-time collaboration
- Integration with Google Drive

First up are GPUs and TPUs.

Free access to GPUs and TPUs

Google Colab provides free access to GPUs and TPUs, which are crucial for accelerating computational tasks, particularly in machine learning and deep learning. When you are learning Python, you might hear a lot about GPUs, especially if you are interested in gaming, graphics, or machine learning. GPU is a piece of hardware that handles lots of calculations simultaneously. This makes it perfect for tasks simultaneously processing large amounts of data, such as creating complex graphics in video games or training machine learning models.

Google Colab provides various resource options, from the free standard tier to the advanced Pro tier. Colab scales with your workload, whether you are running basic data analysis or training large-scale machine learning models. The following is a breakdown of the resources available in each option:

- **Standard option (Free tier):** This option is ideal for small to medium-sized projects, data analysis, and basic machine learning tasks. The free tier offers access to GPU resources sufficient for lightweight deep learning and experimentation without additional costs.

- CPU RAM: 12 GB

- Disk space: 228 GB

- GPU: NVIDIA T4 or similar, with 8 GB of GPU RAM

- TPU: v2 TPU with limited availability, offering 8 TPU cores and 64 GB of TPU RAM

- **L4 GPU option (Available in Colab Pro):** Designed for projects requiring higher performance, such as training moderately sized deep learning models, running complex simulations, or working with larger datasets. The increased resources provide a significant performance boost compared to the standard option.

  - CPU RAM: 43 GB

  - GPU: NVIDIA L4 with 22 GB of GPU RAM

- **A100 GPU option (Available in Colab Pro):** Best for resource-intensive tasks such as training LLMs, image generation models like Stable Diffusion, or large-scale simulations. The A100 GPU is among the most powerful options for deep learning and scientific computing, providing exceptional speed and efficiency for demanding workloads.

  - CPU RAM: 86 GB

  - GPU: NVIDIA A100 with 40 GB of GPU RAM

- **v2-8 TPU option (Available in Colab Pro+ with TPU):** Ideal for large-scale machine learning tasks, especially when working with TensorFlow or PyTorch frameworks optimized for TPU performance. The v2-8 TPU delivers high-speed processing for tasks like natural language processing, image classification, and training deep neural networks with extensive datasets.

  - CPU RAM: 64 GB

  - TPU RAM: 128 GB across 8 TPU cores

- **v5e-1 TPU option (Available in Colab Pro+ with advanced TPU):** Optimized for cutting-edge AI workloads, the v5e-1 TPU offers exceptional computational power for extremely large datasets and state-of-the-art model training. This option is perfect for researchers and professionals working on advanced applications like GPT-scale LLMs, reinforcement learning, or high-resolution image generation models.

  - CPU RAM: 128 GB

  - TPU RAM: 256 GB

Access to a GPU and TPU is essential for the following three reasons.

- **Speed:** The most significant advantage of a GPU is its speed in performing parallel operations. While a **central processing unit (CPU)** has a few cores focused on performing tasks one after the other, a GPU has thousands of smaller cores designed to handle multiple tasks simultaneously. This means functions that can be done in parallel, like processing pixels in an image or handling numerous inputs for a machine learning algorithm, can be done much faster on a GPU.

- **Efficiency in data processing:** In data science and machine learning, you often deal with massive datasets or complex algorithms that require a lot of computational power. GPUs can significantly reduce the time it takes to process this data or train models, making your projects faster to complete and more feasible to iterate and improve.

- **Broader accessibility to advanced computing:** With platforms like Google Colab offering free access to GPUs, even beginners who do not have powerful computers can access state-of-the-art computing resources. This democratizes learning and experimenting with complex computational fields like artificial intelligence, where access to powerful hardware could otherwise be a barrier.

The second major feature for Google Colab is real-time collaboration.

Real-time collaboration

The real-time collaboration feature in Google Colab is a game-changer for team projects and educational settings. It allows multiple users to open and work on the same notebook simultaneously, seeing each other's contributions as they happen. This functionality is enhanced with a built-in chat feature, where team members can directly discuss and coordinate their work within the environment.

Whether tweaking code, sharing insights, or debugging together, this feature ensures that teamwork and knowledge transfer are as smooth and immediate as possible, mirroring the collaborative experience in Google Docs.

Two standout features that make collaboration efficient and real-time are its automatic integration with GitHub and its deep connection with Google Drive. These features simplify sharing, editing, and managing Jupyter Notebooks, making Colab an ideal tool for teams, students, and professionals. By enabling easy access to shared resources and synchronized updates, Google Colab ensures a smooth workflow for collaborative projects, whether you are working on version-controlled repositories or cloud-based files.

- **Automatic integration with GitHub**: Google Colab offers seamless access to GitHub, allowing users to collaborate on Jupyter Notebooks stored in repositories. With just a few clicks, you can import notebooks from GitHub directly into Colab, edit them in real-time, and save your changes to the repository. This feature is particularly beneficial for teams working on shared projects, enabling version control and simplifying merging updates. GitHub integration ensures that all collaborators stay on the same page, making it easy to track changes and maintain consistency across the team's work.

We will discuss shared Google Drive in the next section.

Integration with Google Drive

Integration with Google Drive is another powerful feature of Google Colab that streamlines the workflow of managing data and notebooks. This integration allows users to save their notebooks and access data files stored on Google Drive. Changes to notebooks are automatically saved and backed up in the cloud, ensuring that users' work is secure and retrievable from any location.

Additionally, this connection facilitates easy sharing and publishing of work, as notebooks can be shared amongst users or made public just like any other Google Drive document. This makes managing and organizing files easier and enhances accessibility and collaboration across different users and projects.

First, you need to mount your Google Drive into the Colab environment. This is done using the Google Colab library, which provides a method to authenticate and create a link between your Colab session and Google Drive.

The following figure is an example of how to mount your Google Drive into the Colab:

Figure 2.12: Google Drive on Google Colab

In *Figure 2.12*, line #2 is the friendly prompt we ask GPT-4o. There are full detail explanation of mounting to Google Drive from GPT-4o, but only copy the code to our Jupyter Notebook.

Line #5 imports the function **drive()** from the Python library **google.colab**. Line #6 mount the shared Google Drive accessible by directory path **/content/drive**.

Once you run the above code, there will be a series of pop-up windows asking you to give Jupyter Notebook access to your Google Drive directory.

The sequence of permitting to log in Google Drive is as follows:

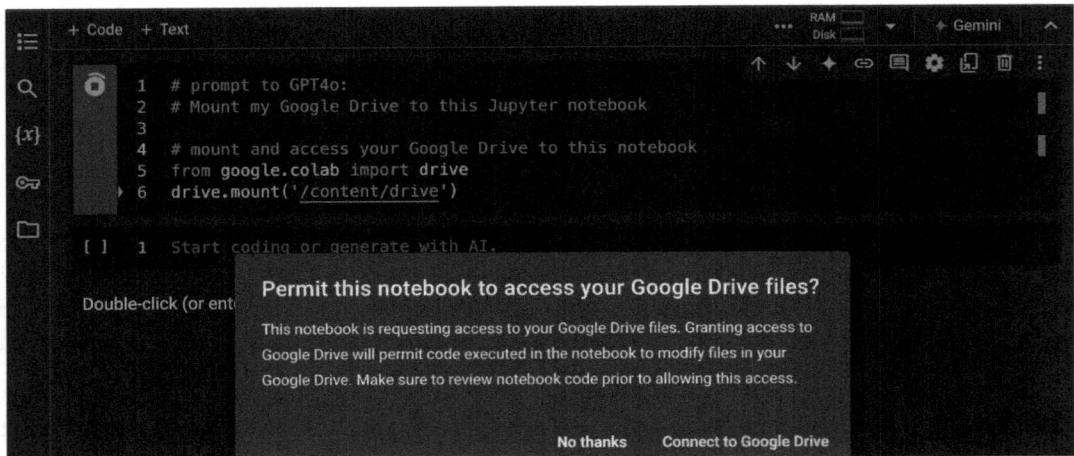

Figure 2.13: Google Drive access permission

Figure 2.13 shows the first popup when you run the `drive.mount()` function. The popup asks for a permit for this notebook to access your Google Drive file. You should click on the **Connect to Google Drive** button to continue, or you can click on **No Thanks** button to stop.

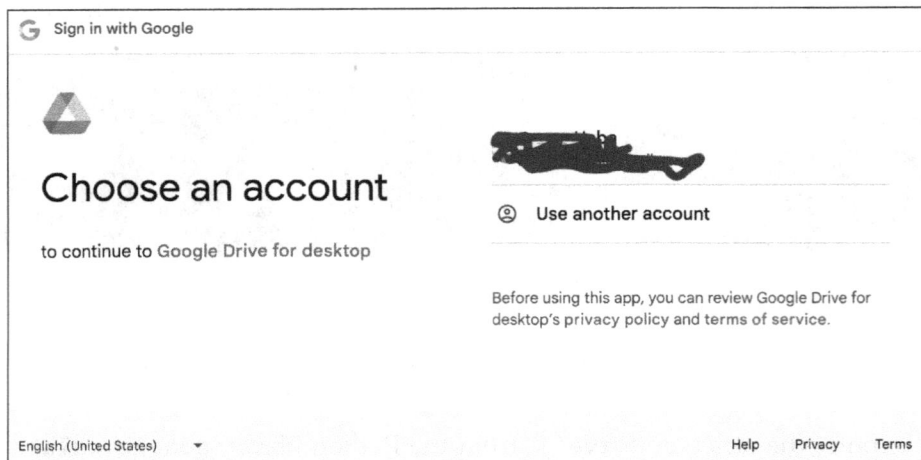

Figure 2.14: Google Drive choose an account

After you choose to connect to Google Drive, you will see a popup asking you to choose which Google account you want to use, *Figure 2.14*. After you select a Google account, you will proceed to the next popup.

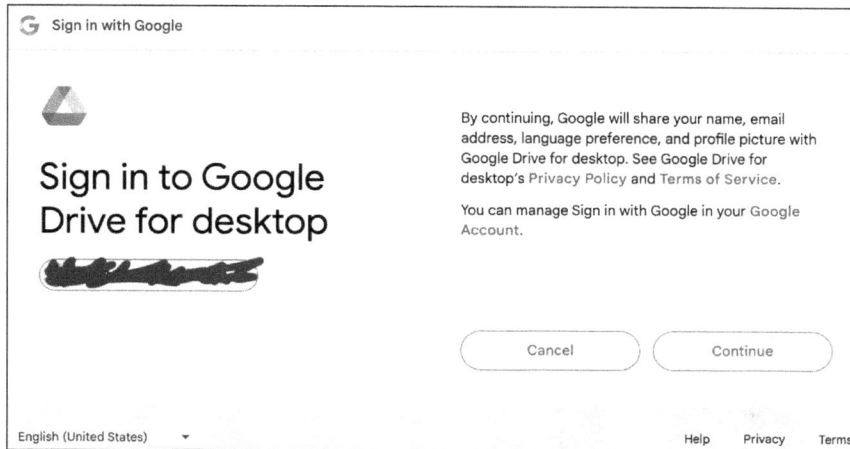

Figure 2.15: *Google Drive sign in for desktop*

Figure 2.15 displays the confirmation that you want to sign in to Google Drive for desktop. It is a security feature, and you can choose to continue or cancel. You should click on the **Continue** button to advance to the last popup.

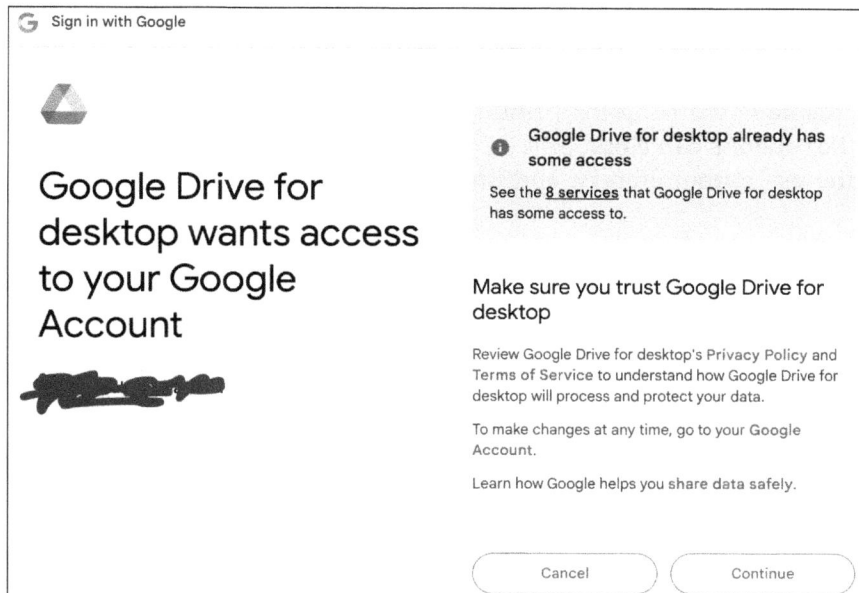

Figure 2.16: *Google Drive for desktop access*

Figure 2.16 is the last popup for Google Drive for desktops that want access to your Google account. It lists the eight services your Jupyter Notebook can access on your Google Drive and includes privacy policy and terms of service links. It is a last chance for you to say **No or Cancel**.

If you are sure to give the Jupyter Notebook access to your Google Drive, click on the **Continue** button.

Once Google Drive is mounted, it is accessible from the directory **/content/drive/My Drive/Colab Notebooks/**. You can read and write files in this directory using standard Python code.

The following figure is an example of how to list files and directories in the root of your Google Drive:

```
[4]   1  # prompt GPT4:
      2  # List the directory of my google drive content in Python code
      3
      4  import os
      5  os.listdir('/content/drive/MyDrive/Colab Notebooks')
      6

    ['fastai_colab_lesson_1_course3_inference_only.ipynb',
     '00_notebook_tutorial.ipynb',
     'fastai_colab_lesson_3_course3_camvid_tiramisu.ipynb',
     'fastai_colab_lesson_3_course3_imdb.ipynb',
     'fastai_colab_lesson_3_course3_camvid.ipynb',
     'fastai_colab_lesson_3_course3_planet.ipynb',
     'fastai_colab_lesson_2_course3_experiment.ipynb',
```

Figure 2.17: Google Drive root folder

Figure 2.17 displays the code for printing the content of your shared Google Drive in the **Colab Notebooks** directory. Line #2 is our friendly prompt request to GPT-4o. Line #4 import the **os** Python library, and line #5 print out the content of the Google Drive directory.

Google Drive integration is beneficial for machine learning or data analysis projects where datasets are too large to upload directly to Colab each time. Having your data in Google Drive lets you quickly load it into your Colab notebooks whenever needed. Additionally, this setup helps keep your work organized and accessible from anywhere, leveraging the cloud storage of Google Drive and the computational power of Google Colab.

Through Google Drive integration, Google Colab becomes a more powerful tool by expanding its file storage and management capabilities, making it easier to handle large-scale projects directly from your browser.

Conclusion

As we wrap up this chapter on Python Jupyter Notebooks and Google Colab, we have journeyed through a landscape where coding meets creativity. From the interactive and modular design of Jupyter Notebooks to the powerful, collaborative features of Google Colab, these tools not only streamline the process of coding and data analysis but also enhance the accessibility of advanced computational resources.

We learn how Jupyter Notebooks facilitate an engaging blend of live code, visualizations, and narrative, allowing users to transform complex code into understandable stories. Similarly, Google Colab's provision of GPUs and TPUs, coupled with its integration with Google Drive and real-time collaboration features, democratizes the ability to perform sophisticated data science tasks.

By now, you should have a solid understanding of setting up and navigating these platforms, leveraging their unique features to boost your productivity and extend your analytical capabilities. As you continue to explore and experiment beyond the core functionalities discussed, remember that the true power of these tools lies in their ability to adapt to and evolve with your growing needs as a programmer or researcher.

In this chapter, we have taken our first steps into coding by exploring the foundational aspects of Jupyter Notebooks and becoming familiar with basic concepts. This gentle introduction is designed to help you ease into the environment and understand the potential of combining narrative, code, and tools like GPT-4o. As we move forward, the following chapters will explore coding deeper, building on these basics to tackle more complex tasks and concepts.

We encourage you to actively use and explore GPT-4o and Jupyter Notebook as much as possible. The more you experiment with these tools, the more natural and intuitive they will become in your learning process. Whether seeking guidance from GPT-4o, testing small pieces of code, or simply exploring the possibilities, this hands-on approach will help you build confidence and make your learning experience productive and enjoyable.

In the upcoming chapters, GPT-4o will become an even more essential part of your learning journey, serving as your guide and assistant as the coding challenges become more complex. Whether debugging errors, offering creative solutions, or explaining complex concepts, GPT-4o will help bridge the gap between understanding and practical application. As the coding tasks increase in difficulty, you will find its support invaluable in keeping you on track and advancing your skills. This journey is just beginning, and with GPT-4o by your side, you are well-equipped to tackle the challenges ahead.

Whether you are a student, educator, or professional, the journey into Python Jupyter Notebooks and Google Colab is one of endless discovery and innovation. Embrace the flexibility and potential of these environments and let them inspire your next project in data science, machine learning, or beyond.

As we conclude our setup in this chapter, we are now ready to explore the essentials of Python and explore how GenAI can become a powerful coding companion in Chapter 3, *Dissect the Calculator App*. Here, we will unveil the Calculator code, get hands-on with app-building, and map out your personalized coding journey.

Join our book's Discord space

Join the book's Discord Workspace for Latest updates, Offers, Tech happenings around the world, New Release and Sessions with the Authors:

https://discord.bpbonline.com

CHAPTER 3
Dissect The Calculator App

Introduction

This chapter involves taking a close look at the elements that go into coding a simple calculator app. We will also take a look at how we can utilize ChatGPT's help in giving detailed breakdowns on what certain lines of code do and what they mean.

By using the calculating app as your gateway to learn Python, you are adopting a playful and hands-on approach that introduces you to the basics of Python syntax in a natural and engaging way. Instead of diving headfirst into tedious memorization of concepts, this method focuses on exploration and discovery. Think of it as a concept of *play first*, where experimentation and curiosity take the lead.

As you interact with the app, you will quickly grasp fundamental Python concepts like variables, functions, and operations, all within a framework that emphasizes practical application over rote learning. This approach allows you to build confidence and familiarity with Python's structure, all while having fun and seeing immediate results from your efforts.

Why is this easier than traditional memorization techniques? Because learning by doing taps into your natural ability to solve problems and apply logic. It transforms Python from an abstract subject into a tangible skill. Each calculation you perform becomes a stepping stone, helping you internalize Python's syntax and functionality without feeling like you are cramming for a test. It is less about forcing knowledge into your brain and more about letting it naturally unfold through practice.

So, as you work with the calculating app, you are not just learning Python. You are mastering it in a way that feels intuitive, empowering, and, most importantly, enjoyable.

Structure

This chapter will cover the following topics:

- Python fundamentals
- Explaining code
- Calculator code reveal
- Understanding Python using GenAI
- Practical applications
- Chart your course

Objectives

In this chapter, we are going to explore and learn about our first project using Python; creating a simple calculator app. While this may sound daunting, do not worry! We will be breaking this down so that everything can be understood individually. This chapter's main objective is to utilize the creation of this calculator app to further understand and break down common variables, functions, and rules of Python. We will be using Juniper notebook and ChatGPT-4 in this section to learn how to code a calculator app using python. By the end of this chapter, we should be able to feel comfortable defining key terms and using them within our own projects. Before we get started, let us first take a look at what topics we are going to be covering in this chapter.

Let us explore learning all about Python fundamentals and GenAI as a coding companion.

Python fundamentals

Before we take a look at creating a calculator app, we first need to familiarize ourselves with a handful of key terms and concepts within Python. This will ensure a better understanding of certain elements of code within the calculator app. We will also go over how GenAI can help us decipher what certain lines of code do.

In this chapter, we expect you to have a solid understanding of the skills introduced in *Chapter 1, Introduction to GenAI,* and *Chapter 2, Jupyter Notebook,* before moving forward. Chapter 1 covers using GPT-4o for coding, troubleshooting, and brainstorming, while Chapter 2 focuses on setting up and using Python Jupyter Notebook for writing and managing code. These foundational skills are essential for tackling the more advanced concepts ahead.

In particular, we will focus on the following key terms and concepts:

- Variables
- If-else decision
- Functions
- Looping
- Class or object

First, let us go over key terms, starting with **variables**.

Variables

Variables are used to store data that can be used and manipulated throughout your program. In Python, you do not need to declare the type of a variable explicitly; the type is inferred based on the value assigned to it.

The following figure is an example that shows **dog_name** as a string variable, and **dog_age** as an integer variable:

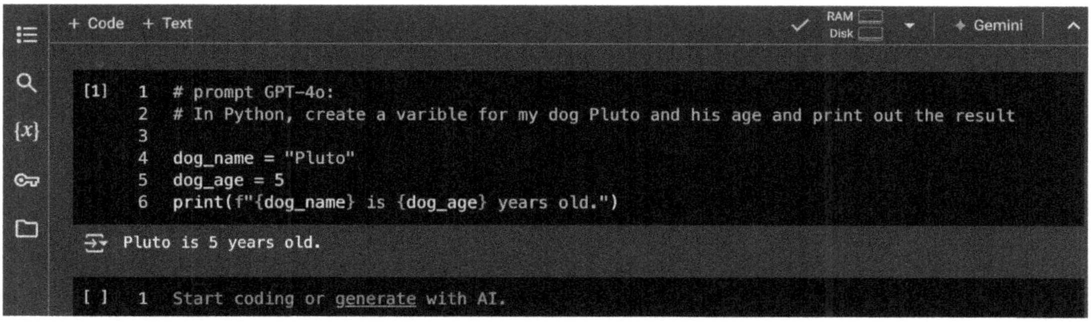

Figure 3.1: Variable example with print function

Figure 3.1 shows the code for Pluto's variables. On line 2, you will see the prompt we typed into GPT-4o. In response, it provided a detailed explanation along with the code. We then copied the code and pasted it into our Jupyter Notebook to continue working with it.

Line 4 defines the **dog_name**, while line 5 sets the **dog_age**. Finally, line 6 prints the result: **Pluto is 5 years old.**

In Chapter 2, *Jupyter Notebook,* you learned that variables in Python go beyond just strings for names and integers for ages. To explore this further, we asked GPT-4o to **use Pluto as the reference and explain other types of Python variables** (the prompt to GPT-4o). Here is what we discovered:

- **Float**: Represents a number with a decimal, useful for precise measurements:

  o Code example: `dog_weight = 25.5 # Pluto weighs 25.5 kilograms`

- **Boolean**: Represents a **True** or **False** value, like whether Pluto is a trained dog:

  o Code example: `is_trained = True # Pluto is a trained dog`

- **List**: Stores multiple values, such as Pluto's favorite toys:

  o Code example: `favorite_toys = ["ball", "bone", "squeaky duck"]`

- **Tuple**: Similar to a list but immutable (cannot be changed), such as Pluto's vaccinations:

  o Code example: `dog_vaccinations = ("rabies", "parvo", "distemper") # Vaccinations Pluto has received`

- **Dictionary**: Stores data in key-value pairs, making it great for grouping Pluto's details:

  o Code example: `dog_details = {"name": "Pluto", "age": 5, "weight": 25.5, "is_trained": True}`

- **None**: Represents the absence of a value, such as when we have not assigned Pluto's microchip ID yet:

  o Code example: `microchip_id = None # We haven't set this value yet`

These variable types let us represent Pluto's characteristics in a clear and practical way, making Python a useful tool for organizing different kinds of data.

Note: In this example, the # used within coding does not impact the output of the code itself. Think of it as a way to organize and explain what the following line or section of code is going to do. In other languages other than Python, // is used instead of # to serve the same purpose, however Python only used the # symbol to signify that the text is a note, explanation, or reminder. Throughout this chapter, when you see the # in front of a line of text, it is providing context or a reminder to the coder. Try using these in your own projects, as they can be extremely helpful, serving as a reminder to why you included certain functions or elements in your code in case you forget.

We have wrapped up variable types, and now it is time to dive into if-else condition statements.

If-else decisions

Decision-making is a crucial part of programming. The **if-else** statements in Python allow you to execute certain pieces of code based on conditions. The following figure shows an example:

```
[3]   1   # GPT-4o prompt:
      2   # Write Python code to demonstrate the if-else condition using Pluto information
      3
      4   # Define Pluto's details
      5   is_trained = True
      6
      7   # Check if Pluto is a trained dog
      8   if is_trained:
      9       print(f"{dog_name} is a trained dog and ready to perform tricks!")
     10   else:
     11       print(f"{dog_name} is still learning and needs more training.")
     12
     13   # Check if Pluto is a senior dog, middle-aged, or young
     14   if dog_age > 10:
     15       print(f"{dog_name} is a senior dog and may need extra care.")
     16   elif 5 < dog_age <= 10:
     17       print(f"{dog_name} is in his prime years and full of energy!")
     18   else:
     19       print(f"{dog_name} is still a young pup, curious about the world!")

     Pluto is a trained dog and ready to perform tricks!
     Pluto is still a young pup, curious about the world!
```

Figure 3.2: If-else condition

Figure 3.2 shows the code for the if-else condition statement. On line 2, we provide the prompt to GPT-4o, and the result is copied into our Jupyter Notebook. Line 5 introduces the **is_trained** Boolean variable.

The **dog_name** and **dog_age** variables were already defined in *Figure 3.1*, so there is no need to redefine them here. Line 8 to 11 check if **is_trained** variable is **True** or **False** and print out the result. Since the value is true the output is: **PLuto is trained and ready to perform tricks!**

Lines 14 through 19 introduce a more complex condition-checking statement. Line 14 checks if Pluto's age is greater than ten. Line 16 evaluates if Pluto is older than five but ten or younger. Finally, line 18 defaults to cases where Pluto is five years old or younger. Since Pluto is five years old, the output is: **Pluto is still a young pup, curious about the world!**

GPT-4o provides the correct answer, but the logic feels more complicated than necessary. Can you simplify the logic for checking Pluto's age to classify him as a puppy, in his prime, or old?

To simplify checking Pluto's age, start by checking **if** Pluto is less than five years old. Next, use an **elif** to check if Pluto is less than 11 years old. Finally, use an **else** for cases where Pluto must be 11 years old or older.

Let us take a moment to highlight an important point that will serve you well as you continue learning. GPT-4o is undeniably one of the most powerful tools available today, capable of generating complex solutions and detailed explanations. However, as impressive as it is, it is important to remember that it is not a substitute for your critical thinking.

While using GPT-4o, if an answer seems overly complicated or does not feel right, take a step back and question it. The tool is designed to assist you, not to think entirely on your behalf. Engage with it by asking follow-up questions, challenging its approach, or even requesting a simpler solution version. In doing so, you ensure that you are not just passively accepting information but actively learning and refining your understanding.

The goal is not just to get the right answer; it is to understand why it is the right answer and how you can apply that knowledge to your projects. By staying curious and critical, you will develop the ability to navigate challenges with or without GPT-4o by your side. Always remember that the tool works best when you pair its capabilities with your insights.

Functions

Functions are blocks of reusable code that perform a specific task. They help to make your code modular and easier to understand. You can define a function using the **def** keyword, as shown in the following figure:

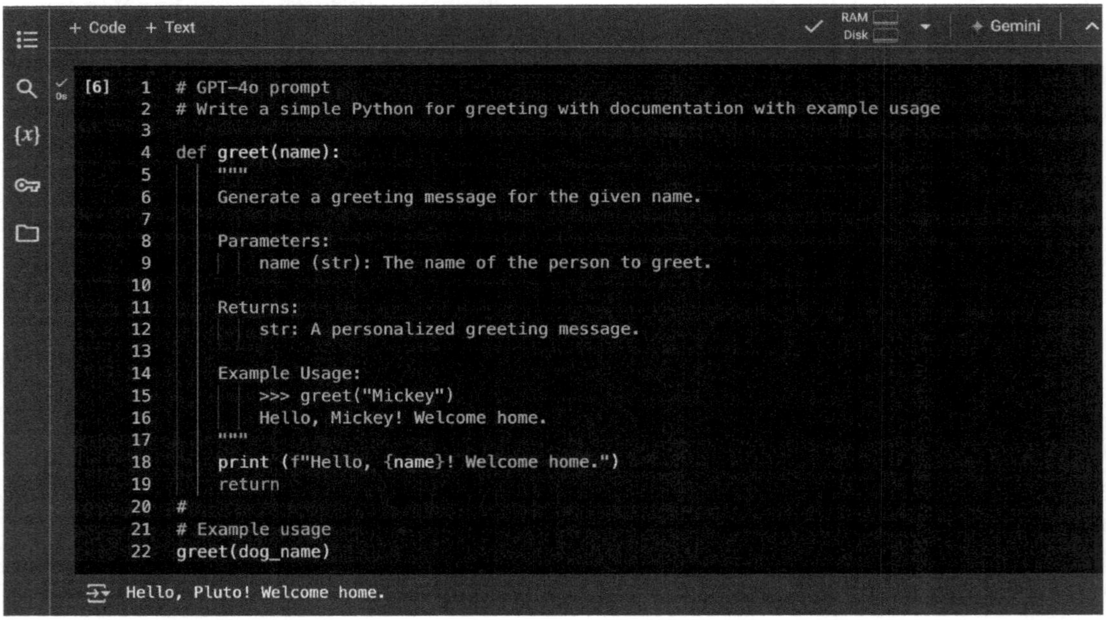

```
[6]  1  # GPT-4o prompt
     2  # Write a simple Python for greeting with documentation with example usage
     3
     4  def greet(name):
     5      """
     6      Generate a greeting message for the given name.
     7
     8      Parameters:
     9          name (str): The name of the person to greet.
    10
    11      Returns:
    12          str: A personalized greeting message.
    13
    14      Example Usage:
    15          >>> greet("Mickey")
    16          Hello, Mickey! Welcome home.
    17      """
    18      print (f"Hello, {name}! Welcome home.")
    19      return
    20  #
    21  # Example usage
    22  greet(dog_name)

    Hello, Pluto! Welcome home.
```

Figure 3.3: Function greet()

Figure 3.3 shows the **greet()** function. Line 2 is the prompt we used to ask GPT-4o to write the Python code. The response included a full explanation, but we only copied the code into our Python Jupyter Notebook.

Notice that we added **with documentation** in the prompt. This inclusion is necessary because GPT-4o automatically includes inline documentation in the code. Lines 5 through

17 show the inline documentation for the **greet()** function, covering the description, parameters, and return values.

Learning to add inline documentation is a crucial skill for beginners learning Python. It helps you understand your code, makes debugging easier, and ensures others can follow what you have written. Getting comfortable with this early on will make your Python journey much smoother.

As you learned in *Chapter 2, Jupyter Notebook,* you can use text cells in Jupyter Notebook for notes and documentation. You can also copy the descriptions and explanations from GPT-4o into your notebook text cell. This way, you have the code and explanation all in one place as you continue learning Python.

Line 4 defines the `greet()` function with the parameter `name`, which is explained in the documentation on lines 8 and 9. Line 18 prints the welcome message. Finally, line 22 calls the function, passing in the parameter `dog_name`, which we previously defined as Pluto in *Figure 3.1*. The output is: **Hello, Pluto! Welcome home.**

The **greet()** function only has one line of code, which is on line 18. While some functions can be much longer, it is a good programming habit to keep them under 40 lines. You can always call other functions within your function. So, if you are working on something complex, break it into smaller functions. This practice makes your code easier to understand and maintain.

For example, many complex programs need to calculate Fibonacci numbers as part of its calculation. Instead of repeating this code in every function, you can create a **get_fibonacci()** function and simply call it from other functions when needed. The following figure shows code for Fibonacci number:

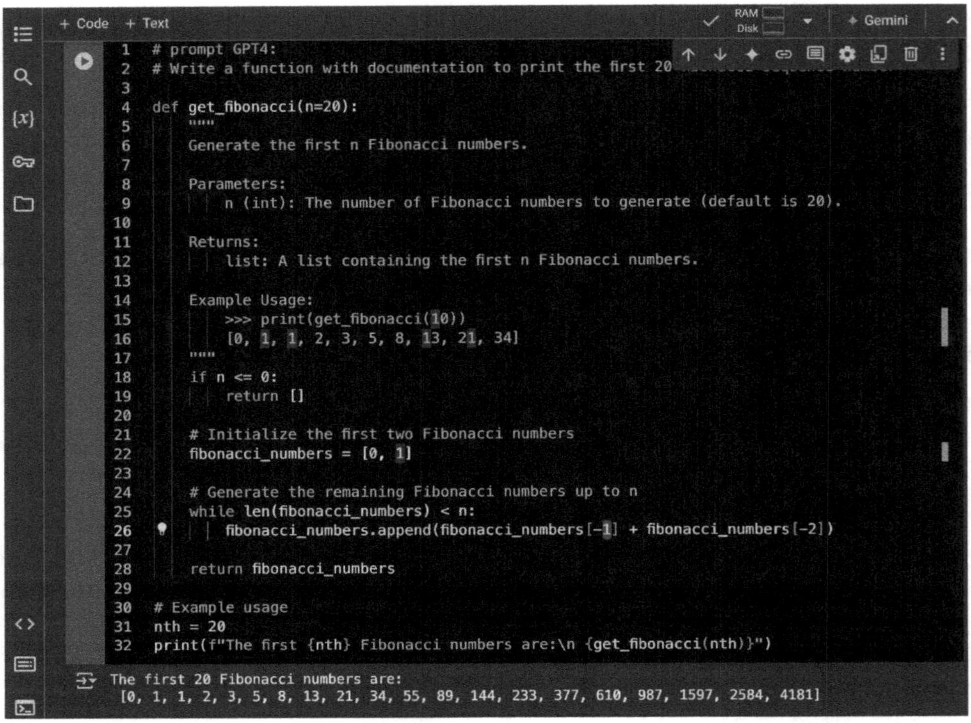

Figure 3.4: *Fibonacci function*

Figure 3.4 shows the Fibonacci function and line 2 shows the prompt for asking GPT-4o to write the Fibonacci number. Lines 5 to 17 display the inline documentation for the function. It includes the function, parameters, returns, and example usage description.

Line 4 defines the **get_fibonacci()** function with a parameter **n** that defaults to 20. This means if you do not provide a number when calling the function, it will assume you mean 20.

Line 18 checks if the passed parameter is zero or a negative number. Line 22 sets the first two numbers in the Fibonacci sequence as 0 and 1. Line 25 uses a **while** loop to generate the sequence, starting at zero and continuing until it is less than the **n** parameter. Line 26 calculates the next Fibonacci number, and finally, line 28 returns the result.

Line 31 and 32 are examples of using the Fibonacci number. The output is:

The first 20 Fibonacci numbers are:

[0, 1, 1, 2, 3, 5, 8, 13, 21, 34, 55, 89, 144, 233, 377, 610, 987, 1597, 2584, 4181]

As mentioned in *Chapter 2, Jupyter Notebook,* text cells are great for adding notes and documentation. We can even ask GPT-4o to write the function explanation in markup language, making it easy to copy and paste into our Jupyter Notebook text cell.

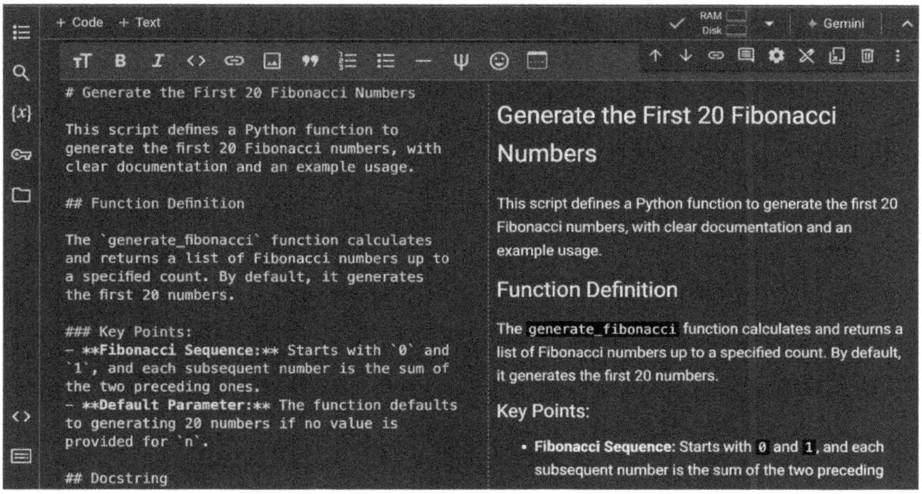

Figure 3.5: *Fibonacci explanation in markup language*

Figure 3.5 shows the output from the GPT-4o prompt: Write the explanation in markup language for a Jupyter Notebook text cell. We took this extra step so we can share the notebook with friends and colleagues, making it easy for them to follow along without needing access to GPT-4o.

That wraps up our discussion on function constructs. Next, we will explore looping structures.

Looping

Loops are used to repeat a block of code multiple times. Python provides several types of loops, with for and while being the most common. For instance, if you want to print a message five times, you can use a for loop.

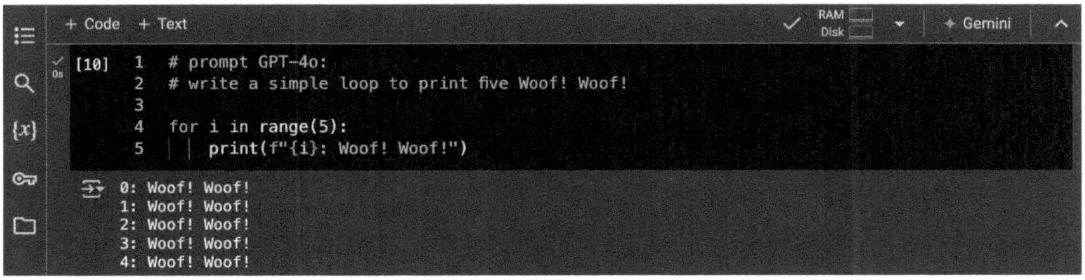

Figure 3.6: *For loop*

Figure 3.6 shows a simple loop that prints five lines of **Woof! Woof!** Line 2 is the prompt we used to ask GPT-4o to write the code. Line 4 contains the **for** loop construct, and line 5 prints the **Woof! Woof!** message. The output is exactly five lines of **Woof! Woof!**

Another type of looping construct in Python is the **while** loop. So, we asked GPT-4o to rewrite the **Woof** function using a **while** loop.

```
[11]  1   # prompt GPT-4o:
      2   # rewrite the Woof looping using while loop
      3
      4   i = 0
      5   while i < 5:
      6       print(f"{i}: Woof! Woof!")
      7       i += 1

    0: Woof! Woof!
    1: Woof! Woof!
    2: Woof! Woof!
    3: Woof! Woof!
    4: Woof! Woof!
```

Figure 3.7: While loop

Figure 3.7 shows the same simple loop, but this time using the while loop construct. Both versions output the same five lines of **Woof! Woof!** Line 2 is the prompt we gave GPT-4o to rewrite the code using a **while** loop.

Line 4 initializes **i** to zero. Line 5 sets up the **while** loop, checking if **i** is less than five. Line 6 prints **Woof! Woof!**, and line 7 increments the value **i** by 1.

For most coding tasks, the **for** loop will work perfectly, but Python has other special looping constructs you might want to explore. Take some time with GPT-4o to learn about these and see how they can be useful.

If you are curious, give these looping constructs a try and practice writing Python code for them. They are mostly for special cases or to make code more compact, so it is okay to skip for now and come back later.

Here are the exotics looping types:

- **Nested loops:** A loop inside a loop.
- **Comprehension loops:** A quick way to create lists, sets, and dictionaries using loop.
- **Break loop:** Use the **break** statements to exit the loop before the loop ends.
- **Continue loop:** Use the **continue** keyword to skip the rest of the code in the loop.
- **Zip loop:** Use the **zip()** function to loop over multiple sequences.
- **Enumerate loop:** Use the **enumerate()** function to return both the index and the value inside a loop.

That wraps up our discussion on loops. Next, we will understand objects.

Class or object

In Python, a class is a blueprint for creating objects. It defines a set of attributes and methods that the objects created from the class will have. Here is how you can create a simple **Dog** class:

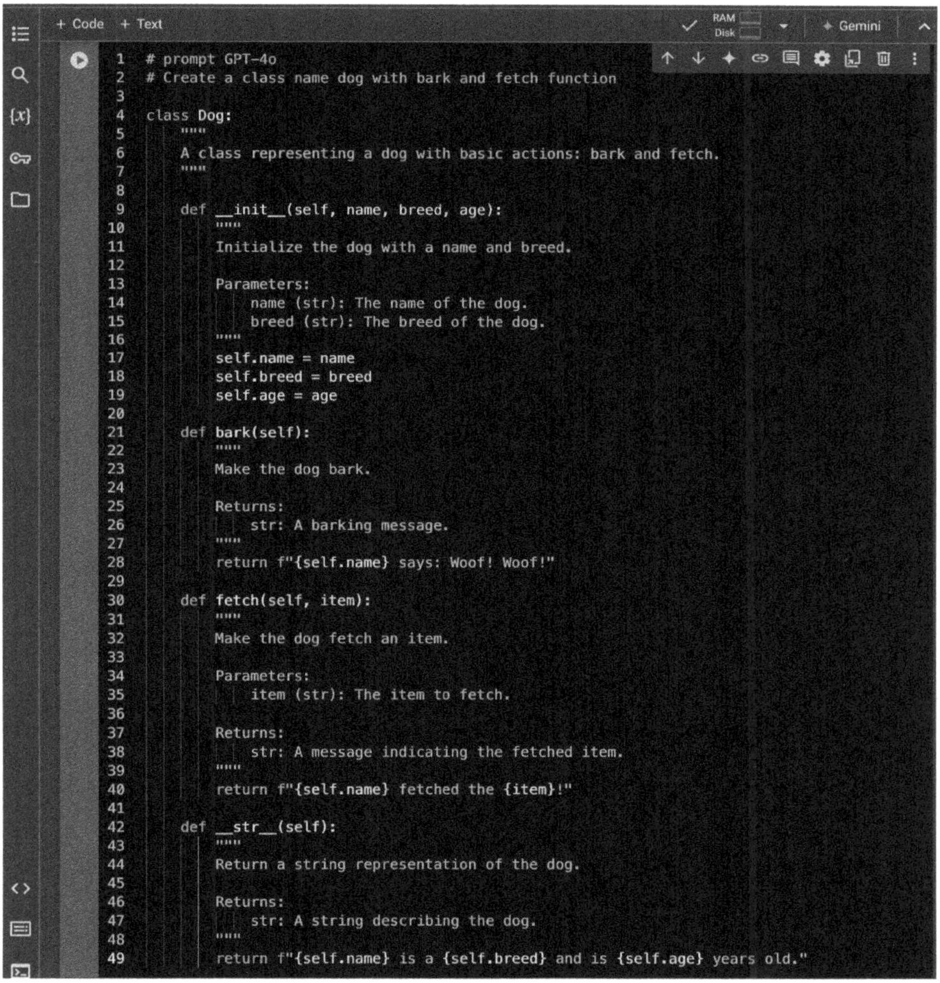

```
1   # prompt GPT-4o
2   # Create a class name dog with bark and fetch function
3
4   class Dog:
5       """
6       A class representing a dog with basic actions: bark and fetch.
7       """
8
9       def __init__(self, name, breed, age):
10          """
11          Initialize the dog with a name and breed.
12
13          Parameters:
14              name (str): The name of the dog.
15              breed (str): The breed of the dog.
16          """
17          self.name = name
18          self.breed = breed
19          self.age = age
20
21      def bark(self):
22          """
23          Make the dog bark.
24
25          Returns:
26              str: A barking message.
27          """
28          return f"{self.name} says: Woof! Woof!"
29
30      def fetch(self, item):
31          """
32          Make the dog fetch an item.
33
34          Parameters:
35              item (str): The item to fetch.
36
37          Returns:
38              str: A message indicating the fetched item.
39          """
40          return f"{self.name} fetched the {item}!"
41
42      def __str__(self):
43          """
44          Return a string representation of the dog.
45
46          Returns:
47              str: A string describing the dog.
48          """
49          return f"{self.name} is a {self.breed} and is {self.age} years old."
```

Figure 3.8: *Class object*

Figure 3.8 shows the code for creating a class named **Dog**. Line 2 is the prompt given to GPT-4o. Line 4 is the class definition. Lines 5 through 7 are the inline documentation for the class.

Line 9 is the class initialization with three parameters: **name**, **breed**, and **age**. Lines 10 through 16 are the inline documentation for the **__init__** function. Line 17 through 19 set the values for **name**, **breed**, and **age**.

Line 21 defines the **bark()** function. Lines 22 through 27 are the inline documentation, and line 28 returns the barking message.

Line 30 defines the **fetch()** function with an **item** as the parameter. Lines 31 through 39 are the inline documentation, and line 40 returns the fetch item message.

Line 42 defines the default function describing the class **Dog**. Lines 43 to 48 are the inline function documentation, and line 49 returns the class description.

In Python, an instance is a specific object created from a class. A class can be thought of as a blueprint for creating objects, and each object created from that class is an instance. The instance contains data (attributes) and methods (functions) defined by the class, but it holds its own unique state.

Understanding Python classes and objects early in your learning journey is a big step toward becoming a confident programmer. Classes and objects are the foundation of object-oriented programming, a core part of Python. They allow you to structure your code in a way that is both organized and reusable, which is especially helpful as your projects grow more complex.

Starting with these concepts early helps you build a solid understanding of how Python works and makes it easier to learn advanced topics later on. Think of it as learning the grammar of a new language—it is not always the most exciting part, but it is essential for writing and understanding anything beyond the basics. By getting comfortable with classes and objects now, you are setting yourself up to write cleaner, more efficient code down the road.

Let us use the **Dog** class to bring our best friend, Pluto, to life.

```
+ Code  + Text                                                    RAM ☐  ▾   + Gemini  ⌃
                                                                  Disk ☐

  [8]  1   # Prompt GPT-4o
  0s   2   # Create an instant Dog name Pluto and invoke its function
       3
       4   pluto = Dog(name="Pluto", breed="Labrador Retriever", age=5)
       5
       6   # Accessing attributes and methods of the Dog class
       7   print(pluto)               # Output: Pluto is a Labrador Retriever and is 5 years old.
       8   print(pluto.bark())        # Output: Pluto says: Woof! Woof!
       9   print(pluto.fetch("ball")) # Output: Pluto fetched the ball!

       Pluto is a Labrador Retriever and is 5 years old.
       Pluto says: Woof! Woof!
       Pluto fetched the ball!
```

Figure 3.9: Using Pluto class

Figure 3.9 shows the code to create our friend, Pluto. Line 2 is the prompt we gave to GPT-4o. We copied the code into our Jupyter Notebook. Line 4 creates an object named **pluto** with the details: **name** as Pluto, **breed** as Labrador Retriever, and **age** as 5.

Line 7 prints Pluto information, and the output is: **Pluto is a Labrador Retriever and is 5 years old.**

Line 8 calls the function **pluto.bark()**, and the output is: **Pluto says: Woof! Woof!**

Line 9 calls the function **pluto.fetch()** with **ball** as the passing parameter, and the output is: **Pluto fetched the ball!**

That wraps up our look at Python fundamentals: variables, if-else, functions, and classes. Now, let us explore the code and break it down in detail.

Explaining code

Code can get confusing, and although many things are named intuitively, sometimes it can be unclear how certain code works. Here are a few examples of common lines of code and what they mean and do, broken down word by word. First up is looping construct.

Loop range

In *Figure 3.6*, line 4, let us break down the code line **for i in range(5)** and explain what it does:

This line is part of a for loop in Python, which is used to repeat a block of code a specific number of times. Here is a detailed explanation of each part:

- **for**: The **for** keyword is used to start a for loop in Python. A for loop allows you to iterate over a sequence (like a list, tuple, string, or range) and execute a block of code for each item in the sequence.

- **i**: **i** is the loop variable. It is a placeholder name and can be replaced with any valid variable name. During each iteration of the loop, **i** will take on the value of the current item in the sequence generated by **range(5)**.

- **in**: The **in** keyword is used to specify the sequence that the for loop will iterate over. In this case, the sequence is generated by the **range(5)** function.

- **range(5)**: **range(5)** is a function that generates a sequence of numbers, starting from 0 and ending at 4. The range function can take one, two, or three arguments:

    o **With one argument (range(5))**: It generates numbers from 0 up to, but not including, 5 (i.e., 0, 1, 2, 3, 4).

    o **With two arguments (range(start, stop))**: It generates numbers from start-up to, but not including, stop. For example, **range(3, 6)** results in sequence (3, 4, 5).

    o **With three arguments (range(start, stop, step))**: It generates numbers from start-up to, but not including, stop, incrementing by step. For example, **range(0, 10, 2)** results in sequence (0, 2, 4, 6, 8)

Putting it all together for loop

In *Figure 3.6*, when you use `for i in range(5)` on line 4, the `for` loop is set to run five times. During each iteration, the variable `i` takes on the next value in the sequence generated by `range(5)`. This sequence starts at 0 and increments by 1 until it reaches 4. So, in the first iteration, `i` is 0. In the second iteration, it becomes 1, then 2 in the third, 3 in the fourth, and finally 4 in the fifth iteration.

Each time the loop runs, the code inside it is executed once, with the current value of `i` controlling the behavior. This makes `for` loops ideal for repetitive tasks where you know exactly how many times the loop should run. In this case, it prints **Woof! Woof!** five times, once for each value of `i`.

You can find both the code and the output example in *Figure 3.6*, showing how the loop works step by step. This simple structure demonstrates how a `for` loop helps automate repetitive tasks efficiently.

We also recommend using GPT-4o to explore other types of loops, like the `while` loop or even nested loops. While `for` loops are great for tasks with a known number of repetitions, `while` loops are better suited for scenarios where the number of iterations depends on a condition. Nested loops, on the other hand, let you perform more complex tasks, like working through lists within lists. Asking GPT-4o for examples and explanations will help you understand these concepts better and see how they can be applied in different coding situations.

Next, we will move on to explaining how functions work.

Function definition

In *Figure 3.8*, let us break down the code line 9, the `def init(self, name, breed, age)`: and explain what it does in the context of a Python class:

- **def __init__ (self, name, breed, age)**: This line defines a special method called the **initializer** or **constructor** for a class. Here is a detailed explanation of each part:
  - **def**: The def keyword is used to define a function or method in Python. In this case, it is used to define the **__init__** method.
  - **__init__**: This is a special method name in Python, also known as a **dunder method** (short for double underscore). This method is called automatically when a new instance of the class is created.

    The purpose of **__init__** is to initialize the new object's attributes and set up any initial state.
  - **self**: self is a reference to the current instance of the class. It is the first parameter of any method in a class and is used to access attributes and methods of the class.

When you create an instance of the class, self refers to that instance. Using self, you can store values in the object's attributes and call other methods defined in the class.

    o   **name, breed, age**: These are additional parameters passed to the **__init__** method. When you create a new instance of the class, you provide values for these parameters, which are then used to initialize the object's attributes.

In this example, name, breed, and age are attributes that will be assigned to the new instance of the **Dog** class.

Putting it all together for function

The **__init__** method is used to initialize an instance of a class with specific attributes. Here is how it fits into a class definition (as seen in *Figure 3.8*):

The following is an example of creating an instance:

In *Figure 3.9*, line 4, here is how you use the **Dog** class to create an instance:

- `pluto = Dog(name="Pluto", breed="Mixed", age=5)`

- This line creates a new instance of the **Dog** class.

- The **__init__** method is automatically called with the arguments **Pluto**, **Labrador Retriever**, and 5.

- Inside the **__init__** method, these arguments are used to initialize the new instance's attributes, *Figure 3.8*, lines 17 through 19.

The **__init__** method is so important because it makes sure every instance of a class starts with the right values. Whether you are creating a simple object or something more complex, the **__init__** method sets everything up by defining the attributes as the object is created. Without it, you would have to manually assign attributes every time you make an object, which can be repetitive and prone to mistakes.

Learning how the **__init__** method works early on helps you understand how Python handles objects and how to customize them. It is a core part of object-oriented programming and something you will use often as you work with classes. By getting comfortable with this now, you will be ready to write cleaner and more organized code as you tackle bigger projects. Think of it as setting the foundation for any object you create. It is a skill that will make your Python journey much smoother.

Function introduction

Lastly, in *Figure 3.8*, line #42, **def __str__(self)**: is a method definition in Python, specifically within a class. Let us take a closer look at the line "**def str(self)**" to understand what is happening within each of these parts:

- **def**: This keyword is used to define a new function or method.

- **str**: The str method is used to define a human-readable string representation of an object. It is called by the **__str__()** built-in function and the **print()** function.

- **self**: This is a reference to the current instance of the class. It is used to access variables and methods associated with the current object.

When you write **def __str__(self)**, think of it as saying, here is how we want our object to introduce itself.

Instead of showing a generic memory address, the **__str__** method allows you to define exactly how your object is represented when printed or converted to a string. It makes debugging, logging, and working with your program much more straightforward.

For example, if you are working with the **Dog** class and define a **__str__** method, you can have it return something like **This is Pluto, a 5-year-old Labrador Retriever**. Instead of seeing something unhelpful like **<Dog object at 0x10abcd>**, you get clear and readable information about the object. It is especially useful when working with multiple objects, allowing you to quickly tell them apart without digging through code.

Using the **__str__** method improves how your program communicates its output, making it easier to understand and share. Anyone looking at your code or output will immediately know what each object represents. Learning how to use the method early on gives you better control over your objects and keeps your code more organized and easier to manage.

Now that we have taken a look at how a few example lines of code can be broken down into easy-to-understand components, it is time to take a look at the project we will be dissecting for this chapter. This next section will go over the calculator code in detail, explaining each element so that we can recreate it ourselves.

Calculator code reveal

Within this simple calculator, our goal is to create something that can add, subtract, multiply, and divide any number that the user needs. First, to introduce the code, we will show our completed calculator so that later we can break down different elements that we have used one at a time. It is strongly encouraged for you to try to write out this code for yourself for some hands-on practice. It is perfectly normal for you to make mistakes or have some questions. If you do have questions about how the calculator works, do not worry, sit tight; our next segment of the chapter explains how to utilize GenAI to help understand specific issues you may have about your code. However, before that, let us first view this completed project.

Seeing the completed code upfront gives you a clear idea of what you are building and makes it easier to follow along as we explain each part. When you write the code yourself, try experimenting with different inputs or adding your own ideas to the project. Doing this helps you understand the concepts better and makes the learning process more engaging. If you run into errors, take some time to review what went wrong and think about how to fix it. Trial and error are an integral part of learning Python. Once you are ready, we will break down the project in detail and show you how to use GenAI to troubleshoot and improve your code.

In particular, we split into three sections which provide an overview of the contents:

- Calculator functions
- User input and operations
- Calculator session

Let us start with introducing the calculating function.

Calculator functions

This section of the code deals with defining different functions and telling the code how we want these words and functions to be used throughout the calculator code. Here is a list of each defined function and what it does specifically:

- **add (x, y)**: Adds two numbers and returns the result.
- **subtract (x, y)**: Subtracts the second number from the first and returns the result.
- **multiply (x, y)**: Multiplies two numbers and returns the result.
- **divide (x, y)**: Divides the first number by the second and returns the result. Raises a **ValueError** if the second number is zero.

The code is long, but it is easy to follow. We will go through it one function at a time. First is the **add()** method.

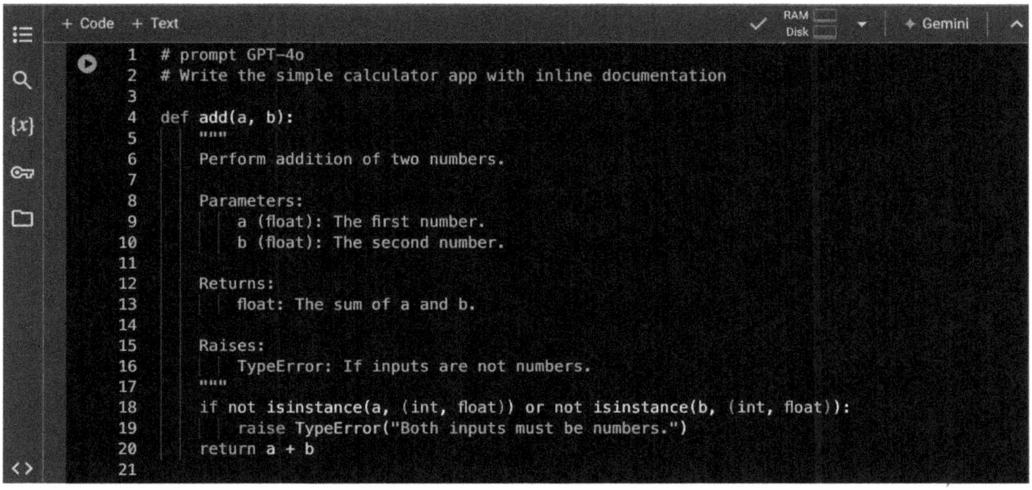

```
1   # prompt GPT-4o
2   # Write the simple calculator app with inline documentation
3
4   def add(a, b):
5       """
6       Perform addition of two numbers.
7
8       Parameters:
9           a (float): The first number.
10          b (float): The second number.
11
12      Returns:
13          float: The sum of a and b.
14
15      Raises:
16          TypeError: If inputs are not numbers.
17      """
18      if not isinstance(a, (int, float)) or not isinstance(b, (int, float)):
19          raise TypeError("Both inputs must be numbers.")
20      return a + b
21
```

Figure 3.10: Calculator app add() method

Figure 3.10 shows the **add()** method from the calculator app. Line 2 is the prompt we gave to GPT-4o. Notice how simple the prompt is. We simply asked it to **write a simple calculator app with inline documentation**, and that was it. GPT-4o generated 127 lines of code along with pages of explanation. This is exactly why learning Python with GPT-4o is such a great experience.

Line 4 defines the **add()** method with two parameters, a and b. A full description of the method, its parameters, and the return value is documented in the block comment from lines 5 to 17. Lines 18 and 19 are for checking the input are number. Line 20 returns the result.

Next is the **subtract()** method.

```
23   def subtract(a, b):
24       """
25       Perform subtraction of two numbers.
26
27       Parameters:
28           a (float): The first number.
29           b (float): The second number.
30
31       Returns:
32           float: The result of a - b.
33
34       Raises:
35           TypeError: If inputs are not numbers.
36       """
37       if not isinstance(a, (int, float)) or not isinstance(b, (int, float)):
38           raise TypeError("Both inputs must be numbers.")
39       return a - b
40
```

Figure 3.11: *Calculator app substract() method*

Figure 3.11 shows the subtract method. Line 23 defines the **substract()** method with two parameters, a and b. A full description of the method, its parameters, and the return value is documented in the block comment from lines 24 to 36. Lines 37 and 38 are for checking the input are number. Line 39 returns the result.

Next is the **multiply()** method.

Figure 3.12: Calculator app multiply() method

Figure 3.12 shows the multiply method. Line 42 defines the **multiply()** method with two parameters, a and b. A full description of the method, its parameters, and the return value is documented in the block comment from lines 43 to 55. Lines 56 and 57 are for checking the input are number. Line 58 returns the result.

Next is the **divide()** method.

Figure 3.13: Calculator app divide() method

Figure 3.13 shows the multiply method. Line 61 defines the **divide()** method with two parameters, a and b. A full description of the method, its parameters, and the return value is documented in the block comment from lines 62 to 75. Lines 56 and 57 are for checking the input are number, and lines 78 and 79 are extra checking for not divide by zero. Line 80 returns the result.

We have defined the methods for the calculator app. Now, let us take a closer look at the app itself.

User input and operations

We have defined the methods for the calculator app, setting the foundation for how it handles each operation. Methods like **add()**, **subtract()**, **multiply()**, and **divide()** form the core functionality of the app. Now, it is time to focus on the app as a whole and see how everything fits together.

The calculator app goes beyond just its methods. It is designed to take user input, process it using the right method, and return a clear result. By looking at the app itself, we can see how all the pieces we have learned so far, variables, methods, classes, and user interaction, work together to create a complete project. Let us take a closer look at how the calculator app works as a single unit.

```python
def calculator():
    """
    A simple calculator app that performs basic arithmetic operations.
    """
    print("Welcome to the Simple Calculator!")
    print("Available operations: add, subtract, multiply, divide")

    while True:
        try:
            # Get user input for the operation
            operation = input("\nEnter operation (add, subtract, multiply, divide or
            'exit' to quit): ").strip().lower()
            if operation == "exit":
                print("Exiting the calculator. Goodbye!")
                break

            # Ensure the operation is valid
            if operation not in ["add", "subtract", "multiply", "divide"]:
                print("Invalid operation. Please try again.")
                continue

            # Get user input for numbers
            num1 = float(input("Enter the first number: "))
            num2 = float(input("Enter the second number: "))

            # Perform the selected operation
            if operation == "add":
                result = add(num1, num2)
            elif operation == "subtract":
                result = subtract(num1, num2)
            elif operation == "multiply":
                result = multiply(num1, num2)
            elif operation == "divide":
                result = divide(num1, num2)

            # Display the result
            print(f"The result of {operation} is: {result}")

        except Exception as e:
            print(f"An unexpected error occurred: {e}")
    return
```

Figure 3.14: Calculator app

Figure 3.14 shows the calculator app. Line 83 defines the **calculator()** function. Lines 84 and 85 include the inline documentation that explains what the function does. Lines 87 and 88 display the welcome message and instructions for using the app.

Line 90 introduces a while true loop that keeps running until it encounters a break statement. The loop exits on line 96 when the user chooses the **exit** option.

Line 91 starts a try block to catch any errors. If something goes wrong, like entering non-numeric values or dividing them by zero, the program moves to the exception handler on line 120 to handle the issue.

Line 99 checks if the user entered a valid option. Lines 104 and 105 then prompt the user to input numbers using the `input()` method so the app can perform the requested calculation.

Line 108 through 115 is the main logic for the calculator app. This segment of the code deals with functions such as `if, elif`, and `else` to define parameters and rules that the code must abide by.

In Python, the `if, elif,` and `else` statements are used to control the flow of the program by making decisions based on certain conditions. These statements allow the program to execute specific blocks of code depending on whether a given condition is true or false. Here is the in-depth explanation of the `if, elif`, and `else` statements:

- **if statement**: The `if` statement evaluates a condition. If the condition is true, the block of code under the if statement is executed. This is the most basic form of decision-making in Python.

- **elif statement**: The `elif` (short for else if) statement allows for additional conditions to be checked if the previous if condition was false. You can have multiple elif statements to handle various scenarios.

- **else statement**: The `else` statement is used as a fallback option if none of the if or elif conditions are true. The code block under else is executed when all previous conditions are false.

These control structures are essential for making decisions within your code, allowing you to define rules and parameters that dictate how your program behaves in different scenarios. For example, in a class method like `__str__`, you might use `if`, `elif`, and `else` to format the output differently based on the attributes of the object. This flexibility makes your code more dynamic and responsive to varying inputs and conditions.

Calculator session

This section is not the code itself, but the output that the code produces. This is an example of how the program would look when it is run and used by the user. By checking the output during the coding process, we are able to see if what we are coding is doing its proper job, displaying the outputs which we want it to.

In this case, we see how the output shows the different options of the calculator app which we are creating.

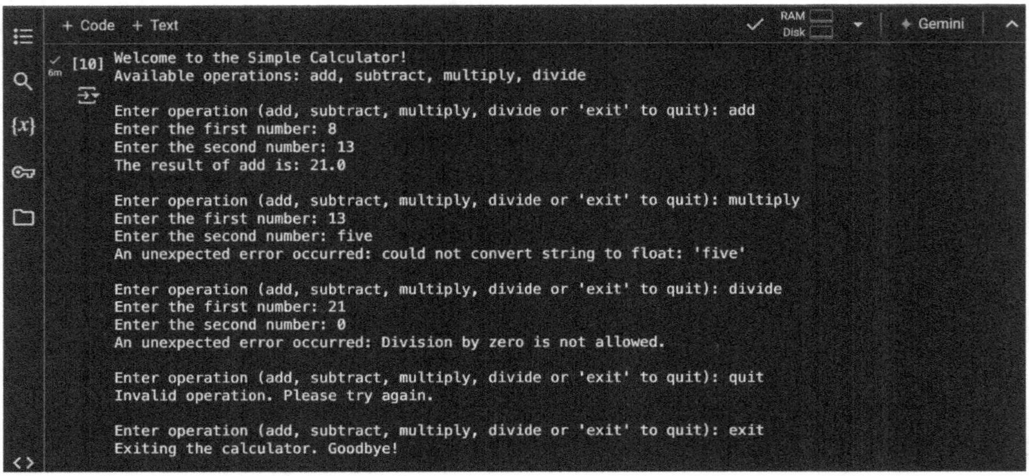

Figure 3.15: Calculator app output

Figure 3.15 displays the output of one of our sample runs.

First, we see the welcome message and the available operations: add, subtract, multiply, and divide.

For the next operation, we chose **multiply** and entered 13 and the word **five**. That triggered an error because the app could not convert the word **five** into a number. The error message was: **An unexpected error occurred: could not convert string to float: five**.

We expected this error because the app treats the word **five** and the number 5 as completely different inputs. This is a simple Python program, not a Generative AI tool like GPT-4o, so it does not understand natural language.

Next, we tried the **divide** operation. We entered 21 for the first number and 0 for the second number, which caused another error. The program correctly raised an exception because dividing by zero is not allowed. It is great to see that the app handles errors like this effectively.

Finally, we attempted to quit the app by typing **quit**, but that did not work because **quit** is not a valid command. The instructions clearly state to use **exit**. Once we typed **exit**, the app stopped gracefully. Everything worked as expected in the end.

Now that we have written our first complete Python app, the simple calculator, we have officially started our journey into learning Python coding. This app is more than just a project—it is a first step in bringing together key concepts and seeing how they work in action. By creating something functional, you have begun to see what it means to turn ideas into working code.

In building the calculator, we worked with foundational programming skills like defining methods, using loops, handling errors, and taking user input. These skills are the building blocks of Python, and you will keep using them as you move forward. More importantly, you have started thinking like a programmer, breaking problems into smaller parts and solving them step by step.

We are just at the beginning. From here, we will build on what you have learned and take on bigger challenges. However, it all starts with this app. Take a moment to appreciate what you have accomplished and prepare for what is next. You have taken the first step toward mastering Python, and there is so much more to discover.

Now that we have a baseline understanding of how these functions operate within the calculator app, let us move onto exploring the different ways in which GenAI can impact our understanding and coding abilities.

Understanding Python using GenAI

GenAI can play a large role in further understanding how this calculator app works, and it can also greatly impact your ability to better understand Python in general. Think of ChatGPT as a personalized teacher. If you have questions regarding one specific line of code within your project, you can ask for it to be explained in more detail.

In Chapter 1, *Introduction to GenAI*, you learned how to use GPT-4o effectively, so now is the perfect time to apply that knowledge here. You can ask GPT-4o to explain different ways to write your code, suggest improvements, or even fix errors in your project. For example, you could request a simpler version of a method, explore why a particular solution works, or find out how to add new functionality. These interactions help you solve problems and teach you new ways to approach programming.

GenAI's ability to adapt to your questions and guide you step by step makes it so powerful. Whether debugging an issue, optimizing your code, or exploring other approaches, GPT-4o can make the process much easier. Treat it as a learning partner, and you will find that you can build your Python skills faster and more confidently.

For example, let us say the raise statement on line 79 of this calculator app as shown in *Figure 3.13* is unfamiliar. By asking ChatGPT-4o to further explain these lines of code and what they do, it will make it easier to recognize how this function is being used in future projects, familiarizing ourselves with the language.

The following is the explanation of the code which ChatGPT gives:

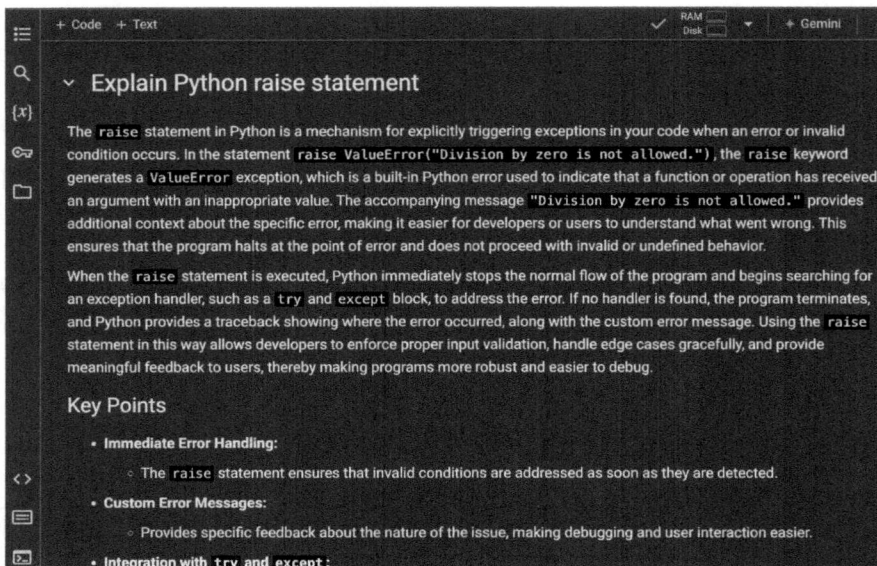

Figure 3.16: ChatGPT response to clarifying "raise" statement

Figure 3.16 shows an explanation for the raise Python keyword in the code: **raise ValueError("Division by zero is not allowed.")**

For fun, we used what we learned in Chapter 2, *Jupyter Notebook,* about Jupyter Notebook text cells and asked ChatGPT-4o to output explanations in markup language. That way, we could copy them directly into a text cell and keep everything organized. *Figure 3.16* only captured a part of the full explanation. In addition to the description and key points, there is a code sample, output, how it works, and an error message section.

To summarize, the **raise** statement in Python is a way to trigger an error when something goes wrong in your code. For example, **raise ValueError("Division by zero is not allowed.")** generates a ValueError to signal that an invalid value was provided. The message, **Division by zero is not allowed**, explains the problem clearly, making it easier to understand what went wrong.

When Python executes the **raise** statement, it immediately stops the program and looks for a way to handle the error, like a **try** and **except** block. If no handler is found, the program stops, and Python displays a traceback along with the error message. Using the **raise** statement helps catch problems early, enforce proper inputs, and provide clear feedback, which makes your programs easier to debug and more user-friendly.

Having explanations in the text cell, right next to the code, makes your project easier to follow. It lets you document what each part of the code does without cluttering it. This setup is helpful when you need to review your work later or share it with others. Keeping the code and explanation together in one place saves time and avoids confusion, especially for more complex projects.

An added benefit is that when you share your code with friends or review it weeks later, neither you nor your friends need access to ChatGPT-4o to understand the project.

Everything, both the code and the detailed explanations, will already be there, ready to guide anyone through the work. By using Jupyter Notebook's text cells and GPT-4o's detailed explanations, you create a project that is functional, well-organized, and easy to share and revisit anytime.

With our understanding of how to prompt ChatGPT in efficient ways, when paired with Juniper notebook, our ability to ask and receive clarification on certain coding elements is exemplified. It becomes much easier to see specific examples that you may have questions about. For example, let us prompt ChatGPT to explain the Python code statement `while True:`

The following figure is a screenshot of ChatGPT's response:

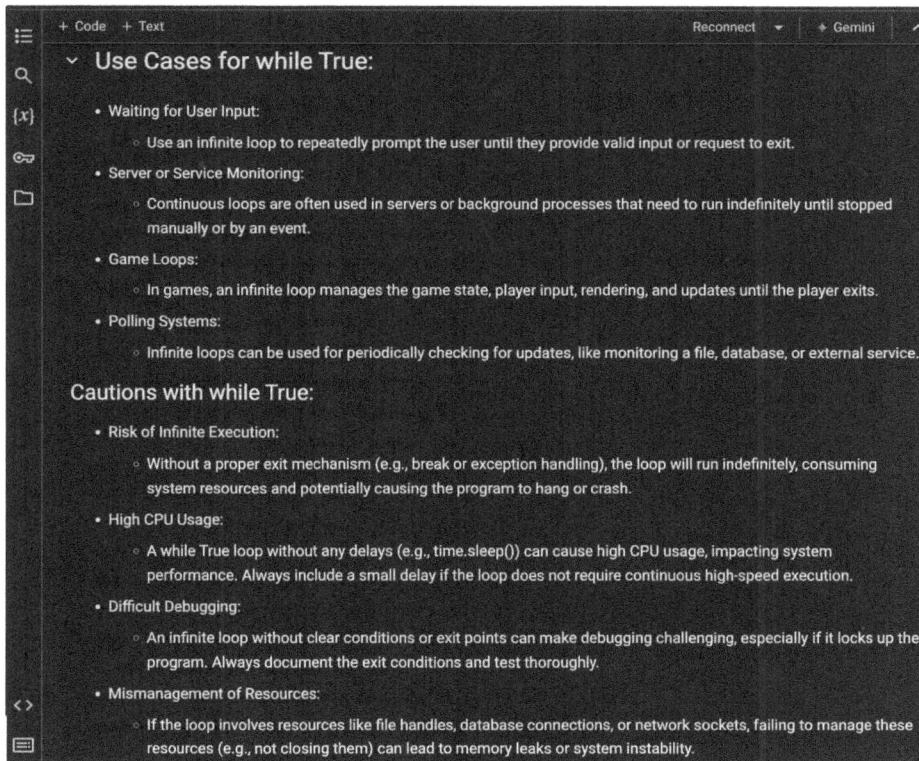

Figure 3.17: *ChatGPT explanation of while True statement*

Figure 3.7 shows the ChatGPT the `while True` explanation. To summarize, `while True` statement is used to create an infinite loop that keeps running until you explicitly stop it. The while loop runs as long as the condition is true, and since True is always true, the loop continues indefinitely. Infinite loops are handy for tasks like waiting for user input, monitoring a system, or managing a server.

To stop the loop, you can use a break statement or another exit mechanism. Without a proper way to stop it, though, the loop will keep running and could use up system resources or even crash the program. Always make sure there is a clear way to end an infinite loop when you use one.

Maybe it is still confusing knowing how this function should be used, and in which cases using this statement would be appropriate. We can ask for examples to clarify when using this statement would be useful and how it should be done.

The following figure is a screenshot of ChatGPT's response to being asked for examples of cases in which the statement `while True`: should be used:

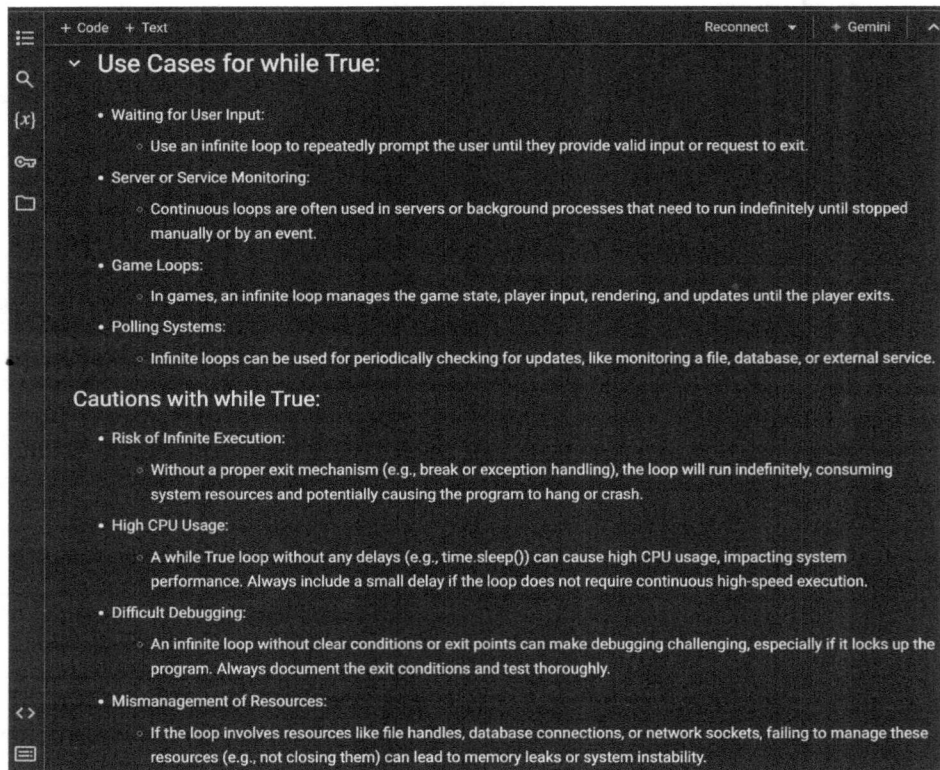

Figure 3.18: ChatGPT further explanation of while True statement

Figure 3.18 shows the output from ChatGPT-4o from us asking when to use the `while True`. The use cases contain descriptions for waiting for user input, server or service monitory, game loops, and polling system. It also lists the cautions, such as the risk of infinite execution, high CPU usage, difficult debugging, and mismanagement of resources.

After asking ChatGPT-4o to explain the raise statement and the `while True` statement in more detail, you can see how helpful it is for understanding coding concepts. You should keep using ChatGPT-4o to explain any part of the code we write for the calculator app. If the explanation does not make sense the first time, do not worry. Learning to code takes time, and understanding often comes after revisiting the concept a few times.

As you learned in *Chapter 2, Jupyter Notebook*, about prompt engineering, you can refine your questions to get clearer answers. If an explanation feels too technical or confusing, try asking ChatGPT-4o to explain it differently. For example, you could ask it to **explain this to a kid or simplify it step by step in Homer Simpson's voice**. Changing the prompt can often make a big difference.

The more you ask and experiment with prompts, the better you will understand both the calculator app and Python. Using ChatGPT-4o helps with specific coding questions and builds your confidence in learning through trial and error. Keep asking questions, exploring, and learning. It is all part of the process.

Next up is your turn.

Practical applications

Try doing these few things to familiarize yourself using GenAI to enhance your understanding of code. Complete this short list to ensure that you have a solid understanding of the calculator app elements before moving onto bigger, more complex projects.

- Alter the **Welcome** and **Thank you** message within the calculator app code.

- Ask ChatGPT to write the code in two different ways. Compare the different examples and take note of what is done differently. Question why it was done differently in each instance and see what ChatGPT's response is.

- Rewrite the calculator app yourself, only asking ChatGPT for assistance when you really feel stuck. Try to troubleshoot issues yourself, be sure to double check your work for mistakes before asking ChatGPT. Coding involves problem solving; be creative!

- Inspired by the calculator app and the concept of classes we discussed earlier in this chapter, we will create an object, either a person or a cat, that acts as an account. This account will help us calculate meal tips, monthly car payments, and yearly compound interest for savings.

Garfield is Pluto's best friend, and he is an excellent and friendly accountant. To bring him into our project, we will create a class called `Accountant` and use it to create an object named `Garfield`. Garfield will be your assistant, ready to help calculate tips, car payments, and even compound interest.

We will show you some steps to create Garfield and the final results. From there, it is up to you to have fun and recreate Garfield in your Jupyter Notebook. You can do it on your own or ask ChatGPT-4o for help. Try experimenting with the class, adding new features, changing Garfield's personality, or expanding his abilities. The best way to learn is by trying things out and making it your own.

Let us get started. We start with code in the following figure.

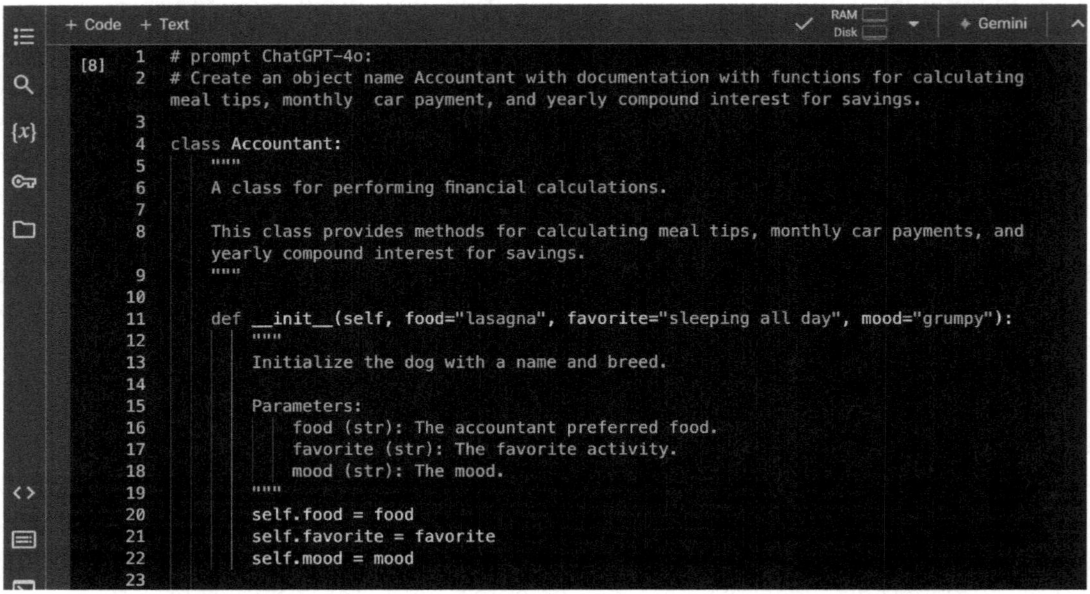

```
# prompt ChatGPT-4o:
# Create an object name Accountant with documentation with functions for calculating
  meal tips, monthly  car payment, and yearly compound interest for savings.

class Accountant:
    """
    A class for performing financial calculations.

    This class provides methods for calculating meal tips, monthly car payments, and
    yearly compound interest for savings.
    """

    def __init__(self, food="lasagna", favorite="sleeping all day", mood="grumpy"):
        """
        Initialize the dog with a name and breed.

        Parameters:
            food (str): The accountant preferred food.
            favorite (str): The favorite activity.
            mood (str): The mood.
        """
        self.food = food
        self.favorite = favorite
        self.mood = mood
```

Figure 3.19: Accountant definition

Figure 3.19 shows the code for the **Accountant** class. Line 2 is the prompt we gave to ChatGPT-4o. It is not the best prompt, but it gets the job done: **Create an object named Accountant with documentation and functions for calculating meal tips, monthly car payments, and yearly compound interest for savings.**

Line 4 is the class declaration. Lines 5 through 9 are the class inline documentation. Line 11 is the **__init__()** method. Lines 12 through 19 are the **__init__** function documentation, and lines 20 through 22 are the class attributes definition.

Are you glad that ChatGPT-4o assists you in writing most of the code and with full explanation?

We made a small edit to line 11 by adding three parameters with default values. This means you do not need to include any values when creating a new accountant. The parameters are **food = "lasagna"**, **favorite = "sleeping all day"**, and **mood = "grumpy"**. These defaults give your accountant a fun personality right from the start.

Next, let us take a quick look at some of the functions.

```
[8]  24      def calculate_meal_tip(self, meal_cost, tip_percentage=0.15):
     25          """
     26          Calculates the tip amount for a meal.
     27
     28          Args:
     29              meal_cost (float): The cost of the meal.
     30              tip_percentage (float, optional): The tip percentage (default is 15%).
     31
     32          Returns:
     33              float: The calculated tip amount.
     34
     35          Raises:
     36              ValueError: If meal_cost is negative or tip_percentage is not within the
     37              range [0, 1].
             """
     38          if meal_cost < 0:
     39              raise ValueError("Meal cost cannot be negative.")
     40          if not 0 <= tip_percentage <= 1:
     41              raise ValueError("Tip percentage must be between 0 and 1.")
     42          return meal_cost * tip_percentage
     43
```

Figure 3.20: Calculate meal tip

Figure 3.20 shows the code generated by ChatGPT-4o. Line 24 is the **calculate_meal_ tip()** method declaration with **meal_cost** and **tip_percentage** as parameters. Lines 25 through 37 are the class inline documentation. Lines 39 through 41 are checking for error condition, and line 42 returns the tip amount.

We did not make any changes to this function. Next is the car payment method.

```
     44      def calculate_car_payment(self, loan_amount, interest_rate, loan_term):
     45          """
     46          Calculates the monthly car payment using the formula:
     47          M = P [ i(1 + i)^n ] / [ (1 + i)^n - 1]
     48          Where:
     49          M = Monthly Payment
     50          P = Principal Loan Amount
     51          i = Monthly Interest Rate (Annual Interest Rate / 12)
     52          n = Number of Payments (Loan Term in Years * 12)
     53
     54          Args:
     55            loan_amount (float): The principal loan amount.
     56            interest_rate (float): The annual interest rate (as a decimal, e.g., 0.05 for
                  5%).
     57            loan_term (int): The loan term in years.
     58
     59          Returns:
     60            float: The calculated monthly car payment.
     61
     62          Raises:
     63            ValueError: If loan_amount, interest_rate, or loan_term are invalid.
     64          """
     65
     66          if loan_amount <= 0 or interest_rate <= 0 or loan_term <= 0:
     67              raise ValueError("Loan amount, interest rate, and loan term must be positive
                  values.")
     68
     69          monthly_interest_rate = interest_rate / 12
     70          number_of_payments = loan_term * 12
     71
     72          monthly_payment = loan_amount * (monthly_interest_rate * (1 +
                monthly_interest_rate) ** number_of_payments) / ((1 + monthly_interest_rate) **
                number_of_payments - 1)
     73
     74          return monthly_payment
     75
```

Figure 3.21: Monthly car payment

Figure 3.21 shows the code generated by ChatGPT-4o. Line 44 is the **calculate_car_payment()** method declaration with **loan_amount**, **interest_rate**, and **loan_term** as parameters. Lines 45 through 64 are the class inline documentation. Lines 39 through 41 checks for an error condition, and lines 69 through 74 calculate and return the monthly car payment.

Once again, we did not change any code for this function.

Did you notice the formular for calculating the monthly payment? It is: **M = P [i(1 + i)^n] / [(1 + i)^n - 1].**

Would it not be nice to see the formula in a more human-readable format? Good news. We can do that! Back in Chapter 2, *Jupyter Notebook*, we learned how to use text cells with LaTeX in Jupyter Notebook. Using that knowledge, we asked ChatGPT-4o to write the formula in LaTeX format. Once it provided the output, we simply copied it into a text cell in our notebook.

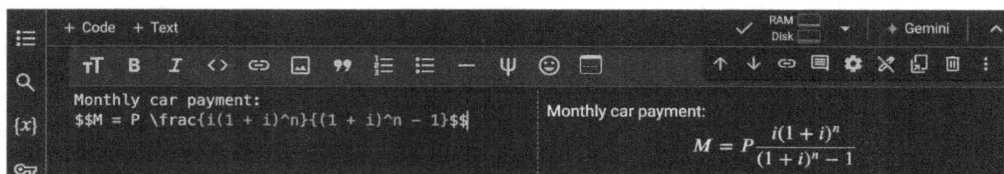

Figure 3.22: *Monthly payment formular in LaTex*

Figure 3.22 shows the monthly payment in LaTeX format. The formula in LaTeX makes it much easier to read and understand, especially for complex calculations. Instead of trying to decipher raw code, you can see the formula as it would appear in a math textbook. This approach is not only helpful for you but also for anyone you share the notebook with. Clear formatting makes a big difference when presenting your work or revisiting it later. You can create a well-documented and professional-looking notebook by combining ChatGPT-4o's capabilities with LaTeX and Jupyter Notebook.

The last method we asked ChatGPT-4o to write is the compound interest. So, let us take a look at that.

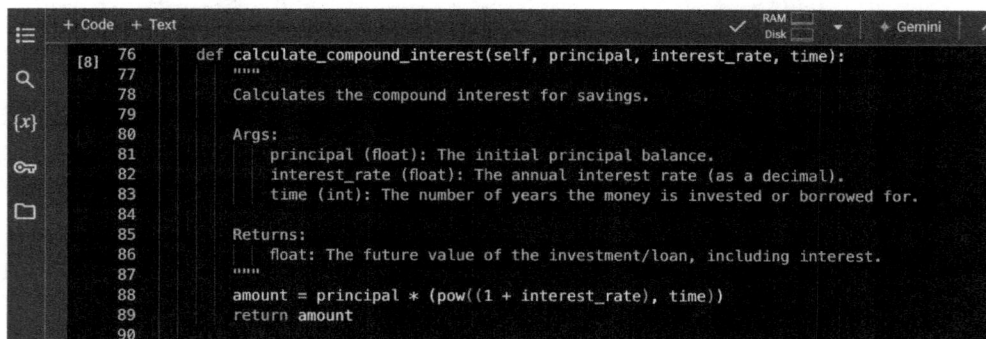

Figure 3.23: *Compound interest*

Figure 3.23 shows the code generated by ChatGPT-4o. Line 76 is the **calculate_compound_interest()** method declaration with **principal**, **interest_rate**, and **time** as parameters. Lines 77 through 87 are the class inline documentation. Lines 88 through 89 calculate and return the compound interest.

We did not make any changes to this function, and that is the amazing part. With just a simple prompt, ChatGPT-4o worked as our assistant and tutor to help us write the **Accountant** class.

This process shows how powerful GenAI can be for both creating and learning. By giving a simple prompt, we got a fully functional **Accountant** class without needing any extra edits. ChatGPT-4o did not just write the code. It also acted as a tutor, making the process easier to understand. It feels like working with a knowledgeable coding partner who is always ready to help.

Even though ChatGPT-4o did the heavy lifting, we still played a critical role by deciding what we wanted and asking the right questions. This back-and-forth lets you learn as you create, building your skills and confidence. As we continue, remember that every prompt you write is another step toward becoming a better Python programmer.

Now that the hard work is done, are you ready to have some fun with the accountant?

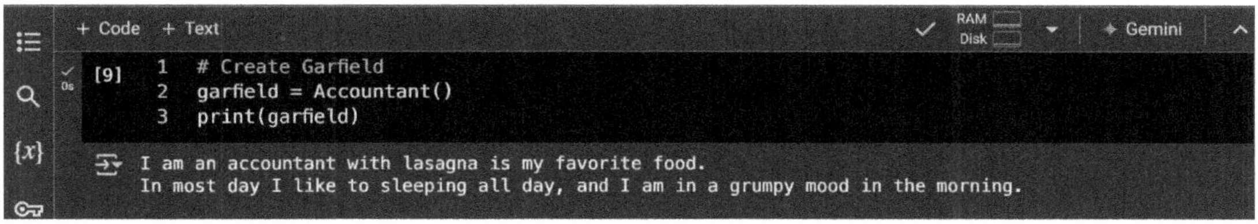

Figure 3.24: *Creating Garfield, the accountant*

Figure 3.24 shows the code for creating an accountant object named Garfield. Line 2 create **garfield** the accountant, and line 3 print the information about Garfield, which is our own edit to the code. The output is: **I am an accountant with lasagna is my favorite food.**

In most day I like to sleeping all day, and I am in a grumpy mood in the morning.

Next, we ask Garfield to calculate the tips for our meal.

```
≡    + Code   + Text                                          ✓ RAM ▭ ▾   ♦ Gemini   ⌃
Q    [ ]   1   # prompt to ChatGPT-4o:
           2   # write example of garfield using its function
{x}        3
           4   # Example usage of Garfield's methods
           5   meal_price = 85
⌕          6   tip_percent = 0.20
           7
▭          8   tip_amount = garfield.calculate_meal_tip(meal_price, 0.2)  # Calculate a 20% tip
           9
          10   print(f"For your meal of ${meal_price}, You want to tip at {tip_percent*100:.2f}%.\nSo
               the tip amount is: ${tip_amount:.2f}\nMaking the total for the meal is ${meal_price +
               tip_amount:.2f}")

     ⇥  For your meal of $85, You want to tip at 20.00%.
        So the tip amount is: $17.00
        Making the total for the meal is $102.00
```

Figure 3.25: Garfield tips calculation

Figure 3.25 shows the code where we ask Garfield to calculate the lunch meal tip. It is not required, but we asked ChatGPT-4o to write a few examples for us in line 2. Line 5 sets the **meal_price** to 85, and line 6 sets the **tip_percent** to 0.20.

Line 8 asks Garfield to calculate the **tip_amount** using the **garfield.calculate_meal_tip()** method, and line 10 prints the result, which is:

For your meal of $85, You want to tip at 20.00%.

So, the tip amount is: $17.00

Making the total for the meal is $102.00

Garfield is a helpful friend when it comes to going out to lunch, but let us ask him something more complex, like how to figure out the monthly car payment if we buy a new car.

```
≡    + Code   + Text                                          ✓ RAM ▭ ▾   ♦ Gemini   ⌃
Q    ▶   1   # ask Garfield for car loan payment
         2
         3   car_loan = 25000
{x}      4   annual_rate = 0.045  # 4.5% interest
         5   loan_years = 5
⌕        6
         7   monthly_payment = garfield.calculate_car_payment(car_loan, annual_rate, loan_years)
▭        8
         9   print(f"You bought a new car at ${car_loan}, with annual rate from the bank at
             {annual_rate*100:.2f}% for {loan_years} year.\nSo your monthly car payment is: $
             {monthly_payment:.2f}")

     ⇥  You bought a new car at $25000, with annual rate from the bank at 4.50% for 5 year.
        So your monthly car payment is: $466.08
```

Figure 3.26: Garfield monthly car payment

Figure 3.26 shows the code for Garfield calculating the new monthly car payment. Lines 3 through 5 set the **car_loan** to be 25000, **annual_rate** equal to 0.045, and **loan_years** equal to 5. Line 7 asks Garfield to calculate the **mothly_payment** using the **garfield. calculate_car_payment()** method. Line 9 prints result, which is:

You bought a new car at $25000, with annual rate from the bank at 4.50% for 5 year.
So your monthly car payment is: $466.08

Lastly, we ask Garfield about how much money will we earn on our bank saving account.

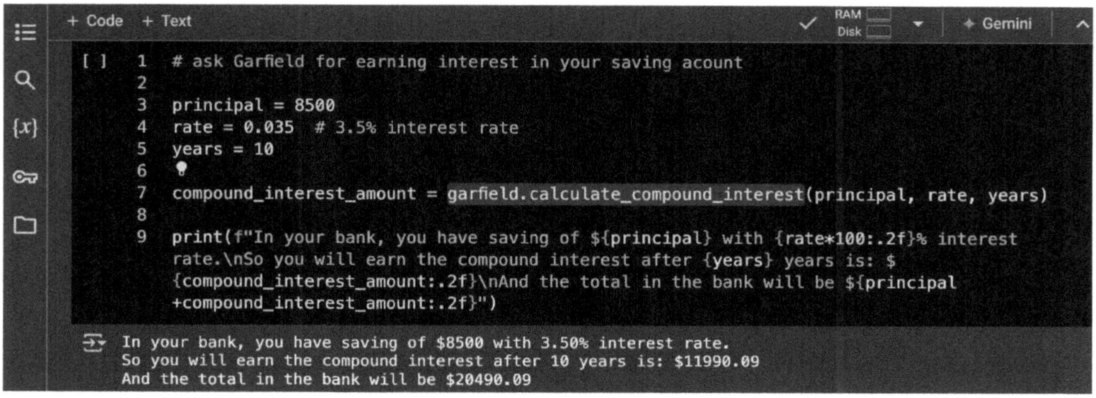

Figure 3.27: *Garfield compound interest*

Figure 3.27 shows the code for Garfield calculating the compound interest in our bank savings account. Lines 3 through 5 set the **principal** equal to 25000, a **rate** equal to 0.035, and **years** equal to 10. Line 7 asks Garfield to calculate the **compound_interest_amount** using the **garfield.calculate_compound_interest ()** method. Line 9 prints the result, which is:

In your bank, you have saving of $8500 with 3.50% interest rate.
So you will earn the compound interest after 10 years is: $11990.09
And the total in the bank will be $20490.09

There is so much more we can do with Garfield. We could add more financial functions to make him an even better accountant, like calculating mortgage payments or tracking expenses. We could use Python's **ipywidgets** library to create a simple graphical interface with buttons and sliders, making it easier for users to interact with Garfield. We could even take it a step further and build a web page where friends can access **Garfield, the Magnificent Accountant**, anytime they need help with numbers. The possibilities are endless, and with Python and a little creativity, Garfield can become a genuinely magical financial assistant.

This next section will discuss other ways to practice strengthening your Python fundamentals using ChatGPT as a tutor and mentor along the way.

Chart your course

After successfully learning how to code a basic calculator app in Python, you have gained a solid understanding of fundamental programming concepts such as variables, functions, conditionals, and loops. The next steps in your Python journey should focus on expanding your skills by tackling more complex challenges and exploring new areas of the language.

Now is the time to push yourself further. You could start experimenting with object-oriented programming to understand how to work with classes and objects more effectively. Try building more advanced projects, like a budgeting app or a to-do list manager, which will help you see how these concepts come together in larger, real-world applications.

You can also explore Python libraries, such as pandas for data manipulation or matplotlib for creating visualizations. These libraries open up new possibilities and give you tools to solve more complex problems. Do not forget to continue using ChatGPT-4o as your tutor and assistant to help you understand new concepts or debug your code along the way.

Every project you complete and every challenge you overcome will build your confidence. So, keep experimenting, keep asking questions, and most importantly, have fun exploring everything Python has to offer.

Here are some ideas on how to continue practicing and growing your Python coding abilities using the knowledge we gained from dissecting and analyzing the calculator app:

- **Creating small projects:** A great way to solidify Python skills is by developing small projects that require applying learned concepts in practical scenarios. Here are some project ideas:

    o **To-do list application**: Design a command-line to-do list that allows users to add, remove, and view tasks. This project offers an opportunity to work with lists and file I/O (input/output) for saving and loading tasks.

    o **Number guessing game**: Develop a game where the program randomly selects a number within a specified range, and the player must guess it. Hints like **higher** or **lower** can be provided after each guess. This project reinforces the use of loops, conditionals, and random number generation.

    o **Simple text-based adventure game**: Create a text-based game where the player navigates through different rooms or scenarios, making choices that influence the outcome. This project offers the chance to explore functions, conditionals, and possibly recursion for more complex decision trees.

    o **Mad libs game:** Build a Mad Libs game where users input words like nouns, verbs, adjectives, and so on, and then the program inserts them into a predefined story template to create a funny or unexpected story. Create a story template with placeholders for different types of words, ask the user to input words to fill in these placeholders, and after all the inputs are collected, print the completed story.

- **Garfield, the Magnificent Accountant mobile app**: Create a beautiful iOS or Android app for Garfield the Magnificent Accountant and sell it on the Apple Store or Google Play. The following figure shows what the app could look like.

Figure 3.28: Imagine Garfield, the Magnificent Accountant app

Between our imagination and ChatGPT DALL-E3, we create a possible iOS app for Garfield, the Magnificent Accountant in *Figure 3.28.*

Remember to practice understanding the code and not relying on the AI to troubleshoot each time. Practice is a key element in familiarizing yourself with Python. Be sure to experiment and exercise creativity throughout the process, as this will lead to greater involvement, interest, and fun with the content. Coding does not have to be serious; it can be practiced in many ways, such as the ones above, to encourage problem solving and critical thinking within your own creations. The possibilities are endless, and with GenAI by your side, exploring any interests or questions is simple to do. Let us wrap up this chapter with a conclusion.

Conclusion

In conclusion, mastering the development of a calculator app in Python provides a solid foundation in essential programming concepts such as functions, conditionals, and loops. This hands-on experience not only enhances coding skills but also deepens the understanding of how to structure and execute a program effectively. Moreover, the integration of GenAI into the learning process serves as a powerful tool for overcoming challenges, offering immediate assistance with coding questions, debugging, and providing alternative approaches to problem-solving. By combining practical coding exercises with the support of GenAI, the journey of learning Python becomes more interactive, efficient, and enriched, paving the way for tackling more complex projects with confidence.

Learning through a project-based approach, like building a calculator app, makes programming concepts more tangible and relatable. Instead of just reading about functions, conditionals, and loops, you see how they work in real scenarios. Defining and calling functions, using logic to handle different situations, and automating tasks with loops all become more meaningful when applied to a practical project. This approach turns abstract ideas into real-world problem-solving that you can use right away.

GenAI, like ChatGPT-4o, makes the process even better. It acts like a guide, helping you debug errors, explore new techniques, and refine your code. If something does not make sense, you can ask for clarification and get an explanation tailored to your level of understanding. It is not just about writing code. It is about thinking critically, experimenting, and learning as you go. ChatGPT-4o creates a supportive environment where you feel confident exploring new ideas without fear of getting stuck.

The skills and confidence you have gained from building a calculator and accounting app and using GenAI set you up for bigger challenges. From creating interactive applications to exploring Python libraries or even building full-fledged software, the possibilities are endless. Every step you take builds on this strong foundation, making your Python journey exciting and full of potential.

The next chapter introduces the concept of **sorting** in coding, covering key algorithms like bubble sort, quicksort, and merge sort. This chapter focuses on how these sorting methods work and their importance in efficiently organizing data in programming.

Join our book's Discord space

Join the book's Discord Workspace for Latest updates, Offers, Tech happenings around the world, New Release and Sessions with the Authors:

https://discord.bpbonline.com

CHAPTER 4

Sorting on
My Mind

Introduction

Sorting is a fundamental function of computer science and everyday life. At its core, sorting is arranging data in a particular order, typically in ascending or descending sequence. This operation can be applied to various data types, including numbers, strings, and complex structures like records or objects.

In practice, sorting is everywhere, quietly powering many of the technologies we use daily. From organizing search engine results to displaying a well-ordered list of contacts on your phone, sorting ensures that information is easy to locate and navigate. Different algorithms, such as quick sort, merge sort, and bubble sort, cater to varying speed, memory usage, and data size requirements. Their selection often depends on the context, whether managing a small dataset in memory or processing massive amounts of data in distributed systems.

Beyond its practical applications, sorting is a foundational concept in computer science education. sorting algorithms are important to understand because they help us learn about algorithm design. By examining their time complexity, stability, and efficiency in different situations, we can improve our problem-solving skills. Sorting is not just a tool for organizing data; it is a gateway to mastering computational thinking and optimizing how we interact with information.

Structure

This chapter is about sorting, and in particular, the following topics:

- History of sorting
- Sorting foundation
- Advanced sorting algorithms
- Performance insights

Objectives

This chapter aims to introduce the importance of sorting in computer science. It also explains various sorting algorithms, including their strengths, weaknesses, and use cases. Moreover, it provides practical guidance on selecting the most suitable sorting algorithm for different scenarios.

In addition, we will learn to use GPT-4o as our tutor and helper to learn about sorting. GPT-4o will explain things clearly and give practical examples, guiding us step-by-step through different sorting algorithms. Whether we start with the basics of bubble sort or explore the more complex merge sort, GPT-4o will adjust to how fast we learn. This way, we will understand both the theory and real-world applications of sorting algorithms. This interactive approach will make learning about sorting both fun and effective.

Let us begin with the sorting history.

History of sorting

The history of sorting algorithms is rich and intertwined with the development of computer science itself. The origins of sorting date back to the early days of computing in the 1940s and 1950s. One of the earliest sorting algorithms, bubble sort, was introduced by *John von Neumann*, a pioneering figure in computer science. Over decades, more sophisticated algorithms were developed as computational power increased and the need for efficient data processing grew.

In the 1960s, *Donald Knuth*'s seminal work *The Art of Computer Programming* cataloged many of the sorting algorithms known today, including quick sort and merge sort, which were independently discovered by *Tony Hoare* and *John von Neumann*, respectively. The 1970s and 1980s saw further advancements with the introduction of algorithms like heap sort and the development of lower-bound theory, which established theoretical limits of sorting efficiency. Today, sorting remains an active area of research, with continuous improvements and optimizations being proposed.

What is particularly fascinating about sorting algorithms is the endless possibility for innovation. While it might seem that every method has already been discovered, history reminds us that breakthroughs often come from creative problem-solving and fresh perspectives. Who knows? Perhaps you could devise a brand-new sorting algorithm that outperforms existing methods.

To make the journey through the world of sorting even more engaging, we will use ChatGPT-4o to create a visual representation of this rich and evolving landscape. Imagine an image capturing the foundational algorithms like bubble sort and merge sort, alongside towering advancements like quick sort and heap sort, all set against the backdrop of computer science history.

The following illustration will serve as a creative lens to view the innovation and potential of sorting, inspiring you to think beyond established methods and explore new possibilities:

Figure 4.1: *DALL-E3, sorting number concept*

Figure 4.1 features a stunning abstract illustration depicting the sorting concept against a colorful swirl background created by ChatGPT DALL-E3.

From *Chapter 2, Jupyter Notebook*, you learn about using Jupyter Notebook's text cells for notes and documentation, it would be helpful to incorporate images into our notebook when sharing our work. Including images can enhance the clarity and professionalism of our sorting documentation, making it more informative and engaging for others. To insert an image in a Jupyter Notebook, you can use the following Markdown syntax in a text cell:

```
![Alt text](path_to_image)
```

Replace **Alt text** with a brief image description, like **sorting number concepts** and **path_to_imag** with the relative path to the image file.

Sorting is essential in computer science. It organizes data for efficiency and accessibility, powering search engines, databases, and countless applications. So, let us explore the significance of sorting.

Sorting significance

Sorting is crucial in computer science for several reasons, such as:

- **Efficiency:** Many algorithms perform better when their input data is sorted. For instance, binary search, which is much faster than linear search, requires sorted data. Sorting can significantly reduce the time complexity of other algorithms, making them more efficient. For example, finding a specific name in a phone book becomes far quicker when the names are alphabetized, allowing you to skip irrelevant sections.

- **Data organization:** Sorted data is easier to work with and analyze. It enables quicker access and retrieval of information, which is essential in databases and information systems. For example, consider a grocery list organized by category: fruits, vegetables, and dairy are easier to manage.

- **Algorithm optimization:** Sorting is often a preliminary step in more complex algorithms. For instance, algorithms for finding the convex hull or closest pair of points usually begin by sorting the input points in computational geometry. For example, sorting a pile of socks by color is quicker if they are already organized by shade.

- **Visualization and understanding:** sorted data can help visualize patterns and trends, making it easier to understand and interpret large datasets. This is particularly important in fields like data science and analytics. For example, organizing your monthly expenses from smallest to largest quickly highlights where most of your money goes.

- **Improving user experience:** Sorted results enhance the user experience by providing relevant and organized information promptly in practical applications such as search engines, e-commerce platforms, and content management systems. For example, when browsing a streaming platform, having movies sorted by genre or popularity helps you find what you are looking for faster. Similarly, shopping online becomes more convenient when products are sorted by price, relevance, or customer ratings.

Sorting is an essential idea in computer science. It has a long history and is very useful real-life situations. Sorting helps us process data efficiently, improves how algorithms work, and is essential for organizing and analyzing data in many different fields.

Sorting foundation

Sorting is a fundamental concept in computer science and data analysis. It involves arranging data in a specific order, usually either ascending or descending. Whether you are organizing a list of names alphabetically, ranking numerical data, or sorting records in a database, grasping how sorting algorithms function is essential. We will introduce you to the concept of sorting, with a focus on using GPT-4o to help you learn bubble sort. It is one of the simplest and most well-known sorting algorithms.

Sorting is not merely about organizing data neatly; it is an essential step in many algorithms and applications. Efficient sorting enhances the performance of other algorithms, including search algorithms and data processing tasks. When data is well-sorted, it can significantly reduce the time complexity of these operations, allowing your programs to run faster and more efficiently.

Once you have mastered bubble sort, you can explore a variety of sorting algorithms, each with its own strengths and weaknesses. Some algorithms are straightforward and easy to understand, while others are more complex but provide better performance in terms of time and space complexity. Here are a few common sorting algorithms:

- **Bubble sort:** A simple, introductory sorting algorithm that repeatedly steps through the list, compares adjacent elements, and swaps them if they are in the wrong order.

- **Selection sort:** An algorithm that divides the input list into two parts: a sorted sublist of items built from left to right and a sublist of the remaining unsorted items.

- **Insertion sort:** Builds the final sorted array one item at a time, with the benefits of being simple and efficient for small datasets.

- **Merge sort:** A divide-and-conquer algorithm that splits the list into halves, recursively sorts each half and then merges the sorted halves.

- **Quick sort:** Another divide-and-conquer algorithm that picks an element as a pivot and partitions the array around the pivot.

Bubble sort serves as the foundation for understanding sorting algorithms, making it the perfect starting point for our exploration of sorting.

Bubble sort

Bubble sort is often the first sorting algorithm that programmers learn due to its simplicity. Despite its simplicity, it provides a solid introduction to the concept of sorting and helps to build a foundation for understanding more complex algorithms. In this section, we will explore bubble sort in detail, covering the following aspects:

- Bubble sort explained
- Pseudocode and implementation
- Loop explanation
- Visual representation
- Practical and limitations

We start by explaining what bubble sort is.

Bubble sort explained

Bubble sort is a straightforward sorting algorithm that works by repeatedly stepping through the list to be sorted, comparing each pair of adjacent items, and swapping them if they are in the wrong order. This process is repeated until the list is sorted. The name bubble sort comes from how larger elements bubble to the top of the list, much like bubbles rising to the surface of a liquid.

The following is a step-by-step process:

1. **Start from the beginning of the list:** Compare the first two elements.

2. **Swap if necessary:** If the first element is greater than the second, swap them.

3. **Move to the next pair:** Repeat the comparison and swap steps for the next pair of elements.

4. **Continue to the end of the list:** Proceed with this comparison and swapping process until the end of the list is reached. At this point, the **largest element** will have bubbled up to its correct position at the end of the list.

5. **Repeat the process:** Ignore the last element (since it is already in its correct position) and repeat the process for the remaining list until no more swaps are needed.

Another way to explain algorithms in computer science, such as bubble sort, is by using the concept of a flowchart. A flowchart is a graphical tool used to represent the sequence of steps in a process or algorithm. It provides a clear and structured way to visualize the flow of tasks, decisions, and outcomes. Each step in a flowchart is depicted using specific shapes.

Flowcharts are especially useful in simplifying complex ideas, making it easier to understand complex algorithms. By breaking down a process into its visual components, flowcharts allow users to see how each step interacts with the others. They are commonly used in fields like computer science, project management, and business analysis to explain algorithms, workflows, or procedures in a visual format that is both intuitive and universally understood.

We encountered an issue that DALL-E3 from ChatGPT-4o could not generate a flowchart for the bubble sorting algorithm. How could you create the flowchart?

Luckily, we have a solution. In *Chapter 1, Introduction to GenAI*, we explore the creative uses of prompt engineering effectively. So, first, we ask ChatGPT-4o which Python library can be used to create flowcharts. It gave us a few options, and we chose the **graphviz** Python library.

The second step in prompt engineering is to ask ChatGPT-4 for the code to display the bubble sort algorithm in **Graphviz**. Then, copy and paste the code into your Jupyter Notebook and run it. Here is the screenshot for the code:

```
[23]  1   # Prompt GPT:
      2   # Write graphviz code to display the bubble sort algorithm
      3
      4   from graphviz import Digraph
      5
      6   # Create a directed graph
      7   dot = Digraph(engine='dot')
      8
      9   # Set graph attributes for a dark gray background and white text
     10   dot.attr(bgcolor="gray20")
     11   dot.attr(fontcolor="white")
     12
     13   # Add nodes with individual web colors, white text, and custom shapes
     14   dot.node("Start", "Start", style="filled", fillcolor="red", fontcolor="white",
              shape="circle")
     15   dot.node("OuterLoop", "Outer Loop i: (0 to n-1)", style="filled",
              fillcolor="forestgreen", fontcolor="white", shape="box")
     16   dot.node("InnerLoop", "Inner Loop j: (0 to n-i-2)", style="filled",
              fillcolor="yellowgreen", fontcolor="white", shape="box")
     17   dot.node("Compare", "IF:\na[j] > a[j+1]\n?", style="filled", fillcolor="chocolate",
              fontcolor="white", shape="diamond")
     18   dot.node("Swap", "Swap: a[j] <--> a[j+1]", style="filled", fillcolor="deepskyblue",
              fontcolor="white", shape="box")
     19   dot.node("NoSwap", "No Swap", style="filled", fillcolor="deepskyblue",
              fontcolor="white", shape="box")
     20   dot.node("EndInner", "Inner Loop End", style="filled", fillcolor="yellowgreen",
              fontcolor="white", shape="ellipse")
     21   dot.node("EndOuter", "Outer Loop End", style="filled", fillcolor="forestgreen",
              fontcolor="white", shape="ellipse")
     22   dot.node("Finish", "Stop", style="filled", fillcolor="red", fontcolor="white",
              shape="circle")
     23
     24   # Add edges with web colors and white text
     25   dot.edge("Start", "OuterLoop", color="white", fontcolor="white")
     26   dot.edge("OuterLoop", "InnerLoop", color="white", fontcolor="white")
     27   dot.edge("InnerLoop", "Compare", color="white", fontcolor="white")
     28   dot.edge("Compare", "Swap", label="Yes", color="white", fontcolor="white")
     29   dot.edge("Compare", "NoSwap", label="No", color="white", fontcolor="white")
     30   dot.edge("Swap", "EndInner", color="white", fontcolor="white")
     31   dot.edge("NoSwap", "EndInner", color="white", fontcolor="white")
     32   dot.edge("EndInner", "InnerLoop", label="Next j", color="white", fontcolor="white")
     33   dot.edge("InnerLoop", "EndOuter", label="j >= n-i-2", style="dashed", color="white",
              fontcolor="white")
     34   dot.edge("EndOuter", "OuterLoop", label="Next i", style="dashed", color="white",
              fontcolor="white")
     35   dot.edge("OuterLoop", "Finish", label="i >= n-1", style="dashed", color="white",
              fontcolor="white")
     36
     37   # Render and display the flowchart
     38   dot.render("bubble_sort_flowchart", format="png", cleanup=True)  # Save as PNG
     39   dot  # Display inline in Jupyter Notebook
```

Figure 4.2: *Graphviz flowchart code*

Figure 4.2 shows the Graphviz code that creates a flowchart for the bubble sort algorithm. We will not explore this code in detail, as our main focus is on the flowchart diagram rather than the code that created it. Line #2 is the prompt to GPT-4o: **Write graphviz code to display the bubble sort algorithm.**

Line #4 is the **graphviz** library import, and lines 7 to 39 draw the bubble sort flowchart. The output is in the following diagram:

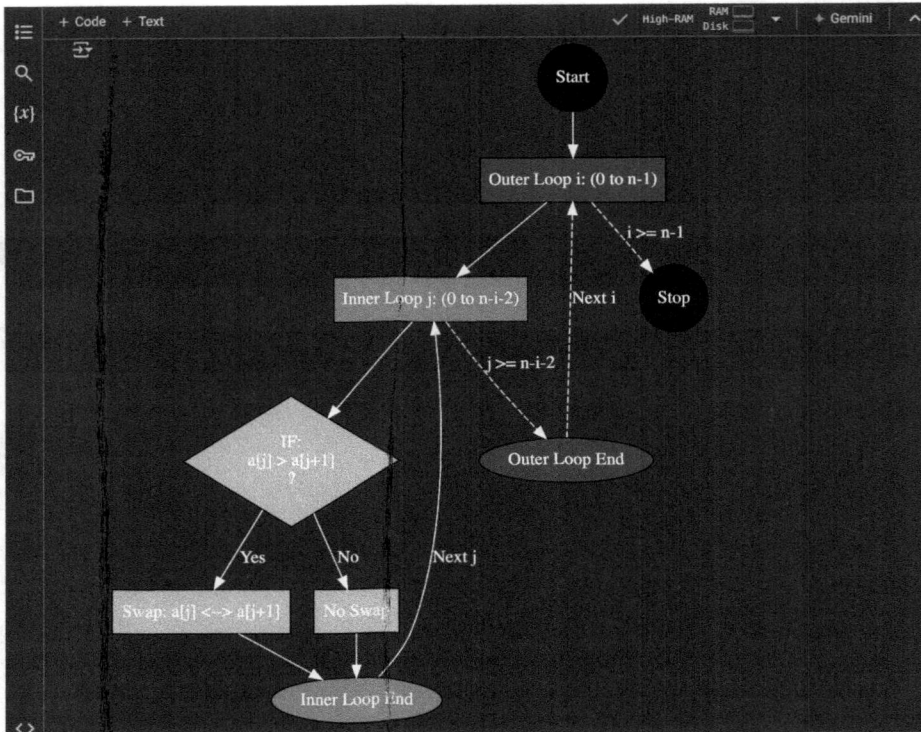

Figure 4.3: Bubble sort flowchart

Figure 4.3 shows the bubble sort flowchart. A flowchart diagram begins with a (red) circle labeled **Start**, showing where the process begins. From there, the flowchart points to the outer loop.

The outer loop handles the overall sorting of the list. It is a rectangle box. Inside it, the (light gray) inner loop compares two adjacent elements, the diamond shape. If the first element is bigger than the second, they are swapped to move the larger one closer to the end of the list. This process repeats for each pair in the list during each pass of the outer loop. After each pass, the outer loop runs again, reducing the number of comparisons, as the largest elements move towards the end.

The beauty of the flowchart is how it simplifies this process into an easy-to-follow visual. By showing the inner loop nested within the outer loop, it is clear how bubble sort works step by step. The arrows guide you through each action: compare two elements, decide if they need swapping, move to the next pair, and repeat.

The flowchart ends with a (black) circle labeled **Stop**, marking the point where the list is fully sorted.

This visual approach makes bubble sort not just logical but beautifully simple to understand. What might feel abstract in code becomes an intuitive sequence of steps, neatly laid out in a way anyone can follow. With a flowchart, learning and appreciating bubble sort becomes accessible and enjoyable.

We use text cells to include documentation or notes, making our work more informative and easier to follow. For our readers with a math background, we can take this a step further by using LaTeX in a text cell to express the logic of bubble sort in a compact, mathematical-style pseudo-formula.

This approach not only bridges the gap between coding and mathematics but also provides a clear, structured way to represent the algorithm's logic for those who appreciate the precision and elegance of mathematical notation.

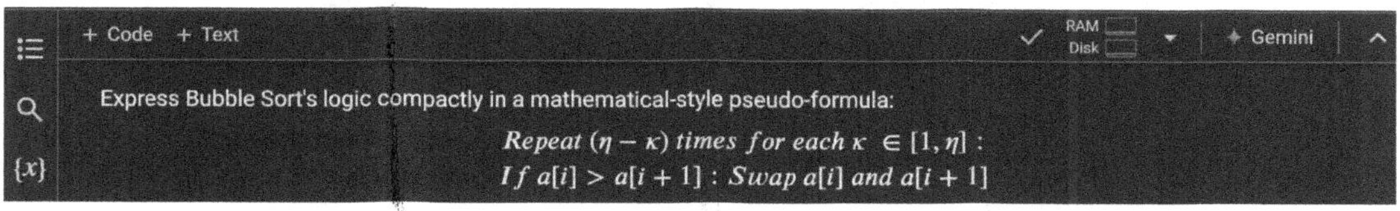

Figure 4.4: *Bubble sort mathematical formula*

Figure 4.4 expresses bubble sort's logic compactly in a mathematical-style pseudo-formula. We explained the bubble sort algorithm in three ways: a step-by-step guide, a flowchart, and a mathematical equation. Each method provides a different perspective to help you understand how and why bubble sort operates. The step-by-step explanation lays the groundwork, the flowchart visualizes the process, and the equation offers clarity for those with a mathematical background.

By now, you should have a clear and thorough understanding of the bubble sort algorithm. This algorithm repeatedly compares and swaps adjacent elements, using an outer and inner loop to sort the entire list. With this solid grasp of the concept, it's time to move beyond theory and put it into practice. Let us start coding bubble sort and bring this algorithm to life.

Pseudocode and implementation

Now that we are ready to learn and apply the bubble sort algorithm, we can use GPT-4o to assist us in the coding process. To get started, we will provide GPT-4o with a clear and straightforward prompt: **Write a simple bubble sort function in Python with inline documentation.**

This prompt will ensure that GPT-4 generates the function and includes helpful comments explaining each code step, making it easy to follow and understand.

Using this approach, we are not just writing code. We are actively learning how to think about the algorithm's logic and how it translates into Python. GPT-4o acts as both a tutor and a collaborator, helping us bridge the gap between theory and implementation. The resulting function, shown in the following figure, will be a starting point for experimenting with bubble sort:

```
1  # prompt GPT:
2  # Write a simple Bubble Sort function in Python with inline documentation
3
4  def bubble_sort(input_list):
5    """Sorts a list using the bubble sort algorithm.
6
7    Args:
8        input_list: The list to be sorted.
9
10   Returns:
11       list: The sorted list.
12   """
13   n = len(input_list)  # Get the length of the list (array)
14
15   # debug statement
16   print(f"Debug log: Length of the input list is: {n}")
17
18   # Traverse through all element in the list
19   # outer loop
20   for i in range(n):
21
22     # Flag to optimize - if no swaps occur, the list is sorted
23     swapped = False
24
25     # debug statement
26     print(f"Debug log: Pass {i}: {input_list}")
27
28     # inner loop
29     for j in range(0, n - i - 1):
30       if input_list[j] > input_list[j + 1]:     # check for swapping
31         input_list[j], input_list[j + 1] = input_list[j + 1], input_list[j]
32         swapped = True
33     if not swapped:
34       break  # If no two elements were swapped in inner loop, the array is sorted
35   return input_list
```

Figure 4.5: *Bubble sort code*

Line #4 defines the **bubble_sort()** function, with **input_list** as its parameter, setting the stage for implementing the bubble sort algorithm. Lines #5 through #12 provide the function's inline documentation, describing the purpose and steps of the code clearly and concisely, making it easier for anyone reading the method to understand its primary function.

Line #13 calculates the length of the **input_list**, an essential step for controlling the outer loop of the bubble sort process. To ensure this calculation is correct and to provide insight into the program's execution, we add debugging code on lines #15 and #16, using the **print()** function to log the length of the list. The debug log is invaluable as it confirms the input is being processed correctly and provides immediate feedback during runtime.

When writing code, it is highly recommended that you use the o function to output debugging statements. These statements allow you to see the intermediate steps of your code and identify where issues may arise. Debugging with **print()** is especially helpful for beginners, as it provides a real-time view of what the code is doing, making the logic easier to follow and troubleshoot.

While tools like debuggers or logging libraries are more advanced alternatives for larger projects, the simplicity and immediacy of **print()** make it a go-to tool for learning and debugging. It is a habit worth cultivating, as it helps you debug and build a deeper understanding of how your code operates step by step. In practice, you could comment out any debug log statements when you deployed the code.

Line #20 defines the outer loop, which controls the number of passes through the list to ensure it is fully sorted. Line #23 includes a flag that tracks whether any swaps have occurred during an outer loop pass. If no swaps are made, it indicates that the list is already sorted, allowing the algorithm to terminate.

Lines #25 and #26 contain the debug log code we added (manually) to improve our understanding of the sorting process. The output log shows how many times the code passes through the outer loop and displays the current state of the input list. This feedback helps us confirm that the algorithm is functioning as intended. Observing how the list changes with each pass provides insight into the step-by-step progress of the bubble sort, making it easier to understand and debug the code.

Debug log statements go beyond simply finding errors. They also involve gaining confidence in your code by seeing its performance.

Line #29 initiates the inner loop, which manages the pairwise comparison of elements in the list during each outer loop iteration. Line #30 checks whether the two adjacent values should be swapped based on their order. If a swap is needed, line #31 executes it, ensuring that the larger value moves closer to its correct position. Following this, line #32 sets a flag indicating a swap occurred during this pass.

These steps are at the core of the bubble sort algorithm. The inner loop systematically compares and rearranges the elements, while the swap flag prevents the algorithm from spending time on sections of the list that are already sorted. This process showcases the elegance of bubble sort, as it progressively sorts the list through repeated passes. Understanding these key code lines reinforces the algorithm's logic and its methodical approach to achieving an ordered list.

In lines #33 and #34, the algorithm checks whether any swaps have occurred during the current pass. If the swapped flag remains **False**, it indicates that the list is already sorted, and the algorithm can exit the loop early, thereby avoiding unnecessary iterations. Line #35 returns the sorted list as the final output, completing the bubble sort process.

This early exit mechanism efficiently enhances the algorithm, ensuring that it does not perform redundant outer loop passes once the list is sorted. By incorporating this step, this version of the bubble sort becomes more intelligent and adaptive, demonstrating how simple improvements can enhance performance and logic.

The idea of tweaking well-established and thoroughly researched code, such as adding a flag to skip unnecessary steps, is incredibly powerful. These minor yet thoughtful adjustments can significantly enhance the efficiency of an algorithm. As you explore bubble sort and other sorting algorithms, you may discover your modifications to improve their performance. This process of experimentation and refinement not only makes coding more engaging but also sharpens your problem-solving skills.

Who knows? Your tweak might even lead to a faster or more optimized version of the algorithm, and you could become famous for improving a sorting algorithm.

Looking back, you can see how the written Python code aligns perfectly with the flowchart in *Figure 4.4*. Every component is represented, including the outer loop that controls the number of passes, the inner loop that manages pairwise comparisons, the condition check for swaps, and the actual swapping of adjacent pairs. This correlation between the visual representation and the code underscores the importance of using a flowchart as a tool for planning a complex coding project.

By mapping out the algorithm visually before writing the code, you gain a clear, step-by-step understanding of the process. A flowchart offers a logical framework that helps you anticipate how each part of the algorithm functions and how the flowchart and the code are interconnected. This approach simplifies the coding process and minimizes errors and confusion, especially when collaborating with a larger software development team.

Using visual graphics like flowcharts reinforces the importance of thoroughly understanding an algorithm before translating it into code. It reminds us that good planning and visualization lead to cleaner, more structured, and effective coding. This practice is especially helpful for complex algorithms, where the visual, logical flow can make a difference in mastering and sharing the concept.

Next, we move on to the exciting part: executing our code and observing the results. This step brings all the theory, planning, and writing to life, allowing us to see the algorithm in action.

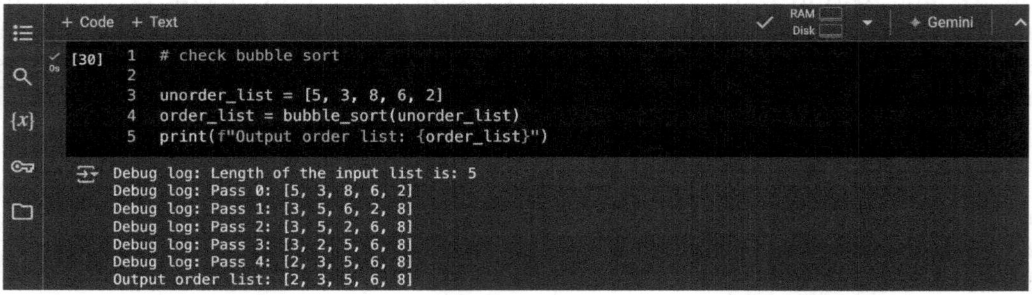

Figure 4.6: Bubble sort output

Figure 4.6 presents the code implementation of bubble sort alongside its output, providing a clear example of how the algorithm works in practice. On line #3, we define the **unorder_list**, a sample input list containing the values **[5, 3, 8, 6, 2]**. This unsorted list serves as the starting point for our bubble sort function.

Line #4 calls the **bubble_sort()** function, passing the **unorder_list** as its parameter. The function processes the list and returns the variable **order_list**.

Finally, line #5 displays the sorted list. This output confirms that the algorithm has correctly ordered the input. The output shows as we expected:

```
Debug log: Length of the input list is: 5
Debug log: Pass 0: [5, 3, 8, 6, 2]
```

```
Debug log: Pass 1: [3, 5, 6, 2, 8]
Debug log: Pass 2: [3, 5, 2, 6, 8]
Debug log: Pass 3: [3, 2, 5, 6, 8]
Debug log: Pass 4: [2, 3, 5, 6, 8]
Output order list: [2, 3, 5, 6, 8]
```

The debug log statements are essential for helping us understand how the bubble sort algorithm works step by step. They provide feedback on the program's state, allowing us to verify our expectations and observe the sorting process.

The first debug log shows that the length of the input list is 5. This result aligns with our expectations since the input list contains exactly five integers. Although this may appear to be a straightforward confirmation, it is crucial for the algorithm to accurately identify the input size. The input list length is essential for determining the number of passes required during the sorting process. There should be at least five passes to order this list.

The following debug log illustrates the state of the list during the first iteration, which we refer to as **Pass 0**. In programming, we typically start counting from zero, representing the first pass through the outer loop. At this point, the list is unchanged and appears exactly as the input list: **[5, 3, 8, 6, 2]**. This result is expected because the algorithm has not yet entered the inner loop for comparing and swapping. In other words, the sorting process has not yet begun, and the list remains in its original, unsorted state.

In the second iteration, **Pass 1**, we see the largest number, 8, move to the end of the list. This result aligns perfectly with our expectations for the inner loop's first complete pass. It should identify the largest value in the unsorted portion of the list and move it to its correct position. Although the rest of the list remains unsorted at this stage, we have made progress by placing the largest number in its proper location.

In **Pass 2**, the second-largest number, 6, moves to its correct position, just before 8. Again, this result is the expected behavior of the bubble sort algorithm as the inner loop continues to process the remaining unsorted portion of the list. With each iteration, the algorithm isolates and sorts the largest values, leaving fewer elements to evaluate in subsequent passes.

Pass 3 reveals the next transformation as the number 5 shifts into its proper position. By now, the algorithm has sorted the three largest numbers, and only the two smallest remain to be placed.

Finally, in **Pass 4**, the last two numbers, 2 and 3, are sorted into correct positions. With this final adjustment, the list is fully ordered. The debug log output for each pass clearly illustrates the systematic progression of the sorting process, showing how the bubble sort algorithm repeatedly narrows its focus and organizes the list step by step.

After the algorithm completes its execution, we reach the end of our debug logs. Finally, as illustrated in line 5 of the code shown in *Figure 4.6*, the ordered list **[2, 3, 5, 6, 8]** is displayed.

The output confirms that the bubble sort function has successfully performed its task, transforming the input list into a correctly sorted output. By examining each pass with the help of the debug logs, we have gained a clear and detailed understanding of how the algorithm operates and achieves its goal.

It was a lot of fun exploring the step-by-step process of bubble sort, but what about the special swapped flag?

This flag is not just an extra line of code. It is an improvement designed to make the bubble sort algorithm run faster. The swapped flag serves as an early exit mechanism. By monitoring whether any swaps occur during a pass through the list, the flag allows the algorithm to detect when the list is already sorted.

The following figure explains the effectiveness of the swapped flag:

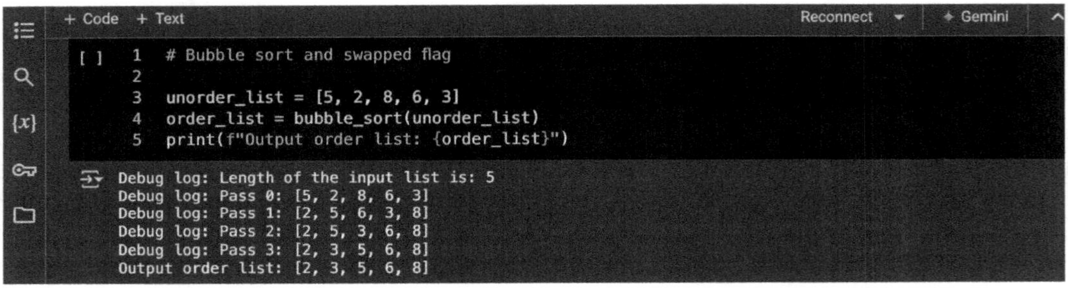

```
# Bubble sort and swapped flag

unorder_list = [5, 2, 8, 6, 3]
order_list = bubble_sort(unorder_list)
print(f"Output order list: {order_list}")

Debug log: Length of the input list is: 5
Debug log: Pass 0: [5, 2, 8, 6, 3]
Debug log: Pass 1: [2, 5, 6, 3, 8]
Debug log: Pass 2: [2, 5, 3, 6, 8]
Debug log: Pass 3: [2, 3, 5, 6, 8]
Output order list: [2, 3, 5, 6, 8]
```

Figure 4.7: Swapped flag in action

Figure 4.7 presents the same code as *Figure 4.6*, but this time with a slightly modified input for the **unorder_list**. Instead of the original order, we have swapped the numbers 2 and 3 positions, making the new **unorder_list**: **[5, 2, 8, 6, 3]**. While the values are identical, this small change in their arrangement provides an excellent opportunity to observe the impact of the swapped flag on the algorithm's behavior.

When we run the code with the new input, the output reveals an interesting result. This time, there are only four passes, from **Pass 0** to **Pass 3**. The algorithm skips one inner loop pass, confirming that the swapped flag functions as intended. By detecting that no swaps are necessary during the final pass, the algorithm recognizes that the list is already sorted and exits early. This adjustment not only avoids unnecessary work but also significantly improves efficiency.

The result shown in *Figure 4.7* not only demonstrates that the flag functions correctly but also highlights the significance of optimization. By eliminating unnecessary steps, the algorithm becomes faster and more efficient while maintaining its simplicity and accuracy. This finding emphasizes the importance of constantly seeking opportunities to refine and enhance algorithms, from the most basic to the most advanced algorithm.

The keen observers among you may have noticed that the swapped flag is not illustrated in the bubble sort flowchart diagram (*Figure 4.3*). This observation is accurate. When we asked GPT-4 to write the code in **Graphviz** language, it produced a standard bubble sort sequence without any additional improvements, but since we have the code, we can update the flowchart diagram.

Here is another case showing the efficiency of the swapped flag.

```
1   # Bubble sort and swapped flag 2
2
3   unorder_list = [8, 2, 3, 5, 6]
4   order_list = bubble_sort(unorder_list)
5   print(f"Output order list: {order_list}")

Debug log: Length of the input list is: 5
Debug log: Pass 0: [8, 2, 3, 5, 6]
Debug log: Pass 1: [2, 3, 5, 6, 8]
Output order list: [2, 3, 5, 6, 8]
```

Figure 4.8: Use case 2 for swapped flag

Figure 4.8 presents the same example run of the bubble sort code as before, but this time, the **unorder_list** has been rearranged.

The values in the list remain the same, but their positions have been rearranged to form a new input: [8, 2, 3, 5, 6]. This change in order allows us to observe how the algorithm functions when the largest number is positioned at the very beginning of the list.

When we run the code, the output reveals some interesting results. There are only two passes in total. **Pass 0** displays the original, unordered input list: [8, 2, 3, 5, 6]. Since **Pass 0** simply shows the initial state of the list, the algorithm performs only one actual pass through the inner loop to sort the values. During this single pass, the largest number, 8, is moved to its correct position at the end of the list, while the remaining numbers naturally fall into order.

This outcome demonstrates the efficiency of the swapped flag once again. By detecting that no further swaps are necessary after the first pass, the algorithm terminates early, skipping the remaining redundant iterations of the outer loop. What would typically require multiple passes with a traditional bubble sort implementation is now accomplished in just one pass through the inner loop.

Let us take a moment to consider the impact of our work with the swapped flag. Sorting algorithms are ubiquitous, functioning silently in nearly every aspect of our daily lives. They are found on your iPhones, online shopping websites, workplace software, and essentially everywhere data needs to be organized.

Consider this, if you have 100 friends saved in your iPhone's contact list, a sorting algorithm works to keep everything in order every time you access that list or add a new contact. Your iPhone likely uses a more advanced and efficient sorting algorithm, which we will discuss in the *Time complexity* section. However, imagine for a moment that it relied on the simple bubble sort algorithm. The computational cost of bubble sort, expressed as $O(n^2)$—a concept we will explore in depth later—would result in approximately 5,950 comparisons and swaps to sort those 100 contacts. While the phone would handle this fairly quickly, with the introduction of our swapped flag to reduce unnecessary passes, you could see that your contact list display is a little faster and smoother.

Now, let us consider a larger scenario. Imagine your college has a list of 10,000 students, and each time someone accesses this list, a sorting algorithm is executed. If we use bubble sort without any optimizations, it will require up to 50 million comparisons and swaps ($O(n^2)$ calculations). This method represents a substantial computational cost, particularly when you think this occurs for every student accessing the list multiple times.

Let us take this a step further. Imagine having access to a database containing 1,000,000 residents in your city. If we used bubble sort to sort this list, it could require an astounding 500 billion operations each time a sort is performed. Now, if we consider how often this database is accessed daily by various systems, such as government services, businesses, or individuals, the level of inefficiency becomes staggering.

This reflection highlights the importance of optimizing sorting algorithms. While bubble sort is an excellent tool for learning the fundamentals of sorting, its inefficiencies become evident as the scale increases. Introducing a swapped flag is a small yet significant step toward reducing computational costs and demonstrates the impact of thoughtful improvements.

There is increasing concern about the carbon footprint produced by large computer server farms that support our digital world. These data centers are crucial for services ranging from streaming video to cloud computing, and they consume significant amounts of energy, much of which still comes from non-renewable sources.

Imagine this, as an ordinary programmer, if you made a minor tweak to a widely used sorting algorithm that reduced its CPU operations by half, this single improvement could lead to global energy savings. When applied across millions of servers handling trillions of operations every second, the carbon footprint of these server farms diminishes, contributing to a greener and more sustainable planet.

It might sound like the premise of a sci-fi movie, but the idea is not as far-fetched as it seems. Programmers hold the power to optimize, innovate, and improve the efficiency of the systems that run the world. A tweak that makes algorithms more efficient is not just about saving milliseconds; it is about reducing computational load, lowering energy consumption, and minimizing the environmental impact of our digital lives.

We programmers might not wear capes, but in our way, we can help drive the world toward a more efficient and sustainable future.

This concludes our discussion on bubble sort, covering its concept, implementation, and optimization using the swapped flag. Next, we will explore looping constructs, which are essential for the bubble sort algorithm.

Loop explanation

Bubble sort functions effectively thanks to its use of nested loops: the outer and inner loops. The outer loop, often represented as **i**, uses the **range(n)** function, where n is the length of the input list. Following typical programming conventions, the loop starts at zero. For example, if the list has five elements, the range would be written as **range(5)** and iterated through the index values 0, 1, 2, 3, and 4.

The inner loop, often represented as **j**, starts at zero and runs up to **n-i-2**. The key phrase here is **up to (but not equal to)**, meaning the loop stops just before reaching **n-i-1**. This process makes the range for the inner loop **range(0, n-i-1)**. In this case, we are using the complete set of parameters for the **range(start_number, up_to_stop_number)** function, which includes both the starting and stopping points. By default, if you omit the **start_number** parameter, Python assumes it to be zero.

To see the outer and inner loops working together in action, we can add a debug log print statement inside the inner loop. By including the line **print(f"Debug log: Inner loop pass {j}: {input_list}")**, we can track the state of the list at every iteration of the inner loop. The following image shows the results:

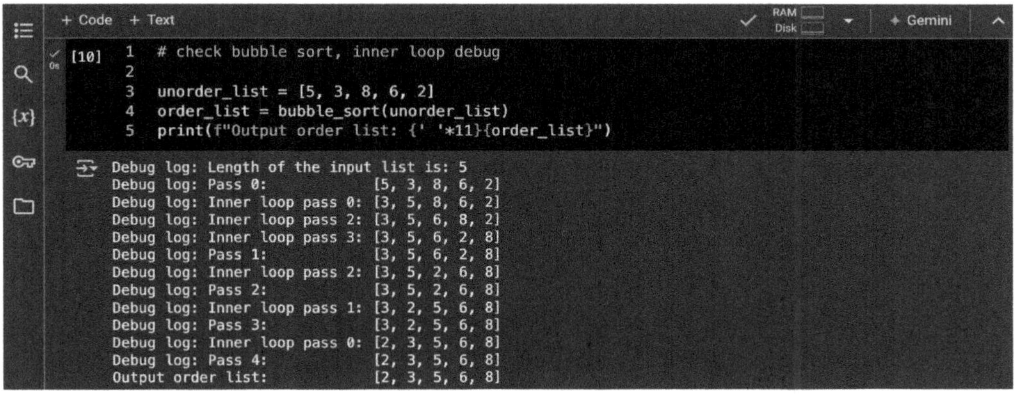

Figure 4.9: Inner loop debug log

Figure 4.9 features the same bubble sort code as before, with one adjustment. Line #3 defines the **unorder_list** as **[5, 3, 8, 6, 2]**. On line #4, we create the **order_list** by calling the **bubble_sort(unorder_list)** function, and line #5 prints the sorted result. What is different this time is that we have added an extra debug log statement to the **bubble_sort()** function (not shown here).

The results, along with the debug print statements that illustrate each pass of the inner loop, clearly demonstrate the step-by-step logic of how the inner loop interacts with the outer loop. During the first cycle of the outer loop, the inner loop makes three passes to move the number 8 to its correct position at the end of the list. In the next cycle, the inner loop completes a single pass to place the number 6 in its proper position. Following this, in the next cycle of the outer loop, one more inner loop pass sets the number 5 correctly.

Finally, during the last cycle of the outer loop, the inner loop swaps the numbers 3 and 2, placing them in their correct positions.

The final sorted list is: **[2, 3, 5, 6, 8]**. This step-by-step progression illustrates how bubble sort systematically processes the list. With each cycle of the outer and inner loops, the order of the elements is refined until the list is completely sorted. The debug logs offer a clear and detailed view of the process, enhancing our understanding of the algorithm's logic.

The next challenge is to visually demonstrate the step-by-step process of bubble sort.

Visual representation

Python is a leading choice for data engineers and scientists, primarily because of its wide range of powerful libraries for data visualization. One of the most popular libraries is Matplotlib, which enables users to create a variety of visualizations, from simple line graphs to complex multi-layered plots. This library makes Matplotlib an essential tool for effectively analyzing and presenting data.

To enhance our exploration of bubble sort, we will use data visualization to see the value from the outer loop output. While we will not review the exact code for generating these graphs here, we strongly encourage you to try it yourself. Experimenting with Matplotlib to visualize the outer loop's operations will deepen your understanding of bubble sort. The following graph displays the results:

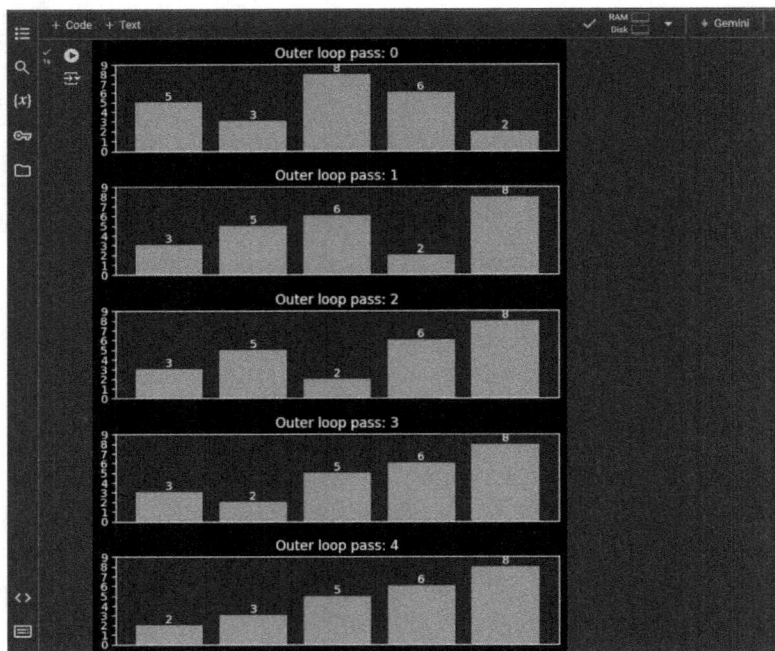

Figure 4.10: Outer loop bar chart

Figure 4.10 shows five bar charts representing the state of the input list after each execution of the outer loop in the bubble sort algorithm. The first bar chart, titled **Outer loop pass: 0**, plots the initial input list **[5, 3, 8, 6, 2]**. At this stage, the list remains unsorted, with the bars representing the values in their original order. This chart serves as a baseline, showing the starting point of the algorithm.

As we progress to **Outer loop pass: 1**, the second chart shows the result after the first full iteration of the outer loop. Here, we can see that the tallest bar, representing the value 8, has moved to the rightmost position in the graph, indicating that the largest value in the list has **bubbled** to its correct spot at the end. The remaining bars still reflect an unsorted order, highlighting that the sorting process is ongoing.

The bar graph **Outer loop pass: 2** shows the second-tallest bar, representing the number 6, shifting to its correct position, settling just to the left of the tallest bar, representing the number 8. This visual movement illustrates how bubble sort systematically identifies and places the next largest value in its proper position with each iteration.

In **Outer loop pass: 3** plot, the bar representing the value 5 moves. The third largest bar slides into its correct position, aligning neatly next to the bars representing 6 and 8. At this stage, the list is almost sorted, with only the two smallest values still out of place.

The final graph, titled **Outer loop pass: 4**, shows the last operation of the algorithm. During this cycle, the bars for 2 and 3 switch places, completing the sorting process. The resulting graph displays a beautiful progression, with the bars now arranged perfectly from the shortest (smallest value) to the tallest (largest value). This orderly, ascending sequence visually confirms that the algorithm has done its job, transforming the unsorted list into an ordered one.

At first glance, this visualization example may seem unnecessary since our list contains only five numbers. With such a small dataset, it is easy to manually track the sorting process and identify any values that are out of order. However, consider what it would be like if your list contained 1,000 numbers or even a million. In those cases, manually spotting which values are out of order could become an overwhelming, if not impossible, task.

Visualization becomes an essential tool in scenarios involving large datasets. When dealing with thousands or millions of values, graphical representations like bar charts can quickly highlight patterns, identify irregularities, and help you understand the overall structure of the data.

Before we move on to more advanced sorting algorithms, let us take a closer look at the practical uses and limitations of bubble sort.

Practical and limitations

Bubble sort is rarely used in practical applications, especially when dealing with large datasets, due to its inefficiency. With a time, complexity of $O(n^2)$, it becomes impractical for sorting anything beyond small lists, as the number of comparisons and swaps increases significantly with larger inputs. In modern programming, faster and more efficient algorithms, such as quick sort or merge sort, are nearly always preferred in real-world situations.

However, bubble sort shines as an educational tool. Its straightforward logic and step-by-step process make it an ideal starting point for beginners learning about sorting algorithms. By working with bubble sort, learners can grasp foundational concepts such as nested loops, comparisons, and swaps. It provides a simple framework for understanding how sorting works, laying the groundwork for more advanced algorithms and critical thinking.

In addition to teaching algorithmic thinking, bubble sort can be valuable in specific niche scenarios. Moreover, it is suitable for environments with extreme memory constraints, as it does not require any additional storage apart from the input list.

The following are the primary features of bubble sort:

- **Inefficiency:** With a time, complexity of $O(n^2)$, bubble sort is impractical for sorting large datasets.

- **Stability:** Bubble sort is stable, meaning it maintains the relative order of equal elements, which can be desirable in specific applications.

- **Memory usage:** Bubble sort is an in-place sorting algorithm that requires only a constant amount of additional memory space, making it memory efficient.

In conclusion, we have thoroughly explored and discussed every aspect of the bubble sort algorithm. We began by explaining its fundamental logic and purpose, followed by a step-by-step breakdown accompanied by a flowchart diagram to represent its process visually. We then expressed its logic in a mathematical-style formula, translating the conceptual framework into a concrete representation. Finally, we implemented the algorithm in Python, enhancing it with a swapped flag to improve its efficiency and performance.

To deepen our understanding, we ran multiple examples and used debug logs to observe the algorithm's inner workings. This approach enabled us to see precisely how the outer and inner loops interact and how the list changes with each iteration. To bring it all together, we created bar charts that visually tracked the sorting process, demonstrating how the algorithm's outer loop systematically organizes the list step by step.

By now, you should be as familiar with the bubble sort algorithm as you are with your favorite cats. It is not just a concept anymore. You have thoroughly explored it from every angle, gaining both theoretical understanding and practical mastery.

Next, we will turn our attention to some of bubble sort's sibling algorithms. While we will not explore the same level of detail, we will still explore their logic, differences, and advantages, equipping you with a broader understanding of sorting algorithms. Let us continue the journey and meet the rest of the sorting family.

Advanced sorting algorithms

Data organization is a dynamic and robust field in computer science. Data engineers and research scientists continuously work to create new sorting algorithms and refine existing ones. There are more than forty well-researched sorting algorithms, each offering unique strengths and applications. These algorithms cater to different needs, whether efficiently sorting small or large datasets, minimizing memory usage, or accelerating the sorting process.

Sorting is a fundamental task that supports numerous applications, including organizing search results, processing transactions, managing the massive demands of social media, and powering our increasingly energy-intensive digital world. With various algorithms available, choosing the proper method for a specific problem involves scientific analysis and artistic judgment. This selection process requires a clear understanding of the trade-offs in speed, complexity, and resource requirements.

The existence of more than forty methods shows how creative and determined the computer science community is in finding better ways to organize information. This continuous improvement ensures that everything from massive computation needed to run the digital world to our iPhone accessing information runs smoother.

The following section highlights the top four popular sorting algorithms.

- Selection sort
- Insertion sort
- Merged sort
- Quick sort

Let us begin with an algorithm similar to bubble sort, the selection sort.

Selection sort

The concept of selection sorting dates back to the early days of computer science, with roots in manual sorting techniques used before the advent of computers. It is one of the oldest and simplest sorting algorithms, often used as an introductory example in computer science education to illustrate basic sorting principles and algorithm design. Despite its inefficiency compared to more later algorithms, its ease of understanding and implementation makes it a valuable educational tool.

Selection sorting is one of computer science's oldest and simplest sorting algorithms. Its origins can be traced back to manual sorting methods before computers were invented. Although it is less efficient, it is faster than our bubble sort.

Selection sort is a straightforward sorting algorithm that repeatedly selects the smallest (or largest, depending on the order) element from the list's unsorted portion and places it in its correct position. Here is how it works, step by step:

1. **Start with the first position (index 0)**: Start with the first element of the input list, whether it is a number, character, or string.

2. **Imagine your list as two sections:** The sorted portion (initially empty) and the unsorted portion (the entire list at the start). Begin at the first position of the list and assume the first element is the smallest.

3. **Find the smallest element in the unsorted portion:** Scan through the rest of the list, comparing each element to the smallest value you have found so far. If you find a smaller value, update your **smallest** marker to that element.

4. **Swap the smallest element with the first unsorted element:** Once you have scanned the entire unsorted portion, swap the smallest element with the first element of the unsorted portion. The smallest value is in its correct position in the sorted portion.

5. **Move to the next position:** Repeat the process but now treat the second element as the start of the unsorted portion. Find the smallest element in this new unsorted section and swap it with the first element of that section. This step expands the sorted portion by one element.

6. **Continue until the list is sorted:** Keep repeating this process, step by step, shrinking the unsorted portion and growing the sorted portion until the entire list is sorted.

Using the prompt to GPT-4o: `Write a Python function with documentation for a Selection sort`, we get the following:

```
1   # prompt GPT:
2   # Write a Python function with documentation for the selection sort
3
4   def selection_sort(input_list, is_debug=True):
5       """
6       Sorts a list using the selection sort algorithm.
7
8       Args:
9           input_list: The list to be sorted.
10
11      Returns:
12          The sorted list.
13      """
14      n = len(input_list)
15      for i in range(n):
16          # Find the minimum element in the unsorted part of the array
17
18          # Debug log
19          if (is_debug):
20              print(f"Debug log: Pass {i}: {' '*26}{input_list}")
21
22          min_idx = i
23          for j in range(i + 1, n):
24              if input_list[j] < input_list[min_idx]:
25                  min_idx = j
26
27                  # Debug log
28                  if (is_debug):
29                      print(f"Debug log: Inner loop pass {j}: Smaller found: {input_list[min_idx]}
                         ")
30
31          # Swap the found minimum element with the first element of the unsorted part
32          input_list[i], input_list[min_idx] = input_list[min_idx], input_list[i]
33      return input_list
```

Figure 4.11: Selection sort

Figure 4.11 presents the selection sort code with a few modifications to include debug log print statements. Line #2 shows the prompt given to GPT-4o for generating the initial function. Line #4 defines the **selection_sort** function. The outer loop is defined on lines #14 and #15, setting up the process for selecting the smallest element in each pass.

Lines #18 and #19 contain the first debug log statement we added, providing a clear view of the algorithm's progress at each step of the outer loop.

Lines #22 through #25 implement the inner loop, which is responsible for finding the smallest value in the unsorted portion of the list. Additional debug log statements, included on lines #27 through #29, offer insights into the comparisons made during the inner loop.

Finally, line #32 performs the swap operation, placing the smallest value in its correct position. It is important to note that the swap occurs outside of the inner loop, ensuring that the operation is only performed after the smallest value has been identified.

Let us run the code:

```
# Testing selection sort

unorder_list = [5, 3, 8, 6, 2]
sorted_list = selection_sort(unorder_list)
print(f'Output ordered list: {" "*24}{sorted_list}')

Debug log: Pass 0:                              [5, 3, 8, 6, 2]
Debug log: Inner loop pass 1: Smaller found: 3
Debug log: Inner loop pass 4: Smaller found: 2
Debug log: Pass 1:                              [2, 3, 8, 6, 5]
Debug log: Pass 2:                              [2, 3, 8, 6, 5]
Debug log: Inner loop pass 3: Smaller found: 6
Debug log: Inner loop pass 4: Smaller found: 5
Debug log: Pass 3:                              [2, 3, 5, 6, 8]
Debug log: Pass 4:                              [2, 3, 5, 6, 8]
Output ordered list:                           [2, 3, 5, 6, 8]
```

Figure 4.12: *Selection sort output*

Figure 4.12 shows the run code and the output for sorting the list [5, 3, 8, 6, 2] step by step:

- **Step 1 (Pass 0):** Start at index 0. The smallest value in [5, 3, 8, 6, 2] is 2. Swap 2 with 5. The list becomes [2, 3, 8, 6, 5].

- **Step 2 (Pass 1):** Move to index 1. The smallest value in [3, 8, 6, 5] is 3. No swap is needed since 3 is already in place.

- **Step 3 (Pass 2):** Move to index 2. The smallest value in [8, 6, 5] is 5. Swap 5 with 8. The list becomes [2, 3, 5, 6, 8].

- **Step 4 (Pass 3):** Move to index 3. The smallest value in [6, 8] is 6. No swap is needed since 6 is already in place.

- **Step 5 (Pass 4):** At index 4, only one element remains, so the list is now fully sorted: [2, 3, 5, 6, 8].

Selection sort is simple because it always follows the same logic: look for the smallest value and put it where it belongs. It does not rely on complex nested loops or advanced data structures.

Insertion sort

Insertion sort is an advanced, intuitive, and effective sorting algorithm that works like organizing a hand of playing cards. You start with one card, compare it to the others, and place it in its correct position relative to the cards you have already sorted. This process repeats until all the cards are in order.

Let us break it down step-by-step. Imagine a list of n elements.

1. Start with the first element in the sorted portion.

2. Take the second element. Compare it with the first; if it is smaller, shift the first element to the right and place the second element in the first position.

3. Move to the third element. Compare it with the sorted portion (now two elements). Shift elements as needed and insert it into the correct position.

4. Repeat this process for the fourth, fifth, and remaining elements until all n elements are sorted.

Let us write the code for the insertion sort:

```python
# prompt GPT4:
# Write a function with documentation for the insertion sort

def insertion_sort(input_list, is_debug=False):
    """
    Sorts an array using the insertion sort algorithm.

    Parameters:
    arr (list): The list of elements to be sorted.

    Returns:
    list: The same list with elements sorted in ascending order.

    Time Complexity:
    - Best Case: O(n) (when the array is already sorted)
    - Worst Case: O(n^2) (when the array is sorted in reverse order)
    """
    # Debug log
    if (is_debug):
        print(f"\nDebug log: Input list: {' '*22}{input_list}")

    n = len(input_list)
    for i in range(1, len(input_list)):
        key = input_list[i]
        j = i - 1

        # Debug log
        if (is_debug):
            print(f"\nDebug log: Outer loop at index {i}: {' '*11}{key}")
        # Check greater than key to one position ahead
        while j >= 0 and input_list[j] > key:

            # Debug log
            if (is_debug):
                print(f"Debug log: Inner loop at index {j}: {' '*11}{input_list[j]} ")

            input_list[j + 1] = input_list[j]
            j -= 1

        input_list[j + 1] = key

        # Debug log
        if (is_debug):
            print(f"Debug log: Outer loop inserted {key} at index {j + 1}: {input_list}")
    return input_list
```

Figure 4.13: Insertion sort

Figure 4.13 presents the Python code for insertion sort. Line #2 shows the prompt provided to GPT-4o to generate the function. Line #4 defines the **insertion_sort** function, with **input_list** as the input parameter. Lines #5 through #17 contain inline documentation. Lines #19 and #20 include the debug log statement.

Line #23 marks the start of the outer loop, which iterates through the list from the second element to the last, progressively expanding the sorted portion of the list.

Line #31 begins the inner loop with the while statement, which compares and shifts elements in the sorted portion to make room for the current element. Lines #33 through #35 are the other debug log statements. Finally, line #40 inserts the variable into its correct position within the sorted portion, completing the iteration for that element.

Let us run the code:

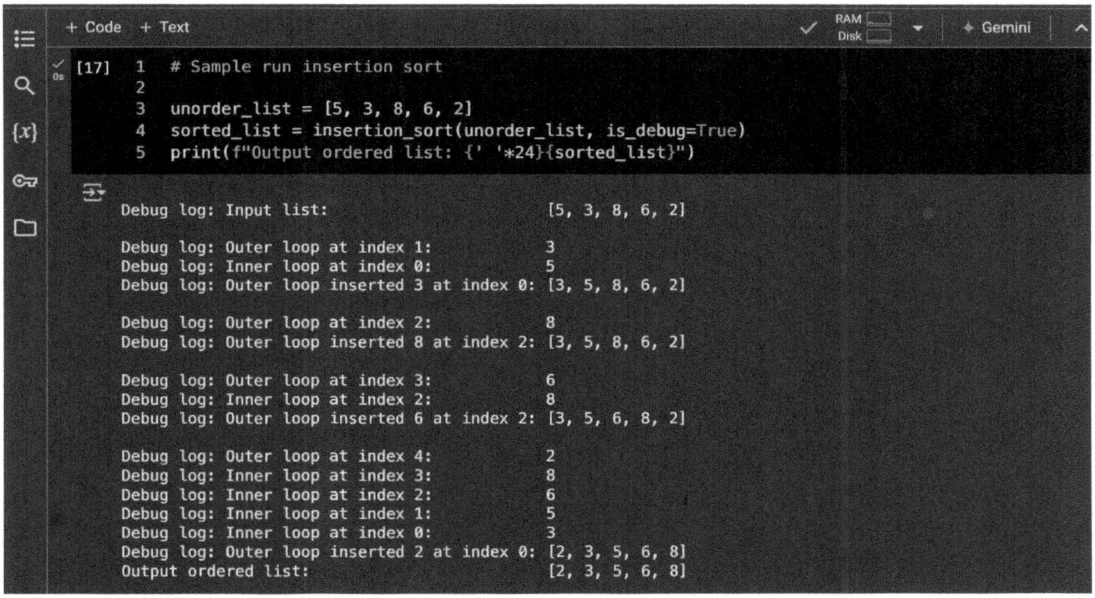

Figure 4.14: *Insertion sort output*

Figure 4.14 shows a sample run of the Insertion sort algorithm using the input list in line #3, which is [5, 3, 8, 6, 2]. Line #4 executes the insertion sort function, and line #5 outputs the sorted list. The output also displays the debug logs as follows:

1. **Start with the first element:** The first element, 5, is already sorted because there is nothing to compare it to. So, we leave it as it is and move to the next element.

2. **Insert the second element into the sorted portion:** Now we look at the second element, 3. Compare it with the elements in the sorted portion (just 5 so far). Since 3 is smaller than 5, we shift 5 one position to the right and insert 3 into the first position. The list now looks like this: [3, 5, 8, 6, 2].

3. **Insert the third element:** Next, take the third element, 8. Compare it with the elements in the sorted portion (3, 5). Since 8 is larger than both, it stays in its current position. The list remains: [3, 5, 8, 6, 2].

4. **Insert the fourth element:** Now look at the fourth element, 6. Compare it with the elements in the sorted portion (3, 5, 8). Since 6 is smaller than 8, shift 8 one position to the right. Compare 6 with 5; since 6 is larger than 5, insert 6 into the correct position between 5 and 8. The list becomes: [3, 5, 6, 8, 2].

5. **Insert the fifth element:** Finally, take the fifth element, 2. Compare it with the elements in the sorted portion (3, 5, 6, 8). Since 2 is smaller than all of them, shift each of these elements one position to the right. Insert 2 into the first position. The list is now fully sorted: [2, 3, 5, 6, 8].

It may be difficult to follow the numbered list with the number index. Thus, we will conduct another sample using the input list with alphabet characters.

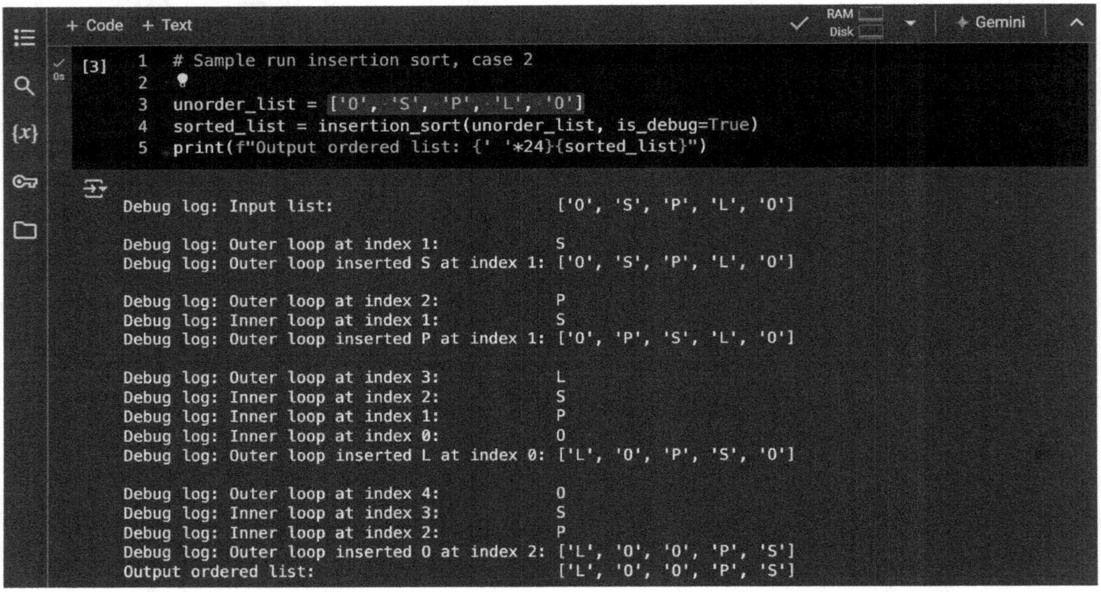

```
# Sample run insertion sort, case 2

unorder_list = ['O', 'S', 'P', 'L', 'O']
sorted_list = insertion_sort(unorder_list, is_debug=True)
print(f"Output ordered list: {' '*24}{sorted_list}")
```

```
Debug log: Input list:                          ['O', 'S', 'P', 'L', 'O']

Debug log: Outer loop at index 1:               S
Debug log: Outer loop inserted S at index 1: ['O', 'S', 'P', 'L', 'O']

Debug log: Outer loop at index 2:               P
Debug log: Inner loop at index 1:               S
Debug log: Outer loop inserted P at index 1: ['O', 'P', 'S', 'L', 'O']

Debug log: Outer loop at index 3:               L
Debug log: Inner loop at index 2:               S
Debug log: Inner loop at index 1:               P
Debug log: Inner loop at index 0:               O
Debug log: Outer loop inserted L at index 0: ['L', 'O', 'P', 'S', 'O']

Debug log: Outer loop at index 4:               O
Debug log: Inner loop at index 3:               S
Debug log: Inner loop at index 2:               P
Debug log: Outer loop inserted O at index 2: ['L', 'O', 'O', 'P', 'S']
Output ordered list:                            ['L', 'O', 'O', 'P', 'S']
```

***Figure 4.15:** Insertion sort output, alphabet*

Figure 4.15 illustrates the execution of the insertion sort algorithm using the input of the alphabet characters ['O', 'S', 'P', 'L', 'O']. The debug log previously described how to read the debug logs. Similarly, this output provides a detailed record of how the function sorted the alphabet list. Unsurprisingly, the output is ['L', 'O', 'O', 'P', 'S']. We encourage you to examine the debug log output for further insights.

Next on the list is the merge sort.

Merge sort

Merge sort was one of the first algorithms to use the divide-and-conquer strategy, a technique now foundational in computer science. Its design principles have influenced the development of many other sorting algorithms and data processing techniques. Despite its early origins, merge sort remains relevant due to its reliable performance and its ability to handle large amounts of data effectively.

Merge sort is effective because it breaks down a larger problem into smaller, more manageable parts, making it efficient and clear throughout the sorting process. It works well for sorting large amounts of data since it has a time complexity of *O(n log n)*, which means it performs consistently. Unlike other sorting methods that use random choices or swaps, merge sort carefully divides the data, sorts it, and then merges it back together, resulting in a reliable sorting outcome.

Let us review a step-by-step process:

1. **Divide the list into two halves:** merge sort starts by dividing the list into two equal halves. If there is an odd number of items, one half will have one more item than the other. This process keeps going until each piece has just one item.

2. **Recursively sort each half:** Once the list has been divided into single element sublists, the algorithm begins the process of sorting. The task now is to merge these sublists back together in a way that maintains order.

3. **Merge the sorted sublists:** The merging process is the main part of the algorithm. It takes two sorted lists and compares their elements one by one. The smallest element from either list is added to a new list, which will be the sorted result for that step. This process keeps happening until all the elements from both lists are combined into one sorted list.

4. **Repeat the merging process until the entire list is sorted:** The merging process continues as larger sorted sublists are combined until the entire list is sorted. In the final step, the two largest sublists, originally from the left and right halves, are merged into one sorted list.

To say it plainly, you start by splitting the list in half and keep doing it until the half's size is just one. That is the recursive loop. The magic happens when you merge and order the smaller left and right halves inside the recursive loop.

As before, we asked our trusty GPT-4o to write the code.

```
☰    + Code  + Text                                          ✓  RAM ▱  ▾  + Gemini  ⌃
                                                                Disk ▱
Q  ✓ [22]  1  # Prompt GPT-4o
   0s      2  # Write a python function with documentation for the merge sort.
           3  # (And many more prompt engineering to break it down to simpler functions)
{x}        4
           5  def split_list(input_list):
☞          6      """
           7      Splits a list into two halves.
           8
□          9      Parameters:
          10      input_list (list): The list to be split.
          11
          12      Returns:
          13      tuple: A tuple containing the two halves.
          14      """
          15      # Split the array into two halves
          16      mid = len(input_list) // 2
          17      left_half = input_list[:mid]
          18      right_half = input_list[mid:]
          19
          20      # print debug log
          21      print(f"Debug log: Split left half:   {left_half}")
          22      print(f"Debug log: Split right helf:  {right_half}")
          23
          24      return left_half, right_half
          25  #
```

Figure 4.16: Merge sort, part I, split list

Figure 4.16 illustrates the first part of the merge sort code, specifically the split function. Lines #2 and #3 show the prompt given to GPT-4o to generate this code. However, what is not immediately apparent is the significant time and effort spent on prompt engineering to gain a deeper understanding of how merge sort works. Although GPT-4o generated a correct response on the first attempt, the initial code and inline documentation are combined in one big function.

The original code was efficient and functional but lacked clarity. It did not clearly distinguish the split and merge functions, making the recursive loop difficult to understand.

The lack of clarity made understanding and learning the algorithm unnecessarily challenging. After spending hours iterating with GPT-4o, we wrote, rewrote, and refined our prompt until we created a functioning merge sort algorithm different from the typical textbook approach. The final result features clearly defined functions for splitting and merging and an easily recognizable recursive loop, making it both functional and significantly easier to understand.

Breaking down one large function into three smaller functions makes the code easier to read and understand. In this case, Line #5 defines the **split_list()** function, with **input_list** as its parameter, creating a clear and focused role for this part of the merge sort process. Lines #6 through #14 contain detailed inline documentation.

Lines #16 through #18 implement the primary logic for splitting the list. Remarkably, this critical operation is completed in just three lines of code, which are clear and easy to understand, making the function both concise and beginner friendly.

Lines #21 and #22 include debug log statements. Finally, Line #24 returns the left and right halves of the split list, completing the function in a clear and organized manner. By isolating the splitting logic into its own function, the overall merge sort code becomes much more structured and easier to understand.

Let us look at the merging function.

```
27  def merge_list(left, right):
28      """
29      Merges two sorted arrays into a single sorted array.
30
31      Parameters:
32      left (list): The left sorted half.
33      right (list): The right sorted half.
34
35      Returns:
36      list: A merged sorted array.
37      """
38      halves_merged_list = []
39      i = j = 0
40
41      while i < len(left) and j < len(right):
42          if left[i] <= right[j]:
43              halves_merged_list.append(left[i])
44              i += 1
45          else:
46              halves_merged_list.append(right[j])
47              j += 1
48
49      # Add any remaining elements from left and right
50      halves_merged_list.extend(left[i:])
51      halves_merged_list.extend(right[j:])
52
53      print(f"Debug log: Merging halves: {' '*3}{halves_merged_list}")
54      return halves_merged_list
55  #
```

Figure 4.17: Merge sort, part II, merging function

Figure 4.17 introduces the **merge_list()** function, which takes left and right lists as input parameters. Lines #28 to #37 are the inline documentation.

The real magic occurs in Lines #41 through #47, where a while loop compares the elements of the left and right lists. The logic is both simple and elegant. The smaller number is appended to the left list, while the larger number is appended to the right list.

Lines #51 and #52 combine the left-half list with the right-half list.

Finally, line #53 contains a debug log statement that monitors the merge operation, while line #54 returns the fully merged and sorted list. By isolating the merging logic into its own function, the code becomes much clearer, and the algorithm becomes easier to understand.

Next is putting the splitting and merging methods into the merge sort function.

```
      ≡        + Code  + Text                                              Reconnect  ▼    ✦ Gemini    ∧
             [ ]  57   def merge_sort(input_list):
      Q            58       """
                   59       Sorts an array using the merge sort algorithm.
    {x}            60
                   61       Parameters:
                   62       input_list (list): The list of elements to be sorted.
    ⊙━             63
                   64       Returns:
    ▢              65       list: A new list containing the sorted elements.
                   66
                   67       Time Complexity:
                   68       - Best/Average/Worst Case: O(n log n)
                   69       """
                   70
                   71       # Base case: A list of zero or one elements is already sorted
                   72       if len(input_list) <= 1:
                   73           print(f"Debug log: Base case reached: {input_list}")
                   74           return input_list      # exit this loop, base case
                   75
                   76       # Split the array into two halves
                   77       left_half, right_half = split_list(input_list)
                   78
                   79       # Recursively sort each half, calling ourself again
                   80       sorted_left = merge_sort(left_half)
                   81       sorted_right = merge_sort(right_half)
                   82
                   83       # Merge the sorted halves
                   84       simi_merged_list = merge_list(sorted_left, sorted_right)
                   85
                   86       return simi_merged_list
```

Figure 4.18: *Merge sort, part III*

Figure 4.18 illustrates the merge sort algorithm. The design choice of separating the splitting and merging methods simplifies the algorithm, making it easier to understand. It starkly contrasts the often dense and complex explanations typically found in programming books about sorting.

Line #57 defines the **merge_sort()** function, with **input_list** as its parameter. Lines #58 to #69 include thorough inline documentation that clearly explains the function's purpose and logic.

The heart of the algorithm is in the following few lines of code. Starting with lines #72 to #74, where it sets the base case for the recursion. This checks if the list has one or no items, determining when to stop the recursion.

Continue to line #77, which invokes the **split_list()** function, dividing the list into two halves. Lines #80 and #81 invoke the **merge_sort()** function on each half. These two lines form two recursive loops. It breaks the input list into smaller parts until the base case is reached.

Lastly, line #84 invokes the **merge_list()** function, which combines the sorted halves into a single ordered list.

And that is it! Our code becomes more intuitive to understand by separating the splitting and merging into distinct functions. Finally, Line #89 returns the fully ordered list.

Let us run the code to see the output.

```
# sample Merge sort run

unorder_list = [5, 3, 8, 6, 2]
print(f"Unorder input list: {' '*10}{unorder_list}")
order_list = merge_sort(unorder_list)
print(f"Order output list: {' '*11}{order_list}")
```

```
Unorder input list:        [5, 3, 8, 6, 2]
Debug log: Split left half:   [5, 3]
Debug log: Split right helf:  [8, 6, 2]
Debug log: Split left half:   [5]
Debug log: Split right helf:  [3]
Debug log: Base case reached: [5]
Debug log: Base case reached: [3]
Debug log: Merging halves:    [3, 5]
Debug log: Split left half:   [8]
Debug log: Split right helf:  [6, 2]
Debug log: Base case reached: [8]
Debug log: Split left half:   [6]
Debug log: Split right helf:  [2]
Debug log: Base case reached: [6]
Debug log: Base case reached: [2]
Debug log: Merging halves:    [2, 6]
Debug log: Merging halves:    [2, 6, 8]
Debug log: Merging halves:    [2, 3, 5, 6, 8]
Order output list:         [2, 3, 5, 6, 8]
```

Figure 4.19: Merge sort output

Figure 4.19 displays the output of the **merge_sort()** function. Line #3 shows the input: [5, 3, 8, 6, 2]. Line #4 executes the function. The output includes the debug log statements presented in a clear format. Let us take a closer look at the output:

1. **Divide the list into halves.** Start by splitting the list into two smaller sublists. In this case: Left sublist: [5, 3] and Right sublist: [8, 6, 2]. If these sublists have more than one element, we keep dividing them further.

2. **Divide again until each sublist has one element.** Break the left sublist [5, 3] into [5] and [3]. Similarly, break the right sublist [8, 6, 2] into [8] and [6, 2]. Then, divide [6, 2] into [6] and [2]. Now we have all the sublists as single elements: [5], [3], [8], [6], [2].

3. **Start merging and sorting smaller sublists.** Now that we have single element sublists, we begin merging them back together, sorting as we go. merge [5] and [3]: Compare the elements, and since 3 is smaller, place it first. The sorted result is [3, 5]. merge [6] and [2]: Compare the elements, and since 2 is smaller, place it first. The sorted result is [2, 6].

4. **Merge the sorted sublists: Continue merging:** merge [2, 6] with [8]. Since 2 is smallest, place it first, followed by 6, then 8. The sorted result is [2, 6, 8]. Now we have two sorted sublists: [3, 5] and [2, 6, 8].

5. **Merge the final two sorted sublists.** Finally, merge [3, 5] and [2, 6, 8]. Compare the smallest elements from both lists. The final sorted list is: [2, 3, 5, 6, 8].

We dedicated extra time to fully understand merge sort because the concept of recursive loops is an extraordinarily powerful tool in computer science. Equally important is learning not to rely solely on the first answer GPT-4o provides for coding advice. While the initial answer was technically correct, it was unnecessarily complicated and lacked clarity.

To address this, we spent hours and efforts that were not visible in the book, refining our prompts (prompt engineering), reworking GPT-4o's suggestions, and repeatedly testing the code in Jupyter Notebook.

The result of this iterative process is a clear, concise, and easy-to-understand implementation of merge sort, with a deliberate separation of the splitting and merging functions. This approach contrasts traditional programming books, where such clarity is often missing. By focusing on simplicity and readability, we have crafted an implementation that is not only functional but also intuitive.

Next, we move to the final sorting topic, the beloved quick sort, another algorithm that elegantly utilizes the power of recursive loops.

Quick sort

Quick sort is a highly efficient sorting algorithm that uses a divide-and-conquer approach to sort elements. Quick sort has an average time complexity of $O(n \log n)$, making it very efficient for large datasets. However, its worst-case time complexity is $O(n^2)$, which can occur with poor pivot selections leading to unbalanced partitions. Despite this, its simplicity, speed, and ability to handle large-scale sorting make quick sort a favorite in practical scenarios. It is a beautiful demonstration of how recursion and divide-and-conquer strategies can solve complex problems efficiently.

Here is a step-by-step breakdown of the quick sort:

1. **Select a pivot element.** The algorithm begins by picking a pivot element from the list, which is used to split the list into two parts. The pivot can be chosen differently, like the first or last element, or randomly.

2. **Partition the list.** Split the list into two parts: one with elements smaller than the pivot and the other with elements larger than the pivot. The pivot is now correctly placed between the two parts, with smaller elements on one side and larger ones on the other.

3. **Recursively apply quick sort to the sublists.** The algorithm divides a list into smaller parts based on a pivot and then recursively applies this process to the smaller parts. A new pivot is chosen for each part, and the division is repeated until the parts are empty or have just one element, which means they are already sorted.

4. **Combine the sorted sublists.** After the recursion, the sorted sublists are merged with the pivot element in their correct positions, resulting in a completely ordered list.

Let us start with the code.

```
1  # prompt GPT-4o:
2  # Write a function with documentation for the quick sort with example run
3
4  def quick_sort(input_list):
5      """
6      Sorts an array using the quicksort algorithm.
7
8      The process is recursively applied to the sub-arrays until the entire array is
       sorted.
9
10     Parameters:
11     arr (list): The list of elements to be sorted.
12
13     Returns:
14     list: A new list containing the sorted elements.
15     """
16     if len(input_list) <= 1:
17         print(f"Debug log: Base case reached: {input_list}")
18         return input_list  # Base case: A list of zero or one elements
19
20     # Choose the pivot
21     # It can be optimized further by selecting a random element or using the median
22     pivot = input_list[len(input_list) // 2]
23     print(f"Debug log: Pivot selected: {' '*3}{pivot}")
24
25     # Partition the array into three parts
26     left = [x for x in input_list if x < pivot]
27     middle = [x for x in input_list if x == pivot]
28     right = [x for x in input_list if x > pivot]
29
30     # Recursively sort the left and right parts, and combine them with the middle part
31     left = quick_sort(left)
32     right = quick_sort(right)
33     order_list = left + middle + right
34
35     print(f"Debug log: Left half: {' '*8}{left}")
36     print(f"Debug log: Right half: {' '*7}{right}")
37     print(f"Debug log: Order list: {' '*7}{order_list}")
38     return order_list
39
```

Figure 4.20: *Quick sort*

Figure 4.20 shows the code for the quick sort. Line #2 is the GPT-4o prompt. Line #4 defines the **`quick_sort()`** function with **`input_list`** as the passing parameter. Lines #5 through #15 are the inline documentation.

Lines #16 through #18 are the recursive loop base case. It is the point where we exit the recursive loop when one or no element is in the list. Line #22 is the pivot calculation. Lines #26 through #28 define the left, middle, and right segments.

Lines #31 and #32 start the recursive loop by calling itself. Line #33 combines it into the **`order_list`**, and line #38 returns it.

Let us run the code.

```
+ Code  + Text                                                    RAM ▭    ▼   + Gemini    ∧
                                                                  Disk ▭

[19]  1  # Example run of quick short
      2
      3  unorder_list = [5, 3, 8, 6, 2]
      4  print(f"Input unordered list: {' '*8}{unorder_list}")
      5  sorted_list = quick_sort(unorder_list)
      6  print(f"Output ordered list: {' '*9}{sorted_list}")

   Input unordered list:        [5, 3, 8, 6, 2]
   Debug log: Pivot selected:   8
   Debug log: Pivot selected:   6
   Debug log: Pivot selected:   3
   Debug log: Base case reached: [2]
   Debug log: Base case reached: [5]
   Debug log: Left half:        [2]
   Debug log: Right half:       [5]
   Debug log: Order list:       [2, 3, 5]
   Debug log: Base case reached: []
   Debug log: Left half:        [2, 3, 5]
   Debug log: Right half:       []
   Debug log: Order list:       [2, 3, 5, 6]
   Debug log: Base case reached: []
   Debug log: Left half:        [2, 3, 5, 6]
   Debug log: Right half:       []
   Debug log: Order list:       [2, 3, 5, 6, 8]
   Output ordered list:         [2, 3, 5, 6, 8]
```

Figure 4.21: Quick sort output

Figure 4.21 shows the output in nicely aligned columns. Line #3 provides the **input_list** as [5, 3, 8, 6, 2], and line #5 calls the **quick_sort()** function. The output explanation is as follows:

1. **Select a pivot:** Choose the middle element as the pivot.

2. **Partition the list:** Divide the list into two sublists based on the pivot 8: Left Sublist (smaller elements): [5, 3, 6, 2]. Right Sublist (larger elements): [] (no elements are larger than 8)

3. **Recursively sort the sublist.** Choose the new pivot as the middle element: 6.

4. **Recursively sort the sublist.** Choose the middle element as the pivot: 3.

5. **Combine the sorted sublists.** The resulting list is [2, 3, 5, 6].

6. **Combine again with the pivot 8.** The final sorted list is: [2, 3, 5, 6, 8].

We have covered a lot of ground exploring sorting algorithms, including bubble, Selection, Insertion, merge, and quick sorting algorithms. Each method employs a unique approach to organizing data, which has helped us understand their logic and implementation. Next, we will compare their speed and efficiency when sorting large input lists.

Performance insights

Performance insights are crucial in software development to understand how efficiently sorting algorithms operate. They assist developers in optimizing speed and resource usage. These insights involve analyzing different aspects of a program's execution, such as its data processing speed, memory consumption, and ability to manage increasing workloads.

By monitoring factors such as CPU usage, input/output operations, and bottlenecks in code execution, developers can gain a clearer understanding of where improvements can be made. Performance profiling tools help identify inefficient code segments or resource-intensive operations. Enhancing performance involves more than just reducing execution time. It also ensures the system can scale efficiently, manage peak loads, and maintain responsiveness under various conditions.

Understanding these insights is essential for creating software that works optimally and reliably, ensuring a better user experience and smoother system operations.

One of the best methods for gaining insight into sorting algorithms is measuring the time it takes to order a large set of unordered data.

Time complexity

Time complexity describes how the running time of a sorting algorithm increases as the size of the input list grows. It provides a measure of an algorithm's efficiency by indicating the number of basic operations (such as comparisons or calculations) it needs to complete its task. By understanding time complexity, we can evaluate how an algorithm will perform as the input size increases, helping us choose the most efficient solution for a problem.

Standard time complexity notations, like $O(n)$ for linear time and $O(log\ n)$ for logarithmic time, allow us to express the expected computation time growth, compare different algorithms, and understand their scalability.

When selecting sorting algorithms, opting for the fastest is not always the best choice. Although speed is an essential factor, other considerations, such as simplicity, memory usage, stability, and the size or nature of the data, are crucial in determining the most appropriate algorithm for a given situation.

quick sort is often praised for its speed, boasting an average time complexity of $O(n\ log\ n)$, which makes it a preferred choice for managing large datasets. However, its worst-case time complexity of $O(n^2)$ can become a significant drawback when poor pivot selection leads to unbalanced partitions. In such scenarios, algorithms like merge sort, which consistently operates at $O(n\ log\ n)$, maybe more reliable, even though they require more memory due to the extra space needed for merging.

Simplicity can sometimes be more important than speed, especially when working with small datasets. For example, while bubble sort and Insertion sort have a time complexity of $O(n^2)$ and may be slower than other algorithms, their straightforward logic and ease of implementation make them practical options when performance is not a critical concern. Additionally, if the data is nearly sorted, Insertion sort can outperform more complex algorithms by reducing unnecessary comparisons and swaps.

The following sections will clarify the specific time complexity notations from fastest to slowest.

- **Big O notation:** It is a mathematical representation used to describe the efficiency of an algorithm by illustrating how its running time or memory requirements increase relative to the input size. Sorting algorithms have best-case, worst-case, and average-case scenarios. When encountering a Big O notation without qualifiers, it is typically understood to refer to the best-case scenario.

- **O(1) constant time complexity:** The algorithm's runtime remains unchanged regardless of the input size. No sorting algorithm achieves *O(1)* time complexity.

- **O(log n) logarithmic time complexity:** It refers to algorithms whose runtime increases gradually as the input size grows, usually by halving the problem size at each step. This complexity is highly efficient for large inputs because the number of operations increases slower than the input size.

- **O(n) linear time complexity**: This indicates that the algorithm's runtime grows directly proportional to the input size. If the input doubles, the time taken also doubles. Very few sorting algorithms, such as counting, radix, and bucket sort, achieve the *O(n)* in the best-case scenario.

- **O(n log n) time complexity:** It is known as **linearithmic time** complexity and describes a situation where an algorithm grows in a way that combines linear and logarithmic patterns. The problem is divided into smaller parts, each handled separately. Two common examples of algorithms with this complexity are merge and quick sort.

- **O(n^2) quadratic time complexity:** The runtime increases quadratically as the input size grows. For example, if the input size doubles, the runtime will increase by four times. This type of complexity is commonly found in algorithms that use nested loops. A typical example is bubble and selection sort.

- **O(n^3) cubic time complexity:** The runtime increases with the cube of the input size. When the input size doubles, the time taken increases by a factor of eight. No known sorting algorithm is this slow.

- **O(2^n) exponential time complexity:** The runtime doubles with each additional input element. This growth rate is extremely rapid. No known sorting algorithm is this slow. You could be famous (or infamous) if you can devise a sorting algorithm that is this slow.

We can evaluate the time complexity of the sorting algorithms discussed in this chapter with the following code:

```
[31]  1  # prompt GTP-4o: c
      2  # Create an random integer list of 18000 range from 0 to 1000000
      3
      4  import random
      5
      6  unorder_list = random.sample(range(0, 1000000), 18000)

[32]  1  %%time
      2  order_list = bubble_sort(unorder_list, is_debug=False)

      CPU times: user 19.7 s, sys: 44.6 ms, total: 19.8 s
      Wall time: 19.9 s
```

Figure 4.22: Evaluate time complexity

Figure 4.22 shows the code for creating an 18,000 random number between zero and a million. Line #2 is the GPT-4o prompt, and line #6 made the **unorder_list**. The following code cell shows we use the Jupyter Notebook magic command **%%time** to measure the bubble sort time. Now shown in *Figure 4.22* is the similar command we use to measure the speed of selection, Insertion, merge, and quick sort.

We draw the bar chart to view the result:

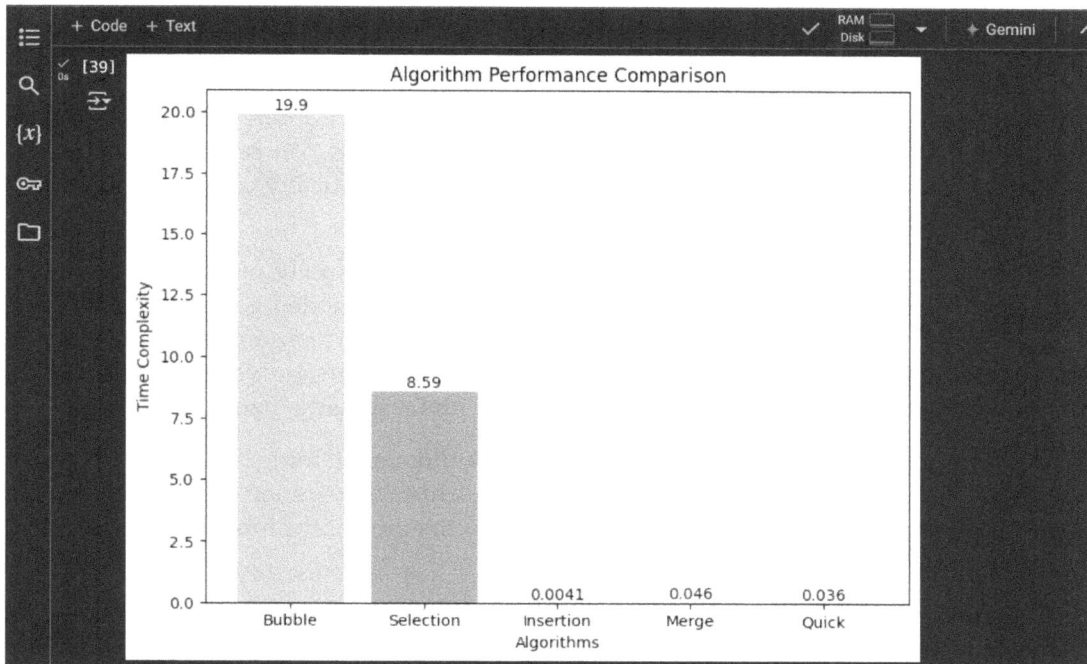

Figure 4.23: Bar chart for time complexity

Figure 4.23 presents a bar chart illustrating the time, in seconds, taken to sort an array of 18,000 random numbers using bubble, selection, insertion, merge, and quick sort algorithms. 18,000 is the average number of students in a college. The graph highlights a striking contrast in performance speed among the different sorting algorithms. The corresponding time values (in seconds) for each algorithm are as follows: [19.9, 8.59, 0.0041, 0.046, 0.036].

Finally, we have reached the end of this chapter. We have thoroughly examined the five popular sorting algorithms, discussing their logic, implementation, and performance. This extensive analysis provides a strong foundation for understanding how these algorithms function and how they compare in various scenarios.

Conclusion

In this chapter, we explored the fundamental role that sorting plays in computer science, from its historical roots to its practical applications today. Sorting algorithms are essential for organizing data and optimizing other algorithms that rely on ordered input. We discussed a range of sorting techniques, from simple approaches like bubble sort and Selection sort to more advanced algorithms like Insertion, merge, and quick sort, each with unique strengths and weaknesses. Understanding how these algorithms work, when to use them, and their performance implications is crucial for developing efficient and effective software.

We dedicated extra time to thoroughly understanding the bubble sort algorithm and analyzing it from various perspectives to ensure clarity and comprehension. First, we detailed its core logic, explaining how the algorithm systematically compares and swaps adjacent elements to sort a list gradually.

To clarify the process further, we created a flowchart that visually represents the bubble sort algorithm's step-by-step operation. The information provided gave us a clear, high-level understanding of how bubble sort functions. We also took an additional step by expressing the algorithm using pseudo-mathematical equations, providing an abstract yet concise explanation of its mechanics for those who prefer a mathematical perspective.

We then implemented the bubble sort function in Python, explaining each part of the code and its relevance to the overall structure of the algorithm. To deepen our understanding, we included debugging log statements that allow us to monitor the inner workings of both the outer and inner loops during execution.

We tested the function using two different sample input lists, carefully analyzing the output at each step. This approach allowed us to observe how the algorithm processes and transforms the data in real-time. We took the extra step of using a bar chart to visualize how each number in the list was sorted. By observing and explaining these results, we not only confirmed that the function worked correctly but also gained deeper insights into the behavior of the algorithm. Through this comprehensive approach, we have established a solid foundation for understanding bubble sort as well as Selection, Insertion, merge, and quick sort algorithms.

In this chapter, we extensively utilized GPT-4o to help us write code, provide detailed explanations, and assist with debugging. However, we did not accept its responses without question. Instead, we exercised our judgment to guide the process, refining and adjusting the output to achieve our desired level of understanding. By actively engaging with GPT-4o's suggestions, such as reviewing, modifying, and testing, we ensured that the content remained accurate and precise, turning its assistance into a valuable learning experience.

The chapter also highlighted the importance of selecting a suitable sorting algorithm for the task at hand. Factors such as dataset size, memory constraints, and the need for stability can significantly impact algorithm choice. Using the wrong algorithm can lead to poor performance, mainly when working with large datasets or resource-limited systems. By mastering various sorting algorithms, you can optimize not just the sorting process but also improve the overall performance of your applications.

In summary, sorting is more than just a technical requirement—it is a tool that enhances data organization, algorithm efficiency, and user experience across various computer science fields and real-world applications. Whether building complex systems or working with small datasets, understanding the sorting principles equips you to choose the most appropriate solution for the problem.

The next chapter takes our journey of learning Python code deeper into the Pandas library.

Join our book's Discord space

Join the book's Discord Workspace for Latest updates, Offers, Tech happenings around the world, New Release and Sessions with the Authors:

https://discord.bpbonline.com

CHAPTER 5

Pandas, the Data Tamer

Introduction

In this chapter we will explore how to use Python's Pandas library with GPT-4o. Whether you are a beginner or an experienced programmer, this chapter aims to unlock the potential of data manipulation and analysis in Python. By the end of this chapter, you will be equipped with valuable skills to manipulate data effectively and efficiently using the Pandas library. Furthermore, you will learn to use GPT-4o to explore and explain Pandas concepts and syntax.

Throughout this chapter, we will explore the core functionalities of the Pandas library, from DataFrames and Series to intricate data manipulation techniques. You will learn how to read, clean, and visualize data while GenAI provides tips, explanations, and code examples. By combining the interactive learning experience that GenAI offers with hands-on practice in Jupyter Notebooks, you will gain a comprehensive understanding of Pandas engagingly and efficiently.

Python is recognized for its simplicity and readability, which contributes to its popularity among both beginners and experienced developers. Many beginner books on Python cover fundamental concepts such as variables, control structures, functions, and file I/O but often exclude the Pandas library. The reason is that Panas is considered too complex for beginners, but not for us, with the help of GenAI and Jupyter Notebook.

GPT-4o is a game-changer for beginners who are learning Pandas. It offers contextual explanations that simplify complex concepts and tailor them to each individual's level of understanding. Unlike static examples, GPT-4o provides an interactive learning experience where students can ask questions, request specific examples, and get help with errors in their code. This dynamic learning process enhances understanding and retention, making it easier to master Pandas.

Customized examples generated by GPT-4o align with a learner's interests or specific tasks, making the learning process less abstract and more engaging. Additionally, it provides real-time feedback on code to correct misunderstandings early and reinforce the learning process.

Note: Wes McKinney created Pandas in 2008, short for Panel Data, not for a cute black-and-white panda bear or Kung Fu Panda.

Figure 5.1: GPT-4o and DALL-E3 depict a Panda in a futuristic office

Figure 5.1 illustrates the rapid advancements in GenAI, including GPT-4o. In 2023, GPT-3.5 was limited to responding with text and did not have an accompanying image model. However, it has now evolved to generate images as well. Looking ahead, GPT-4o is expected to advance further, with capabilities that will include text-to-music, text-to-speech, text-to-animation, and text-to-movie functionalities.

Before we get sidetracked with generating picture, let's get back to discussing the Pandas library. While Pandas can be quite complex, GenAI helps make it easier for beginners to understand. As always, we'll start with a clear and structured approach.

Structure

This chapter is about learning the Pandas library, and in particular the following topics:

- Pandas' foundation

- Manipulating Pandas data
- Data analysis superpower
- Chart your Pandas path and beyond

Objectives

By the end of this chapter, you will have a solid foundation in using the Pandas library for data manipulation and analysis. You will learn how to create DataFrames and Series, which are the core components of Pandas, and perform essential operations such as adding and deleting rows and columns. Additionally, you will explore advanced transformation techniques that enable you to reshape, filter, and aggregate data efficiently to meet your specific needs.

Furthermore, you will learn how to display your data in a clear, table-like format, making it easier to interpret and share insights. To enhance your data presentation, you will also discover how to create informative graphs that provide valuable perspectives on your datasets. We will advance beyond a small sample dataset, typical of most computer books about Pandas. Instead, we will access real-world datasets from the Kaggle website.

We will not stop there. This chapter will also guide you in leveraging GPT-4o as your personal Python tutor. You will learn how to ask GPT-4o for assistance in writing and explaining Python code, tailoring its responses to your level of understanding while also enjoying the process. Whether you are troubleshooting an error or looking for a new perspective, GPT-4o will assist you and enhance your Python coding experience or goof off along with you.

We will start at the bottom, the foundation.

Pandas' foundation

Before learning the functions of Pandas, we recommend that you review *Chapter 1, Introduction to GenA,* for guidance on how to get started with GPT-4o and how to use the prompt engineering technique. Additionally, *Chapter 2, Jupyter Notebook*, provides valuable tips and step-by-step instructions for navigating and coding on the Python Jupyter Notebook. This chapter heavily relies on the mastering of GPT-4o and the Python Jupyter Notebook.

Remember, becoming proficient in new tools and languages is a journey. Every expert was once a beginner. So, take your time and explore Chapters 1, *Introduction to GenAI*, and 2, *Jupyter Notebook*. Before you know it, you will be an expert working with GPT-4o and Jupyter Notebooks.

In particular, we will cover the following subtopic in Pandas' foundation.

- Pandas' definition

- Python's community
- Pandas' first coding

Let us start with the definition.

Pandas' definition

Like the previous chapter, this chapter relies on GPT-4o and information from academic papers and books. To understand the basics of the Pandas library, we asked GPT-4o several questions and summarized the answers here. We encourage you to read this chapter and explore further with the assistance of GPT-4. In Chapter 2, *Jupyter Notebook*, you learn about prompt engineering techniques, so no question is too basic or silly. Remember, GPT-4o is a machine. It will not laugh or roll its eyes at you. Here are some initial questions we asked:

- *Explain what Python Pandas is in a knowledgeable and conversational tone.*
- *Explain Pandas in contrast to other main libraries such as Matplotlib and Numpy.*
- *Give a few examples of other essential Panda's libraries.*
- *Explain why Pandas are important for students to learn first in a kid's friendly tone.*
- *What is the history of Python Pandas?*
- *What are the essential components of Pandas, such as DataFrame?*
- *Write ten fun headlines to explain Python Pandas, starting with "Pandas is...".*
- *If you are stuck on a deserted island, what is one Panda function you should take?*
- As an example of a funny answer to the above question, GPT-4o wrote: *groupby() is the Swiss Army knife of Pandas functions—it slices, it dices, and it helps you survive.*

You can ask GPT-4o to draw a picture in watercolor style in landscape format of a Panda in the futuristic office reading an Excel spreadsheet with plants and flowers on the desk.

Here are the highlights from our many sessions with GPT-4o. Pandas is a Python library that provides high-level data structures and a wide range of functions for quickly and efficiently manipulating and analyzing data. The two key components of Pandas are Series and DataFrame are:

- A Series is a one-dimensional labeled array that holds any data type, such as integers, strings, or floating-point numbers. For computer science students, it is similar to a one-dimensional array but with an added feature: each data value is associated with a label (index). You can think of it as a single column from a spreadsheet, like a daily list of your hometown's temperatures or the Super Bowl winners, where each data point has a meaningful label, such as a temperature or a winner list.

- A DataFrame is a two-dimensional labeled data structure comparable to a table or spreadsheet. It comprises rows and columns, where each column is a Series and can hold different data types. Think of it as a buffet table, where each food section represents a column, and the rows represent individual plates of food. For instance, a column could list different types of salads (Caesar, Greek, Caprese, and Cobb), while another might describe their calorie counts. DataFrames are incredibly versatile, allowing you to organize, clean, analyze, and visualize diverse datasets in one place.

In addition, Pandas is a popular tool in data science that provides easy-to-use features for data management and manipulation. It allows users to access various data sources, such as Excel files, CSV files, and databases effortlessly. With Pandas, you can perform complex data transformations, aggregations, merge datasets, and create pivot tables, all with minimal lines of code.

Pandas is one of many libraries in the open-source community.

Python's community

The Python community is incredibly robust and continues to grow at an impressive pace. As of November 2024, the **Python Package Index (PyPI)** hosts over 350,000 libraries, catering to a wide range of use cases. However, it is important to note that developers do not use all available libraries in a single project, which is far from it. Most projects typically employ five to eight libraries, chosen carefully based on the specific requirements of the task, excluding any additional dependencies these libraries might bring.

For example, the choice of libraries will differ significantly depending on the project's goals. A simple tic-tac-toe game may only require one or two lightweight libraries while predicting global warming trends or fine-tuning a **Convolutional Neural Network (CNN)** for image classification might involve a combination of data science, machine learning, and visualization libraries. Python's strength lies in its adaptability, allowing developers to tailor their toolkit for projects ranging from basic applications to cutting-edge research.

Let us have some fun with GPT-4o. We challenged GPT-4o to explain the standard Python library in a fun and kid-friendly way. When you can break down these complex libraries in a way that a child can understand, you know you have mastered their intended functions.

The following are definitions of essential Pandas's library in a kid-friendly and Christmas tone:

- **Pandas:** Imagine you have a giant toy box from Santa Claus. Pandas help you organize and sort your toys, find your favorite ones quickly, and even clean them up if they are messy. Pandas are like super elves helping to organize the toys.

- **NumPy:** Numpy is a super-fast calculator that can do math on lots of numbers at once. It is a great toy when you have to count how many elves' helpers Santa needs or do some quick calculations on how many toys Santa needs for Christmas.

- **Matplotlib:** If you ever wanted to draw how many cookies you have eaten over the week in a nifty chart, Matplotlib is your friend. It turns numbers into pictures, like graphs and charts, so Santa can see which kids are naughty or nice.

- **Scikit-learn:** Imagine teaching your robot to recognize your drawings or to play a game with you. Scikit-learn is like putting your teacher inside the robot. She will make decisions or predictions, like guessing your favorite color, which toys are popular in your neighborhood, or whether mom and dad will allow you to watch a TV cartoon before bedtime.

- **Dask:** When a puzzle is too big to fit a table, Dask helps you solve it piece by piece. Another example is when Santa cannot fit all the elves in one building. Dash will tell some elves to work in the daytime and some at night.

- **GeoPandas:** GeoPandas are like elves helping Santa's reindeer to know where to fly so Santa can deliver toys to children all over the world, from your neighborhood to cities like New York City, Los Angeles, London, Amsterdam, Kyoto, Dakar, Sydney, Santiago, and Kyiv.

That was a wonderfully clear and engaging explanation of six popular Python libraries, making them accessible to learners of all ages and backgrounds. Whether you are a curious beginner or a seasoned programmer, a fun explanation can unlock the potential of these libraries in intuitive and exciting ways.

GPT-4o truly excels in this context. Its ability to break down technical concepts and tailor explanations to your specific level of understanding is a game changer. Whether you need an analogy to help an idea click, a detailed line-by-line explanation of code, or just a refresher on syntax, GPT-4o adapts to your needs. It transforms complex topics into digestible and relatable insights, making Python easier to learn and enjoyable to explore.

Now, let us take a look at some Pandas coding.

Pandas' first coding

We begin by asking GPT-4o to generate Python Pandas code for creating a DataFrame that includes eight individuals along with their names, ages, heights, and college majors.

The next step is to copy the code generated by GPT-4o into a Jupyter Notebook and run it. The following are the code and its output:

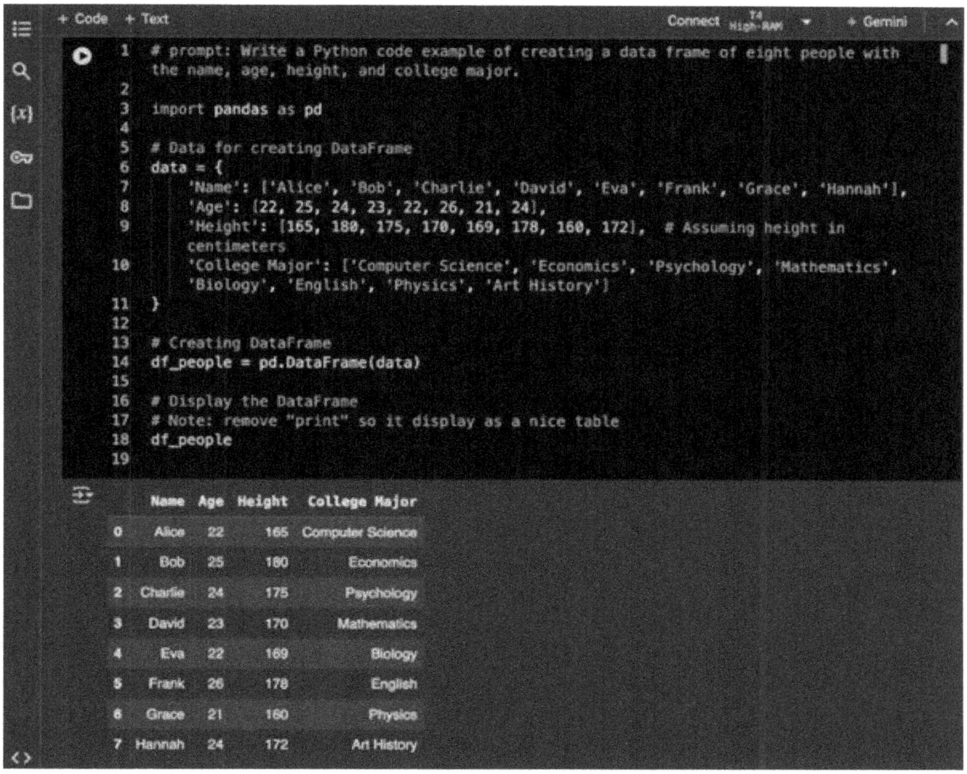

Figure 5.2: Pandas code and output for creating a DataFrame

In *Figure 5.2*, line #1 contains the prompt asking GPT-4 to write the code. Line #3 shows the import statement for the Pandas library, using **pd** as the shorthand for **pandas**. It is worth noting that the command to install the Pandas library, **!pip install pandas**, is sometimes unnecessary because Google Colab automatically includes the Pandas library as a standard library loaded at startup.

Lines #6 through #11 define the data as a dictionary type, with attributes are Name, Age, Height, and College Major representing a college student. You can also manually add new attributes, such as Nationality and Gender. Line #14 creates a **DataFrame** named **df_people** using this data as input. Finally, line #18 displays **df_people** in a well-formatted table.

The output is a table displaying the data like a spreadsheet, with the leftmost column representing the record row index number. Each column has a title at the top and values per row. There are eight rows of values in total. The demonstration in *Figure 5.2* may seem easy, but it showcases a powerful capability. For an experienced Python programmer, creating a simple list of students with just a few lines of code is routine. However, consider the challenge of manually writing code for a table that contains thousands of records. This task can quickly become tedious and is prone to errors. In such situations, GPT-4o proves to be invaluable. You can generate the required sample data without hassle by simply adjusting the prompt to create a table with a million records instead of eight.

To test how easily Pandas handles data manipulation, let us ask GPT-4o to sort the table by the **Age** column. We use a prompt such as sorting the **df_people** based on age.

GPT-4o efficiently produces a correctly sorted table but does not display the corresponding Python code. To address this, we refine the prompt using the prompt engineering techniques explained in Chapter 2, *Jupyter Notebook*, such as: Show me the Python code.

With the code ready, the next step is the same as before: copy it into Jupyter Notebook and execute it. The result is a sorted table showing ages in increasing order, exactly as intended.

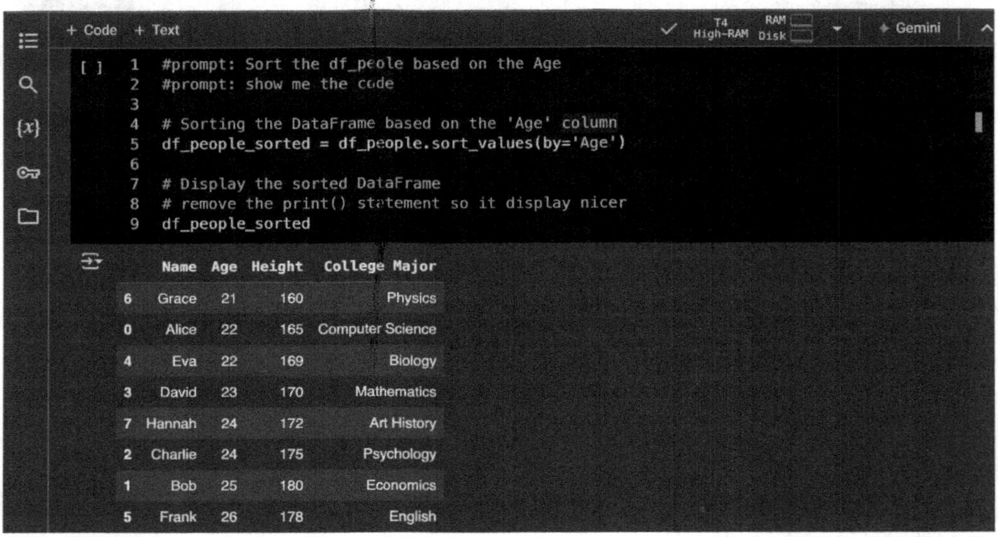


```
1 #prompt: Sort the df_peole based on the Age
2 #prompt: show me the code
3
4 # Sorting the DataFrame based on the 'Age' column
5 df_people_sorted = df_people.sort_values(by='Age')
6
7 # Display the sorted DataFrame
8 # remove the print() statement so it display nicer
9 df_people_sorted
```

	Name	Age	Height	College Major
6	Grace	21	160	Physics
0	Alice	22	165	Computer Science
4	Eva	22	169	Biology
3	David	23	170	Mathematics
7	Hannah	24	172	Art History
2	Charlie	24	175	Psychology
1	Bob	25	180	Economics
5	Frank	26	178	English

***Figure 5.3:** Sort by age*

Figure 5.3 shows the code and the output of the sorted list of students based on the age in ascending order. Lines #1 and #2 are the GPT-4o prompts. Line #5 is the Pandas' **sort_value(by='Age')**, and line #9 displays the result.

The output data remains unchanged but is now organized by age. Grace, who is 21 years old, is listed first, followed by the others, with Frank being the last at 26.

After gaining an understanding of Pandas creating DataFrame, the next step is to explore how to manipulate data using Pandas' built-in functions.

Manipulating Pandas data

The previous section discussed how Pandas' Dataframe and Series are the foundation objects that constitute a table with rows and columns. This section will explain the Pandas library standard functions.

The theme of this book revolves around relying on GPT-4o for guidance while allowing you to choose your preferred learning approach. We will explain how to use GPT-4o for learning and why it fulfills our curiosity. The main objective of this section is to help you feel confident in mastering essential Pandas functions.

GPT-4o offered a clear and straightforward explanation of coding standard Pandas functions. Here is our recommended list of Pandas methods.

- Creating a DataFrame
- Selecting rows and columns
- Adding columns
- Dropping columns
- Renaming columns
- Sorting data
- Basic statistics
- Handling missing data
- Grouping and aggregating
- Merging and joining

We are already covered the fundamentals of creating DataFrames and Series, laying a solid foundation for working with data in Pandas. Now, it is time to take the next step: learning how to select specific rows and columns.

Pandas truly excel in providing a range of powerful and flexible methods for accessing and manipulating data with minimal coding. Whether you are working with a small dataset or analyzing millions of rows, mastering row and column selection allows you to concentrate on the most relevant information. In a later section, we will import a real-world dataset containing millions of records. From slicing rows based on index positions to filtering columns by their names or attributes, these techniques open up new possibilities for efficiently organizing and analyzing your data.

Selecting rows and columns

Let us begin by extracting the first three rows from the **df_people** dataset. This method will allow us to examine the initial entries more closely and better understand the structure and contents of our dataset. If the dataset contains millions of records and we are unfamiliar with it. Analyzing the first few records will give us insights into the data types, available columns, and the kind of information we are working with. This foundational step is crucial for any further data manipulation or analysis we plan to conduct.

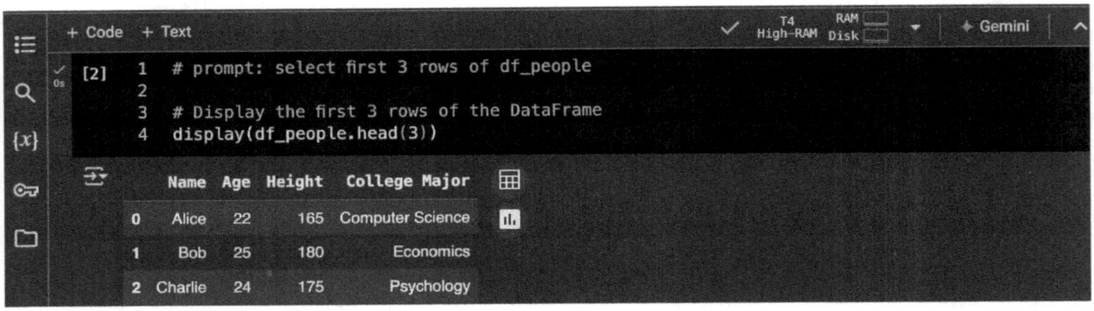

Figure 5.4: First three records

Figure 5.4 displays the code for the first three records of a DataFrame. Line #1 contains the prompt sent to GPT-4. Line #4 is the method **df_people.head(3)** to retrieve and display the first three records from the DataFrame.

You can easily change the number in the parentheses if you want to show a different number of records. For instance, if you replace three with five, the code will display the first five records instead. Similarly, changing it to ten will show the first ten records.

This flexibility highlights one of the key advantages of using the Pandas library. The standard methods are designed to be intuitive and straightforward, making it easier for users to work with data. In our example, **df_people** refers to the DataFrame, and by simply calling the **.head()** method, we can access a portion of that data with minimal effort.

There is no need for complicated setups or lengthy coding practices, like writing out looping structures to display records. This simplicity saves time and makes it easier for anyone to analyze data effectively, even if they are not highly experienced programmers.

The output is the first three records of **Alex, Bob, and Charlie** in a nice table format. The leftmost column is the record index. Notice that the index starts with zero and not one. Starting an index with zero is the programmer's preferred way to index a list. Along with the person's name, the other columns are **Age, Height**, and **College Major**.

Next, we will look at retrieving the tail-end records.

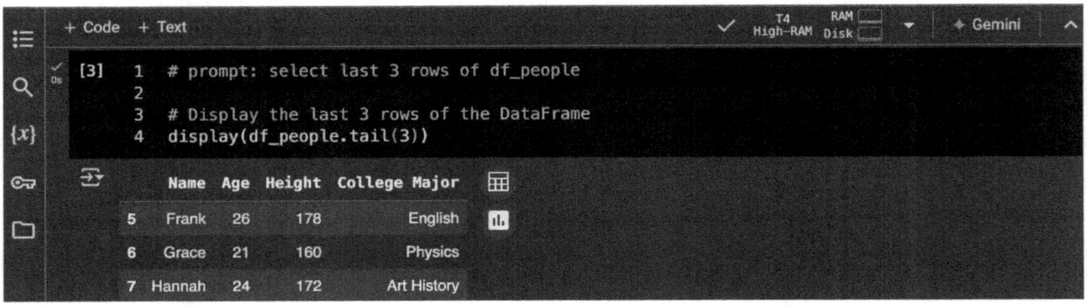

Figure 5.5: Last three records

Figure 5.5 displays the code used to show the last three records. Line #1 contains the GPT-4o prompt, while Line #4 retrieves the last three records using the method **df_people.tail(3)**. Once again, the simplicity and intuitiveness of Pandas methods facilitate quicker learning. Similarly to the **head()** method, you can replace three with twelve to view the last dozen records.

The output is a nicely structured table displaying information for **Frank, Grace, and Hannah**. The leftmost column shows the record index in the dataset, not the record count. Hence, the indexes are 5, 6, and 7.

We have printed the head and tail of the dataset; how about the middle?

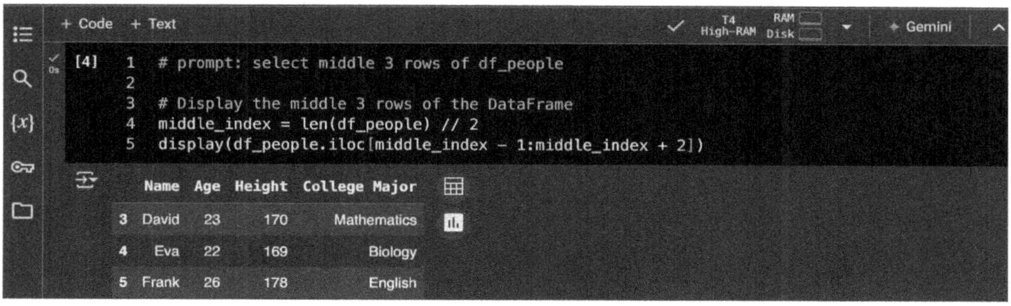

Figure 5.6: *Middle three records*

Figure 5.6 shows the code for displaying three middle records from the **df_people** DataFrame. Line #1 contains the GPT-4o prompt. Line #4 calculates the middle index, and Line #5 shows the three middle rows. Note that there is no built-in **middle()** function; however, the calculation is straightforward.

The output is a well-structured table that presents the middle records for **David, Eva, and Frank**. Now that we are comfortable displaying selected rows, we will do the same for displaying selected columns.

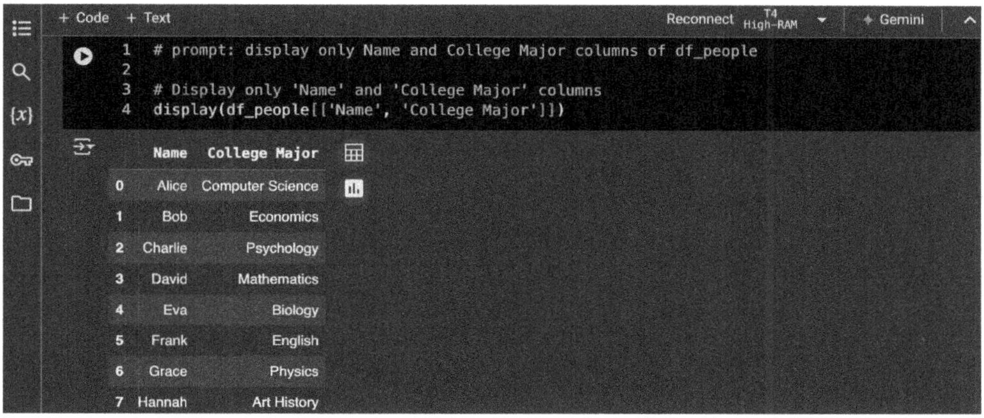

Figure 5.7: *Selected columns*

Figure 5.7 shows the code and output for displaying selected columns. Line #1 contains the GPT-4 prompt. Line #4 displays the columns: **Name** and **College Major**. The output presents a neatly structured list of student names and college majors.

Once again, notice the ease and intuitiveness of using Pandas to display records. It takes just one line of simple code without any if-else or looping statements.

Next is the conditional display technique.

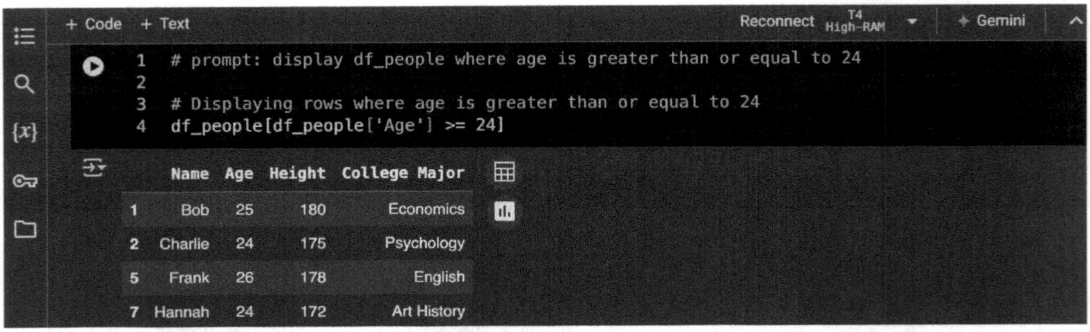

Figure 5.8: *Conditional display*

Figure 5.8 shows the code and output for a conditional display. Line #1 contains the GPT-4o prompt, while line #4 specifies the condition for displaying only students who are 24 years old or older. The output is a well-structured table with **Bob, Charlie, Frank, and Hannah**. All of whom are 24 or older. Note that the leftmost column contains the actual record index numbers.

Checking for ages greater than or equal to 24 is just one example of applying a condition in Pandas. You can easily customize this approach to suit your specific needs. For instance, you could apply a condition to any column, such as **Name, Height, or College Major**, and use a variety of comparison operators to filter the data. Here's a quick overview of the options available:

- Greater than (**>**)
- Less than (**<**)
- Greater than or equal to (**>=**)
- Less than or equal to (**<=**)
- Equals (**==**)
- Not equals (**!=**)
- AND (**&**)
- OR (**|**)
- NOT (**~**)

These operators provide incredible flexibility, allowing you to build complex conditions and precisely filter your data. Whether isolating students above a certain height, selecting records by college major, or combining multiple conditions, these tools make it easy to extract the data you need.

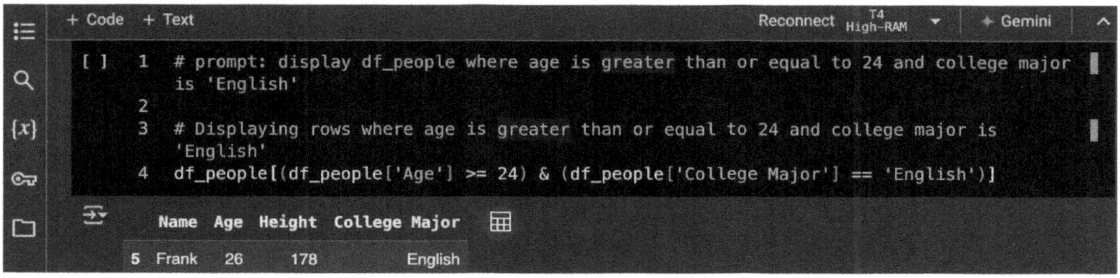

Figure 5.9: *Multiple condition*

Figure 5.9 shows the code and output for selecting from multiple conditions. Line #1 is the GPT-4o prompt, and line 4 displays the record for anyone 24 or older who majors in **English**. The output is a nice table with **Frank** being the only one who meets those conditions.

We are moving on to adding a column.

Adding columns

Adding new columns to a Pandas DataFrame is essential to working with data. It lets you add more information to your dataset, making it more useful. This process is flexible, so you can change your DataFrame to fit your analysis needs.

You can add new data, create columns using the existing ones, or make changes to your data. By learning to add columns, you can better organize your data and prepare for in-depth analysis.

To enhance our student records, we added a few additional columns.

```
+ Code   + Text                                           Reconnect  T4        ▼    ✦ Gemini      ⌃
                                                                    High-RAM
  ▶   1  # prompt: Add two new columns to df_people 'Gender' and 'ethnicity' with sample data
      2
      3  # Add 'Gender' column with sample data
      4  import random
      5  genders = ['Male', 'Female']
      6  df_people['Gender'] = random.choices(genders, k=len(df_people))
      7
      8  # Add 'Ethnicity' column with sample data
      9  ethnicities = ['White', 'Asian', 'Black', 'Hispanic', 'Other']
     10  df_people['Ethnicity'] = random.choices(ethnicities, k=len(df_people))
     11
     12  # Display the updated DataFrame
     13  df_people
```

	Name	Age	Height	College Major	Gender	Ethnicity
0	Alice	22	165	Computer Science	Male	Other
1	Bob	25	180	Economics	Female	Asian
2	Charlie	24	175	Psychology	Female	Black
3	David	23	170	Mathematics	Female	Hispanic
4	Eva	22	169	Biology	Female	Black
5	Frank	26	178	English	Female	Black
6	Grace	21	160	Physics	Female	White
7	Hannah	24	172	Art History	Male	White

Figure 5.10: *Adding columns*

Figure 5.10 displays the code and output for adding new columns to a DataFrame. Line #1 contains the prompt to GPT-4o. In line #4, the library named random is imported. Line #5 defines the male and female genders, while line #6 creates a new Gender column in the **df_people** DataFrame, randomly assigning either male or female to each individual. Similarly, line #9 defines the possible values for ethnicities, and line #10 randomly assigns these values to each person. Finally, line #13 displays the results.

The output presents a well-organized table of our eight students, now including the additional columns for **Gender and Ethnicity**.

First, we add, now we drop.

Dropping columns

Removing columns from a Pandas DataFrame is an important task that helps you focus on relevant data and eliminate unnecessary information. This is especially helpful when working with large datasets, as it can simplify and speed up your analysis.

Pandas make it easy to drop columns so you can choose which ones to remove. Whether you want to delete a single, multiple, or even columns based on certain conditions, you can tailor your DataFrame to your needs.

Removing unneeded columns can reduce clutter, improve performance, and ensure your analysis is centered on the most critical information. This step is key to creating clean data for your projects.

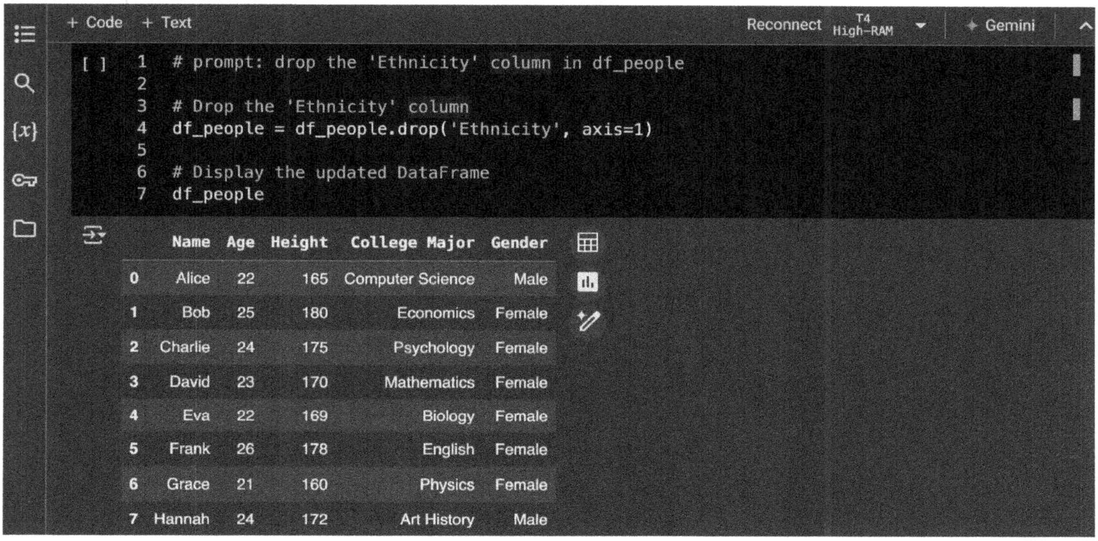

```
1  # prompt: drop the 'Ethnicity' column in df_people
2
3  # Drop the 'Ethnicity' column
4  df_people = df_people.drop('Ethnicity', axis=1)
5
6  # Display the updated DataFrame
7  df_people
```

	Name	Age	Height	College Major	Gender
0	Alice	22	165	Computer Science	Male
1	Bob	25	180	Economics	Female
2	Charlie	24	175	Psychology	Female
3	David	23	170	Mathematics	Female
4	Eva	22	169	Biology	Female
5	Frank	26	178	English	Female
6	Grace	21	160	Physics	Female
7	Hannah	24	172	Art History	Male

Figure 5.11: Drop column

Figure 5.11 shows the code and output for removing a column. In line #1, we see the GPT-4o prompt. Line #4 uses the Pandas function **drop()** to delete a column named **Ethnicity** and **axis=1**.

In Pandas, the **axis** keyword defines the direction of the operation. When you set **axis=0**, the operation affects rows, working vertically. If you use **axis=1**, it affects columns, working horizontally. For example, in the **drop()** function, using **axis=1** means you want to remove columns, not rows.

The output is a nicely structured table for all students without the **Ethnicity** column.

We add. We dropped, and now we rename.

Renaming columns

Renaming columns in a Pandas DataFrame is essential for making your data easier to understand. Often, column names can be confusing, inconsistent, or not descriptive enough for your needs. By renaming them, you can ensure that the names accurately reflect what the data represents.

Pandas make it easy to rename one or multiple columns at a time. Renaming and standardizing columns helps your colleagues quickly understand the meaning behind the data.

Figure 5.12: Rename column

Figure 5.12 shows the code and output for renaming a column. Line #4 rename the column Gender to be **Birth_Gender** using the build-in function **rename()**, and line #7 display the result. The output is a same table of student information but the right most column has been renamed to **Birth_Gender**.

We looked at sorting earlier, but we are now expanding on it.

Sorting data

Sorting data in a Pandas DataFrame is a fundamental technique that allows you to organize and analyze your data more effectively. Whether you are arranging rows in ascending order based on a single column or sorting by multiple columns with varying criteria, this operation helps bring clarity and structure to your dataset.

Sorting is not just about organizing. It is about uncovering patterns, highlighting trends, and ensuring your data is presented in a logical and meaningful order. For instance, arranging sales data by revenue from highest to lowest can help you identify top-performing products while sorting timestamps chronologically ensures a clear sequence of events.

Pandas provides a flexible and efficient way to sort rows and columns, allowing you to customize the operation to suit your needs. Whether you need to sort by numerical values, strings, or a combination of both, mastering this skill will make your dataset easier to explore, interpret, and share.

We have added three additional records to our student files, so first, we will look at a simple sort by college major.

```
[32]   1   # prompt: sorting df_people based on College Major
       2
       3   # Sorting the DataFrame based on the 'College Major' column
       4   df_people_sorted_major = df_people.sort_values(by='College Major')
       5
       6   # Display the sorted DataFrame
       7   df_people_sorted_major
```

	Name	Age	Height	College Major	Birth_Gender
7	Hannah	24	172	Art History	Female
4	Eva	22	169	Biology	Female
9	Ashley	22	175	Business Communication	Female
0	Alice	22	165	Computer Science	Female
8	Duc	46	175	Computer Science	Male
10	Evan	19	188	Computer Science	Male
1	Bob	25	180	Economics	Female
5	Frank	26	178	English	Female
3	David	23	170	Mathematics	Male
6	Grace	21	160	Physics	Male
2	Charlie	24	175	Psychology	Female

Figure 5.13: *Sort by college major*

Figure 5.13 shows the code and output for sorting student records by college major. Line #1 contains the GPT-4o prompt. Line #4 sorts the student records by the **College Major** column using the built-in function **sort_values()**, while line #7 prints the result.

The output is a well-organized table with all the students ordered by their college majors in ascending order. For instance, **Hannah**, who majors in **Art History**, appears as the first record, while **Charlie**, who majors in **Psychology**, is listed last.

There are numerous examples of sorting demonstrate the flexibility and power of Pandas' built-in methods. For example, if you want to sort a dataset first by gender and then by age, you can use the command: **df_people.sort_values(by=['Birth_Gender', 'Age'])**. This type of multi-level sorting is extremely useful for organizing data in a way that reveals relationships or trends across multiple categories.

In Chapter 4, *Sorting on My Mind*, we spend much time studying, prototyping, and experiencing different sorting algorithms. It is humbling to have the Pandas library perform these tasks for you through an intuitive and easy-to-use function.

We encourage you to explore Pandas sorting techniques using GPT-4o and Jupyter Notebook. By trying different sorting scenarios, you will learn how to adapt your approach to fit your specific analysis needs. With GPT-4o providing clear explanations and examples and Jupyter Notebook offering an interactive space for practice, mastering Pandas sorting will be achievable and enjoyable. The more you practice, the more confident and skilled you will become at uncovering insights from your data.

When the dataset is large, such as containing thousands or millions of records, the next topic in statistics is a must-read.

Basic statistics

Understanding a dataset's basic statistics is a crucial first step in any data analysis project, especially for large datasets of millions of records. In Pandas, the **info()** method is a powerful tool that provides a quick and comprehensive summary of your DataFrame, helping you assess its structure and content at a glance.

By using **info()**, you can instantly see key details about your dataset, such as the number of rows and columns, the names and data types of each column, and the count of non-null values. This method is beneficial for identifying missing data, understanding the composition of your dataset, and ensuring that each column's data type aligns with your analysis requirements.

In the later section, *Data analysis superpower*, we will use this **info()** method when discussing real-world datasets.

This diagnostic tool overview provides a snapshot of your data's overall health. For example, suppose a column contains many missing values or has an unexpected data type. In that case, you can resolve these issues before proceeding with a more in-depth analysis.

Here is the code to examine our student records.

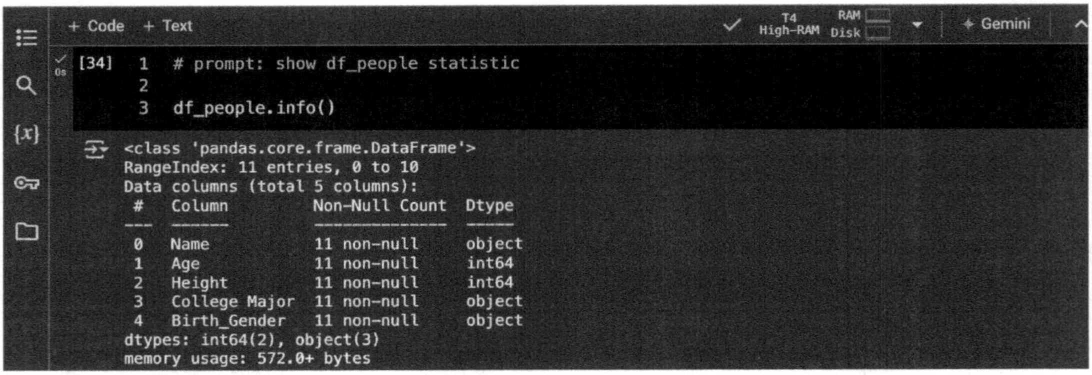

Figure 5.14: Info statistics

Figure 5.14 shows the code and output for the function for displaying the **df_people** statistic. Line #1 is the prompt to GPT-4o, and line #3 is the **info()** function. The output shows that we have eleven records, five columns named **Name, Age, Height, College Major, and Birth_Gender**, and no null value.

It is essential to understand that **None** and **NaN** are different from **null**. When we use the value of **None** (string type) or **NaN** (numeric type), we indicate that the cell has no value.

In contrast, null serves as a default for missing data. In other words, with **None** or **NaN**, we acknowledge that there is no value, and **null** means missing value.

Next, we will discuss how to handle missing data.

Handling missing data

Identifying and handling missing data in a Pandas DataFrame is essential to avoid errors and inaccuracies in your analysis. Missing data can disrupt critical operations, such as drawing graphs, where gaps in the dataset may result in misleading or incomplete visualizations. For instance, a line graph with missing values can break the continuity, making trends harder to interpret, or bar charts might entirely omit categories due to missing entries.

Beyond visualization issues, missing data can also cause calculation errors, skew statistical summaries, and negatively impact the performance of machine learning models. Left unaddressed, these gaps can undermine the validity of your analysis and lead to flawed insights.

Pandas provide powerful tools to address missing data, enabling you to clean your dataset effectively. Whether you drop rows or columns, fill gaps with default values.

Here is the code to create a new column in our student record and purposely add missing values.

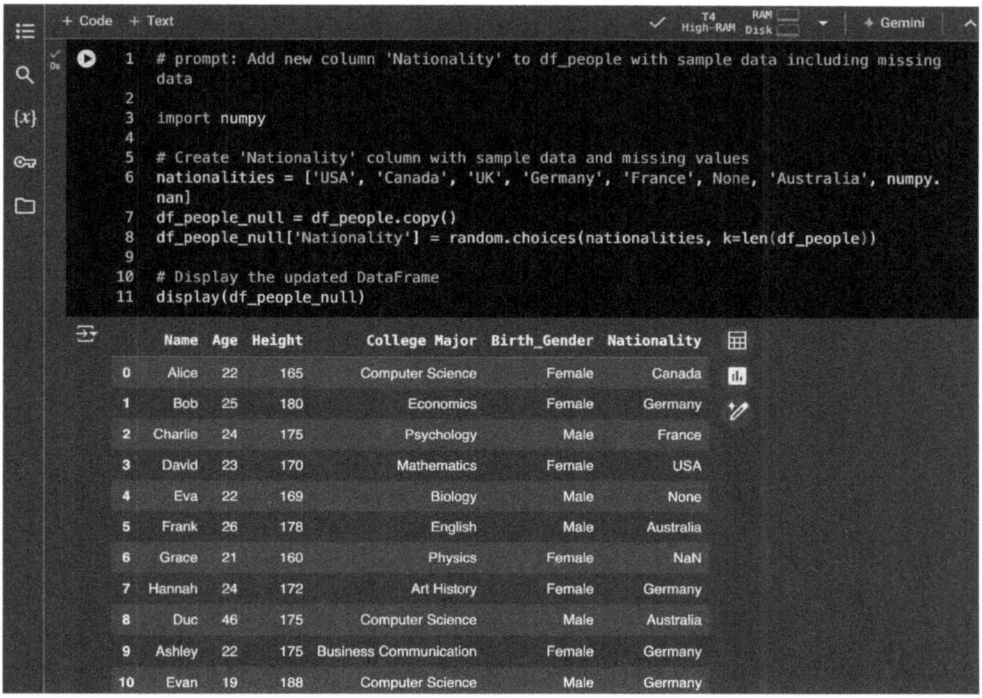

```
# prompt: Add new column 'Nationality' to df_people with sample data including missing data

import numpy

# Create 'Nationality' column with sample data and missing values
nationalities = ['USA', 'Canada', 'UK', 'Germany', 'France', None, 'Australia', numpy.nan]
df_people_null = df_people.copy()
df_people_null['Nationality'] = random.choices(nationalities, k=len(df_people))

# Display the updated DataFrame
display(df_people_null)
```

	Name	Age	Height	College Major	Birth_Gender	Nationality
0	Alice	22	165	Computer Science	Female	Canada
1	Bob	25	180	Economics	Female	Germany
2	Charlie	24	175	Psychology	Male	France
3	David	23	170	Mathematics	Female	USA
4	Eva	22	169	Biology	Male	None
5	Frank	26	178	English	Male	Australia
6	Grace	21	160	Physics	Female	NaN
7	Hannah	24	172	Art History	Female	Germany
8	Duc	46	175	Computer Science	Male	Australia
9	Ashley	22	175	Business Communication	Female	Germany
10	Evan	19	188	Computer Science	Male	Germany

Figure 5.15: *New column with missing data*

Figure 5.15 presents the code and output for adding a new **Nationality** column containing some missing values. Line #1 is the GPT-4o prompt. Lines #6 to #8 randomly assign a nationality to each student, including options for missing values such as **None** and **NaN**. Line #11 displays the output. The resulting table neatly displays the students' information, showing that **Eva and Grace** have missing nationalities.

Since **None** and **NaN** can cause problems, we can change the value to a safe value, such as the string **not_declared**.

```
[42] 1 # prompt: Replace None and nan values in Nationality df_people_null with 'not_declare'
     2
     3 # Replace None and NaN values in the 'Nationality' column with 'not_declared'
     4 df_people_null['Nationality'] = df_people_null['Nationality'].fillna('not_declared')
     5 df_people_null['Nationality'] = df_people_null['Nationality'].replace({None:
       'not_declared'})
     6
     7 # Display the updated DataFrame
     8 display(df_people_null)
```

	Name	Age	Height	College Major	Birth_Gender	Nationality
0	Alice	22	165	Computer Science	Female	Canada
1	Bob	25	180	Economics	Female	Germany
2	Charlie	24	175	Psychology	Male	France
3	David	23	170	Mathematics	Female	USA
4	Eva	22	169	Biology	Male	not_declared
5	Frank	26	178	English	Male	Australia
6	Grace	21	160	Physics	Female	not_declared
7	Hannah	24	172	Art History	Female	Germany
8	Duc	46	175	Computer Science	Male	Australia
9	Ashley	22	175	Business Communication	Female	Germany
10	Evan	19	188	Computer Science	Male	Germany

***Figure 5.16:** Replace with safe string value*

Figure 5.16 shows the code and output for replacing missing values that could lead to errors with a string value. Line #1 contains the GPT-4o prompt. Line #4 uses the Pandas built-in method **fillna()**, while line #5 utilizes the built-in function **replace()** to change the missing values to the string **not_declared**. Line #8 displays the output, a well-structured table indicating that the nationality values for **Eva and Grace** are **not_declared**.

You also have the option to drop the records for **Eva and Grace** using a built-in function of Pandas. We will leave that exercise up to you. The final topic for manipulating Pandas data is grouping techniques.

Grouping and aggregating

Grouping and aggregating are essential concepts in data analysis. They allow you to organize and summarize data to identify patterns and trends. Grouping involves dividing a dataset into smaller groups based on shared characteristics, while aggregating involves applying operations to these groups to extract meaningful insights.

In Pandas, the **groupby()** function is a powerful tool for performing these operations. It lets you group your data by one or more columns and analyze each group independently. Similarly, the **merge()** function helps you combine multiple DataFrames into a single, unified dataset, making it easier to combine related information for deeper analysis.

These functions work together, enabling you to organize, summarize, and combine data efficiently. Here are sample codes for the **groupby()** function.

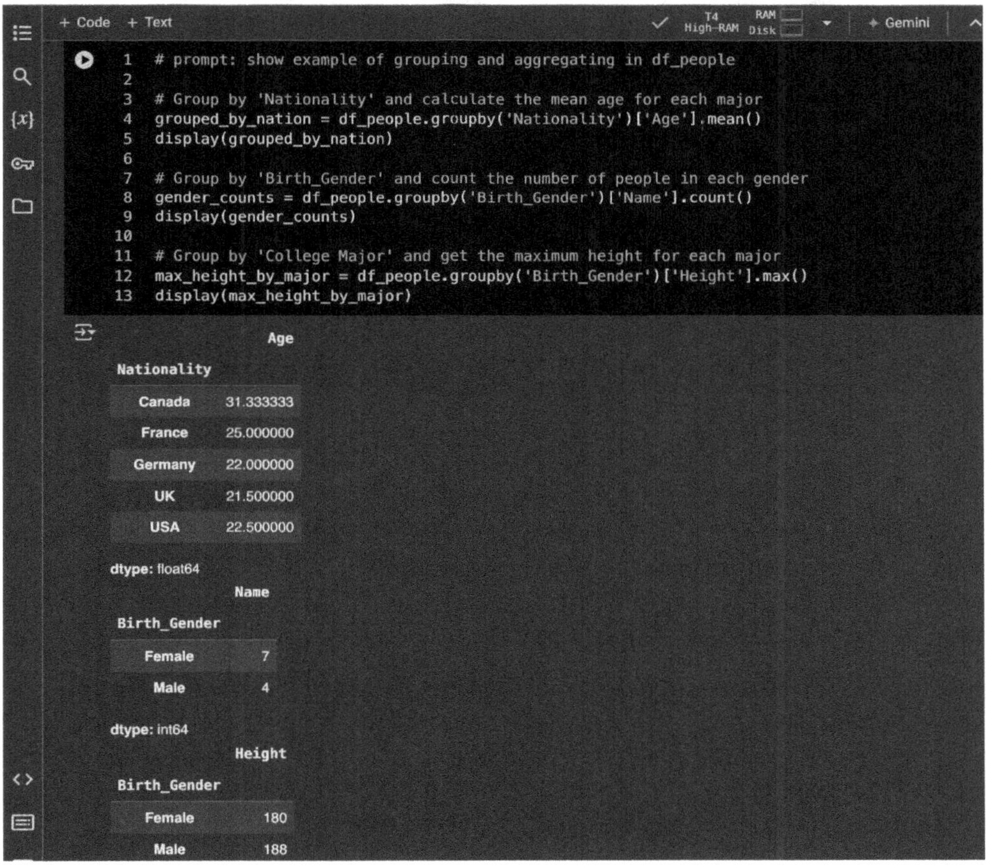

Figure 5.17: Groupby() function

Figure 5.17 shows the code and output for three different grouping functions. Line #1 contains the GPT-4o prompt. Line #4 defines the grouping by **Nationality** and calculates the average age for each **Nationality** using the **mean()** function. Line #8 defines the grouping by **Birth_gender** and calculates the number of males and females using the **count()** function. Lastly, in line #8, the data is grouped by **Birth_gender**, and the tallest male and female are found using the **max()** function.

The first output shows the **Nationality** and average age, where **Canada's** average age is 31.3, and the **USA's** is 22.5. The second output shows the gender and the count, where we have seven females and four males in our group. Lastly, the third output shows that the tallest female is 180 cm (or about 5.9 feet), and the tallest male is 188 cm (or about 6.1 feet).

Next, we look at the aggregating technique.

```
1  # prompt: Show example of Merging using df_people
2
3  # Create a sample DataFrame (df_other) for merging
4  data_other = {
5      'Name': ['Alice', 'Bob', 'Charlie', 'David', 'Eva'],
6      'City': ['New York', 'Los Angeles', 'Chicago', 'Houston', 'Phoenix']
7  }
8  df_other = pd.DataFrame(data_other)
9
10 # Merge df_people and df_other based on the 'Name' column
11 merged_df = pd.merge(df_people, df_other, on='Name', how='inner')  # 'inner' join
12
13 # Display the merged DataFrame
14 merged_df
```

	Name	Age	Height	College Major	Birth_Gender	Nationality	City
0	Alice	22	165	Computer Science	Female	USA	New York
1	Bob	25	180	Economics	Female	France	Los Angeles
2	Charlie	24	175	Psychology	Female	UK	Chicago
3	David	23	170	Mathematics	Male	USA	Houston
4	Eva	22	169	Biology	Female	Germany	Phoenix

***Figure 5.18:** Merge() function*

Figure 5.18 illustrates the code and output for aggregating the **`df_people`** DataFrame with a new dataset. Line #1 is the prompt to GPT-4o. Lines #4 to #8 create a new DataFrame called **`df_other`**, which includes the columns **Name** and **City**. Line #11 merges the two datasets using the Pandas **`merge()`** function, pivoting on the **Name** column and applying an **`inner`** merge. Finally, line #14 displays the resulting dataset.

The output is a well-structured table that combines the two datasets and includes the new City column from the data labeled **`df_other`**. For instance, the output has **Alice** as the first student listed in **New York City**. It is important to note that only five students are in the output, so what happens to the other students? It occurs because we performed a pivot operation on the **Name** column and used an **`inner`** join.

An **`inner`** join includes only the rows where the keys match both DataFrames. If a row exists in one DataFrame but not the other, it is excluded from the result. It is useful when you want to focus solely on the standard data shared between the two DataFrames. In this case, **Alice, Bob, Charley, David, and Eva** are on both lists. Hence, the other students are dropped.

Three other types of join are **`outer`**, **`left`**, and **`right`** joins. An **`outer`** join includes all rows from both DataFrames, regardless of whether the keys match. For rows where no match is found, missing values are filled with **NaN**. The join is ideal when you want a comprehensive view of all data, including unmatched rows, while still aligning the keys. The output will include all the students, but Ashley, Duc, Evan, Frank, Grace, and Hanna are missing the city value.

A `left` join includes all rows from the left DataFrame and only the matching rows from the right DataFrame. If there is no match, the columns from the right DataFrame will be filled with NaN values. The join is beneficial when you want to retain all the data from the left DataFrame while supplementing it with information from the right DataFrame. In this example, the result is the same as an `outer` join because the left DataFrame, `df_people`, includes all the names in the right DataFrame, `df_other`. If the right DataFrame includes a name such as **Xavier**, then **Xavier** will not appear in the output list.

Lastly, a `right` join is the mirror image of a `left` join. It includes all rows from the right DataFrame and only the matching rows from the left DataFrame. Unmatched rows in the left DataFrame are filled with `NaN`. This join is helpful when the right DataFrame is the primary focus of your analysis. In our example, the output matches that of an `inner` join. If the right list contains **Albert**, then he is excluded.

We have thoroughly explained all the methods for manumitting a DataFrame using our small student list. Now, it is time to graduate to a real-world dataset.

Data analysis superpower

Exploring data analysis with Python's Pandas library often involves working with real-world datasets. One of the most reliable sources for such datasets is **Kaggle**, a platform known for its data science competitions and extensive collection of datasets. As of November 2024, Kaggle offers over 300,000 datasets covering a wide range of topics, including text, images, audio, and video. Whether you are a beginner looking to gain practical experience or an experienced programmer tackling advanced projects, Kaggle provides datasets suited for diverse needs.

Data analysis using Python's Pandas library is vital in extracting insights from data to support decision-making. Pandas' flexible and intuitive tools allow users to manipulate, clean, and analyze large datasets efficiently.

Throughout the previous section, we will explore essential Pandas functions to help you manage and analyze data effectively, preparing you to handle real-world datasets confidently. The Kaggle website offers a wide variety of datasets in fields like finance, biology, social media, and more.

Beyond its datasets, Kaggle is also a hub for a global community of data scientists and enthusiasts. It hosts competitions focusing on real-world challenges in GenAI, deep learning, and other advanced topics, making it an invaluable resource for anyone applying data analysis in practical scenarios.

The following four topics will guide you in learning how to use the Pandas library effectively to work with real-world datasets.

- Searching and choosing a dataset
- Importing the data
- Drawing plots and graphs
- Generating summarizes reports

By this point in the book, you are already familiar with using GPT-4o to generate and explain Python code, as well as testing it in Jupyter Notebook. Since you know the basics of these tools, we will focus on a few key prompts moving forward. Now, open a new browser tab and head over to the Kaggle website.

Searching and choosing a dataset

The Kaggle website hosts over 300,000 real-world datasets. For this example, we have chosen *Muhammad Jawad Awan's Global Warming Trends (1961-2022)* dataset, available under the **Open Database License (ODbL)**. As of November 2024, this dataset is available and an excellent choice for exploring climate-related data.

The following figure is a screenshot of the Kaggle website in November 2024:

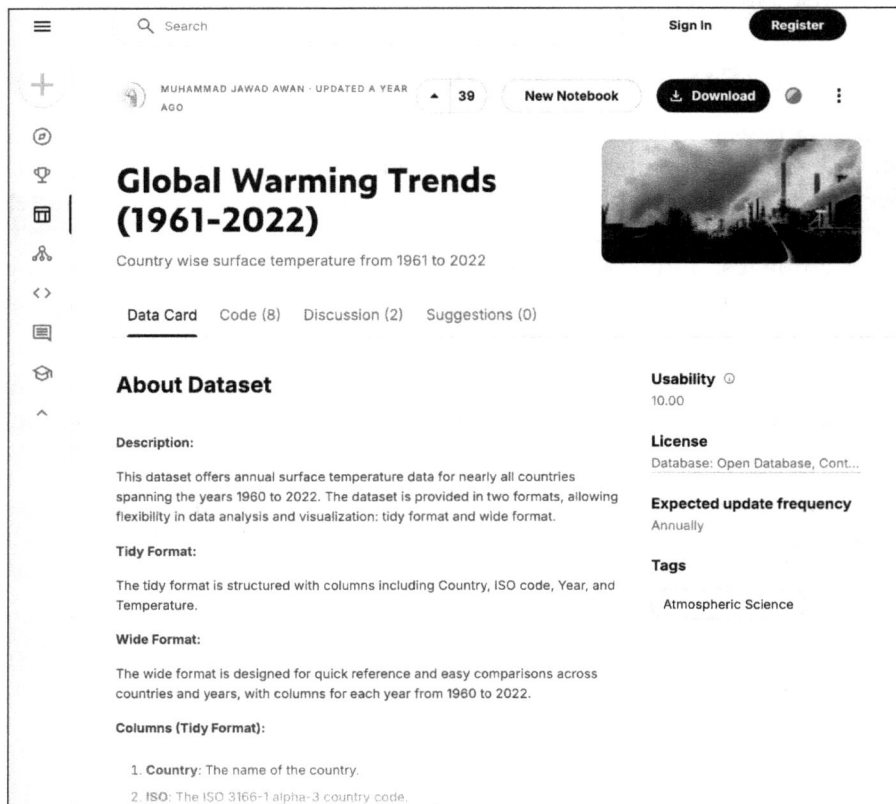

Figure 5.19: Kaggle screenshot

Figure 5.19 is a screenshot of the global warming dataset on the Kaggle website. Global warming, caused by human emissions of greenhouse gases, is resulting in a long-term increase in Earth's average surface temperature. It has significant environmental, economic, and social impacts. It leads to more severe weather events, rising sea levels that endanger coastal areas, and ecological disruptions that threaten species extinction and affect vital ecosystem services such as pollination and water purification. These changes also threaten agricultural productivity and food security, and health risks can arise from heat waves and the spread of infectious diseases.

Furthermore, they result in substantial economic costs due to damage to infrastructure and the need for adaptation across multiple sectors. Without significant global action to reduce emissions and adapt to changing climates, these impacts will only intensify, highlighting the urgent need for international cooperation and sustainable practices.

We have chosen the dataset, and now it is time to import it into Pandas.

Importing the data

There are several methods to access data from Kaggle. Still, one of the simplest and most convenient approaches we have found is to download the dataset directly from the Kaggle website and upload it to a personal GitHub repository. Hosting the dataset on GitHub becomes easily accessible via a public URL.

This method also works seamlessly with GPT-4o. Once the dataset is uploaded to GitHub, GPT-4o can generate the Python code to load the data directly into a Pandas DataFrame by fetching it from the GitHub link. The method eliminates the need for manual file transfers between local directories and your coding environment, streamlining the entire process.

Here is the code to import the dataset into a Pandas DataFrame from GitHub.

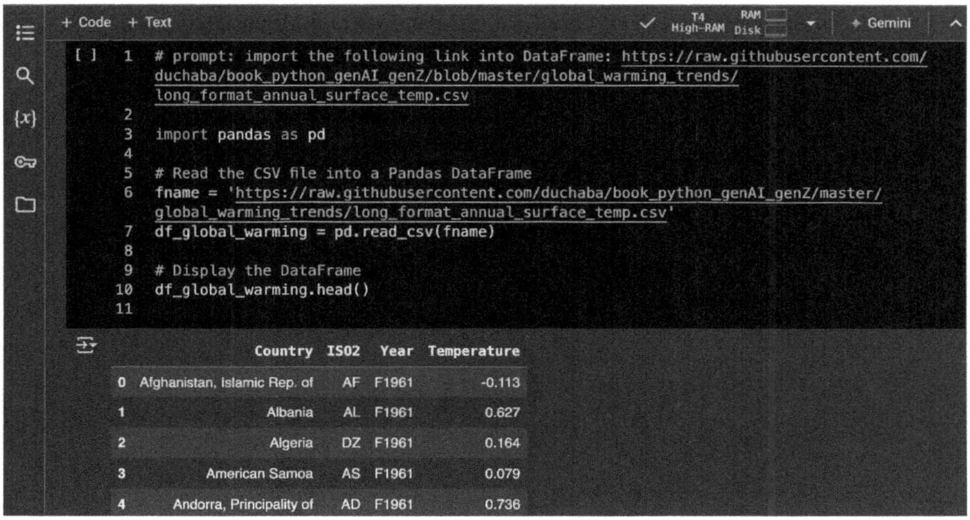

```
# prompt: import the following link into DataFrame: https://raw.githubusercontent.com/duchaba/book_python_genAI_genZ/blob/master/global_warming_trends/long_format_annual_surface_temp.csv

import pandas as pd

# Read the CSV file into a Pandas DataFrame
fname = 'https://raw.githubusercontent.com/duchaba/book_python_genAI_genZ/master/global_warming_trends/long_format_annual_surface_temp.csv'
df_global_warming = pd.read_csv(fname)

# Display the DataFrame
df_global_warming.head()
```

	Country	ISO2	Year	Temperature
0	Afghanistan, Islamic Rep. of	AF	F1961	-0.113
1	Albania	AL	F1961	0.627
2	Algeria	DZ	F1961	0.164
3	American Samoa	AS	F1961	0.079
4	Andorra, Principality of	AD	F1961	0.736

Figure 5.20: *Import global warming dataset*

Figure 5.20 shows the code and output for importing the global warming dataset. Line #1 is the GPT-4o prompt. Line #6 defines the URL string for the dataset, and line #7 imports the data with the **read_csv()** function. The main syntax code is only one line. This compact coding is precisely why we use the Pandas library. It makes even the most challenging tasks quick and effortless. Lastly, line #10 displays the first five records.

The output is a table listing the first five rows of data beginning with the country name: **Afghanistan, Islamic Rep. Of**, followed by the ISO2 code, **AF**, the year, **F1991**, and the temperature **–0.113**.

As we begin to analyze the global warming dataset, we will approach it as if we are entirely unfamiliar with its structure and contents. This scenario is common in real-world data analysis, where the techniques we have previously covered will prove invaluable. We will apply much of our prior knowledge about data manipulation and exploration to uncover insights from this new dataset.

If you find any part of the following code difficult to understand, do not worry. You can always refer to the earlier sections, where we worked with simpler datasets, such as the small student records example, to build a solid foundation. We design the examples to help you understand the concepts step by step, so feel free to revisit them to reinforce your understanding before tackling the global warming dataset. Each step we take builds on that foundational knowledge, guiding you toward confidently working with real-world datasets.

Note: Did you know that the URL for viewing a file on GitHub differs from the one used to download the raw file? The link for viewing the file starts with www.github. com, while the link for downloading it starts with raw.githubusercontent.com. In case you were wondering, I learned this fun fact from GPT-4o.

After importing the dataset from the Kaggle website and displaying the first five rows, the next step is to inspect them. The following prompt and code explain the dataset:

```
[ ]  1   # prompt: display information about df_global_warming
     2
     3   df_global_warming.info()
     4

<class 'pandas.core.frame.DataFrame'>
RangeIndex: 11222 entries, 0 to 11221
Data columns (total 4 columns):
 #   Column       Non-Null Count  Dtype
---  ------       --------------  -----
 0   Country      11222 non-null  object
 1   ISO2         11222 non-null  object
 2   Year         11222 non-null  object
 3   Temperature  11222 non-null  float64
dtypes: float64(1), object(3)
memory usage: 350.8+ KB
```

Figure 5.21: Global warming data information

Figure 5.21 shows the code and output for printing the global warming data. Line #1 is the GPT-4o prompt. Line #3 is the **info()** function for displaying the **df_global_warming** dataset. The **info()** method is our go-to method for examining imported data when we do not know what is in the data.

The output tells us that we have 11,222 records of the **Country, ISO2, Year**, and the average **Temperature** in Celsius. There is no missing data, i.e., no non-null cell. However, we have identified some anomalies or inaccuracies in the data. For instance, the **Year** column contains a string that begins with the letter **F**, which is incorrect. The reason for this error is unclear, but we should remove it.

Use the following code to remove the **F** and convert the **Year** into an integer. The type was a string:

```
# prompt: remove the leading "F" in the Year column in df_global_warming

df_global_warming['Year'] = df_global_warming['Year'].str[1:]
```

```
# prompt: convert the year column in df_global_warming into an integer

df_global_warming['Year'] = df_global_warming['Year'].astype('int64')
df_global_warming.head()
```

	Country	ISO2	Year	Temperature
0	Afghanistan, Islamic Rep. of	AF	1961	-0.113
1	Albania	AL	1961	0.627
2	Algeria	DZ	1961	0.164
3	American Samoa	AS	1961	0.079
4	Andorra, Principality of	AD	1961	0.736

Figure 5.22: *Clean the year column*

Figure 5.22 shows the code and output for correcting the Year column. In the first code cell, Line #1 is the GPT-4o prompt, and line #3 is the code for removing the first letter from the Year column. In the second code cell, line #1 is the GPT-4o prompt. Line #3 converts the Year from a string to an integer type, and line #4 prints out the first five records using the **head()** function.

The output is a well-structured table with the correct data type in the Year column. For example, Albania with ISO2 registers the accurate year 1061.

Fortunately, this real-world dataset is relatively clean, with only a minor issue in the Year column that requires adjustment. Beyond that, there is no missing or inconsistent data, making it an excellent resource for analysis without needing extensive cleaning.

Despite its cleanliness, this dataset offers plenty of opportunities for exploration and investigation. We can explore deeper by selecting specific rows and columns to focus on particular aspects of the data, sorting the dataset to highlight trends or patterns, or grouping the data to analyze it at a higher level of granularity. Each technique helps uncover valuable insights and improves our understanding of global warming trends.

The clean structure of this dataset allows us to focus on analysis and visualization rather than data preparation. We will explore its full potential while practicing the essential skills of selecting, sorting, and grouping data for deeper insights. There is much to learn from this dataset about global warming, and each step brings us closer to understanding the story it tells.

We will use graphs to help us visualize this large real-world dataset.

Drawing plots and graphs

Pandas offers a wide range of functions for analyzing global warming data and extracting meaningful insights from large datasets. One of the most effective ways to understand the data is through visualization. Plotting the data allows you to see trends and patterns that might not be obvious from numbers alone. Learning to create charts in Python follows the same approach we have used before, which is asking GPT-4o for the code, copying it into Jupyter Notebook, and reviewing the output.

If the graph does not look quite right, refine your request using the prompt engineering techniques covered in Chapter 2, *Jupyter Notebook*. The process is not just about running analyses. It is about the excitement of uncovering new insights, understanding the story behind the data, and improving your Python skills.

Given the focus on global warming, we will put it to the test. Create a graph showing the average temperature for each country from the first year, 1961, to the last year, 2022. A clear upward trend in the graph indicates that global warming is a reality. The practical exercise combines data analysis, visualization, and Python coding while exploring critical skills.

Below, we show the GPT-4o prompts, Python code, and the resulting output from Jupyter Notebook.

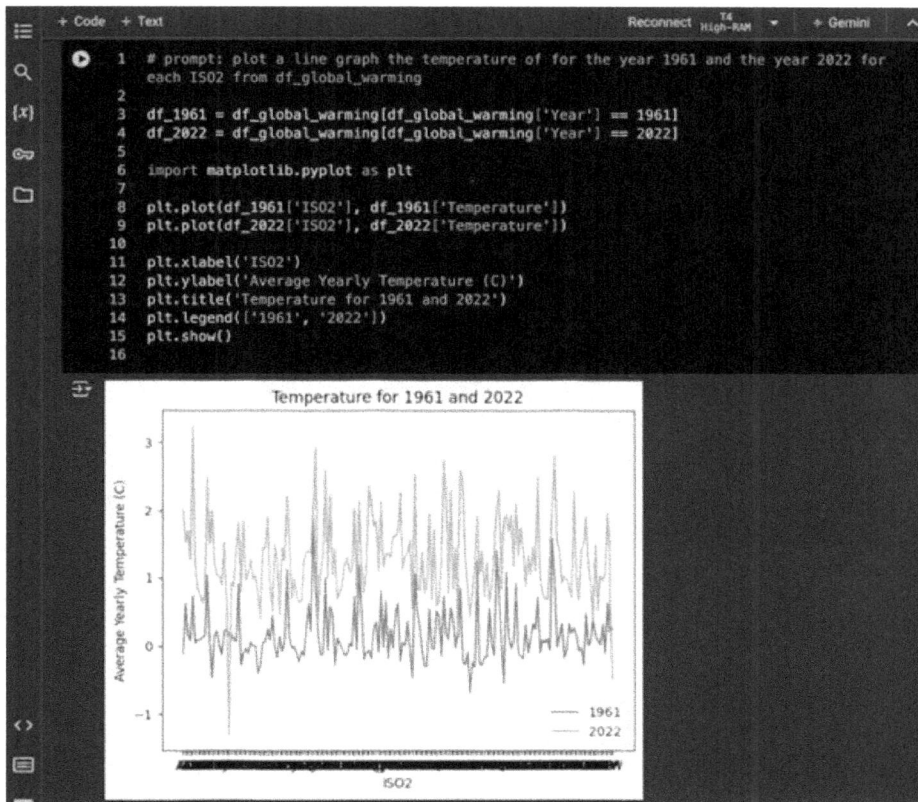

Figure 5.23: *Global warming, 1961 and 2022*

Figure 5.23 shows the code and output from graphing the global warming temperature. Line #1 is the GPT-4o prompt. Lines #3 and #4 extract records for 1962, the oldest year, and 2022, the most recent year. The technique is the same as in our earlier discussion on selecting rows and columns on the small student list.

In line #6, we import the Matplotlib library, while lines #8 and #9 plot the graph using the **plot()** function from Matplotlib. The first line in the graph, the bottom line, represents the average temperature. The second line, displayed in orange for color print, indicates the temperature for the year 2022. Note that we do not select and plot all the years between 1962 and 2022. Lines #11 through #15 add a title and labels for the graph.

The output confirms it. The world is getting hotter, as shown in *Figure 5.23*. It is a global trend, with all nations, except for two, showing a rise in the average yearly temperature from 1961 and 2022. ISO2 is a two-character abbreviation used to represent a country name. For instance, the United States shorthand is *US*, while Algeria is *DZ*. The bottom line, blue line, on the graph indicates the temperature in 1961, while the top line, represents the temperature in 2022. The code is easy to understand, which highlights the strength of the Pandas library.

Note: It is hilarious to hear GPT-4o explain line #8, the figsize() function, in Homer Simpson's voice. You should try it yourself. Since the data is in the DataFrame, it is easy to isolate a country and graph its yearly average temperature against time. For example, the prompt, code, and output for the United States of America (US) are as follows:

Here is the code for examining the temperature just for the United States.

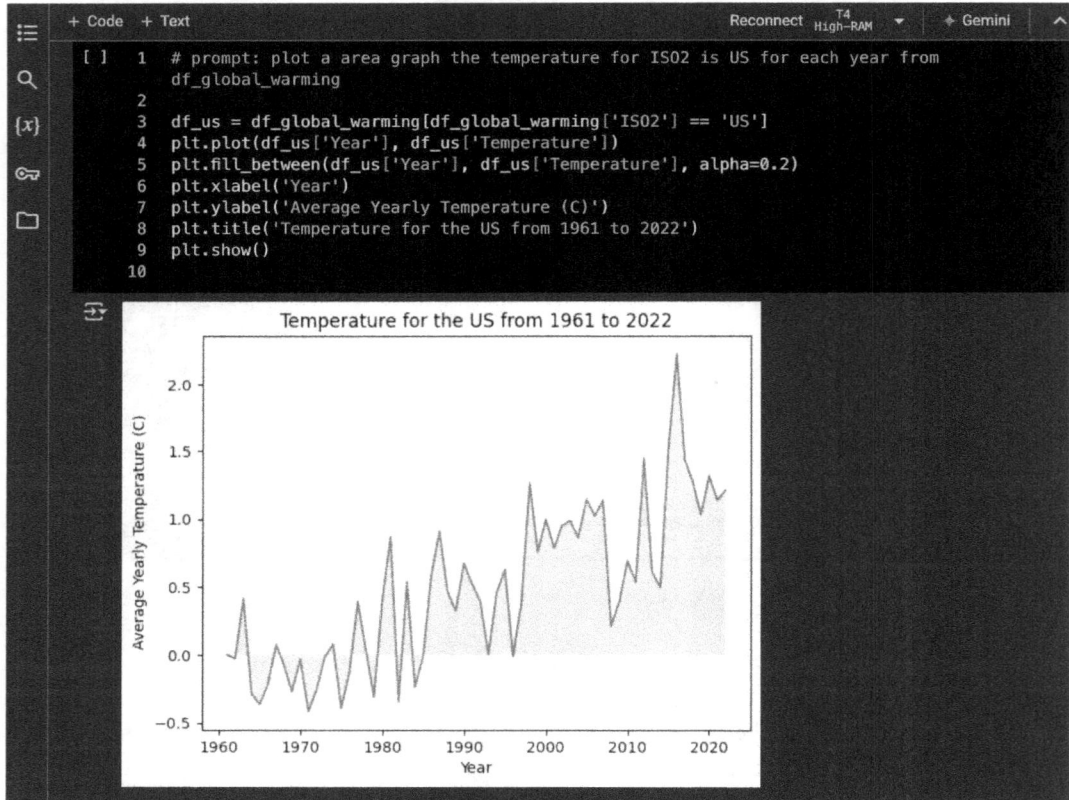

Figure 5.24: USA temperature from 1961 to 2022

Figure 5.24 shows the code and output for the United States' temperature from 1962 through 2022. Line #1 is the GPT-4o prompt. Line #3 extracts the record only for the US out of 11,222 records, and line #4 displays the area graph.

The output area graph shows that the USA has been getting warmer over time. However, there is a pattern in the data where the average temperature dips back to normal every 10 or 12 years. It is worth exploring whether the years with lower temperatures have caused a decrease in farming, transportation, or industrial carbon output. If we can find a correlation between the drop in temperature and the actions taken by Americans, we should investigate them.

The code uses Pandas DataFrame and Matplotlib to streamline the data analysis process, making it straightforward and efficient. For example, line #3 effortlessly extracts the US data, while lines #5 and #6 generate the area graph.

It is noteworthy to reflect on the significance of the extensive data set we have at our disposal, which consists of a staggering 11,222 records. This wealth of information allows us to explore deeper into the global warming crisis affecting the world. With just two lines of simple code, we can effectively filter and analyze this complex data for the US, illuminating critical trends and insights that might otherwise go unnoticed.

This approach not only simplifies the data but also makes it accessible, enabling stakeholders, from policymakers to the general public, to grasp the urgency and impact of climate change.

You can do so much more with plotting data by applying the manipulation techniques we previously explored with the student dataset. Now, it is your turn to expand and experiment on your own. Take the next step by exploring visualizations deeper and uncovering meaningful insights through graphs and reports. It is your opportunity to explore, analyze, and let the data tell its story.

Generating summarizes reports

In this section, we will use the global warming dataset as a practical tool to enhance your coding skills with the Pandas library. With the guidance of GPT-4o as your coding assistant, researcher, and tutor, we will navigate through various stages of data analysis, from writing and debugging code to discovering new Pandas functions and applying them effectively.

The goal here is to master Python syntax and Pandas functionalities, not to produce a climate report. We will select the use case, and you are encouraged to find one that resonates with you. While the USA, Canada, and Mexico may differ politically, economically, and culturally, they share the same continent. Through this example, you will learn how to use Python to explore whether these shared geographical conditions are reflected in their average yearly temperatures. This hands-on approach bridges coding practice with real-world data, offering technical growth and valuable insights.

The prompt, code, and output are as follows:

```
[15]  1  # prompt: plot a area graph the temperature for ISO2 equal US for each year from the
          df_global_warming dataframe.
      2  # Add Canada, ISO2 = 'CA'
      3  # Add Mexico, ISO2 = 'MX'
      4
      5  plt.figure(figsize=(15,4)) # increase graph size
      6
      7  df_us = df_global_warming[df_global_warming['ISO2'] == 'US']
      8  plt.plot(df_us['Year'], df_us['Temperature'])
      9  plt.fill_between(df_us['Year'], df_us['Temperature'], alpha=0.2)
     10
     11  df_canada = df_global_warming[df_global_warming['ISO2'] == 'CA']
     12  plt.plot(df_canada['Year'], df_canada['Temperature'])
     13  plt.fill_between(df_canada['Year'], df_canada['Temperature'], alpha=0.2)
     14
     15  df_mexico = df_global_warming[df_global_warming['ISO2'] == 'MX']
     16  plt.plot(df_mexico['Year'], df_mexico['Temperature'])
     17  plt.fill_between(df_mexico['Year'], df_mexico['Temperature'], alpha=0.2)
     18
     19  plt.xlabel('Year')
     20  plt.ylabel('Average Yearly Temperature (C)')
     21  plt.title('Temperature for the US from 1961 to 2022')
     22  plt.show()
     23
```

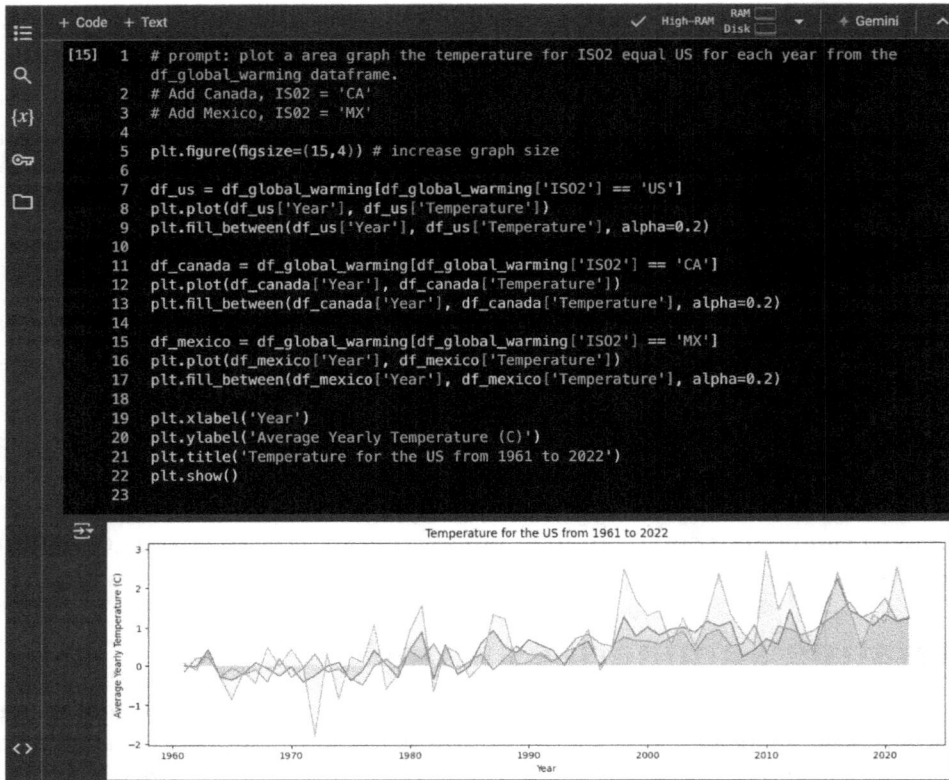

Figure 5.25: USA, Canada, and Mexico temperature

Figure 5.25 shows the average temperature for the USA, Canada, and Mexico average temperature from 1961 through 2022. Line #1, #2, and #3 are the prompts we give to GPT-4o. The first prompt and two follow-up prompts use the prompt engineering technique from Chapter 2, *Jupyter Notebook*.

Lines #7 through #9 extract the US data from the 11,222 records and plot it. Lines #11 to #13 do the same for Canada, and lines #15 to #17 do it for Mexico. Lines #19 to #22 create the title and labels for the graph.

The output is a vibrant area graph illustrating the average temperatures of three countries. In a color print, the United States is represented in blue, Canada in orange, and Mexico in green.

Sometimes, mastering coding with GPT-4 can feel as exhilarating as navigating the Starship Enterprise—especially if you are a *Star Trek* fan. It transforms seemingly complex tasks into simple steps, creating almost magical experiences. The Python Pandas library simplifies operations that traditionally require complicated conditions, loops, and structures, resulting in just a few intuitive function calls. For example, line #7 extracts the US data, line #8 generates the line chart, and line #9 shades the area beneath it. All accomplished in a fraction of the time it would take to write these operations manually.

Note: Ask GPT-4o to rewrite the code in Figure 5.25 without using Pandas functions. You will be amazed at how complex the code becomes.

If writing a report, we can conclude that after analyzing the USA, Canada, and Mexico temperature trends from *Figure 5.25*, they all follow the same pattern of peaks and valleys. This finding implies that the effects of global warming are not limited to one country but rather have a global impact. It is essential to recognize that one country's actions can directly impact the temperature of neighboring countries.

As shown in *Figure 5.25*, Canada, represented by the orange line, is experiencing a more rapid increase in temperature compared to the USA and Mexico. This graph raises an intriguing question: **Why is Canada's temperature rising at a faster rate?** It is a puzzle that invites further exploration and analysis.

The next use case is to calculate the average temperature of all countries per year and generates a bar chart. Afterward, we increased the global temperature to one degree Celsius and compared the charts.

The prompts, code, and output are as follows:

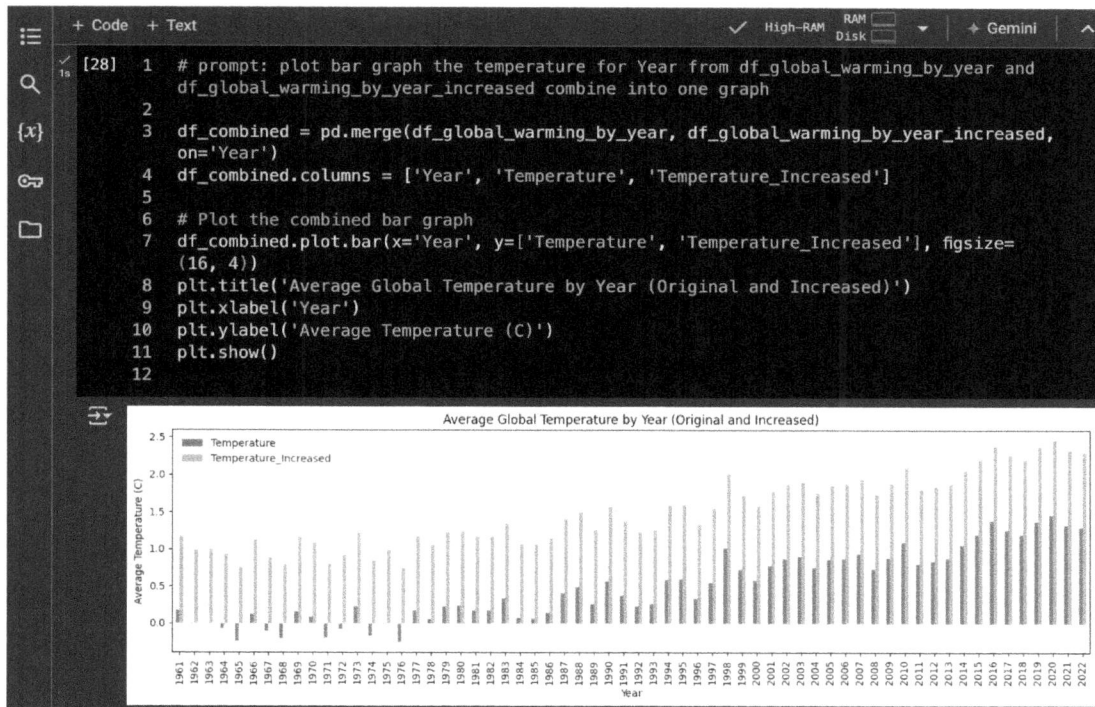

```python
# prompt: plot bar graph the temperature for Year from df_global_warming_by_year and
df_global_warming_by_year_increased combine into one graph

df_combined = pd.merge(df_global_warming_by_year, df_global_warming_by_year_increased,
on='Year')
df_combined.columns = ['Year', 'Temperature', 'Temperature_Increased']

# Plot the combined bar graph
df_combined.plot.bar(x='Year', y=['Temperature', 'Temperature_Increased'], figsize=
(16, 4))
plt.title('Average Global Temperature by Year (Original and Increased)')
plt.xlabel('Year')
plt.ylabel('Average Temperature (C)')
plt.show()
```

Figure 5.26: Average global temperature increases by 1C

Figure 5.26 illustrates the Earth's global average temperature, independent of country and boundary. Line #1 represents the GPT-4o prompt. Line #3 combines the DataFrames **df_**

global_warming_by_year and **df_global_warming_by_year_increased**. We created these two DataFrames using various data manipulation techniques, such as adding, dropping, selecting, renaming, sorting, grouping, and aggregating data. We learned these techniques through working with a smaller student dataset and are now applying them to larger, real-world data.

Line #4 renames the column. Line #7 generates the bar graph. Note that we directly use the **plot.bar()** function from Pandas; this is possible because Pandas utilizes Matplotlib under the hood. This technique serves as a shortcut. Lines #8 through #11 create the graph's title and labels. The beauty of this code lies in the simplicity of using Pandas and Matplotlib functions, which simplify the process by abstracting away the underlying complexity.

Writing effective GPT-4o prompts takes practice and experimentation. It is about asking the right question and refining your approach until you get the desired outcome. Dedicate time to replicating the examples shown here using your prompts. This hands-on practice will not only improve your prompt-writing skills but also deepen your understanding of how to leverage GPT-4o effectively.

The output graph tells a compelling story. The evidence is clear: As the Earth's average temperature increased by just one degree Celsius from 1961 to 2022, the impact on global warming became undeniable. This visualization is a stark reminder of the importance of data-driven insights in understanding critical issues like climate change.

While we have made significant progress, we must acknowledge that we are only scratching the surface of what Pandas can do. So far, we have explored about 10 to 15 percent of its functionality. Pandas is a vast library with countless tools and techniques for learning. Still, the key takeaway is this: continuous learning through GPT-4o and Jupyter Notebook is the most critical skill you can develop. Mastering Pandas is not a quick task. It is a journey that may take weeks or months of practice. With persistence and the tools at your disposal, you will gain proficiency and unlock this powerful library's full potential.

The following section moves beyond the Pandas library.

Chart your Pandas path and beyond

The Pandas library, alongside TensorFlow, Matplotlib, NumPy, and Scikit-learn, is a cornerstone of Python's ecosystem. It enables users to turn raw data into meaningful insights. Each of these libraries serves a specific purpose, yet together, they form a seamless pipeline for analyzing, visualizing, and modeling data across countless fields of study.

Imagine starting with a raw dataset, perhaps climate records, sales figures, or patient medical histories. The first challenge is making sense of it all, and that is where Pandas excels. With its ability to clean, structure, and manipulate data effortlessly, Pandas transforms scattered information into well-organized tables ready for analysis. This foundation is critical because, without clean data, the rest of the process falters.

Once the data is prepared, the next step often involves understanding it visually. Matplotlib brings the numbers to life, turning columns of data into meaningful charts and graphs. Whether it is a simple line graph showing temperature changes over time or a complex scatterplot revealing hidden relationships, visualization helps you see the story your data is trying to tell.

For numerical calculations, NumPy quietly works in the background, performing the heavy lifting. It handles complex computations and large datasets with remarkable speed and precision. Whether you are calculating averages for a survey or solving equations for a physics simulation, NumPy ensures that your results are accurate and efficient.

However, data is rarely just about numbers. Often, the goal is to make predictions or uncover patterns, and that is where Scikit-learn and TensorFlow shine. Scikit-learn simplifies machine learning, offering tools to build predictive models with ease. Whether you are identifying customer behavior or clustering wildlife migration patterns, it provides a user-friendly way to apply powerful techniques. TensorFlow takes it further, enabling deep learning models to tackle advanced problems like image recognition, natural language processing, and disease diagnosis.

These libraries are not just tools. They are enablers of discovery. In fields as diverse as biology, economics, engineering, and the social sciences, they empower researchers, students, and professionals to ask better questions and find clearer answers. The beauty of this ecosystem is its accessibility. Open-source by nature, these libraries encourage collaboration and innovation, allowing anyone with curiosity and determination to dive in and contribute.

Mastering these libraries is more than a technical achievement. It is a journey of exploration, a way to uncover truths hidden in data and transform them into actionable insights. With Pandas, TensorFlow, Matplotlib, NumPy, and Scikit-learn, you are not just working with data but unlocking its potential to make a difference in the world.

Now that you have been introduced to these essential libraries and their incredible capabilities, it is time to get hands-on experience. Start by selecting a dataset that sparks your interest, whether it pertains to climate change, social behavior, financial trends, or even your fitness data. The main goal is to choose something that excites you, as enthusiasm is the best motivation for learning.

Begin with Pandas. Practice cleaning and organizing your dataset until it feels intuitive. Experiment with filtering rows, grouping data, and creating new columns. Once your data is structured, use Matplotlib to bring it to life. Draw graphs, explore trends, and let the visualizations guide your curiosity.

When you are ready to explore further, use NumPy to handle complex numerical operations and Scikit-learn to create your first predictive model. Do not worry if it feels daunting at first. Start simple, test your code, and ask GPT-4o for help when stuck. It is there to guide you, like a patient tutor, offering examples and explanations tailored to your pace.

Finally, challenge yourself to explore TensorFlow when ready to tackle advanced topics. Build a small neural network or train a model on an image dataset. It might seem complex at first, but the satisfaction of making it work will be worth the effort.

The most important thing is to take one step at a time. Coding is not about perfection. It is about persistence, exploration, and learning from each step. Open Jupyter Notebook, ask questions, test ideas, and do not be afraid to make mistakes. Each challenge you solve will deepen your understanding and bring you closer to mastering these tools.

The journey ahead is yours to shape. Start small, stay curious, and keep experimenting. Every line of code you write is not just a skill. You build a foundation to transform data into knowledge, insights, and meaningful change.

Conclusion

As this chapter concludes, the study of Python's Pandas library, enhanced by the advanced capabilities of GPT-4o and Jupyter Notebook, has provided you with essential skills for advanced data manipulation and analysis. This journey began with the basics, where you learned about DataFrames and Series, and progressed to more complex procedures such as data manipulation, grouping, cleaning, transforming, and visualizing.

We begin with a small student dataset to learn the fundamental functions of Pandas. These functions are a powerful tool that simplifies complex and lengthy Python code. With detailed examples and interactive exercises, you can quickly master these functions. One of the key advantages of Pandas is its ability to read data from various sources, perform advanced transformations, sort data, and efficiently merge datasets. These practical skills will significantly enhance your Python programming, making you more effective and efficient in real-world data scenarios.

After mastering the basic Pandas functions with the student dataset, we downloaded and imported a real-world global warming dataset, which contains 11,222 records.

Furthermore, GPT-4o integration allows you to learn the Pandas library in the beginner Python book, a unique feature not found in any other beginner Python book. It is unheard of for a beginner Python programmer to generate code to process extensive real-world data and Pandas library, but you learned this skill in this chapter.

The skills acquired in this chapter will serve as a solid foundation for further Python coding study. Whether you plan to explore data analysis, machine learning using the Scikit-learn library, or enhance data visualization with Matplotlib, the expertise gained in Pandas will be crucial for your continued development in data science.

Mastering a new library like Pandas is a valuable investment for any Python programmer. Keep experimenting, learning, and asking insightful questions. Practice the code in Jupyter Notebook, and let this chapter be your guide to Python coding and data manipulation. The next chapter will introduce the CNN. So, hold on to your hat.

C‌HAPTER 6

Decipher
CNN App

Introduction

This chapter marks a significant milestone in your learning journey. By now, you have built a solid foundation in Python coding, including key concepts and tools. In *Chapter 1, Introduction to GenAI*, we introduced GenAI, such as GPT-4, as your coding assistant and tutor, along with techniques for prompt engineering. *Chapter 2, Jupyter Notebook*, guided you through Jupyter Notebooks, which is an essential Python development environment. *Chapter 3, Dissect the Calculator App*, covered standard Python syntax and even introduced a calculator application. In *Chapter 4, Sorting on My Mind*, we explored various sorting algorithms, while *Chapter 5, Pandas, the Data Tamer*, delved deeper into the Pandas library for data manipulation and analysis.

Now, it is time to take things to the next level. In this chapter, we will venture into the exciting and advanced world of **machine learning** (**ML**), focusing on **Convolutional Neural Networks (CNNs)**. This leap into ML builds on your critical thinking skills and solving complex problems in image recognition.

CNN is an advanced topic generally reserved for college graduate-level CS classes. *So why is CNN in a coding Python book for beginners?*

ML, especially CNNs, significantly departs from traditional decision trees and sequential logic. While the former adheres to explicit, human-defined rules, algorithms, and sequences, ML algorithms such as CNNs can learn to recognize patterns and make decisions based on data. This capacity for learning independently and adapting reshapes industries and fuels innovation in ways that static logical systems cannot, leading to the advance of GPT-4o, Gemini Ultra, Claude 3.5, and other GenAI.

In today's rapidly evolving AI technological landscape, it is crucial to understand that ML is just as important as mastering programming fundamentals. Integrating AI into various sectors, from healthcare to finance to entertainment, requires programmers to have at least a foundational understanding of how these intelligent systems work. Introducing CNNs early in the learning process provides a glimpse into the powerful tools shaping our future.

For beginner programmers, this advanced topic is accessible through GenAI tools like GPT-4o. These tools simplify complex concepts, offer step-by-step guidance, and even help troubleshoot issues, enabling newcomers to grasp and experiment with machine-learning coding techniques. This method improves your coding skills and prepares you for the AI-driven world ahead.

A friendly note before we begin: this chapter is not meant to replace a graduate-level course in ML or CNNs. While it is impossible to condense years of study into one chapter, this section provides a beginner-friendly introduction to CNN coding. Do not worry if some of the concepts or code seem challenging. This chapter, along with GPT-4o as your tutor, will help you build a solid foundation.

By working through the following exercise, you will gain valuable insights into the basics of CNNs and their practical applications. It might even spark an interest that leads you to pursue AI and ML as a college major or career path. For now, it is your starting point in exploring this fascinating AI field.

This chapter promises mind-bending concepts of ML and CNN, but first, we review the chapter's structure.

Structure

This chapter introduces ML and CNN concepts, algorithms, and coding. In particular, we will cover the following topics:

- Machine learning and CNN foundation
- Fast.ai library and framework
- Snakes' dataset
- Training the model

Objectives

By the end of this chapter, you will have a foundational understanding of ML concepts and algorithms, with a particular focus on CNNs. You will learn why ML techniques fundamentally differ from traditional programming logic, where rules are explicitly defined and instead rely on data-driven models that learn patterns and make decisions based on training.

This chapter will also guide you on how to find and download real-world datasets suitable for ML tasks. You will explore practical steps for preparing data for training and learn the importance of cleaning, organizing, and splitting datasets to ensure reliable and accurate model performance.

Additionally, you will write Python code using the Fast.ai libraries and frameworks to develop a CNN capable of classifying snake species as poisonous or non-poisonous. Along the way, you will gain hands-on experience setting up the training process, fine-tuning the model, and evaluating its performance. By blending theory with practical coding exercises, this chapter equips you with the tools to take your first steps into the exciting world of ML and CNN applications.

We begin at the bottom, the foundation.

Machine learning and CNN foundation

Understanding the theory behind ML and CNNs becomes much easier when we compare it to standard sequential logic. By examining the differences, we can see why ML requires an entirely different approach to problem-solving. Before diving into the specifics, let us take a moment to reflect on what we have covered so far and set the stage for exploring a problem that can only be solved using ML techniques.

In *Chapters 3, Dissect the Calculator App,* and *Chapter 4, Sorting on My Mind,* you learned about sequential logic through examples like a calculator and the bubble sort algorithm. These examples rely on clearly defined step-by-step instructions. Each operation or condition follows a predetermined path, which you visualize using a flowchart. Sequential logic is deterministic. It means that a given input always produces a specific, predictable output. This approach works perfectly for problems with explicit and straightforward rules, such as performing arithmetic calculations or sorting a list of numbers.

However, not all problems fit neatly into this framework. Imagine trying to write sequential logic to classify images of snakes as poisonous or non-poisonous. The rules for identifying subtle differences in patterns, shapes, and colors are too complex and nuanced to encode manually. It is where ML and CNNs step in. Instead of relying on predefined rules, they learn from data, analyzing patterns and relationships within the dataset to make predictions.

In this section, we will focus on:

- Sequential logic
- Machine learning
- Top level AI terminology
- CNN versus sequential coding

Sequential logic

We will now explore a real-world coding problem that cannot be addressed using sequential logic alone. By exploring how machine learning handles such challenges, you will see why it is an entirely different paradigm. It is no longer about writing exact instructions; it is about training a model to recognize patterns and make decisions based on the data it has seen. This shift in thinking is at the heart of ML, and understanding this difference is key to grasping the power of CNNs.

We first exam the typical usage of programmer logic in a flow chart.

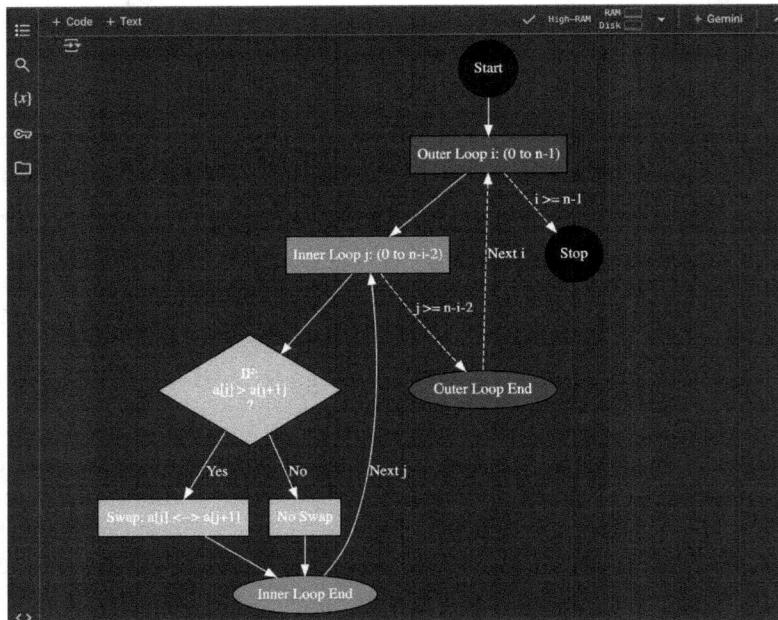

Figure 6.1: Programming logic flowchart

Figure 6.1 illustrates a classic programming logic flowchart showcasing the bubble sort algorithm we explored in Chapter 4, *Sorting on My Mind*. This flowchart highlights the structured, step-by-step logic humans create through critical thinking. It has a clear start, an outer loop, an inner loop, a condition check, a swap operation, and a stop point when the sorting process is complete. Every element of the flowchart represents a deliberate choice made by the programmer to solve a specific problem, while the computer merely executes these instructions as designed.

The algorithm begins by defining the list length or array of unordered values. The outer loop iterates through the list, and the inner loop compares adjacent index values. If one value is larger than the next, they are swapped. This process continues until all elements are sorted, with both loops systematically running to their end. The computer does not understand why this process works. It simply follows the precise logic we have defined.

This sequential log showcases the beauty of programming languages. They faithfully execute human-designed logic written in languages such as Python, C, C++, Fortran, Java, JavaScript, or Swift. The bubble sort algorithm can run millions of cycles without error. For over five decades, flowcharts have been used to represent the logic behind countless programs and algorithms, from calculating U.S. census data to powering popular gaming apps on Apple devices. Flowcharts have become a cornerstone of early programming education, as professors have relied on them to introduce students to data structures and algorithms. The prevailing belief is that we can represent any concept, problem, or process through a flowchart.

What happens when a problem cannot be effectively represented by a flowchart? What if the rules are too complex, the patterns too subtle, or the logic too abstract for a simple step-by-step process? These scenarios highlight the limitations of traditional programming. While flowcharts are useful for structured problems with clear rules, they fall short when it comes to problems that require learning from data or adapting to subtle nuances. Addressing these challenges demands a new paradigm that shifts the focus from creating explicit logic to designing systems that learn and infer patterns, marking the beginning of ML.

Note: Historians credited the first written algorithm to English mathematician and writer Ada Lovelace. In 1843, she wrote an algorithm intended to be executed by Charles Babbage's Analytical Engine, but the technology for building the Analytical Engine was not possible in the 1800s. The first modern program for the Electronic Numerical Integrator and Computer (ENIAC), 1945, often recognized as the first general-purpose electronic digital computer, was written by a team led by John W. Mauchly and J. Presper Eckert. The programming team consisted of Kay McNulty, Betty Jennings, Betty Snyder, Marlyn Wescoff, Fran Bilas, and Ruth Lichterman. It was an all-woman programmer team. The ENIAC's first task was to compute artillery firing tables for the United States Army's Ballistic Research Laboratory.

Machine learning

ML is the foundation of Generative AI models like GPT-4, Gemini, and Claude, allowing them to tackle complex problems that traditional programming cannot handle effectively. For instance, image classification presents challenges that highlight the limitations of sequential flowchart-based methods. A simple task, such as determining whether an image depicts a dog or a cat, clearly illustrates the necessity of machine learning.

At first glance, distinguishing between a dog and a cat may seem trivial. Humans can quickly tell them apart with just a quick look. However, programming a computer to perform the same task is a different challenge. One might start by creating a flowchart highlighting their distinguishing features: the shape of the ears, the presence of whiskers, the structure of the head, and the length and size of the body, legs, and tail. While this method may work for comparing two images, it becomes impractical in real-world scenarios.

Consider the immense diversity of thousands of dog and cat species, captured in millions of photos taken from countless angles and under various lighting conditions, poses, and backgrounds. Attempting to account for all these variations in a flowchart is not only impractical but also impossible. Flowcharts depend on explicit, rigid, and sequential rules, which cannot accommodate the complexity, variability, and subtle nuances found in real-world images.

Even when trying to describe a single feature, like an ear, using a flowchart highlights the problem. A computer lacks an innate understanding of what an ear is, its location, or how its shape varies across different species. To a computer, an ear is merely a collection of pixels. Translating that concept into a step-by-step process is overwhelming. Traditional programming methods rely on predefined conditions and sequential instructions and are fundamentally inadequate for handling the vast complexity and variability involved in tasks like image classification.

Machine learning plays a crucial role in the context of image classification. Instead of relying on human-defined rules, machine learning enables the computer to learn patterns and features directly from the data itself. It does not need us to explain what an ear looks like or create a rule for every angle or shape. A machine learning model can identify patterns, relationships, and unique features that distinguish dogs from cats by training on thousands or even millions of labelled images. It learns from the data and generalizes adapting to new images it has not seen before.

Machine learning represents a paradigm shift in how we approach problem-solving in computer science. It allows us to tackle challenges too complex, dynamic, or nuanced for traditional flowchart-based programming methods. Rather than creating logic for the computer, we train *the computer to discover the logic itself*, making ML the only viable solution for tasks like image classification. It powers modern AI systems and advances our ability to solve real-world problems.

We have reviewed the flowchart for the bubble sort algorithm, which uses sequential logic, in *Figure 6.1*. The next figure describes a general flow diagram for the CNN algorithm.

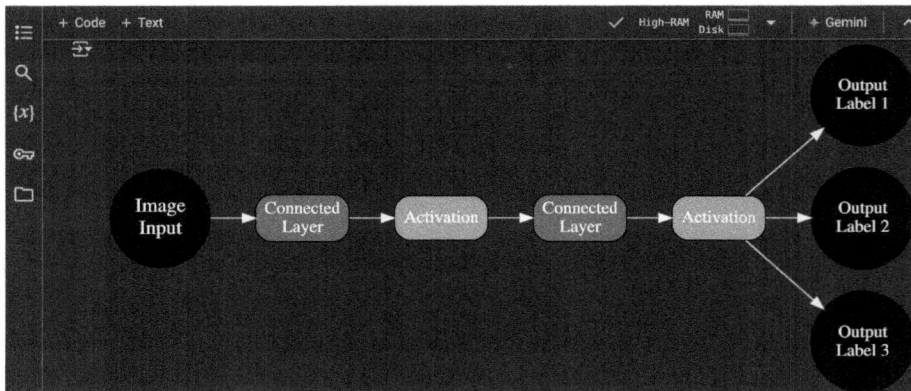

Figure 6.2: CNN coding process

Figure 6.2 illustrates the fundamental concept of programming a CNN model widely used in image classification tasks. Leveraging the **Graphviz** library introduced in *Chapter 4, Sorting on My Mind*, the CNN diagram visually represents the architecture of a deep learning model. The Python This architecture consists of multiple layers, including convolutional layers, pooling layers, activation functions, and fully connected layers, which work together to process and classify images.

In a typical application of CNNs, such as identifying whether an image contains a dog or a cat, the process begins with an input image passed through the network, referred to as the AI model. There are hundreds of models available for image classification, including ResNet34 and ResNet100. The CNN performs a series of convolutions by applying learned filters to detect various features within the image, such as edges, textures, and patterns. After several convolutional and pooling layers, which reduce the dimensionality of the data while preserving important features, the output is flattened and fed into fully connected layers.

These fully connected layers ultimately combine the high-level features extracted by the earlier layers to make classification decisions. The final output of the network is a set of labels, like dog or cat, along with a confidence percentage for each classification. This confidence score indicates the likelihood that the input image belongs to each predicted category, helping inform users of the model's certainty in its predictions. A CNN learns to optimize weights and biases across its layers through training on large datasets, improving its accuracy in distinguishing between different classes over time.

By using a pre-trained CNN model, such as **ResNet34**, you do not need millions of pictures of dogs and cats. Instead, approximately three to five thousand images are sufficient to predict whether an image contains a **dog** or a **cat** with an accuracy of 96% or higher.

In a slightly more technical explanation, the CNN flow diagram offers a comprehensive understanding of the ML process using the CNN algorithm. This method deconstructs an image into its pixel values, which serve as network input. These pixel values are then passed through multiple layers of artificial neurons, each with weights and activation functions. As the data moves through these layers, the model identifies patterns and features within the image, ultimately producing an output that indicates the likelihood of the image belonging to specific categories, such as dog or cat.

What is remarkable about CNNs is their ability to learn from vast datasets. By providing the network with thousands, or even millions, of labelled images, the algorithm starts recognizing patterns, such as the shape of ears, fur texture, and body proportions. The outcome is a model that can accurately identify objects in images it has never seen before. Unlike traditional programming, there is no need to write explicit rules or logic for the network. The computer learns these patterns independently.

The process used to identify dogs or cats in images can also be applied to entirely different tasks, such as detecting cancer cells in medical imaging. The core algorithm and structure of the CNN remain the same; the only difference lies in the input dataset. For instance, instead of training on photos of animals, the network may analyze microscopic images of skin cells to classify them as healthy or cancerous.

This paradigm shift can be challenging for developers accustomed to traditional programming. The sequential logic methods rely on explicitly defined logic, often represented in flowcharts, where the programmer has direct control and can debug the code step by step. CNN and other ML algorithms, however, operate differently.

In ML algorithms like CNN, the developer does not explicitly write the step-by-step logic. Instead, the computer learns it through a training process. The debugging focuses on interpreting the model's performance rather than examining individual lines of code. For many experienced developers, relying on the computer to learn independently can feel counterintuitive and uncomfortable. The shift away from sequential logic, like the bubble sort, is precisely why CNNs are included in this beginner Python book. The goal is to introduce beginner programmers to the new coding paradigm for today's AI world.

The next step is to familiarize ourselves with the terminology and labels used in AI and CNNs. Understanding these concepts will be essential for grasping how they function.

Top level AI terminology

Understanding ML begins with mastering standard AI terminology. Terms such as AI, ML, deep learning, ANN, CNN, RNN, NLP, LLM, GenAI, and AGI are foundational. These are not just buzzwords. They represent the building blocks of knowledge essential for anyone working in the programming field.

Think of AI terminology as a shared language, much like the specialized vocabulary used in other professions. Just as a biologist must understand terms like DNA, genome, and cell division, or an engineer needs concepts like torque, stress, and load, programmers and AI practitioners must grasp these key terms to effectively communicate ideas, solve problems, and contribute to advancements in the field.

Much like a college major, each sub-field equips practitioners with specific skills and methodologies tailored to a particular area of expertise. By understanding the terminology, you gain clarity about the distinct goals of each sub-field and build the ability to navigate and connect them.

In AI programming, understanding these terms is not just academic; it is practical. It allows you to communicate effectively with peers, interpret documentation, and make informed decisions about which tools and approaches to use for specific challenges. More importantly, it prepares you to contribute meaningfully to one of the most transformative fields of our time.

The following figure provides an overview of the structure to help clarify this terminology:

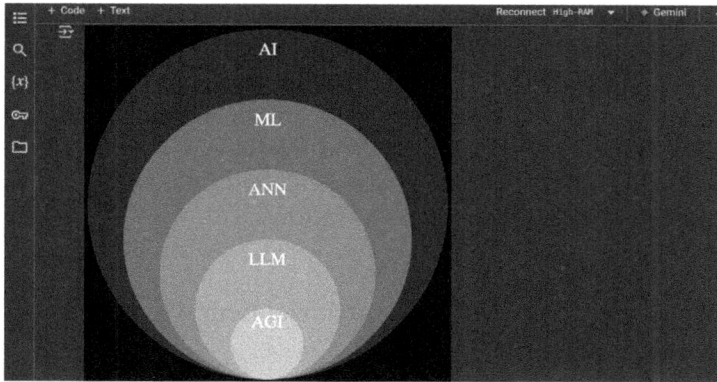

Figure 6.3: *AI classification*

Figure 6.3 provides a visual representation of the hierarchy of the top-level AI classification using nested circles. Each larger circle represents a broader concept, while the smaller circles narrow the scope, defining more specific disciplines. The design captures the relationship between overarching ideas and the specialized fields under its umbrella.

We used GPT-4o to generate Python code with the **Graphviz** library to create this diagram. It took a few iterations and some careful prompt engineering, as described in Chapter 1, *Introduction to GenAI*, to achieve the final result. While the Python code is not included here, this is an excellent opportunity for you to try replicating the diagram using GPT-4o and Jupyter Notebook. It is a fun challenge and reinforces your understanding of AI classification and your ability to guide GPT-4o to create visualizations.

Each nested circle reflects the progression from general concepts to more specialized disciplines, highlighting how broad AI principles give rise to increasingly focused discipline. Understanding this hierarchy is crucial for grasping the landscape of AI and its subfields. Visualizing these relationships allows you to see how concepts like CNNs fit within the broader context of AI and appreciate the connections between disciplines.

The definition of each circle is as follows:

- **Artificial intelligence (AI)** refers to machines designed to *simulate human intelligence*. These systems are capable of thinking and learning similarly to humans. AI encompasses a wide range of applications, from simple games like checkers to advanced technologies that can drive cars. There is no universally accepted definition of AI, which means it can include ML systems and sequential logic. As a result, any program that mimics human intelligence can be classified as AI. Marketers often label various apps, services, products, or games as AI, and they are not incorrect since a formal definition of AI does not exist. It is essential to note that the ML field mentioned below is not the only sub-field within AI. Other disciplines outside of ML still considered part of AI, which is not shown in the diagram, include expert systems, rule-based systems, symbolic reasoning, knowledge representation, search algorithms, and sorting algorithms.

- **Machine learning (ML)** is a subset of AI (nested inside the bigger AI bubble). It enables computers to learn from data and make decisions based on it. Rather than being programmed with specific instructions for every task, ML algorithms identify patterns and use inference to enhance their performance over time. Unlike AI, ML has a strict definition and must adhere to one of the ten published algorithms, which have been peer-reviewed and documented in scholarly papers. The ten popular ML algorithms are as follows:

  o Apriori algorithm

  o Deep learning, also known as **artificial neural networks (ANN)**

  o Decision trees

  o K means clustering algorithm

  o **K-Nearest Neighbors (KNN)**

  o Linear regression

  o Logistic regression

  o Naive Bayes classifier algorithm

  o Random forests

  o **Support Vector Machine (SVM)**

- ANN, often called **deep learning**, are a specialized subset of machine learning. Note that ANN is one of the possible ML algorithms listed above. Other ML algorithms are not displayed in the diagram. ANN algorithms are inspired by the structure and function of the human brain, consisting of layers of interconnected nodes, or neurons, that process data. Each connection between neurons has a weight, which adjusts during the learning process. This adjustment allows the network to identify patterns, adapt to new data, and make predictions with increasing accuracy. ANN's ability to learn and generalize from complex datasets makes it such a powerful tool in modern AI. Here are the popular algorithms under ANN:

  o CNN, which is the topic of this chapter.

  o **Feedforward Neural Networks (FNN)**

  o **Recurrent Neural Networks (RNN)**

  o **Long Short-Term Memory Networks (LSTM)**

  o **Gated Recurrent Units (GRU)**

  o **Generative Adversarial Networks (GANs)**, used by *DeepFake*

  o Transformer Networks, also known as **LLM**, which is used by GPT-4o, Gemini, Claude and all other LLMs

  o **Radial Basis Function Networks (RBFN)**

  o Boltzmann Machines

- ○ **Graph Neural Networks (GNN)**
- ○ **Deep Belief Networks (DBN)**

- **Large Language Models (LLMs)**, often referred to as **Generative AI** or **GenAI**, are a specialized subset of ANN. It is the smallest inner circle in the nested bubbles in *Figure 6.2*. While LLMs are one of many ANN algorithms as seen in *Figure 6.3*. The others are not shown in the diagram. LLMs are specifically designed to process, understand, and generate human language, leveraging the Transformer algorithm at their core. Trained in massive amounts of text data, LLMs can perform various tasks, including language translation, summarization, question answering, text-to-image, text-to-audio, text-to-music, and text-to-video. Their ability to model the intricacies of human language sets them apart from other ANN algorithms, making them an essential tool in natural language processing and a transformative technology in AI. There are dozens of commercial and open-source LLM. Here are a few examples:

  - ○ OpenAI GPT-4o
  - ○ Google Gemini
  - ○ Meta Llama-3
  - ○ Apple Intelligence
  - ○ Microsoft Copilot
  - ○ Anthropic Claude
  - ○ And many others.

- **Artificial General Intelligence (AGI)** is often viewed as an advanced form of AI, closely related to LLMs but much broader in scope. AGI refers to highly autonomous systems that can perform most tasks at a level equal to or surpassing human ability. Unlike specialized AI systems, AGI has the ability to generalize knowledge across different domains and adapt to entirely new challenges without human intervention. While some theorize that AGI may eventually attain a form of consciousness, it remains a theoretical concept rather than a practical reality. Despite significant advancements in AI, AGI exists more as a future possibility than current technology.

Using GPT-4o for research and learning is highly recommended, particularly when exploring topics in AI, ML, CNN, and LLM. GenAI tools like GPT-4o are particularly effective at simplifying complex concepts into understandable explanations. Whether you need a technical definition, a relatable analogy, or real-world examples, GPT-4o can adapt to your specific needs.

That said, understanding CNNs or LLMs at a deep, foundational level typically requires two to four years of focused study in college or equivalent experience. These are intricate topics that go beyond the basics of AI and involve advanced mathematics, programming, and algorithmic thinking. While this chapter provides an introduction, it is crucial to consider the scope. If AI is a mountain-sized iceberg, this chapter is merely a hand-held snowball taken from the tip of that iceberg. This chapter gives you a feel for the subject but barely scratches the surface of the vast and complex field beneath.

GPT-4o is an excellent guide to help you explore this snowball and understand its place in the larger AI ecosystem. You will build a strong foundation in AI programming by asking questions, exploring examples, clarifying terminology, and using prompt engineering techniques in Chapter 1, *Introduction to GenAI*. However, mastering these disciplines, whether CNNs, LLMs, or other AI specialties, takes time, practice, and commitment.

Once you are comfortable with the basic concepts and terminology, you can move on to coding CNNs. Combining theoretical understanding with hands-on practice will give you a glimpse of what lies beneath the tip of the iceberg, helping you appreciate the depth and breadth of AI as you continue your Python learning journey.

CNN versus sequential coding

The Python syntax for coding a CNN uses the same if-else statements, looping techniques, and algorithms as traditional programming, but the approach fundamentally differs from sequential logic programming. In sequential logic, you typically begin by designing a flowchart to outline the steps or algorithms at a high level and then translate those steps into Python or another programming language. This process is entirely driven by the explicit instructions that you, the programmer, create.

In contrast, coding a CNN shifts the focus from building step-by-step logic to enabling the model to learn patterns and make decisions from data. The core steps involve cleaning and augmenting your dataset, feeding it into an AI-based model, and iteratively optimizing its accuracy. Instead of explicitly defining every rule, you create an environment where the model learns these rules on its own.

It is like the difference between writing out a detailed, step-by-step guide for baking a cake versus simply asking an AI for a great cake recipe. With the latter, the AI uses its training to suggest the best approach, saving you from having to define every single step. In CNN programming, the emphasis is on preparing the model and data, allowing the AI to handle the logic through its training process. This shift in focus represents the fundamental difference between traditional programming and ML.

The CNN coding process involves several key steps as follows:

1. **Set up Python coding environment:** Similar to the process explained in Chapter 2, *Jupyter Notebook,* set up the Python Jupyter Notebook and choose Python-based libraries such as Pandas, NumPy, Transformers, TensorFlow, PyTorch, and Fast.ai.

2. **Prepare train dataset:** CNNs require large datasets to learn effectively. You will need a dataset, typically images for CNN, to preprocess and split into training and validation sets. The Kaggle website has thousands of real-world datasets available.

3. **Transfer learning:** Instead of spending a year or two in CS graduate study to learn to build a CNN model from scratch and compile it, you can use prebuilt models like ResNet34. Hundreds of prebuilt CNN and RNN models are available in the PyTorch Image Models (TIMM) collections.

4. **Learn rate:** You can determine the best learning rate using the model and input dataset.

5. **Train the model:** Once you have the dataset, learning rate, and based model, you can train it. This step involves feeding the data into the model and adjusting the hyper-parameters and loss function to improve accuracy.

6. **Evaluate the model:** After completing the training, it is essential to study the model's performance using metrics such as the F1 score and the Confusion matrix. Furthermore, testing the model with new, unseen data is crucial to evaluating its generalization.

7. **Making predictions:** Finally, you can use your trained model to make predictions on new data. This is where you see the real-world application of your CNN model.

To enhance clarity, we will represent the seven steps discussed above with a process flow diagram. This visual representation will outline the CNN workflow in a way that highlights the sequence of operations, from data preparation to model optimization. However, the critical difference between a CNN flow diagram and traditional programming diagrams lies in the absence of explicit logic.

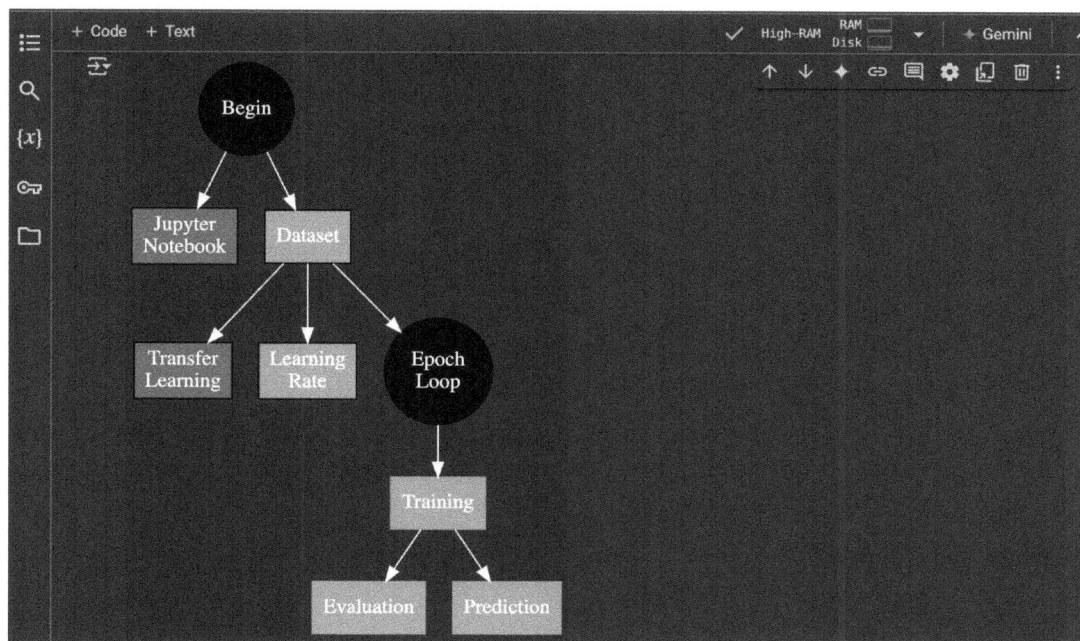

Figure 6.4: Process flow CNN

Figure 6.4 illustrates the process steps for coding a CNN model. We used the Graphviz library to create diagrams and applied prompt engineering techniques with GPT-4o. While the Python code for generating the diagram is not included here, this presents an excellent opportunity for you to experiment with GPT-4o. Challenge yourself to ask GPT-4o to create a similar diagram, honing your prompt engineering and visualization skills.

The flow reflects the key steps we discussed earlier, starting with using Jupyter Notebook as the development environment. It proceeds through essential stages, including selecting and preparing the dataset, training the model, evaluating its performance, and making predictions.

Note the differences between the flow of a CNN and the sequential bubble sort algorithm. In sequential programming, a flowchart has to clearly define characteristics, such as what constitutes an ear or a tail when distinguishing between a dog and a cat. It would lay out specific rules and conditions that describe these features in detail, dictating how the computer should interpret them. In contrast, CNNs function on a different principle. The flow diagram for a CNN does not include explicit definitions for features like ears or tails. Instead, the model automatically recognizes these features by analyzing patterns within the training data.

The absence of predefined rules makes CNN incredibly powerful and distinct from traditional logic-based programming. Providing the model with thousands of labeled images, it learns to differentiate between a dog and a cat without relying on human-defined instructions.

Figure 6.4 highlights essential steps, including dataset cleaning, data augmentation, feeding data into the network, and iteratively optimizing the model for accuracy. Instead of being hard-coded by the programmer, the CNN model learns the logic through the data it processes. This shift in approach fundamentally alters the role of the programmer. Rather than defining every rule and exception, the focus shifts to creating conditions that allow the model to learn effectively.

As we conclude this section, it is necessary to remember that this chapter is designed to introduce you to the fundamentals of CNN programming. Mastering CNN coding does not happen overnight. It takes time, practice, and persistence. If everything does not click right away, it may take a year or two; that is perfectly normal. The key is to keep learning and building on what you have gained so far.

Stay curious, keep experimenting, and embrace the challenge of learning something new. The world of CNN programming is as rewarding as it is fascinating, and every step you take brings you closer to mastering it. Enjoy the journey.

We begin our coding journey by importing the Fast.ai library and taking a closer look.

Fast.ai library and framework

Ready to dip your big toes into CNN coding? It is deceptively easy, almost too easy, with the Fast.ai library and framework. You can create your CNN model with just four lines of code. It does not use API from a costly private AI model or a simple toy demo app. You build a world-class CNN model that you can license. A few years ago, it would have taken forty pages of Python code, four months to develop, and four million dollars.

Fast.ai is a Python library and framework developed by *Professor Jeremy Howard* and *Dr. Rachel Thomas* to make deep learning accessible to everyone. Professor Howard taught an online course, and the book *Deep Learning for Coders with fastai and PyTorch: AI Applications Without a PhD,* is available on *Amazon Book*s. It aspires to bring advanced deep learning within reach, regardless of your background or expertise. The Fast.ai library provides high-level components that help you construct models quickly and effectively, helping you achieve impressive results with minimal effort. We will explore why Fast.ai is a game-changer and a wise beginner choice.

First and foremost, Fast.ai is based on PyTorch, a robust deep-learning framework. PyTorch can be overwhelming for beginners because of its complexity, but Fast.ai simplifies the process without sacrificing PyTorch's power. This framework allows you to focus on learning and applying deep learning concepts while staying aware of the underlying complexity.

The two sub-sections are as follows:
- CNN cats and dogs code
- CNN cats and dogs result

We start with the code.

CNN cats and dogs code

One of the standout features of Fast.ai is its user-friendly code. The library is designed to be intuitive and straightforward, allowing you to build intricate models with just a few lines of code. For instance, writing code for a CNN for image classification can be as effortless as the following:

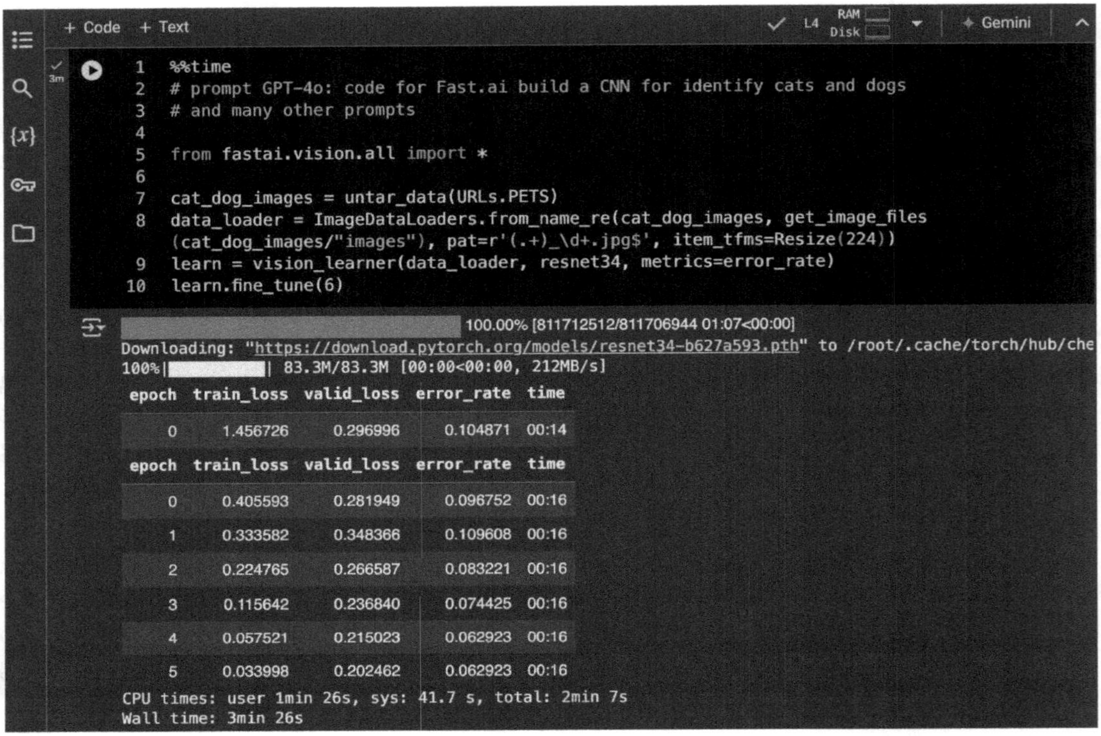

Figure 6.5: Fast.ai code for CNN dogs and cats breed

Figure 6.5 presents the code and output for creating a CNN model to identify different dog and cat breeds. The process begins with Line #1, where the Jupyter Notebook is instructed to track the time spent executing this code cell. Lines #2 and #3 display the initial prompts used to generate the code, although many other prompts are not shown here. Line #4 imports the Fast.ai library, which provides the necessary tools for building and training the CNN model.

Line #7 downloads the dataset containing images of cats and dogs, along with their corresponding breed labels. Line #8 creates the Fast.ai data loader to prepare the data for training and validation. Line #9 initializes the Fast.ai vision learner object, which sets up the CNN model for training. Finally, Line #10 begins fine-tuning the model over six epochs, gradually enhancing its performance on the dataset.

The output includes status messages and a well-organized table displaying key metrics, such as the epoch count, training loss, validation loss, error rate, and time taken. After completing six epochs, the final row of the table indicates an error rate of 0.062923, which corresponds to an accuracy of 93.7% in correctly identifying whether an image depicts a cat or a dog and determining its breed. The entire training process took three minutes and 26 seconds to complete, nearly totaling four minutes.

Wait, what?

It only takes four lines of code and four minutes to train a CNN model. You type four lines of code and make a cup of tea, and it is done. *What happened to all the discussions about needing two to four years of college, a completely new coding paradigm, complex algorithms, and extensive mathematical knowledge?* Just four years ago, this same task would have required forty pages of code and millions of dollars in resources to accomplish. *How is this even possible?*

Well, none of that was a lie, and here is why: Behind those four lines of code lies a mountain of concepts, intricate algorithms, and advanced mathematics that enable it. From the moment you set up Jupyter Notebook with a *Nvidia* GPU equipped with 16 GB of RAM, you begin the process of cleaning, augmenting, labeling, and organizing 25,864 images of cats and dogs. Each step depends on a solid understanding of ML workflows and years of experience.

The data loader object structures the data for the model. The default learning rate of 0.003 is meticulously tuned for training, and the Resnet34 architecture is selected from thousands of available models as the base model for transfer learning. Additionally, it involves concepts like transfer learning, fine-tuning, and epoch loops. Each element represents a complex puzzle piece that has been streamlined to make those four lines of code possible.

For example, in *Chapter 4, Sorting on My Mind,* we spent hours, even days, learning about various sorting algorithms such as bubble, insertion, and quick sort. We explored their strengths, weaknesses, and applications in depth. Then, in *Chapter 5, Pandas, the Data Tamer,* we utilized the Pandas library, which automatically selects the best sorting algorithm for the data when we choose the built-in **sort()** function. Fast.ai operates similarly, but it does so on a much more advanced level. It abstracts away the complexities, handling all the heavy lifting behind the scenes, and is significantly more powerful than Pandas.

The reason we study sorting algorithms instead of jumping straight to the Pandas **sort()** method is straightforward: someone dedicated months, or even years, to perfecting that **sort()** function so it could be as efficient, reliable, and elegant as it is today. As a programmer, you have the opportunity to be that person. By doing this, you enable future programmers to benefit from your hard work, allowing them to accomplish their tasks with the simplicity of calling a single function.

The same principle applies to the study of CNNs. Libraries like Fast.ai make coding CNNs seem almost magically simple. Their elegance hides the years of effort, trial, and error required to perfect the techniques behind them. If your goal is to push the boundaries of AI, to improve the concepts, or to create entirely new techniques, then you must invest years of study and experimentation. By doing so, you can make those breakthroughs that will simplify complex tasks for the next generation of programmers. They, in turn, will build on your work, just as we stand today on the shoulders of the giants who came before us.

Here is the best part. You can become one of those giants in the field. By committing yourself to mastering these concepts and understanding not just how things work but why they work, you position yourself to advance the field and contribute something meaningful to the world of programming. Every improvement you make, no matter how small, has the potential to impact countless others, enabling them to achieve more with less effort. That is the beauty of this field. It is a cycle of continuous learning, innovation, and contribution, and you have the power to be a part of it.

Those four lines of code in *Figure 6.5* metaphorically stand on the shoulders of years of research and technological advancements. They represent not just a coding paradigm shift but the culmination of hard work from thousands of researchers, developers, and mathematicians. While the code might be simple to write, understanding what happens beneath the surface still requires years of study and practice. Fast.ai makes cutting-edge AI accessible, but the foundational concepts remain as intricate as ever. Next is looking at the results from the training cycle.

CNN dogs and cats result

With Fast.ai, you can generate results simply by calling the **show_result()** function. Each time you run it, the displayed images will vary, providing fresh results with every execution. The following code and output demonstrate this in action.

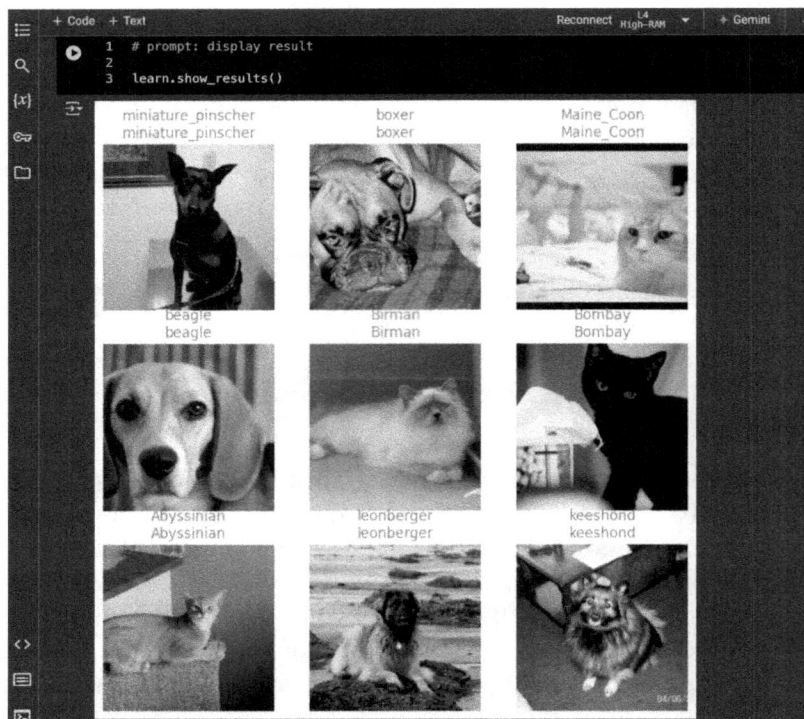

Figure 6.6: Display learner results

Figure 6.6 displays the results of the CNN training. It shows nine dog images, each labeled with its predicted breed at the top and the actual label below. Most predictions are correct, thanks to the model's 93.7% accuracy from training on 25,864 images. The occasional mismatches, which make up 6.3% of the error rate, can be isolated and displayed using other methods if you want to focus on analyzing the mistakes.

It is necessary to note that this dataset does not include thousands of cat and dog breeds. To better understand the scope of our data, we will examine the number of unique breeds represented in the dataset.

```
# prompt: print the list of dog breeds in the dataset

learn.dls.vocab
```

```
['Abyssinian', 'Bengal', 'Birman', 'Bombay', 'British_Shorthair', 'Egyptian_Mau', 'Maine_Coon',
 'Persian', 'Ragdoll', 'Russian_Blue', 'Siamese', 'Sphynx', 'american_bulldog',
 'american_pit_bull_terrier', 'basset_hound', 'beagle', 'boxer', 'chihuahua',
 'english_cocker_spaniel', 'english_setter', 'german_shorthaired', 'great_pyrenees', 'havanese',
 'japanese_chin', 'keeshond', 'leonberger', 'miniature_pinscher', 'newfoundland', 'pomeranian', 'pug',
 'saint_bernard', 'samoyed', 'scottish_terrier', 'shiba_inu', 'staffordshire_bull_terrier',
 'wheaten_terrier', 'yorkshire_terrier']
```

Figure 6.7: *List of dog breeds*

Figure 6.7 shows the code and output for looking up the count of breeds in the dataset. There are a total of 37 dog and cat breeds, starting with Abyssinian and ending with Yorkshire Terrier.

37 breeds fall far short of the thousands of dog and cat breeds worldwide. However, it is not the function of the CNN model to determine how many breeds it can classify. It is the data itself that dictates this. The model's ability to classify breeds is directly tied to the diversity and size of the dataset. This profound insight underscores the core principle of ML: the model learns what we teach it through data.

For instance, in our current dataset, we have 25,864 images representing 37 breeds, achieving an accuracy of 93.7%. If we were to scale up the dataset to cover 20,000 cat and dog breeds worldwide while maintaining a similar data density per breed, we would require approximately 13.98 million images. This projection highlights the immense need for data when attempting to classify a significantly larger number of categories.

To summarize, if we want to increase the model's accuracy or expand its ability to classify more breeds, the solution is not to rewrite the CNN code. The CNN architecture remains the same. Instead, we must expand and diversify the dataset. With more breeds represented in the training data and more images per breed, the model will naturally learn to recognize and classify a wider variety of breeds more precisely. Power lies not just in the algorithm but in the quality and quantity of the data.

Explaining why this works so effectively would require an entirely separate book. It involves diving deep into the relationship between data diversity, data quality, feature learning, and neural networks' capacity to generalize from training examples. For now, it is enough to appreciate that a CNN's strength is its elegant code and ability to adapt and scale with the data.

Fast.ai is known for its thorough documentation and supportive community. The team has created extensive tutorials, courses, and forums. *Professor Howard's* and *Dr. Thomas's* courses stand out as they take a top-down approach to teaching deep learning. The online course is free, and you can purchase the *Deep Learning for Coders with Fastai and PyTorch: AI Applications Without a Ph.D* on Amazon. The course and book provide an approach that focuses on the big picture before exploring specifics, making the learning process more manageable.

Fast.ai is designed to implement best practices in deep learning and is continuously updated by an active GitHub community. The library incorporates cutting-edge techniques such as data augmentation, learning rate schedules, and mixed-precision training to improve model performance. With regular updates from a dedicated AI developer community, Fast.ai ensures your development process is faster, aligned with industry standards, and keeps you at pace with the latest AI advancements.

Fast.ai provides a straightforward and user-friendly approach to deep learning, making it accessible for beginners and experienced practitioners. By simplifying the complexities involved in building and training models, Fast.ai allows users to concentrate on learning and experimenting. Its comprehensive documentation, active community, and powerful transfer learning features make it a reliable and essential tool in your deep learning toolkit.

Are we ready to code CNN using our own set of real-world data? It is time to see if we can find snakes on the plane.

Snakes' dataset

Are we ready to take our CNN coding knowledge one step further? To clarify our intention for this section, the code is not a substitute for attending CNN courses. Instead, think of it as an introduction to a high-level concept. We will start by selecting an image dataset from the Kaggle website. You may recall exploring Kaggle in *Chapter 5, Pandas, the Data Tamer,* when we searched for global warming data for our Pandas DataFrame study. This time, however, we are specifically looking for an image dataset.

In CNN image classification, the input data significantly influences the accuracy of the resulting model. Furthermore, around 80% of the coding can be reused for multiple projects. In simple terms, the differentiating factor in tasks such as identifying poisonous snakes, classifying dogs or cats, categorizing skin cancer cells, determining people's ethnicity, and selecting the best college for you lies in the input datasets.

Thanks to the highly intelligent GPT-4o acting as an instructor and coding assistant, we can confidently work with a large, real-world dataset in this beginner Python book. Before we dive into the snake images dataset, feel free to choose your image dataset to work with, whether shoes, rice grain types, apples, skin cancer classifications, celebrity faces, or any other area that interests you. Exploring a topic you are passionate about will make the learning process even more engaging and rewarding.

The section has the following:

- Find new real-world dataset
- Clean dataset
- Data loader

We start with finding the snakes data.

Find new real-world dataset

We are drawn to identifying poisonous snakes because we instinctively fear them and often assume all snakes are dangerous. In reality, most non-poisonous snakes play a vital role in maintaining ecological balance. To explore this further, we choose the real-world dataset, specifically *Yash Goel's Snakes Species* dataset from the Kaggle website.

The code in this section will be longer than the four lines shown previously because we begin to unpack what magic lies beneath.

This dataset is particularly valuable because identifying snake species and distinguishing between poisonous and non-poisonous ones is challenging, even for most humans. With 135 species of poisonous or non-poisonous included, the task highlights the intelligence of CNNs and their ability to recognize patterns far beyond human capability.

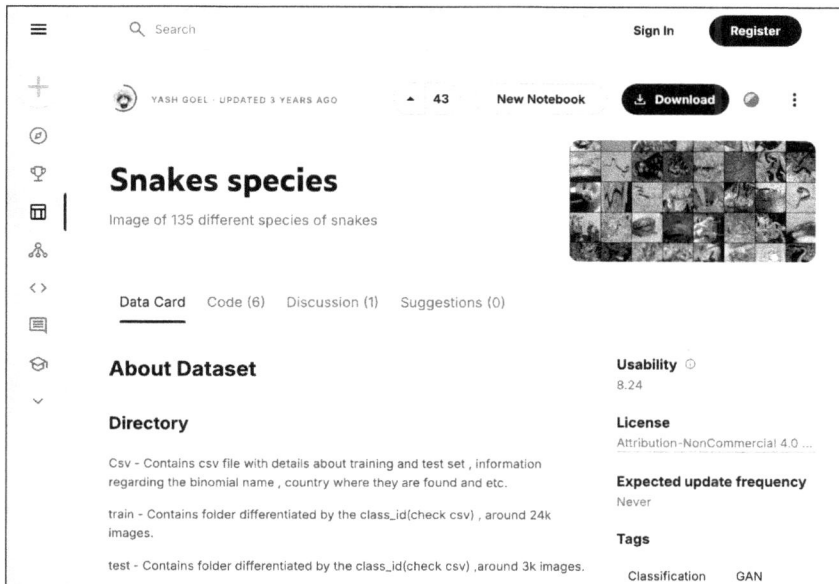

Figure 6.8: Kaggle website, snake species

Figure 6.8 displays the snake species datasets page on Kaggle. Kaggle has a specific method for downloading datasets. Therefore, the first step is to request our trusty GPT-4o for assistance in writing the code to download Kaggle data.

```
+ Code  + Text                                           Reconnect  L4          + Gemini
                                                                    High-RAM

[ ]   1    # prompt: write a python function to download kaggle data
      2    #    from https://www.kaggle.com/datasets/goelyash/165-different-snakes-species
      3
      4    import os
      5    import kaggle
      6
      7    def download_kaggle_dataset(dataset: str, download_path: str):
      8        """
      9        Downloads a dataset from Kaggle.
     10
     11        Parameters:
     12            dataset (str): The Kaggle dataset URL or dataset identifier.
     13            download_path (str): The local path where the dataset should be downloaded.
     14        """
     15        # Check if the download path exists, if not, create it
     16        if not os.path.exists(download_path):
     17            os.makedirs(download_path)
     18
     19        # Use Kaggle API to download the dataset
     20        kaggle.api.dataset_download_files(dataset, path=download_path, unzip=True)
     21        print(f"Dataset downloaded and extracted to {download_path}")
     22        return
     23
     24    # Example usage
     25    download_kaggle_dataset('goelyash/165-different-snakes-species', './snakes_dataset')
     26

⮑  Warning: Your Kaggle API key is readable by other users on this system! To fix this, you can run 'chmo
    Dataset URL: https://www.kaggle.com/datasets/goelyash/165-different-snakes-species
    Dataset downloaded and extracted to ./snakes_dataset
```

Figure 6.9: Download snakes dataset

Figure 6.9 shows the code and output for a function to download data from the Kaggle website. Lines #1 and #2 display the initial prompts provided to GPT-4o. Not shown here are additional prompts used to guide the process, such as creating an account on Kaggle, retrieving the Kaggle API key, and installing the Kaggle library.

Lines #4 and #5 import the OS and Kaggle libraries necessary for managing file paths and interacting with Kaggle's API. Line #7 defines the **download_kaggle_dataset()** function with two parameters: **dataset** and **download_path**. Lines #8 through #14 provide inline documentation for the function, explaining its purpose and usage. Lines #16 and #17 check for the existence of the specified local **download_path** and create the local directory if it does not already exist.

Line #20 using the Kaggle's API to download the data using the function **dataset_download_files()**. We set **unzip** equal to **True** to unpack the dataset automatically. Lastly, line #25 downloads the snake's dataset.

The output shows the images download successfully in the local directory **./snakes_dataset.**

The next step is to import the data into a Pandas DataFrame. We will use all the fun methods from Pandas that we learned in *Chapter 5, Pandas, the Data Tamer*.

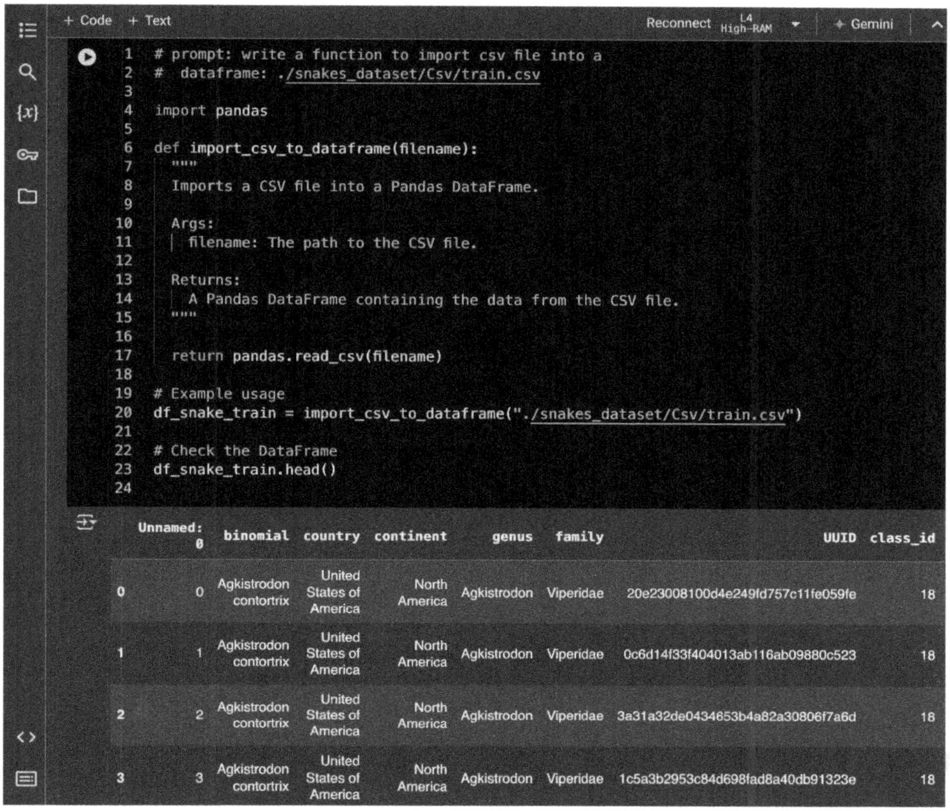

Figure 6.10: *Import snake data to DataFrame*

Figure 6.10 displays the code and output for importing the metadata file from the snake dataset into a Pandas DataFrame. Before we could do that, we had to do some detective work. Downloading and unzipping data from Kaggle is just the first step—the real challenge lies in understanding the dataset's structure. Unlike curated datasets from official organizations, Kaggle datasets come from researchers and individuals worldwide, meaning there is no standard format. The data is raw, often messy, and requires investigation before use.

After exploring the downloaded files, we found two CSV files containing metadata for the dataset. We first asked GPT-4o to import **train.csv**, as seen in Lines #1 and #2. The second file, **test.csv**, contains additional metadata and follows a similar structure.

The following code should feel familiar since we studied the Pandas library in *Chapter 5, Pandas, the Data Tamer*. Line #4 imports the Pandas library. Line #6 defines the **import_csv_to_dataframe()** function, taking **filename** as an input parameter. Lines #7 through #15 provide inline documentation explaining the function's purpose. Finally, Line #17 reads the CSV file into a Pandas DataFrame and returns it. This simple function allows us to load and explore the dataset efficiently, setting the stage for further analysis.

Line #20 calls the **import_csv_to_dataframe()** function to create the **df_snake_train** DataFrame, and Line #23 displays the first five records using the Pandas **head()** function.

The output presents a neatly structured table containing the metadata of the image set. Our first look at the dataset reveals its columns: **Uname: 0, binomial, country, continent, genus, family, UUID, class_id**, and a few more that extend off-screen to the right. The first record includes values such as **0, Agkistrodon contortrix, United States of America, North America, Agkistrodon, Viperidae, 20e23008100d4e249fd757c11fe059fe, 18**, along with additional data to the right. The second, third, and subsequent records follow a similar structure.

At first glance, the dataset appears messy, containing information we may not need for our CNN model. It is a common challenge with real-world data, and before moving forward, we need to clean and refine it to ensure we are working with relevant and structured information. We start with the data-cleaning process.

Clean dataset

Our goal for the CNN model is simple: determine whether a snake in an image is poisonous or safe. To do this, we only need two key pieces of information: the image location and a label indicating whether the snake is poisonous or not.

As we learned in *Chapter 5, Pandas, the Data Tamer*, the best way to start working with a dataset is by understanding its structure. We will begin by inspecting the records using the **info()** function to see what we are working with before cleaning and refining the data.

```
# prompt: print df_snake_train info

df_snake_train.info()
```

```
<class 'pandas.core.frame.DataFrame'>
RangeIndex: 23816 entries, 0 to 23815
Data columns (total 14 columns):
 #   Column            Non-Null Count  Dtype
---  ------            --------------  -----
 0   Unnamed: 0        23816 non-null  int64
 1   binomial          23816 non-null  object
 2   country           23816 non-null  object
 3   continent         23816 non-null  object
 4   genus             23816 non-null  object
 5   family            23816 non-null  object
 6   UUID              23816 non-null  object
 7   class_id          23816 non-null  int64
 8   snake_sub_family  23816 non-null  object
 9   poisonous         23816 non-null  int64
 10  X                 23816 non-null  float64
 11  Y                 23816 non-null  float64
 12  height            23816 non-null  float64
 13  width             23816 non-null  float64
dtypes: float64(4), int64(3), object(7)
memory usage: 2.5+ MB
```

Figure 6.11: Snake image dataset metadata

Figure 6.11 presents the code and output for inspecting the training dataset. Line #1 shows the GPT-4o prompt, while Line #3 runs the Pandas **info()** method to examine the data structure.

The output reveals that the dataset contains 23,816 records across 14 columns with no missing values. The columns include **Unnamed: 0, binomial, country, continent, genus, family, UUID, class_id, snake_sub_family, poisonous, X, Y, height, and width**. Since there are no **null** values, we do not need to handle missing data before training the model.

We followed the same process to inspect the **test.csv** file and found a similar structure with fewer records. This dataset will serve as our validation data when training the CNN model, ensuring we can test its performance on unseen images.

However, one crucial detail is missing. The dataset does not explicitly tell us how each metadata entry maps to an image file. A bit of detective work reveals that the image path is constructed by combining the base directory with the **class_id** (column 7) and **UUID** (column 6). The next step is to add an image path column to the DataFrame. The following code and output show how we accomplish this.

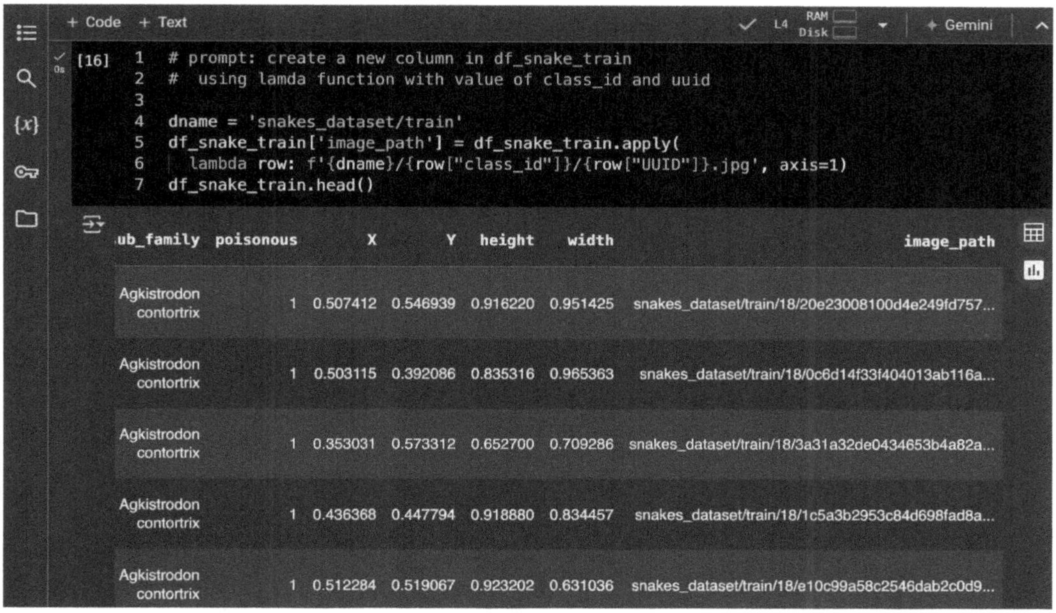

Figure 6.12: Adding image_path column

Figure 6.12 shows the code and output for creating a new column for the image path. Lines #1 and #2 are the final GPT-4o prompt. There are other try-and-error prompts not shown. When interacting with GPT-4, it is essential to understand that experimentation is a valuable part of the process. We learned prompt engineering techniques in *Chapter 1, Introduction to GenAI,* so do not hesitate to try and make mistakes. They are a natural part of learning and refining your techniques.

Line #5 defines the starting image path name. Lines #5 and #6 create a new column and assign a new path for each record using a **lambda** function.

It is necessary to emphasize that relying on GPT-4o does not mean turning off our critical thinking. While GPT-4o is a powerful tool for generating code, explaining concepts, and accelerating development, it does not replace the need for careful investigation and logical reasoning.

GPT-4o cannot determine how image paths are structured. We did that ourselves. By analyzing the existing records, identifying patterns, and cross-referencing column values, we deduced that the image path is formed by combining the base directory, **class_id**, and **UUID**. This step required human intuition, problem-solving, and an understanding of how datasets are typically organized.

It is crucial to distinguish that GPT-4o can execute instructions and generate solutions based on known patterns. Still, it lacks true reasoning or specific domain insight unless provided with the proper context. The AI can suggest possible file structures, but we must verify whether those structures align with the dataset at hand.

In real-world AI development, this balance between automation and human expertise is fundamental. We use GPT-4o to streamline repetitive tasks and fill in knowledge gaps, but we remain responsible for the interpretation, validation, and decision-making that drive the project forward. Understanding this relationship makes us more effective AI developers. Ones who use AI as a tool, not a crutch.

Now that we have established how to construct the image path. We test whether our logic and code are correct by displaying a snake image using the **image_path** column. The code and output are as follows.

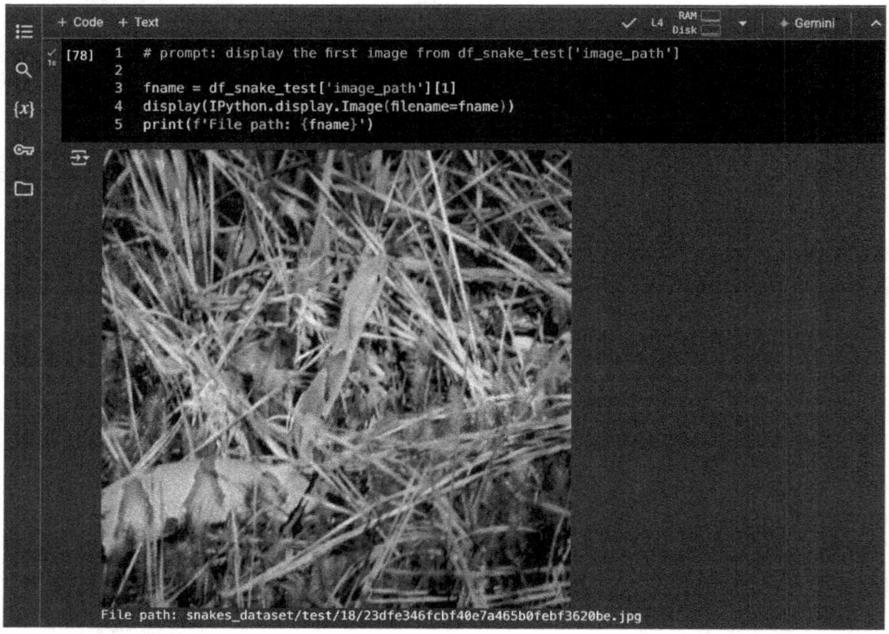

Figure 6.13: Display a snake image from the train dataset

Figure 6.13 shows the code and output for displaying an image using the new image path column. Line #1 is the GPT-4o prompt. Line #3 takes the second record of the file path name, index value 1. Line #4 displays the image, and Line #5 prints the path name.

The output is an image of a snake, and the file path name is: **snakes_dataset/ test/18/23dfe346fcbf40e7a465b0febf3620be.jpg.**

The next step is to merge the training and test DataFrames. To keep track of them, we create a new column called **is_valid** and mark the test dataset as **True** and the training dataset as **False**.

Continue cleaning the data, we notice the **poisonous** column currently uses one for poisonous and zero for non-poisonous, which works fine for the model but is not human-friendly value. To make the data easier to read, we will replace these values with **poisonous** and **safe**, making it clearer at a glance.

Next, we will clean up the dataset by dropping all unnecessary columns and keeping only the ones, we actually need: the image path, the poisonous or safe label, and **is_valid**, which indicates whether the image belongs to the training or testing set. The last step is shown as follows:

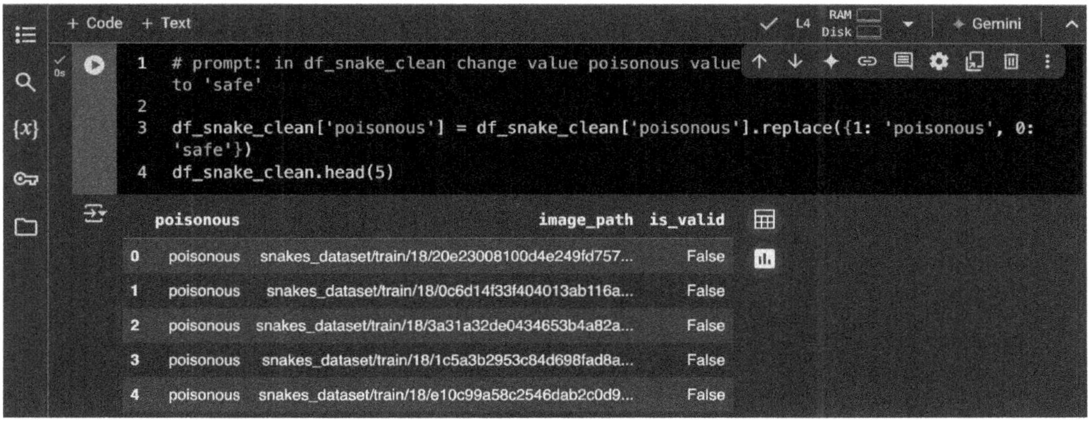

Figure 6.14: Cleaned snake metadata

Figure 6.14 presents the code and output for the final step in cleaning the dataset metadata. Line #1 contains the GPT-4o prompt. Line #3 updates the values in the poisonous column, changing one to poisonous and zero to safe, making the data more readable. Line #4 then displays the first five records using the **head()** function.

The output is a well-structured table containing the columns we need for the CNN model training, with the correct values in place. The final dataset consists of only three essential columns: **poisonous**, **image_path**, and **is_valid**.

You are left to explore the behind-the-scenes cleaning steps, such as merging the train and test datasets and dropping unnecessary column. The cleaning process involves the same

Pandas functions and techniques covered in Chapter 5, *Pandas, the Data Tamer*, making it an excellent opportunity to reinforce your understanding by replicating the process independently.

The data loader is essential for several key tasks, including batching, shuffling, and data augmentation. Batching groups multiple images together for each training step, enhancing both speed and stability in the training process. Shuffling randomizes the order of the data, preventing the model from memorizing specific patterns. Data augmentation modifies images in various ways to improve the model's generalization ability.

In summary, the data loader is crucial in CNN's training. It ensures the data is well-organized, properly formatted, and ready for the model to learn, making large-scale training more efficient and manageable. The code and output for creating the data loader are as follows.

```
1  # prompt: creat data loader using Fast.ai with df_snake dataframe,
2  #  X (image) value in column 1 and Y (label) value in column 0,
3  #  and use column 2 to denote validation set.
4  #  AND use many other prompts.
5
6  import fastai
7  import fastai.vision
8  import fastai.vision.data
9
10 # use Fast.ai ImageDataLoaders() function
11 dloaders_snake = fastai.vision.data.ImageDataLoaders.from_df(
12    #1 source
13    df_snake_clean, path='./',
14    #2 (ImageBlock, CategoryBlock), get_x, get_y
15    fn_col=1, label_col=0,
16    #3 spliter, not using random 80/20
17    valid_col=2,
18    #4 transform and image augmentation
19    item_tfms=fastai.vision.augment.Resize(512),
20    batch_tfms=fastai.vision.augment.aug_transforms(do_flip=True, flip_vert=False),
21    #5 batchsize, dataloader
22    bs=32
23 )
```

Figure 6.15: Create the data loader

Figure 6.15 shows the code used to create the data loader from the cleaned snake dataset. Developing this was not a straightforward process. After multiple iterations of refining our prompts for GPT-4, we eventually consulted Dr. Howard's Fast.ai book to establish the correct data loader setup. The result is a few code lines encapsulating potentially required months of deep learning expertise.

Lines #1 through #4 provide a portion of the prompt used to generate the code. Line #7 defines the data loader utilizing Fast.ai's **from_df()** method. Line #13 inputs the cleaned dataset, **df_snake_clean**, which includes only the necessary columns. In Line #15, the input data, commonly called X in CNN, is defined. The label, often called Y, is also defined in the same line. Finally, Line #17 specifies the **is_valid** column, indicating whether an image belongs to the training or validation set.

Line #19 applies item augmentation, ensuring all images are resized to a uniform 512×512 pixels. Line #20 defines batch augmentation, introducing transformations such as flips or color adjustments to help the model generalize. Finally, Line #22 sets the batch size to 32, meaning the model will process 32 images simultaneously, balancing computational efficiency and learning stability.

At first glance, this code may seem deceptively simple, but it could take months of deep learning. Do not worry if you do not fully understand every concept right away. Studying each component, such as image preprocessing, batch training, and data augmentation, will take time to master the concepts behind the code. Fully explaining each of these elements would require an entire book. For now, it is essential to recognize that the data loader is not just responsible for loading data. It is a carefully designed system that ensures the CNN model receives structured, well-prepared input for effective learning.

If all works correctly, we can ask the data loader to display an image batch.

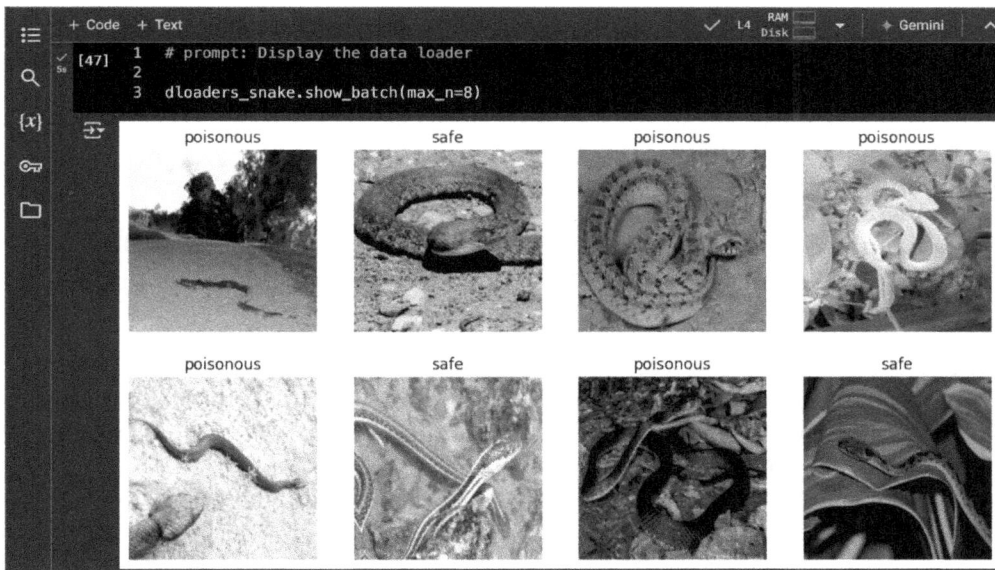

Figure 6.16: Display data loader batch

Figure 6.16 displays the code and output for visualizing a data loader batch. Line #1 contains the GPT-4o prompt, while Line #3 uses Fast.ai's **show_batch()** function to display a batch of eight images from the data loader. The batch size used for training was 32, which does not limit how many photos we can display. The batch size for visualization is independent of the model's training configuration.

The output consists of eight thumbnail images of snakes, each labeled at the top as either poisonous or safe. Each time the **show_batch()** function runs, a new set of randomly selected images appears, enabling us to glimpse the entire dataset. Some photos clearly show the snake, while in others, the snake is barely visible, blending into the background, coiled under leaves, or mostly obscured by shadows. These are not carefully curated research images taken in a controlled setting. They are raw, real-world images captured in nature, where even human eyes may struggle to spot the snake, let alone classify it.

This dataset perfectly illustrates the power of CNN image classification. Most of us are not snake enthusiasts or ophiologists, yet we can train a machine to do a task that requires years of training and practice. The ability to teach AI to recognize patterns that humans may overlook is what makes CNNs transformative in fields from medical diagnostics to wildlife conservation.

It is noteworthy to highlight that in CNN image classification and segmentation, preparing a clean, organized, and accurately labeled dataset typically takes up 50% to 65% of the effort in a typical CNN project. Getting the data ready for training is often the most challenging aspect. Now that we have accomplished this, it is time to celebrate! Let us break out the disco music and dance. The arduous part is behind us. Now, we do the fun part and train the model.

Training the model

Now comes the moment we have been working toward. It is time to unveil the magic and train your snake classification CNN using the Fast.ai library. This process is where deep learning truly comes to life. Fast.ai is a powerful library and platform that abstracts away much of the complexity behind CNNs, allowing you to focus on building effective models without spending two years in a CS graduate program just to understand the fundamentals.

Teaching CNNs is not a one-size-fits-all process. Every professor, researcher, and book take a slightly different approach. Professor *Jeremy Howard*, the creator of Fast.ai, emphasizes hands-on learning, teaching CNNs from the ground up with real-world examples. While this book introduces CNN coding, it is not a comprehensive technology study of CNN. If you want to master CNNs, *Deep Learning for Coders with Fastai and PyTorch* by Professor Howard is an essential read.

During this process, GPT-4o has been a great help in writing code and understanding the structure and best practices of Fast.ai. It provides quick explanations and helps debug errors, making it feel like having a personal tutor. After thorough research with GPT-4o and other resources, we have pinpointed three key components needed to build a CNN model successfully using the `dloader_snake` data loader from the previous section.

The three components are as follows:

- Selecting a base model
- Finding the learning rate
- Fine-tuning the model

We will begin by selecting the model.

Selecting a base model

A base model such as ResNet34 is a pre-trained neural network trained on extensive datasets like the ImageNet dataset. These models comprise various layers, including convolutional layers, pooling layers, and fully connected layers, each designed to capture different levels of feature abstraction.

Using a pre-existing model is known as **transfer learning** or **fine-tuning**. This method enables the scientific community to avoid the extensive effort and cost of building a new CNN or LLM model from the ground up. Training a CNN or LLM model from scratch would require tens of millions of dollars and access to large computer server farms for months. In other words, most programmers and researchers must use transfer learning methods to work with CNN or LLM.

ResNet34, short for Residual Network with 34 layers, is a highly effective base architecture. Its key innovation is the introduction of residual connections, or shortcuts that allow the model to bypass one or more layers. This architecture enables ResNet34 to learn complex patterns more effectively and with greater stability. There are hundreds of pre-trained models that you can use as a base architecture. They are grouped into families such as ResNet, EfficientNet, DenseNet, and many more.

These pre-trained models contain learned parameters from extensive training. The weights reflect the model's understanding of different features from the diverse training data. When you use a pre-trained model, you leverage these optimized weights, which can significantly accelerate the training process for your specific task. Instead of starting from random initial weights, which require significant data and time for optimization, you begin with weights that already capture valuable patterns.

In summary, a base model like ResNet34 is a pre-trained neural network that has already learned patterns from large datasets like ImageNet. Instead of training from scratch, which is costly and time-consuming, most developers use transfer learning to adapt existing models.

The following code and output demonstrate how to create the Fast.ai learner object, using the data loader, **dloaders_snake**, from the previous section.

```
# prompt: define learner using fast.ai

import torchvision
base_model = "torchvision.models.resnet.resnet34"
learner_snake = vision_learner(dloaders_snake,
  torchvision.models.resnet.resnet34,
  metrics=fastai.metrics.error_rate)
```

Figure 6.17: Learner object

Figure 6.17 shows the code for defining a learner object. Line #1 contains the GPT-4o prompt. Additional prompts and several hours of consulting Professor Howard's book informed the subsequent lines. Line #3 imports the **torchvision** library.

Line #4 defines the ResNet34 model, while lines #5 through #7 create the learner object named **learner_snake** using the data loader **dloaders_snake** mentioned in the previous *Data Loader* section.

Before proceeding to the next section, we take a closer look at the Fast.ai learner object. We used GPT-4o and Jupyter Notebook and dedicated several hours to asking questions and running code in Jupyter Notebook, aiming to explore its intricacies. Below, you will find the code and output from our efforts.

```python
1  # prompt: display learner data
2  # and many other tries (prompt engineering technique)
3
4  def print_learner_meta_info(learner):
5      print(f"{str('Learner epoch'):20} : {learner.n_epoch}")
6      print(f"{str('Learner momentum'):20} : {learner.moms}")
7      print(f"{str('Learner rate'):20} : {learner.lr}")
8      print_dloader_meta_info(learner.dls)
9      return
10
11 # sample run
12 print_learner_meta_info(learner_snake)
```

```
Learner epoch        : 1
Learner momentum     : (0.95, 0.85, 0.95)
Learner rate         : 0.001
Batch size           : 32
Dataset Train size   : 23816
Dataset Valid size   : 3138
Vocab size           : 2
Vocab first label    : poisonous
Vocab last label     : safe
```

Figure 6.18: Print learner metadata

Figure 6.18 shows the code and output for printing the learner attributes. Lines #1 and #2 are the GPT-4o prompts. Line #4 defines the function **print_learner_meta_info()**. Lines #5 through #8 print the learner object attributes, and line #12 runs the function.

Among other information, the output shows that the batch size is 32, the training dataset has 23,816 photos, the valid (or test) dataset has 3,138 snake photos, and the vocab has poisonous and safe values. It tells us that the learner object is created correctly with the information from the data loader, **dloader_snake**.

The default learning rate is 0.001. Next, we will find an optimized learning rate.

Finding the learning rate

The second step in training your CNN is finding the optimal learning rate. It is the speed at which the model learns. If the learning rate is too high, the model jumps around chaotically and never settles. If it is too low, learning drags on forever without making much progress. Fast.ai simplifies this process with a single line of code to automatically find the best learning rate. By default, Fast.ai sets it to 0.001, but it also provides functions to adjust learning rates dynamically based on the dataset.

Think of the learning rate as adjusting the water temperature in a shower. If you turn the knob too far, the water becomes scalding, causing you to jump away quickly. The process resembles an unstable model that never converges. Conversely, if the adjustment is minimal, the water stays cold, leading to a long wait to warm up. The analogous model learns too slowly. The key is to find the right balance, just like tweaking the knob until the water feels comfortable. In deep learning, techniques such as adaptive optimizers, including AdaGrad, RMSprop, and Adam, and learning rate schedules help fine-tune this balance, ensuring the model learns efficiently and effectively.

The code for calculating the optimal learning rate for the snake datasets are as follows:

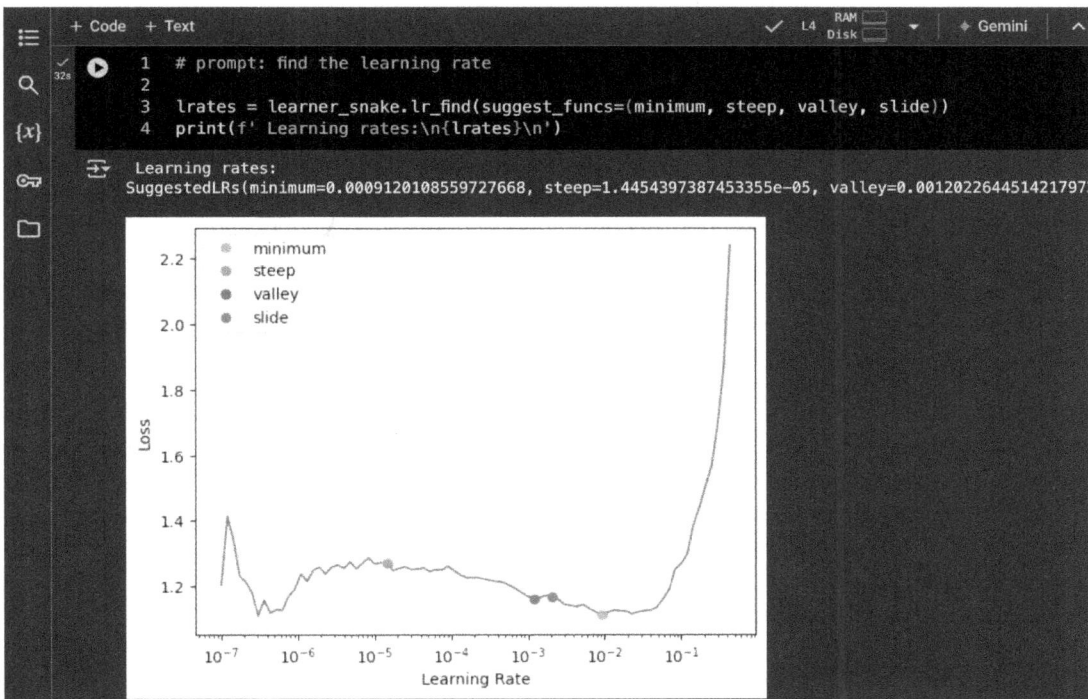

Figure 6.19: Learning rate finder

Figure 6.19 shows the code and output for finding the optimal learning rate specifically for the snake image dataset. Line #1 is the GPT-4o prompt. Line #3 defines the learning rates using Fast.ai **lr_find()** function, and line four print the output.

The output shows the beautiful line graphs for the four possible learning rate values specifically for the snake dataset. On the graph, from left to right, the learning rate are

steep, 1.4454e-05, the most conservative learning rate, then the **valley** learning rate, follow by the **slide** learning rate, and finally the left most, the **minimum** learning rate, the most aggressive learning rate, 9.1201e-02.

After research using book and GPT-4o, we conclude to choose the second to the most aggressive learning rate, which is the **slide** learning rate, 2.0892e-03. Notice every dataset will have different order and value for the four learning rates.

We have selected a base architecture, established the learner object, and calculated the optimal learning rate for the snake image dataset. It is time to free it and learn.

Fine-tuning the model

Looking back at our progress, we have downloaded the real-world snake image dataset from the Kaggle website, imported the metadata into a DataFrame, cleaned and augmented the metadata, created a data loader, selected the base architecture ResNet34, initialized the learner, calculated the learning rate, and chose the Slide learning rate. The final step is to train the model to predict whether the snake is poisonous or not.

To provide more insight, we have built a fully functional deep-learning pipeline. The snake dataset has been carefully chosen, ensuring each image is correctly labeled as poisonous or safe and mapped to its corresponding metadata. The data loader is set up to efficiently feed images into the model in batches, applying necessary transformations like resizing and augmentation. The choice of ResNet34 as our base model leverages pre-trained knowledge, drastically reducing the time and data needed for effective training. The learner object is fully initialized, and the learning rate has been optimized to balance fast convergence with stable performance.

Now, we are moving into the most exciting phase: training the model. All the previous steps come together in this stage, enabling the CNN to refine its ability to distinguish between poisonous and safe snakes based on the patterns learned from the dataset. With the fine-tuning process, the model will adjust its final layers to our specific dataset and then gradually update all layers to improve classification accuracy. Each epoch will bring incremental improvements, fine-tuning the network's ability to recognize subtle differences between poisonous or safe snakes.

Training a CNN involves more than simply executing a function; it requires a deep understanding of how the model learns and the ability to make adjustments throughout the process. Monitoring training performance, fine-tuning hyperparameters, and evaluating accuracy are all essential steps. By the end of this process, we will have a trained model for snake classification that can make predictions on new, unseen images, showcasing the effectiveness of transfer learning in real-world AI applications.

The code for fine-tuning the snake image classification model is as follows.

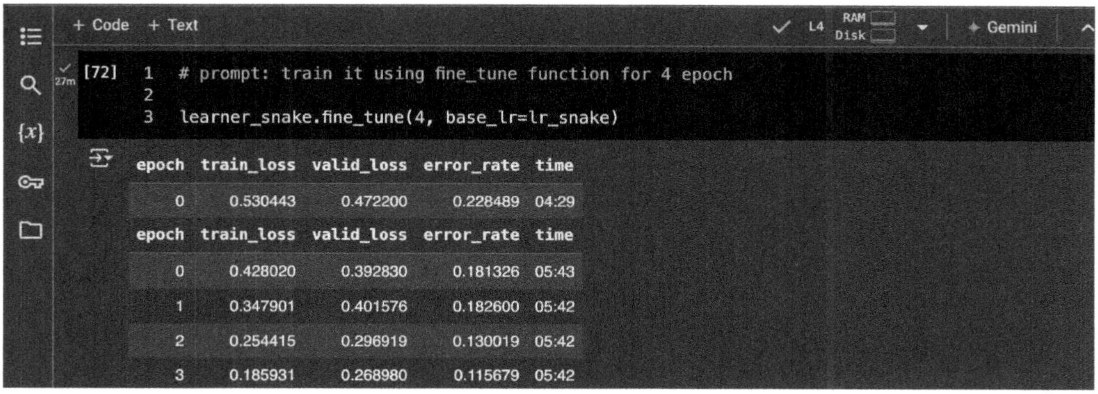

```
[72] 1 # prompt: train it using fine_tune function for 4 epoch
     2
     3 learner_snake.fine_tune(4, base_lr=lr_snake)
```

epoch	train_loss	valid_loss	error_rate	time
0	0.530443	0.472200	0.228489	04:29

epoch	train_loss	valid_loss	error_rate	time
0	0.428020	0.392830	0.181326	05:43
1	0.347901	0.401576	0.182600	05:42
2	0.254415	0.296919	0.130019	05:42
3	0.185931	0.268980	0.115679	05:42

Figure 6.20: *Fine tune snake classification model*

Figure 6.20 presents the code and output of the fine-tuning process for our snake classification CNN model. The training process begins in Line #1, where we prompt GPT-4o for assistance. Line #3 trains the model using Fast.ai's **`fine_tune()`** function.

The output table displays key training metrics, including epoch, training loss, validation loss, error rate, and time taken. Each row represents an epoch, illustrating how the model improves with each training cycle.

After fine-tuning, the final error rate is 0.115679, which translates to an accuracy of 88.4% in classifying a snake as either poisonous or safe. The entire training process took approximately 26 minutes using Google Colab Nvidia GPU with 16 GB of GPU RAM. In contrast, if the training were conducted on a CPU-only server or laptop, it would take significantly longer, ranging from 14 to 24 hours. Utilizing GPUs for deep learning tasks demonstrates a substantial advantage.

Examining the training and validation loss values, we see no signs of overfitting. The results indicate that our decision to apply data augmentation during the data loader setup is effective. If we want to increase accuracy beyond 88.4%, we have several options: increase the number of epochs or adjust the learning rate. However, the most significant improvement in accuracy would come from expanding and cleaning our dataset by adding more diverse images of snakes in the wild.

Central to the CNN process is a shift in our approach to problem-solving. Instead of identifying poisonous snakes using sequential logic, like finding the snake in the photo and analyzing their size or pattern, we let the model do the work. It learns from data and makes predictions on its own.

The transition from sequential programming to ML is precisely why CNNs are featured in this beginner Python book. By embracing AI's capacity to recognize patterns that may elude human perception, we can tackle complex tasks that might otherwise be impossible. Snake enthusiasts or herpetologists may have problems identifying non-curated snake photos as poisonous. While humans struggle to recognize subtle patterns, the CNN algorithm can detect features we might overlook.

Next, we will review the output of the CNN model.

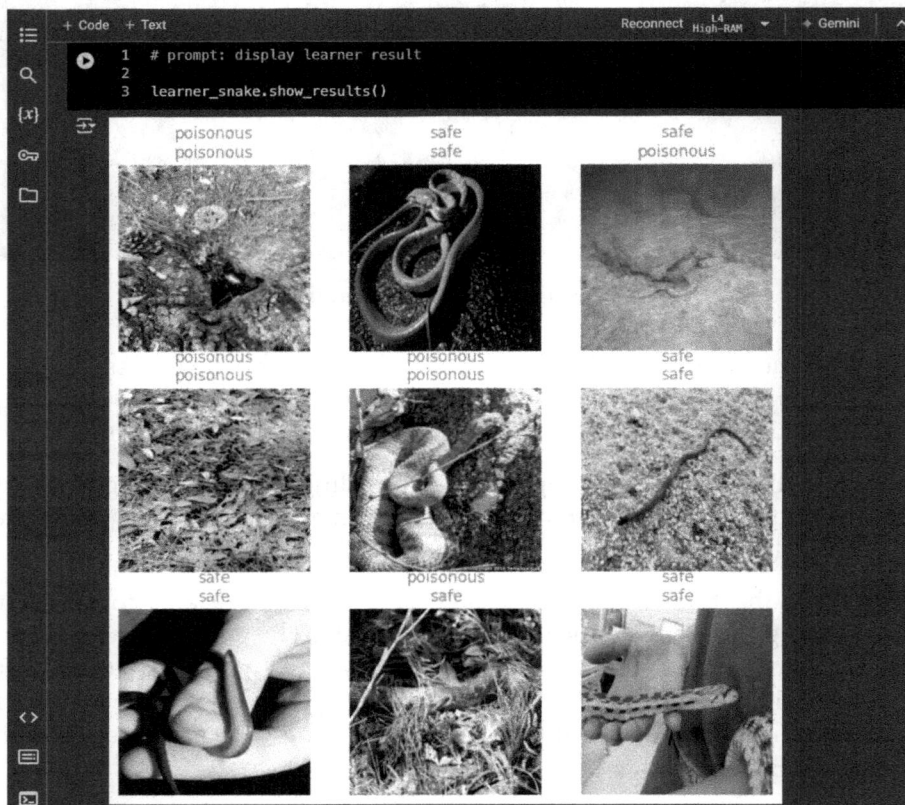

Figure 6.21: Result of snake CNN model

Figure 6.21 displays the code and output of our trained snake classification CNN model. Line #1 is the GPT-4o prompt, and line #3 uses Fast.ai's **show_result()** function to visualize the model's predictions. Each time you run **show_result()**, a new set of images is displayed, allowing you to see different predictions in action.

The output consists of nine thumbnail images of snakes, each with two labels. The top label shows the model's prediction, while the bottom label displays the actual truth. When both labels match, the model got it right; if they differ, it was an incorrect prediction.

With 88.4% accuracy, our model can identify whether a snake is poisonous or safe better than most humans. Recognizing a snake in the wild is no easy task, even for trained experts. Lighting, angles, camouflage, and background noise all make identification difficult. Yet, our CNN model has learned to analyze subtle patterns and key features, distinguishing between poisonous or not with impressive precision.

This level of accuracy puts our model on par with the top 1% of snake identification experts and herpetologists. People who have spent years studying reptiles in the field. *The difference?* Your model can do it instantly, at scale, and without fatigue. It does not need years of training, just well-labeled data and a few lines of optimized code.

That is no small achievement, and you will not find many beginner Python books that take you this far. Most introductory books focus on simple Python scripts or basic data analysis. In this case, you have built an AI-powered classification model using real-world datasets and advanced deep-learning techniques. You have not just learned Python; you have also ventured into the realms of AI, ML, and practical problem-solving with CNNs.

We have accomplished our task. Let us bring it together with a conclusion.

Conclusion

In this chapter, you embarked on a stimulating journey through the concepts and algorithms of ML and CNNs, uncovering why these techniques stand apart from sequential programming logic, like the bubble sort algorithm. You see firsthand how ML solves problems beyond the reach of standard sequential programming, shifting from explicit algorithms to models that learn from data. Along the way, you used GPT-4o as your tutor and coding assistant, making the complex world of AI more interactive, accessible, and efficient.

Beyond theory, you take practical steps of searching for, downloading, and structuring real-world image datasets from Kaggle, including the snake classification dataset. You wrote Python code using Fast.ai to train a CNN model capable of distinguishing poisonous from non-poisonous snakes. The process was not just about coding. It involved understanding how each step, including data preparation, augmentation, model selection, and training, contributes to building an AI system that can make intelligent predictions.

Through Jupyter Notebooks, you tested and refined your model, transforming complex theories into hands-on, practical skills. Unlike many beginner Python books that stop at simple scripting, this chapter has equipped you with real-world AI tools, bridging the gap between introductory programming and applied ML. In the end, you successfully built a CNN model with 88.4% accuracy, surpassing most human experts in snake poisonous identification.

This journey has also changed the way you think about programming. You learned the differences between traditional flowchart logic and the layered structure of CNNs, where fully connected nodes and activation functions allow the model to extract patterns independently. Along the way, you developed a solid understanding of key AI terminology, including AI, ML, deep learning, CNNs, LLMs, and Generative AI, which positions you well for further exploration in this field.

Fast.ai has been a game-changer, simplifying CNN programming while leveraging state-of-the-art techniques. Handling real-world datasets from Kaggle has become second nature, and you made informed choices, selecting ResNet34 as your base architecture and fine-tuning your model by optimizing the learning rate. What once took months and millions of dollars can now be done in minutes with a few lines of Python, thanks to transfer learning and pre-trained models.

The true achievement goes beyond simply coding a CNN. It involves a fundamental shift in mindset. Rather than manually defining rules for identifying snakes, you have created a model that learns from experience, adapts, and improves independently. You no longer need to be an expert in snakes to classify them accurately. Your CNN model accomplishes this for you. The power of AI lies in utilizing machine intelligence to address complex problems at scale.

This chapter was not just about learning CNNs. It was about transforming your approach to problem-solving. You entered a field where artificial intelligence is not merely theoretical. It is a practical tool that you can utilize to unlock possibilities that extend far beyond traditional sequential programming. Now, it is up to you to take this knowledge further.

The next chapter is about Hugging Face deployment.

Join our book's Discord space

Join the book's Discord Workspace for Latest updates, Offers, Tech happenings around the world, New Release and Sessions with the Authors:

https://discord.bpbonline.com

CHAPTER 7

Gradio and Hugging Face Deployment

Introduction

Deploying Python projects to a website is a crucial milestone in your Python programming journey. This book is about learning by doing, applying real-world experience rather than memorizing syntax. We began by building a calculator, exploring sorting algorithms, and practicing and exploring the Pandas library. Eventually, we developed a **Convolutional Neural Networks (CNNs)** model to classify poisonous snakes using photos taken by users. Now, as a natural progression, we are ready to take the next step: deploying our applications to the web.

Unlike other beginner Python books that force-feed algorithms and advanced Python built-in functions like `zip()`, we focus on practical skills that matter. Memorization fades, but exploration and application build lasting expertise. *Besides, why memorize everything when GPT-4o is your personal tutor, armed with the collective knowledge of thousands of programmers?* Instead of drilling abstract exercises, you will learn how to build, deploy, and share real applications because that is what coding is all about.

As of November 2024, countless platforms claim to make building web pages and apps effortless, offering drag-and-drop dashboards that let you piece everything together without writing a single line of code. Just click, drag, and your app is live. No coding is required. That sounds tempting, but the reality is that if you are here to learn Python, simply clicking buttons or dragging images will not help you learn.

We use Hugging Face, a platform specifically designed for Python developers who want complete control over their applications. It is tailored for AI projects, making it easy to deploy models, test ideas, and launch real-world applications. With tools like Jupyter Notebook and the Python Gradio library, it is particularly well-suited for Python beginners.

You are not doing this alone. GPT-4o is here as your tutor and coding assistant, guiding you through every step. Whether you need help debugging, optimizing performance, or troubleshooting deployment, GPT-4o is your on-demand mentor. Instead of just following instructions, you will be learning how to think like a developer, making decisions, solving problems, and understanding why things work the way they do.

By choosing Hugging Face, Gradio library, and Python, you are not just building an app. You are developing the skills to create and deploy anything you imagine. That is the difference between being a user and becoming a programmer.

As with every chapter, we start this one with a clear and structured layout to guide our journey.

Structure

You will learn how to deploy your Python application on the Hugging Face website, and in particular, the following topics:

- Deployment trio
- Deployment code
- Deploy on Hugging Face
- Create Hugging Face space
- Design with Gradio

Objectives

The goal of this chapter is to demystify deployment, giving you a practical understanding of what it takes to bring your Python projects online. You will explore deployment fundamentals, covering both server-side and browser-side programming, and see how APIs connect everything together. Rather than just discussing concepts, you will write actual Python code, build APIs, and deploy them directly from Jupyter Notebook to the Hugging Face platform.

An essential part of this process is learning Gradio, a Python library designed to create interactive web interfaces for AI models and applications. Instead of building complex front-end components from scratch, Gradio allows you to integrate user-friendly UI elements with just a few lines of code. By the end of this chapter, you will understand how deployment works and have hands-on experience in making your Python projects accessible on the web.

Your journey begins with three key players: server-side programming, client-side interaction, and APIs, the foundation of modern mobile and web applications.

Deployment trio

Before we start coding, it is essential to break deployment down into its three core components: client-side, server-side, and APIs. Understanding these concepts will give you a clear mental model of how web, iPhone, and tablet applications function before we learn to write Python code.

Consider deployment as a conversation among different parts of a system. The client side is where users interact with the web page, iPhone, or tablet, which includes buttons, text fields, images, and everything else visible. The server side is responsible for the heavy lifting, handling the logic, database interactions, and AI processing that power the application. The API connects these two sides, which acts as a middleman, ensuring smooth communication between the client and the server.

To clarify these concepts, we will use the following diagram, created using the Python Graphviz library, as a visual guide. Bridging the gap between theory and practice will set the stage for the code we are about to write.

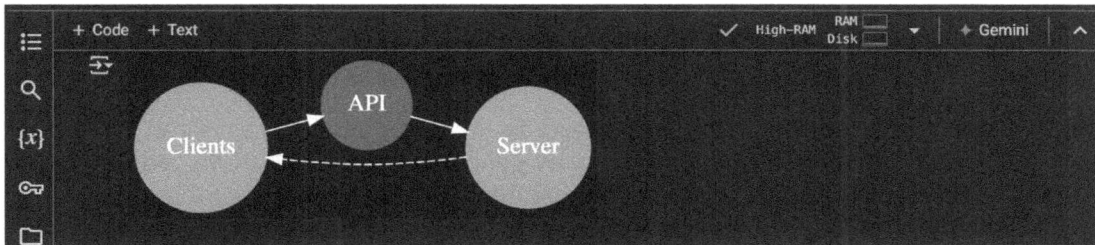

Figure 7.1: Deployment process

Figure 7.1 presents the output of a flow diagram generated using the Graphviz library. The Python code is not shown because our focus here is learning deployment, not drawing process flows. If you need a refresher on Graphviz, we covered it in *Chapter 4, Sorting on My Mind*, where we used it to visualize sorting algorithms.

The figure illustrates how a web application communicates across its three core components: the client, the API, and the server. On the far left, the client circle represents a user requesting data. For example, the action could be someone clicking a button on an app or entering a search query. The request is sent across the network, represented by an arrow pointing to the API circle, which acts as the middleman, transferring the request to the server circle. The server processes the request, retrieves the necessary data or performs computations, and returns the response. A dotted line returning from the server to the client represents the processed data being sent back to the user.

This simple flow is the foundation of every modern web and mobile application. In the next section, we will break down these concepts in more detail, ensuring you understand how each part works before we start writing code. The three components are as follows:

- Client side
- API
- Server side

The initial start is with the users on the client side.

Client side

The client-side refers to the **Graphical User Interface (GUI)**, which includes everything a user interacts with when using a web or mobile app. The UI component may contain text fields, images, animations, buttons, dropdown menus, lists, links, or interactive forms. Essentially, anything visible and clickable is part of the client side.

The method for building a client-side application depends on the platform. Native mobile apps require different programming languages depending on the operating system. For example, developers use Swift language in iPhone or iPad apps, while Android apps use Kotlin or Java language. On the other hand, the foundation for applications running in a web browser are HTML, CSS, and JavaScript, which work across all major browsers, including Google Chrome, Apple Safari, Microsoft Edge, and Firefox.

This chapter focuses on building web-based applications using Python and the Gradio library. Gradio makes it easy by automatically generating the HTML, CSS, and JavaScript needed for our app. Focusing on one coding language, like Python, is more practical for beginner programmers. It does not require you to learn additional front-end languages. Gradio acts like a bridge, translating our Python code into a format that web browsers can understand.

You might wonder why one would not learn HTML, CSS, and JavaScript directly. The answer lies in efficiency. Many developers specialize in a single programming language and utilize frameworks or libraries for other aspects of development. Languages such as Python, PHP, and Java are frequently employed to create dynamic user interfaces without writing extensive front-end code.

In this chapter, we will build the GUI for a calculator app, a practical example of how Python can create interactive web applications. Before beginning coding, it is meaningful to take a sneak peek at both the rendered UI and the underlying HTML and CSS code generated by Python.

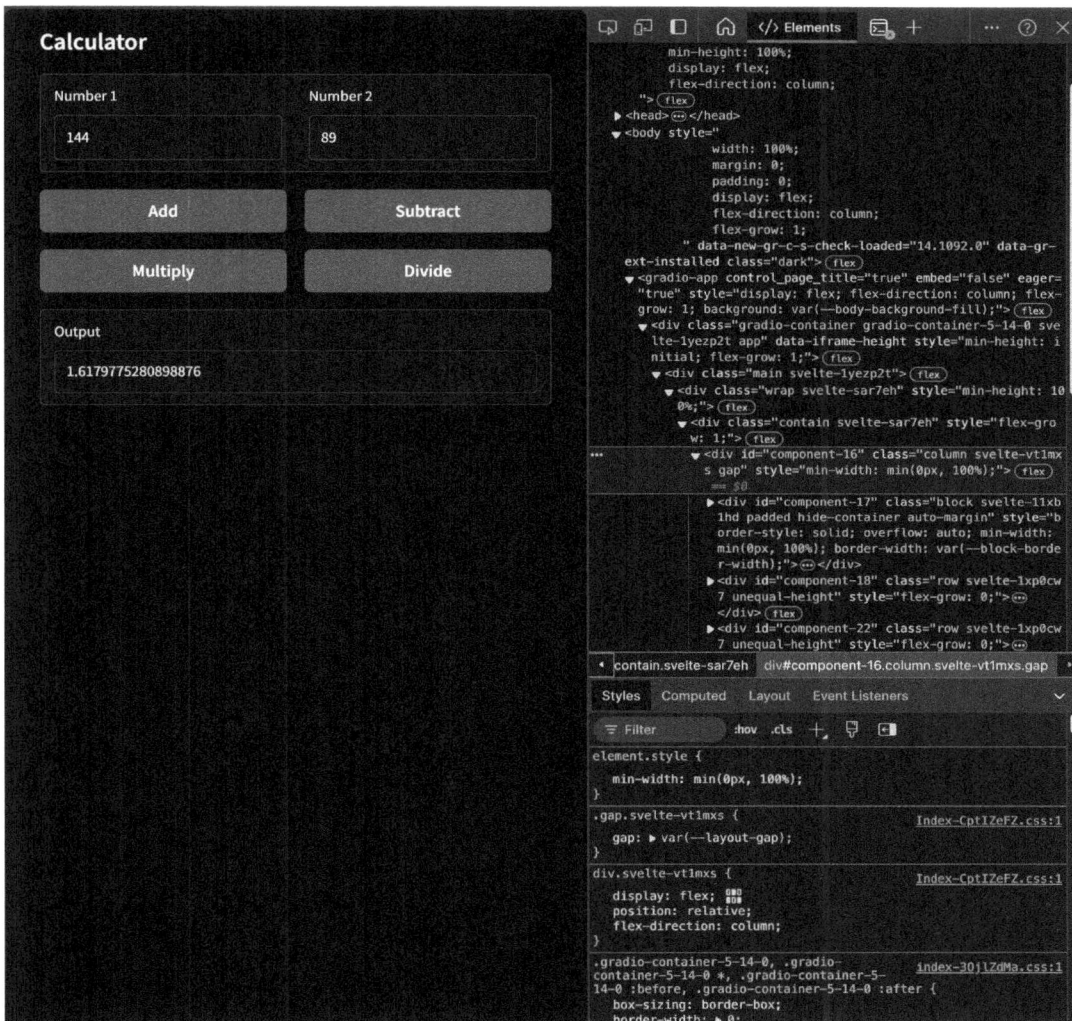

Figure 7.2: Calculator web app and underline code

Figure 7.2 shows the GUI of the calculator application alongside a snippet of the underlying code that powers it. On the left side, we see the fully functional calculator interface, which includes input boxes and four buttons. On the right side, we have a small portion of the HTML, JavaScript, and CSS that comprise the web page. If the entire code were printed, it would span several pages, highlighting the complexity of manually coding a front-end application from scratch.

We will not explore the specifics of the HTML or explain how each element functions. The primary takeaway from this screenshot is to have a sneak peek of what the Gradio library accomplishes behind the scenes. With just a few lines of Python code, Gradio automatically generates all the necessary front-end components, transforming Python functions into a fully interactive web application. The automation removes the need to write HTML, JavaScript, or CSS manually while providing a professional and functional interface.

You will notice a similar concept when using online website builders like Wix or Squarespace. These platforms enable users to design web pages visually while handling the generation of the HTML, CSS, and JavaScript that make the pages function. Gradio offers the same functionality for Python developers, bridging the gap between back-end programming and front-end web development without needing expertise in multiple programming languages.

By using Gradio, we are not merely creating a basic web interface. Instead, we are leveraging modern tools that allow Python applications to be deployed as fully featured web apps while remaining focused on coding in Python.

It is crucial to address a common mistake that beginners often make in programming: placing logic on the client rather than handling it on the server side. Implementing client-side logic can be perfectly adequate for simple applications like a basic calculator. In these cases, JavaScript can perform all calculations directly within the user's browser, eliminating the need for a backend server.

The approach provides several advantages: there is no requirement to define APIs, host backend services, or manage complex deployment infrastructure. However, the client-side logic method falls apart quickly when the application requires access to a database or needs to perform complex processing before sending a response. Most real-world applications avoid placing critical logic or sensitive data on the client side because it exposes proprietary algorithms, business rules, or confidential information to anyone accessing the webpage's source code.

A good rule of thumb is that client-side processing is acceptable if the application is simple and does not involve proprietary logic or sensitive data. However, if it requires access to data storage, authentication, or complex computations, the logic should be handled on the server side. Nearly all modern applications, from Facebook to online tax filing software, rely on server-side processing to ensure security, efficiency, and scalability.

API

An **application programming interface (API)** is a defined set of rules that dictates how the client and server sides of an application interact. It is not a physical entity like a server or database but rather a formal method of communication that ensures systems can exchange data consistently and efficiently.

Think of it as a contract between two teams. The front-end developer works on the client side, and the back-end developer manages the server. The API specifies what data the client needs to send and how the server should respond, allowing both sides to develop independently without disrupting each other's work. In the case of our calculator app, the API expects two numbers and an operation as input and returns the calculated result as output.

One of the APIs' fundamental advantages is their flexibility. A front-end developer can build the user interface using any programming language or framework, whether HTML, Swift, or Java. Meanwhile, the back-end engineer can implement the server logic in Python, PHP, Java, or any other language of their choice. This separation allows developers to work with the best tools for their specific tasks, making applications more adaptable and scalable.

At a technical level, APIs enable the web browser (client) to communicate with the server by sending requests and receiving well-formatted responses, typically in **JavaScript Object Notation (JSON)**. It ensures that the client receives data in a format that is easy to read, interpret, and display.

When drafting APIs, it is essential to be mindful of potential security risks they may introduce. If an API is not adequately secured, malicious users can exploit vulnerabilities to access, modify, or steal sensitive data. To prevent such threats, developers must implement authentication, authorization, encryption, and validation mechanisms, ensuring that only legitimate requests are processed.

Representational State Transfer (REST) API and GraphQL are popular approaches for building APIs for the following reason:

- **REST API** uses standard HTTP methods (GET, POST, PUT, DELETE). Data is typically returned in JSON or XML format. Although REST is straightforward and widely used, it can be inefficient when multiple endpoints are needed to fetch related data. The majority of APIs on the internet use the REST method.

- **GraphQL,** developed by *Facebook*, allows clients to request specific data with a single query, reducing the number of network requests and minimizing over-fetching and under-fetching. It provides a flexible and efficient way to interact with APIs, especially in complex applications where data needs to be aggregated from multiple sources.

Finally, the user request arrived at the server side.

Server side

The core logic of an application is executed on the server side. Unlike the client side, which handles user interactions and displays information, the server is responsible for processing requests, performing calculations, retrieving and storing data, and ensuring everything runs securely and efficiently.

For example, in the Facebook app, the server handles core logic and data processing. When a user posts a status update, likes a photo, or sends a message, the client (either the mobile app or web browser) sends a request to the server through an API call. The server processes this request, updates the database, and sends a relevant response. This response could confirm that a post has been published, update the like count, or deliver a message to the recipient. Facebook's backend infrastructure utilizes a mix of technologies, including Python, PHP, and C++.

Why is the logic handled on the server? Moving computations to the server ensures consistency, security, and scalability. If we were to keep all the logic on the client side, the calculations would depend on the user's device, which could introduce inconsistencies across different browsers and platforms. Worse, if an attacker modifies the client-side code, they could manipulate the results or exploit vulnerabilities. By centralizing logic on the server, we maintain control, accuracy, and security.

Beyond enhancing security, server-side processing enables significant performance optimizations. Unlike a user's smartphone or laptop, which may have limited processing power, a server can be equipped with high-performance CPUs, GPUs, and dedicated computing resources. Understanding the significance of efficient processing is essential, especially for applications that involve complex operations, such as AI models, large-scale financial calculations, or real-time data processing. The server effectively manages these tasks, ensuring the millions' user experience remains smooth and responsive daily.

Another significant advantage of using a client-server model with APIs is scalability. A web application might start with just a handful of users, but as it grows, it could need to handle thousands or even millions of requests per second. With cloud-based architecture, servers can automatically scale up or down based on demand. Allocating additional computing power during traffic spikes ensures the application remains fast and responsive. Meanwhile, the client remains lightweight, focusing only on displaying the UI and handling user interactions, regardless of the number of users accessing the system.

Nearly all modern web and mobile applications follow the client-server cloud-based architecture. Whether it is Facebook, online banking platforms, or e-commerce websites, the pattern remains the same: the client sends requests through an API, the server processes the logic, and the results are returned to the client. The architecture enables apps to be efficient, secure, and highly scalable.

Understanding the roles of client-side, server-side, and APIs is crucial for building robust, secure, and scalable applications. In modern applications, the client side offers a user-friendly interface, the server side handles secure and accurate processing, and the API connects the two. This separation of responsibilities improves performance, security, and flexibility, making it the preferred architecture for contemporary web applications.

Now that you have mastered the concept of client-server deployment with APIs, it is time to implement that knowledge. The following section will explore the deployment code and see how everything comes together in practice.

Deployment code

At first glance, the client-server model and APIs might seem overwhelming, especially considering the number of technologies involved. Traditional deployment methods require knowledge of HTML, CSS, JavaScript, Docker, YAML, and Bash scripts and extensive coding to integrate everything. While mastering these technologies is valuable, it is not the only path forward. Instead of reinventing the wheel, a wiser approach is to leverage existing tools and frameworks that handle much of the complexity for us.

Gradio is a Python library designed to simplify web interface development. Instead of manually writing front-end code or configuring deployment environments, Gradio automates these processes, allowing you to focus on building functionality rather than managing infrastructure. With Gradio, your Python application can instantly support a user-friendly web interface without requiring expertise in traditional web development. It supports various input and output types, including text, images, and audio, making it versatile for a wide range of applications.

The first step in working with Gradio is installing and importing the library.

```
[4]  1  # prompt: install and import gradio and print gradio version
     2
     3  !pip install gradio
     4  import gradio
     5
     6  # print version
     7  print(f'Installed Graido version: {gradio.__version__}. As of November 2024, we are
        using Gradio version: 5.14.0.')

     Installed Graido version: 5.14.0. As of November 2024, we are using Gradio version: 5.14.0.
```

Figure 7.3: Install and import Gradio library

Figure 7.3 presents the code and output for installing and importing the Gradio library, a crucial step in integrating Python applications with a web interface.

The process begins with Line #1, where we use GPT-4o to generate and explain the installation and import code. Instead of searching through documentation manually, GPT-4o provides a concise, step-by-step guide, ensuring that we understand how to install Gradio and why each step matters.

Line #3 executes the **!pip install gradio** command. You can skip this step if Gradio has already been installed on your system. However, if you encounter issues later, reinstalling Gradio using this command ensures you work with the latest compatible version.

Line #4 imports the Gradio library, making its functions available in our Python scripts. This step is necessary regardless of whether Gradio was pre-installed or freshly installed.

Line #7 checks and prints the installed version of Gradio, confirming that we are working with Gradio version 5.14.0 as of November 2024. Updating Gradio is recommended to avoid compatibility issues if your output shows an older version. If a newer version is installed, most of the code should still run correctly, but there may be minor differences in function calls or parameters due to ongoing updates in the library.

Keeping libraries up to date ensures access to the latest features and improvements while reducing potential security risks. With Gradio now installed and ready, we can move on to writing our first interactive Python-powered web app.

We will write the GUI using Gradio library for the following three apps:

- Calculator app
- Quick sort app
- CNN snake classification app

We start with the easiest one first, the calculator app.

Calculator app

In *Chapter 2, Jupyter Notebook*, we created the calculator app with simple text input to test it. Now, we are upgrading it with a GUI, as shown in the following code:

```
# prompt: using gradio to create two numbers input side by side. below it have 4
buttons for add, subtract, multiply, and dive, add title Calculator

import gradio as gr

with gr.Blocks() as calculator_app:
    gr.Markdown("## Calculator")
    with gr.Row():
        num1 = gr.Number(label="Number 1")
        num2 = gr.Number(label="Number 2")
    with gr.Row():
        add_btn = gr.Button("Add")
        subtract_btn = gr.Button("Subtract")
        multiply_btn = gr.Button("Multiply")
        divide_btn = gr.Button("Divide")
    output = gr.Textbox(label="Output")

    add_btn.click(calculator, inputs=[num1, num2, gr.Textbox(value="add", visible=False)], outputs=output)
    subtract_btn.click(calculator, inputs=[num1, num2, gr.Textbox(value="subtract", visible=False)], outputs=output)
    multiply_btn.click(calculator, inputs=[num1, num2, gr.Textbox(value="multiply", visible=False)], outputs=output)
    divide_btn.click(calculator, inputs=[num1, num2, gr.Textbox(value="divide", visible=False)], outputs=output)

calculator_app.launch()
```

Figure 7.4: Calculator app GUI code

Figure 7.4 presents the code for creating a GUI for the calculator app using Gradio. Line #1 is the GPT-4o prompt that generated the initial code, but getting the perfect layout was not instant. It took a few iterations and tweaking the design until we arrived at the most user-friendly version. Initially, we experimented with placing the input fields on the left side and the output on the right, but it did not feel intuitive. We also tried different UI elements for selecting operations, including radio buttons and dropdown lists, but neither provided the best experience. Ultimately, we found that keeping the input fields at the top, the operator buttons in the center, and the output displayed below created the most natural and user-friendly layout.

If you want to personalize the interface, we highly encourage you to experiment and apply prompt engineering techniques from *Chapter 1, Introduction to GenAI*. Designing a GUI is not just about making something functional. It is about creating an interface that feels natural to users. By adjusting prompts and iterating through different layouts, you will learn how small changes in the UI can enhance usability.

Another valuable insight is how well GPT-4o explains the code it generates. While the Gradio documentation and various online resources exist, GPT-4o provides more practical and easier-to-follow explanations. It breaks down concepts step by step, adapting the explanation to your level of understanding. If something is unclear, you can always ask follow-up questions, making it an interactive learning experience that goes beyond static documentation.

Line #3 imports the Gradio library, making its tools available for building the UI. Lines #5 through #15 define the title, input boxes, output display, and four operator buttons (addition, subtraction, multiplication, and division). These elements are what the user interacts with, and their placement determines the overall feel of the application.

Lines #17 through #20 link each operator button to the **calculator()** function, which handles the actual math operations. The function itself is not shown in this code cell because we have already written and studied it earlier. Since we are focusing on the GUI, there is no need to display the function again. However, this is an excellent example of separating logic from the user interface, reinforcing the best practices we have been following throughout this book.

Finally, line #22 launches the application, bringing everything to life. The Gradio library generates a fully functional web app with a single command, making deployment incredibly simple.

The following figure is the output:

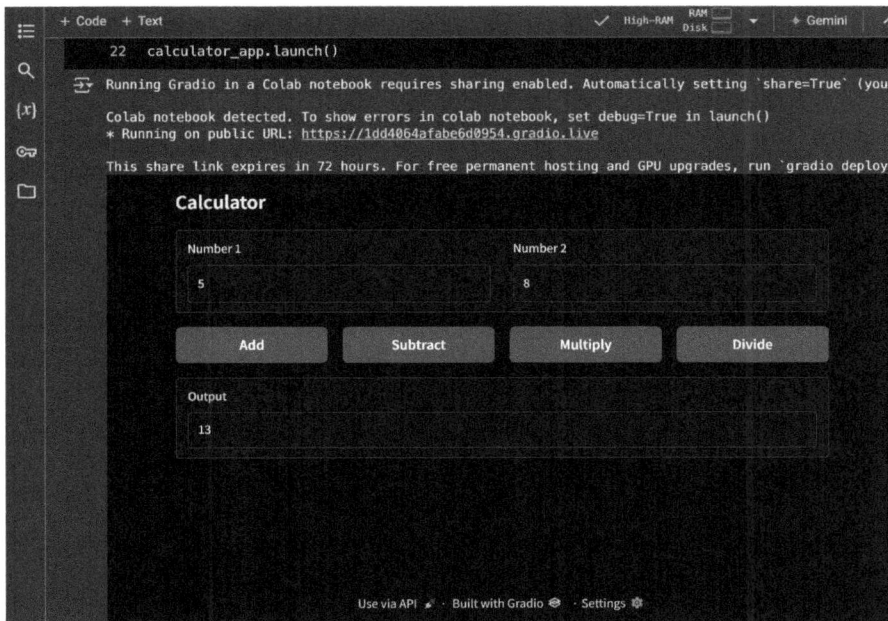

Figure 7.5: Calculator app GUI on Notebook

Figure 7.5 displays the fully functional GUI output generated by the code in *Figure 7.4*. When we run the code, Gradio automatically detects that we are working within Google Colab's Jupyter Notebook and renders the GUI directly inside the notebook. Unlike a static image, this is a live, interactive web app, meaning we can input numbers, click buttons, and see real-time calculations, just as we would in a standalone web application.

The layout is simple yet effective. The top row contains two input boxes where users enter numbers. The middle row consists of four operator buttons: **Add, Subtract, Multiply, and Divide**. Each button ties to its respective function. The bottom row is the output display, showing the result of the selected operation. For example, when we input 5 and 8, then click the **Add** button, the output immediately updates to 13, confirming that everything is working as expected.

It feels too easy, which is the beauty of using Gradio and GPT-4o together. In just fifteen minutes, we wrote and tested a fully functional GUI for our calculator app. Traditionally, building a simple web interface requires manually writing HTML, CSS, and JavaScript, setting up event listeners, handling form inputs, and debugging layout issues across browsers. Here, we bypassed all of that complexity, letting Gradio handle the front-end work while we focused entirely on Python logic. The native web app code, including HTML, CSS, and JavaScript, is there, as seen when we sneak peek in *Figure 7.2*. However, we did not write it ourselves.

Owing to the combination of modern libraries and AI-assisted coding, what used to take hours or even days now takes minutes. This shift is not just about convenience. It is about empowering developers, especially beginners, to move from concept to execution faster than ever before. Instead of getting bogged down in tedious syntax, we can test ideas, refine our designs, and iterate quickly, all while deepening our understanding of Python and web development.

Throughout this book, we have seen the power of GPT-4o in action. It continues to amaze us with how quickly it accelerates learning, simplifies complex concepts, and enhances the fun of coding in Python. The combination of Python, Gradio, and GPT-4o makes coding feel less like a chore and more like a creative process where you can bring your ideas to life faster.

There is more. The Gradio library simplifies the deployment process by automatically providing a public URL, as shown in *Figure 7.5*. By clicking on the live URL link, we can view our app, which is accessible on the World Wide Web for everyone to see. In accordance with Gradio's policy, you can share this link with your friends for the next 72 hours. As part of this chapter, we will learn to write code to deploy our app on the Hugging Face website to replicate Gradio's functionality.

The following figure shows the live calculator app.

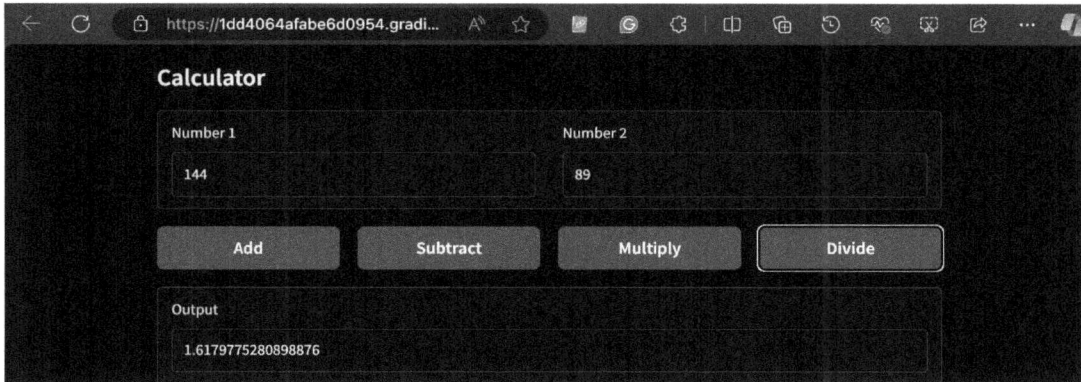

Figure 7.6: *Calculate app on the World Wide Web*

Figure 7.6 shows the calculator web app live on the web, just as it appears in *Figure 7.5* from the notebook. We expected the exact same displays to happen, which is the deployment goal. To test it out, we entered 144 and 89 and then clicked the **Divide** button. The result is 1.6179775280898876, which represents the **golden ratio**.

Wait, there is more. Remember our discussion about APIs and REST interfaces? Well, Gradio handles that too. Your Python application is not just limited to a web-based GUI. It has a fully accessible API, allowing other applications to interact with it programmatically.

Think about the possibilities. Someone developing a custom web app with a different framework, or even a native iPhone app using Swift or an Android app using Kotlin, could connect directly to your calculator's API. Instead of reinventing the wheel and writing their calculator logic, they can send a request to your API, retrieve the result, and display it in their interface.

At the bottom of your Gradio app, you will find a **Use via API** link, as shown in *Figure 7.5*. Clicking this reveals the pre-generated API code, providing everything needed to integrate your calculator into other applications.

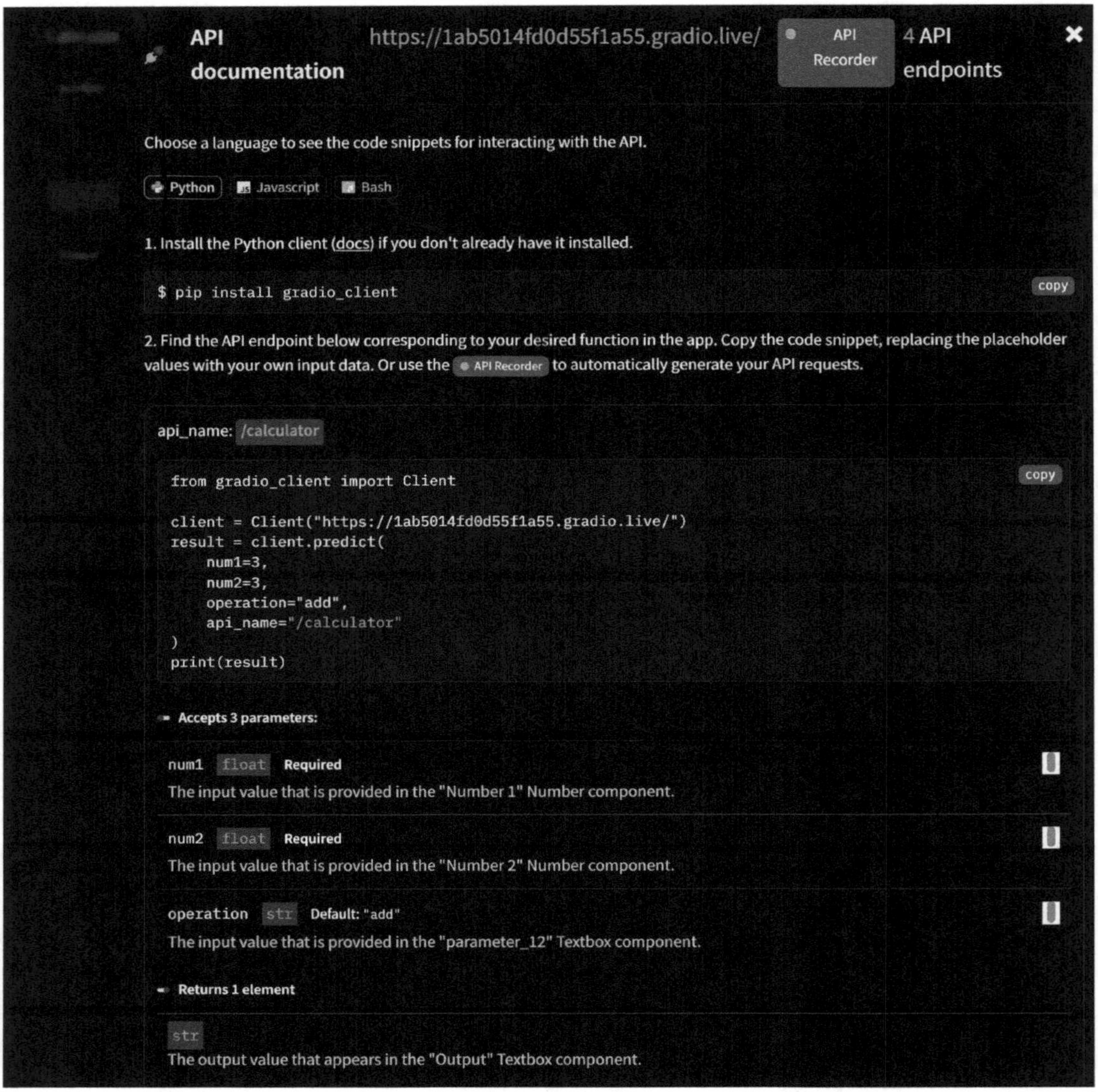

Figure 7.7: Calculator Python API

Figure 7.7 shows the Python code and documentation for the calculator app. There is full documentation and a code sample for the API. The top has three language options: **Python, JavaScript**, and **Bash**. We chose the Python option. Next, we copy the code into our Jupyter Notebook and test it.

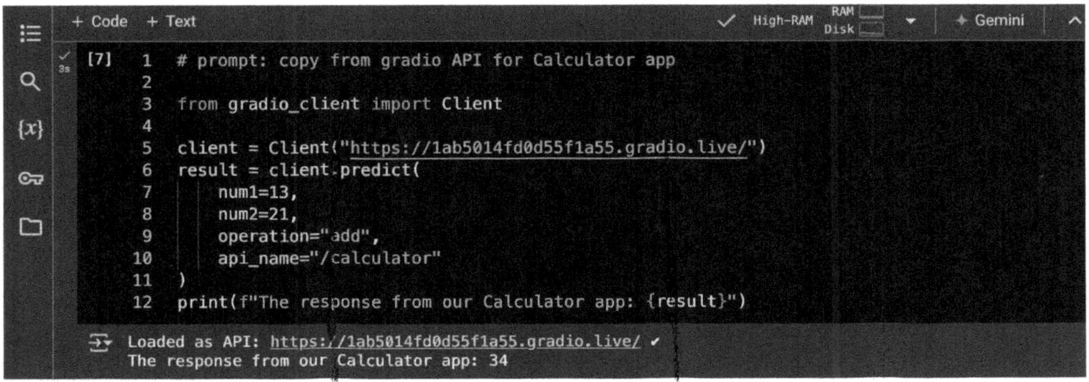

```
+ Code   + Text                                              ✓  High-RAM  RAM      ▼   + Gemini   ∧
                                                                        Disk
  [7]  1   # prompt: copy from gradio API for Calculator app
       2
       3   from gradio_client import Client
       4
       5   client = Client("https://1ab5014fd0d55f1a55.gradio.live/")
       6   result = client.predict(
       7       num1=13,
       8       num2=21,
       9       operation="add",
      10       api_name="/calculator"
      11   )
      12   print(f"The response from our Calculator app: {result}")

   ⥁  Loaded as API: https://1ab5014fd0d55f1a55.gradio.live/ ✔
      The response from our Calculator app: 34
```

Figure 7.8: Testing the calculator app Python API

Figure 7.8 shows the code and output for testing the calculator app using Python API. Line #1 said you copy the Python code from the example in *Figure 7.7*. Line #3 import the **gradio_ client** library. Line #5 define the clients with the URL: **https://1ab5014fd0d55f1a55. gradio.live/**.

Line #6 defines the output result using the Gradio **predict()** method, which sends a request to our calculator API server. Lines #7 and #8 specify the two inputs, which we set as 13 and 21. Line #9 defines the operation, where we choose the **add** operation. There are three other options available: **subtract, multiply,** and **divide**. Line #10 specifies the API name, which is **/calculator**. Finally, line #12 prints the result.

The output the answer for 13 plus 21, which is **34**.

We will look at the two other option to use API, but we will not explain the API using JavaScript or Bash, but here is a picture of invoking the API from JavaScript.

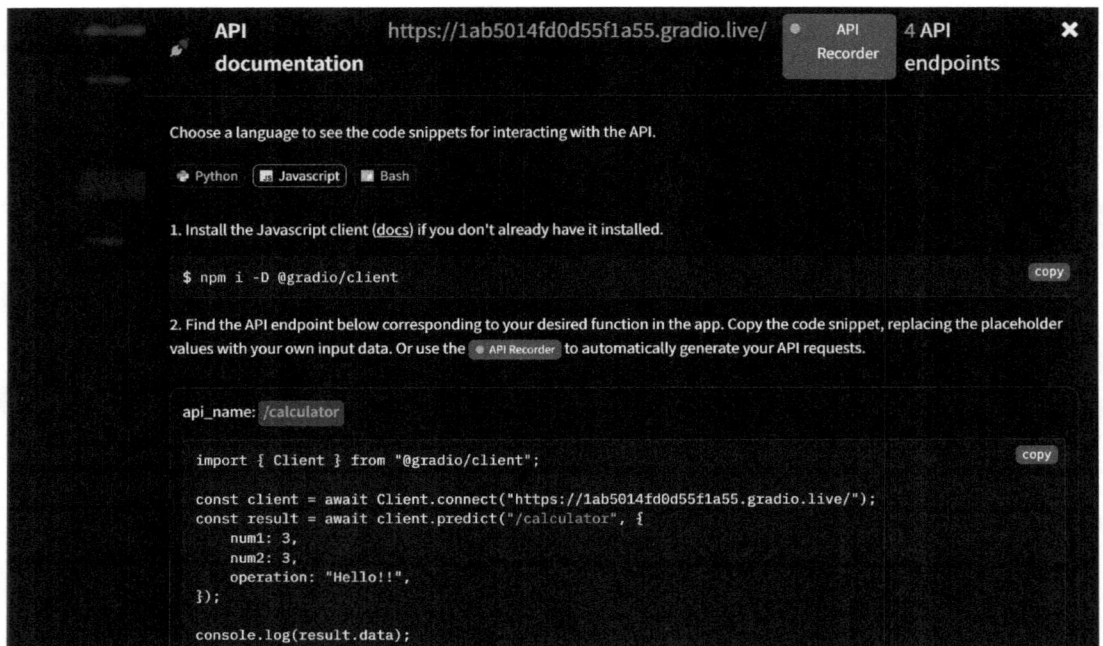

Figure 7.9: *Calculator JavaScript API*

Figure 7.9 presents the JavaScript documentation and code sample for using the API in a JavaScript-based application. While we are not focusing on JavaScript in this book, it is crucial to understand that the API remains the same regardless of the programming language used on the client side. This consistency is what makes APIs fundamental to modern software development.

The server-side logic does not change whether the client is a web app written in JavaScript, a mobile app built in Swift for iPhones, or a desktop application coded in Python. The API acts as the bridge, allowing different applications to send requests and receive responses in a standardized format.

With this approach, your Python-powered calculator is no longer just a standalone web app. It becomes a service that can be integrated into multiple platforms. A JavaScript developer working on a finance dashboard could call your API to perform instant calculations. A mobile developer building an expense tracker could use it to compute totals and tax rates. Even a CNN assistant could integrate the API to identify poisonous snakes from users' iPhone images.

APIs eliminate the need to rewrite business logic in every programming language. Instead, developers build a single, well-structured API that is the foundation for multiple applications. Most modern software is built using API. Google Maps, OpenAI's GPT, and payment processors all follow this model, enabling thousands of applications to interact with them without needing to rewrite the core functionality.

The calculator app GUI came together effortlessly, proving just how powerful and intuitive Gradio is for creating interactive web applications. Now that we have seen how smoothly the process works, it is time to apply the same approach to building a GUI for the sorting algorithms we explored in *Chapter 4, Sorting on My Mind*.

Sorting algorithms are foundational in computer science, and while we have already implemented them in Python, they were purely command-line based. Users had to input data manually and read the output in raw text form. But what if we could elevate the experience by giving our sorting functions a visual, interactive interface?

Quick sort app

Quick sort is an efficient sorting algorithm that utilizes the divide-and-conquer approach. It begins by selecting a pivot element from the list. Then, it partitions the list into two sublists: one containing elements smaller than the pivot and another containing elements greater than the pivot. After the partitioning, quick sort recursively sorts these two sublists. This algorithm is one of the fastest for handling large datasets and is widely used in various real-world applications, as we study in *Chapter 4, Sorting on My Mind*.

We follow the same process for deploying our quick sort web app as we did with the calculator app. The first step is prompting GPT-4o to generate the deployment code. Unlike the calculator app, where we experimented with different GUI layouts, this time, we let GPT-4o handle the UI design entirely. Instead of specifying how the interface should look, we define the input and output requirements, and GPT-4o constructs the GUI to match those needs.

All we need to provide is a clear description of the functionality: the user inputs an unsorted list of numbers, selects quick sort, and receives the sorted list as output. GPT-4o translates this into an interactive Gradio interface, ensuring it is functional and user-friendly.

The approach streamlines development, allowing us to focus on the sorting logic rather than spending time manually designing the UI. GPT-4o and Gradio can move from concept to a working web app in minutes. It is time to generate the code and deploy our quick sort application.

```
1  # prompt: Write a Gradio interface for the quick short where the input is an unorder
   list and the ouput is an ordered list. Including the title and description.
2
3  import gradio as gr
4
5  def sort_list(input_data):
6      if isinstance(input_data, list):
7          return quick_sort(input_data)
8      elif isinstance(input_data, str):
9          try:
10             input_list = [int(x.strip()) for x in input_data.split(',')]
11             return quick_sort(input_list)
12         except ValueError:
13             words_list = [x.strip() for x in input_data.split(',')]
14             return sorted(words_list)
15     else:
16         return "Invalid input type. Please provide a list of integers or a
           comma-separated string of numbers or words."
17
18 sort_app = gr.Interface(
19     fn=sort_list,
20     inputs=gr.Textbox(placeholder="Enter numbers or words separated by commas, like: 9,
       3,8,1"),
21     outputs=gr.Textbox(),
22     title="Quick Sort Algorithm",
23     description="Enter a list of numbers or words, comma-spearated and get the sorted
       result.",
24 )
25 sort_app.launch()
```

Figure 7.10: Quick sort GUI code

Figure 7.10 presents the GPT-4o-generated code for the quick sort GUI. Line #1 is the prompt given to GPT-4o. It is common for the initial prompt not to yield the exact result you want. Part of the process involves refining the prompt until GPT-4o understands and executes it correctly. Unlike human assistants, GPT-4o does not get tired, frustrated, or impatient. It will keep generating solutions until you are satisfied.

Line #3 imports the Gradio library, ensuring we have the necessary tools to build and launch the GUI. Lines #5 to #16 check whether the input is a list of numbers or a list of words, ensuring that quick sort processes the data correctly. The sorting function itself is referenced in Line #12, where it calls **quick_sort()**, a function defined in another code cell. It is not displayed here since we have already written and tested the **quick_sort()** function.

Lines #18 to #23 define the GUI interface, setting up the input and output elements. **Submit** and **Cancel** buttons are included by default in Gradio, so they are not explicitly written in the code. The interface remains clean and intuitive, ensuring users can input an unsorted list and quickly receive a sorted result with minimal effort.

Now that our quick sort web app is ready, it is time to test it in action. Next, we will see how well it performs with different data typs.

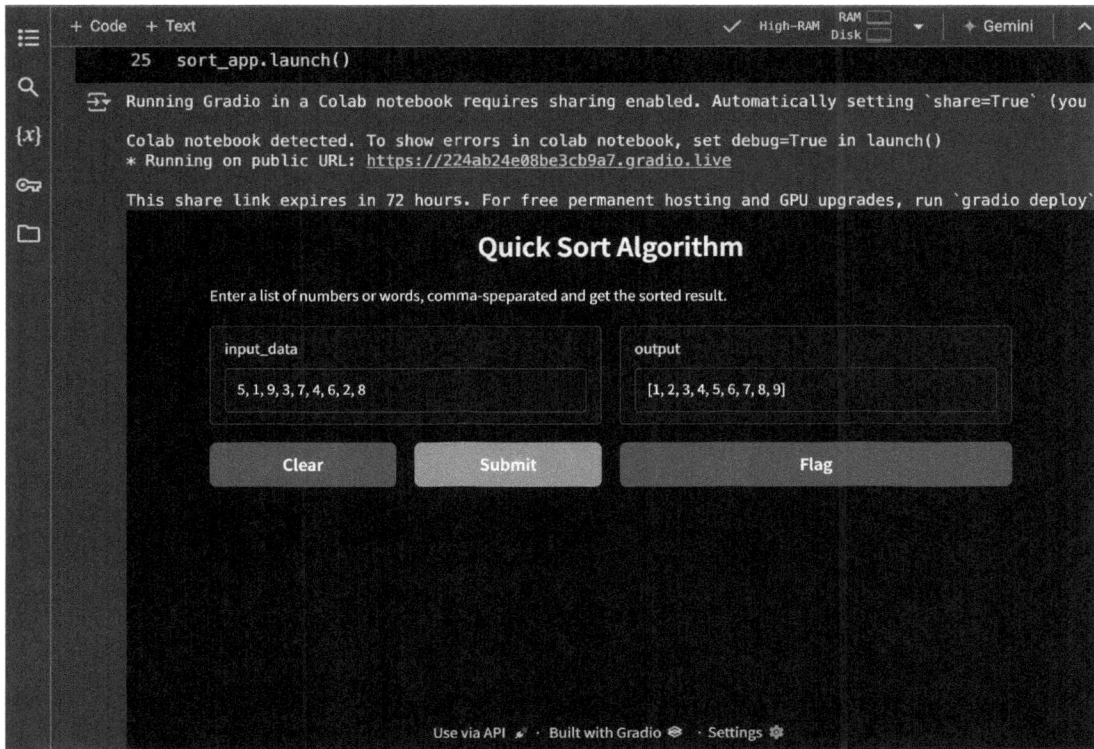

Figure 7.11: Quick short GUI interface

Figure 7.11 displays the output of the quick sort GUI interface. On the left side, an input box with **Submit** and **Clear** buttons is located beneath it. The ordered list output appears on the right side, while the title and instructions are printed at the top of the interactive form.

We entered the following numbers in the input box: **5, 1, 9, 3, 7, 4, 6, 2, 8**, and then clicked **Submit**. The resulting output is **[1, 2, 3, 4, 5, 6, 7, 8, 9]**. The design of the interface is intuitive, and we find it acceptable. For testing the sorting of a word list, we entered forty words, as shown as follows:

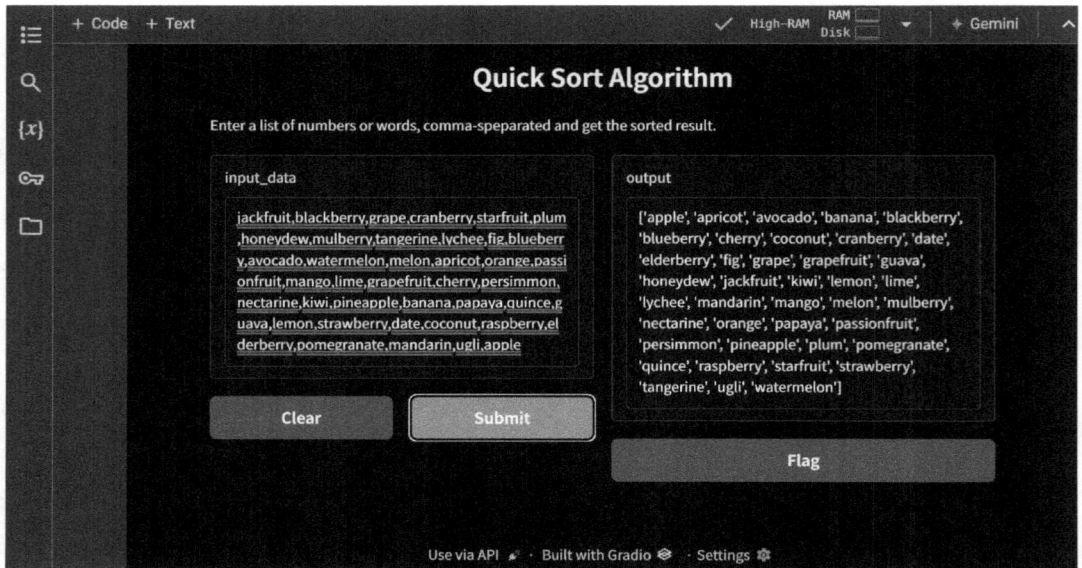

Figure 7.12: Quick sort using number list

Figure 7.12 displays the quick sort interface in action, sorting a list of forty words. The unordered list of fruits starts with **jackfruit** and **blackberry** and ends with **ugli** and **apple**. After clicking **Submit**, the output updates to a properly sorted list, beginning with **apple, apricot** and ending with **ugli, watermelon**. The transformation happens instantly, demonstrating the efficiency of quick sort when applied through a simple Gradio-powered web interface.

Like the calculator app, the quick sort web app has a live URL on Gradio, allowing you to test it in real-world apps. An API version is also available, enabling developers to integrate the sorting functionality into other applications. We leave both of these for you to explore at your own pace.

Now, we shift to something even more exciting: deploying our CNN-based snake classification app. Unlike a simple quick sort interface, no online drag-and-drop GUI builder, like Wiz or SquareSpace, can compete in this area. Deploying an advanced machine learning model as a web app requires a different level of integration.

CNN snake classification app

We have successfully developed a CNN-based model for classifying snakes, determining whether a snake in a photo taken on an iPhone or Android device is venomous or safe. It is not just another beginner-friendly coding exercise but a significant achievement. CNNs are typically covered in graduate-level computer science courses, yet we are building a fully functional machine learning model within a beginner Python book. No other introductory book takes you this far into real-world AI applications.

We have achieved more than simply writing Python code; we completed an end-to-end machine learning project. Instead of using pre-made toy datasets, we downloaded a real-world dataset from Kaggle. We processed thousands of images, cleaned and structured the metadata, trained a CNN model using Fast.ai, and deployed it as a fully interactive web application. This workflow mirrors the practices employed by professionals and researchers who develop AI-powered applications in various industries, ranging from medical imaging to self-driving cars.

Deploying a CNN image classification model cannot be accomplished using traditional drag-and-drop website builders like Wix, Squarespace, or Webflow. While these platforms are excellent for creating static and dynamic websites, they cannot host and execute AI models in real time. Instead, we turn to Fast.ai and Gradio, two powerful libraries specifically designed for machine learning and AI deployment.

Fast.ai simplifies deep learning, allowing us to train and fine-tune complex models without months of study. Gradio bridges the gap between AI models and web applications, enabling us to create interactive interfaces that let users upload images and receive predictions instantly. These tools allow you to deploy real-world AI applications without requiring expertise in web development or years of study. However, if you want to pursue machine learning and CNN, consider investing two to four years of study to become proficient in the field.

As with the same as the calculator and quick sort app, we begin looking at the deployment code.

```python
# prompt: Create interface for the Snake CNN Clasification using the export fast.ai
learner_snake, and the input is a picture and the output is prediction of poisonous
or safe.

import gradio as gr
from fastai.vision.all import load_learner, PILImage

# Load the trained model
learner = load_learner('learner_snake.pkl')

def classify_snake(image):
    pred, _, probs = learner.predict(PILImage.create(image))
    return f"Prediction: {pred}, Confidence: {probs.max():.4f}"

cnn_snake_app = gr.Interface(
    fn=classify_snake,
    inputs=gr.Image(type="pil"),
    outputs=gr.Textbox(),
    title="Snake Poisonous Classifier",
    description="Upload an image of a snake, and the model will predict if it is
    poisonous or safe.",
)

cnn_snake_app.launch()
```

Figure 7.13: CNN deployment code

Figure 7.13 presents the code for deploying our CNN-based snake classification model, which determines whether a snake in a picture is poisonous or safe. Line #1 is the GPT-4o prompt. As with previous projects, it took several iterations to arrive at a prompt that produced a clean, functional deployment script to our satisfaction. While the other code suggestions work, they do not align with our preferred style. Fine-tuning prompts is an essential skill when working with AI-assisted coding, and through this process, we learned how to refine our requests to get optimal results.

Additionally, we are programmers, not just users. Therefore, we can copy the suggested code and refine or debug it ourselves. In other words, the code suggested by GPT-4 serves as a foundation for what we want to create. It does not have to be the final version.

Lines #3 and #4 import the necessary libraries: Gradio for building the interactive web interface and Fast.ai for managing the pre-trained CNN model. Line #7 loads the learner object that we previously exported after training. It is important to note that deployment does not need any data, unlike the training phase, which requires thousands of images and the data loader. The learner object is often referred to as the inference engine. The inference engine allows us to make real-time predictions without access to the original dataset.

Lines #9 to #11 define the core prediction function. The **predict()** function takes an uploaded image, runs it through the CNN model, and returns the classification result, which is poisonous or safe. Unlike sorting numbers or calculating equations, this function performs a high-level AI task, analyzing image features in ways that are beyond human-written logic rules.

Lines #13 to #18 set up the Gradio interface, ensuring a user-friendly experience. Users simply upload an image instead of typing text or numbers, and the model does the rest. This type of AI-powered image classification is widely used in medicine, agriculture, security, and wildlife conservation, making our snake classifier a real-world AI application rather than just a coding exercise.

Finally, line #21 launches the **cnn_snake_app**, making it live and interactive. In just 21 lines of code, with the help of GPT-4o, we have built and deployed a fully functional deep-learning web application. It is an incredible milestone. A few years ago, deploying an AI model required extensive backend development, GPU infrastructure, and cloud server configurations. Today, with Fast.ai and Gradio, we can accomplish this in just a few minutes.

Now that our CNN model is deployed, it is time to test the app and see how well it identifies poisonous snakes.

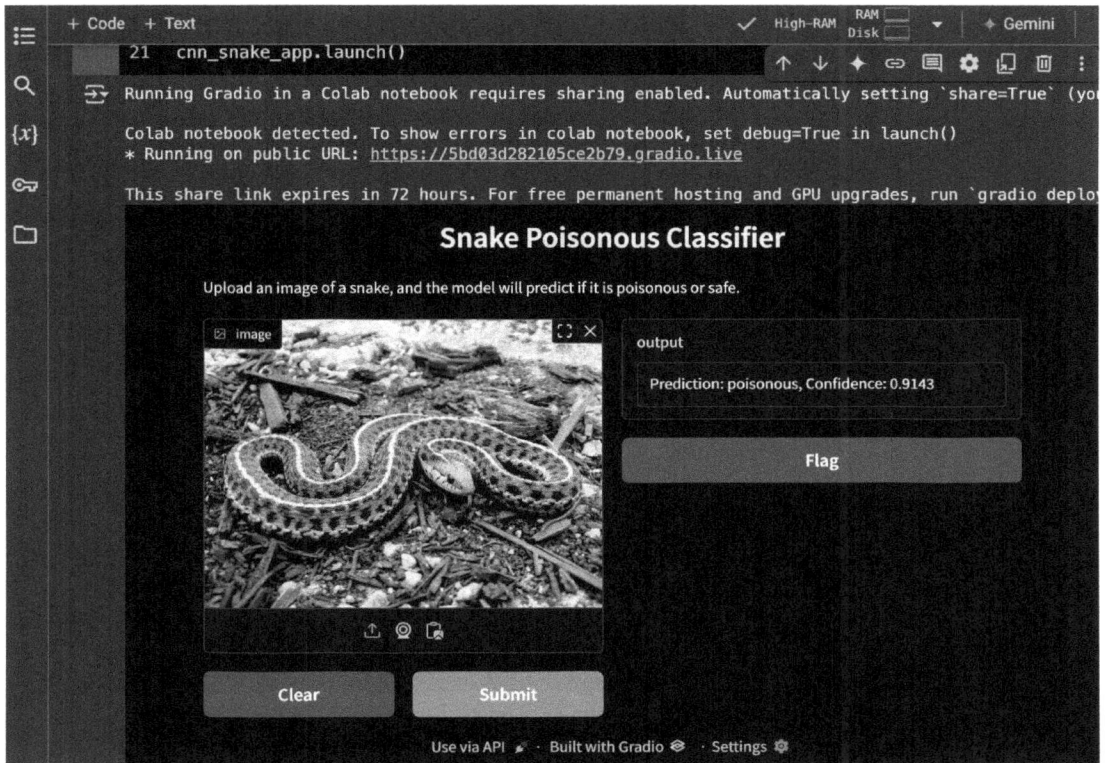

Figure 7.14: *Testing CNN image classification with poisonous snake*

Figure 7.14 displays the GUI for our CNN-based snake classification app, now fully deployed and ready for real-world testing. To evaluate its accuracy, we retrieved a few snake images from the web that were not part of the training dataset. This step is crucial in testing AI models, as it helps determine whether the model generalizes well to new, unseen snake photos.

We select a snake image from our local device using the **upload** button icon. Gradio also provides a camera option, allowing users to take a photo in real-time using their phone or webcam, making the app more versatile for field use. Once the image is uploaded, we click **Submit**, and in less than a second, the model processes the image and displays the classification result in the output box on the right.

For this particular snake image, the model confidently predicts poisonous with a probability score of 0.9143, meaning it is 91.4% certain that the snake in the picture is venomous. The speed and accuracy of the classification are remarkable. Achieved without writing hundreds of lines of code or configuring complex server infrastructure. It marks an important milestone. Our AI-powered app is now making real-time, high-confidence predictions on new images, just as it would in an actual field application.

To validate the model further, we continue testing with different snake images. Eventually, we find a picture of a non-poisonous snake, and as expected, the model correctly classifies it as safe, reinforcing the reliability of our CNN deployment.

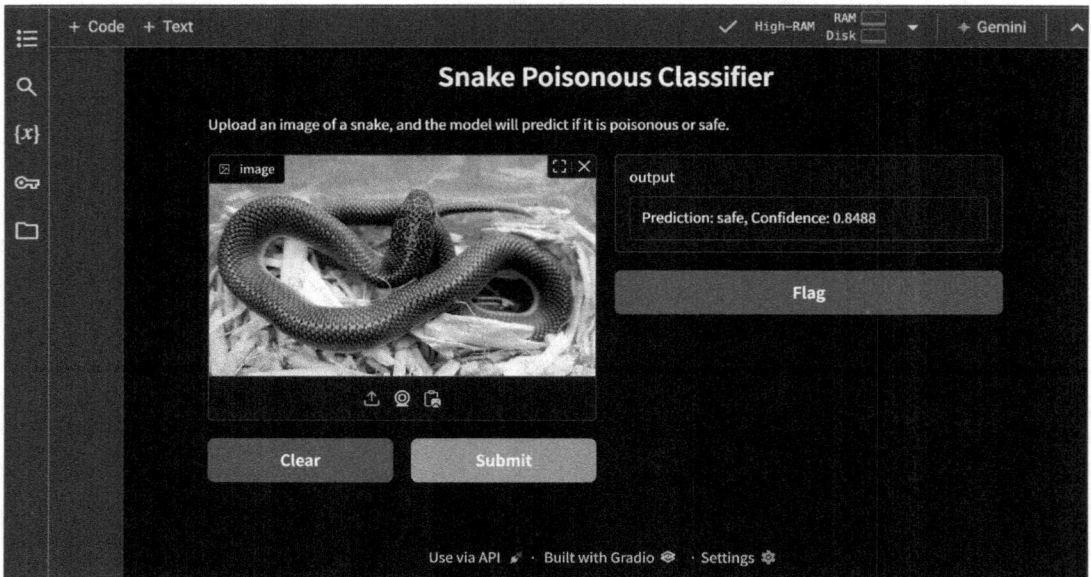

Figure 7.15: *Testing CNN image classification with non-poisonous snake*

Figure 7.15 shows the same GUI for the CNN image classification as in *Figure 7.14*, but this time, we uploaded an image of a non-poisonous snake. After we click on the **Submit** button, the prediction is **safe** with a confidence of 0.8488, which is 84.9% confidence that the snake in the photo is non-poisonous.

Similar to the calculator app, our CNN image classification application features a Gradio live URL, enabling us to deploy it on the internet and share it with others. This app is not just a local project running in a Jupyter Notebook. It is now a fully functional web application that anyone can access from anywhere in the world.

Excited to see how well it performs outside of our testing, we sent the link to a few friends, inviting them to try it. Within minutes, they opened the app on their iPhones and began testing it with their own snake images. The results left them genuinely impressed.

Our friends' response was immediate and enthusiastic. They were genuinely impressed by how accurately the app could determine whether a snake was poisonous. All admitted that the model outperformed their ability to identify venomous species.

The app now runs on an iPhone and can make real-time predictions with a photo uploaded or taken with the iPhone camera. We have progressed from training a deep learning model to deploying an interactive AI-powered web app, making it accessible to anyone with a smartphone.

The possibilities extend far beyond snake identification. This same approach can be applied to medical imaging, wildlife conservation, food recognition, or security applications. Here is an iPhone photo of it.

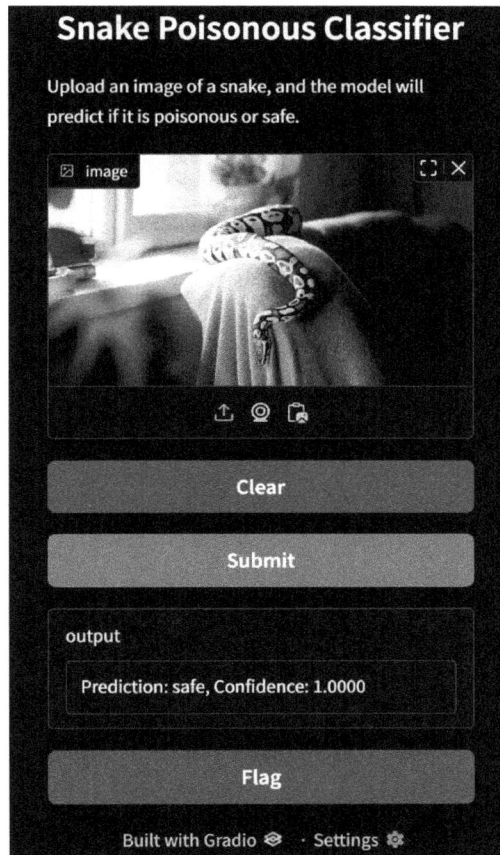

Figure 7.16: CNN snake image classification app on iPhone

Figure 7.16 shows our CNN snake image classification app running on an iPhone SE. The photo shows a large yellow and black snake slithering on top of an armchair. The app predicts that the snake is safe with confidence at 1.0, which is 100% certain that it is non-poisonous.

The Gradio interface is designed with modern flexibility, automatically adjusting and rearranging itself to fit the iPhone screen format. The interface remains intuitive and responsive across all screen sizes and orientations, from laptops and tablets to iPhones and Android phones, ensuring an intuitive user experience.

We have learned to write GUI code using the Gradio app for the calculator, quick sort, and CNN snake image classification app. So, we are moving on to deployment on Hugging Face.

Deploy on Hugging Face

Hugging Face is a platform that simplifies server-side deployment and is ideal for beginner Python coders. It is known for its extensive library of pre-trained AI and machine learning models and provides tools that make deploying these models as web applications straightforward. The framework eliminates the complexity of setting up and managing servers, allowing you to focus on writing and refining your Python code. You can use your application, AI or not, in the deploying process.

The platform integrates with Gradio, allowing you to convert Python functions into user-friendly web applications quickly. You can write a function, add Gradio's interface, and deploy it on Hugging Face within minutes. The supportive community and GPT-4o provide numerous tutorials and documentation to assist you throughout the process.

Hugging Face provides practical, hands-on experience for deploying models, handling API requests, and managing application deployment. It is beginner-friendly and supports advanced features, enabling you to scale and deploy in production environments as your skills improve.

We have used the Gradio live URL link to deploy the app on the server, so why are we learning how to deploy on Hugging Face?

The key concept here is scalability, which is essential for understanding deployment across various cloud servers. As the number of users grows, potentially reaching millions daily, the complexity of server-side infrastructure increases. An application deployed on Gradio may be sufficient for a few hundred users, but it may not be able to scale effectively. For instance, Facebook accommodates millions of users accessing the platform daily. We will explore the fundamental deployment concepts with scalability in mind.

The deployment concept applies to any server infrastructure, whether it be Google App Engine, AWS, Microsoft Azure, Hugging Face, or many others. We will discuss the following four topics in particular.

- Requirements text file
- Application code
- Container
- Transport layer

We will start by addressing the first step, creating a requirements file.

Requirements text file

A Python project's requirements.txt file is crucial for managing dependencies. It lists all the external libraries and packages the project requires to function correctly. This file ensures that anyone setting up the project on a different machine or environment can install the correct versions of these packages, maintaining consistency and preventing potential issues due to version mismatches.

The file that lists dependencies in a Python project does not necessarily have to be named **requirements.txt**, but the requirement.txt name is a standard convention. This convention is widely recognized and supported by many tools as the default name. In other words, we can use the **my_cat_eats_tulips.txt** file as a dependency file, but most developers will not guess it is intended for listing library dependencies.

The dependencies file contains the names of Python libraries, occasionally accompanied by version numbers or constraints. The version details indicate the specific package versions needed, which is essential for maintaining compatibility and stability within the project. For instance, we can specify an exact version to prevent unexpected issues from updates.

The **requirements.txt** file has a simple format, with each line listing a library name and, if needed, its version constraints. You can also add comments to give more context or notes. To install the dependencies listed in **requirements.txt**, you must run a command that reads the file and installs all the specified packages. This process standardizes the setup and guarantees that the software performs consistently across various systems and servers, such as AWS, Azure, or Hugging Face servers.

Although you can create the requirements file using a text editor, the goal of this book is for you to learn Python. Therefore, why not use Python code to create the requirements text file? The code for creating a requirements text file is as follows:

```
[8]  1  # prompt: create an array with value "gradio==5.12.0, fastai>=2.7.18" and write to
        the requirement.txt file
     2
     3  requirements = ["gradio==5.12.0", "fastai>=2.7.18"]
     4
     5  with open("requirements.txt", "w") as f:
     6      for requirement in requirements:
     7          f.write(requirement + "\n")
     8
     9  !cat requirements.txt

gradio==5.12.0
fastai>=2.7.18
```

Figure 7.17: *Create the requirement file*

Figure 7.17 displays the code and output for generating the requirements file, which ensures our deployment runs with the correct library versions. Line #1 is the GPT-4o prompt, used to generate the code and explain the necessary dependencies.

Line #3 defines the required versions for the Gradio and Fast.ai libraries. The Gradio library is locked to version 5.12.0, while Fast.ai must be version 2.7.18 or higher. Instead of automatically allowing the system to install the latest versions, we explicitly specify these versions because all our code was written and tested in November 2024. By pinning these versions, we guarantee compatibility and ensure that the deployment works exactly as expected. It does not mean that newer versions will not work, but updates can sometimes introduce breaking changes, requiring additional testing and modifications.

Lines #5 through #7 write the **requirements.txt** file to a local or network disk, storing the necessary dependencies for deployment. Finally, line #9 prints out the content of the file, allowing us to verify that the correct versions have been saved. The file print output is what we expected.

After the requirement file, the application file is the next prerequisite for deployment.

Application code

The application file, typically called **app.py**, is essential for deploying a Python application. It contains the primary code, including the core logic and functions, and manages input and output data. The **app.py** file consists of pure Python code. All references to the imported libraries must be defined in the **requirement.txt** file.

Sensitive information, such as database credentials, API keys, or passwords, should never be hardcoded within the application file. Instead, these details should be stored in environment variables or separate configuration files. Additionally, the application file should not contain testing code or unnecessary code. You should write separate files for testing, debugging scripts, and non-essential code.

In our calculator app example, the application file contains the calculator logic function, the Gradio UI components, and the launch statement.

There are various methods for exporting or creating an application file from a Jupyter Notebook. One option is to copy and paste the code from the Jupyter Notebook into a text editor. Alternatively, you can use the Jupyter Notebook magic command **%%write** to export the file directly. The code is as follows:

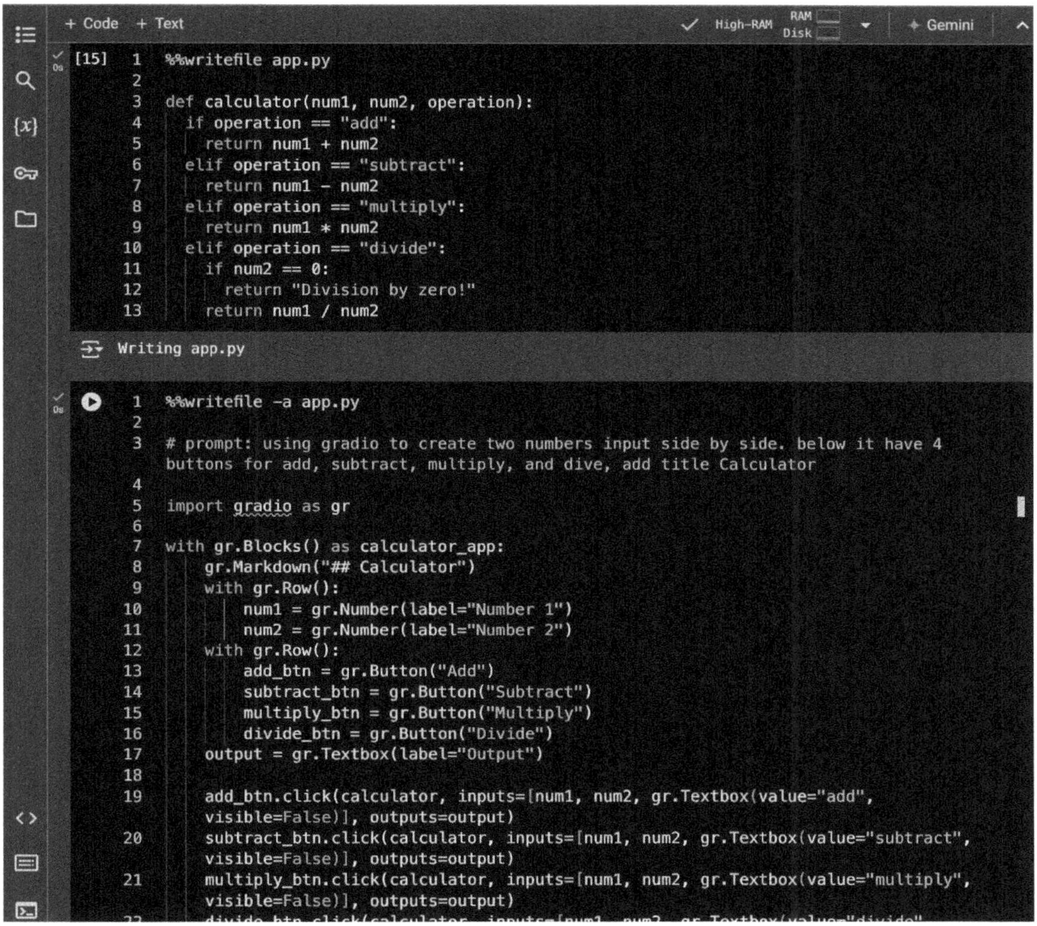

```
[15] 1 %%writefile app.py
     2
     3 def calculator(num1, num2, operation):
     4     if operation == "add":
     5         return num1 + num2
     6     elif operation == "subtract":
     7         return num1 - num2
     8     elif operation == "multiply":
     9         return num1 * num2
    10     elif operation == "divide":
    11         if num2 == 0:
    12             return "Division by zero!"
    13         return num1 / num2

Writing app.py

 1 %%writefile -a app.py
 2
 3 # prompt: using gradio to create two numbers input side by side. below it have 4
   buttons for add, subtract, multiply, and dive, add title Calculator
 4
 5 import gradio as gr
 6
 7 with gr.Blocks() as calculator_app:
 8     gr.Markdown("## Calculator")
 9     with gr.Row():
10         num1 = gr.Number(label="Number 1")
11         num2 = gr.Number(label="Number 2")
12     with gr.Row():
13         add_btn = gr.Button("Add")
14         subtract_btn = gr.Button("Subtract")
15         multiply_btn = gr.Button("Multiply")
16         divide_btn = gr.Button("Divide")
17     output = gr.Textbox(label="Output")
18
19     add_btn.click(calculator, inputs=[num1, num2, gr.Textbox(value="add",
    visible=False)], outputs=output)
20     subtract_btn.click(calculator, inputs=[num1, num2, gr.Textbox(value="subtract",
    visible=False)], outputs=output)
21     multiply_btn.click(calculator, inputs=[num1, num2, gr.Textbox(value="multiply",
    visible=False)], outputs=output)
```

Figure 7.18: Export the application file

Figure 7.18 shows how to export the code from the two code cells for the calculator app. On the first code cell line #1, export the code to the application file using the **`%%write app.py`** command. In the second code cell, line #1, append the code to the application file using the **`%%writefile -a app.py`** command.

The output is the file **`app.py`** created in our local or network disk drive. Next a discussion on the container.

Container

In the context of deploying software, a container is a lightweight, portable, and self-sufficient environment containing an application and its dependencies. Containers ensure that the software runs consistently across various environments, from a developer's local machine to testing and production environments.

Containers contain everything required to run an application: the code, runtime, system tools, libraries, and settings. This isolation helps to avoid issues related to software running differently due to variations in the underlying infrastructure. For example, suppose an application runs properly on a developer's laptop or online development environment but fails in production. In that case, containers can prevent such discrepancies by maintaining a consistent environment throughout development and deployment.

However, containers are not always necessary. Traditional deployment methods may be sufficient for simple applications or environments with well-managed consistency. Containers add complexity and overhead that might be unnecessary for smaller projects or teams. Containers are typically written in Docker format using the **Go programming language (Golang)**. The docker-compose is commonly written in the **Yet Another Markup Language (YAML)** file.

Lucky for us, the Hugging Face platform will automatically generate the appropriate container file. All it requires is for us to upload the `requirements.txt` and `app.py` files, which is the next step.

Transport layer

Copying code from a laptop or cloud storage to a production server is the final application deployment step, the transport step. There are several methods to accomplish this, with one typical approach being **File Transfer Protocol (FTP)**. FTP allows direct file transfer between the local machine and the server. An FTP client, such as FileZilla or WinSCP, is used to connect to the FTP server on the production machine. This setup enables manual file uploads, often through a simple drag-and-drop interface. FTP is useful for uncomplicated file transfers and speedy deployments.

However, Hugging Face does not prefer FTP. The preferred method is GitHub, the most popular platform for version control and collaboration. Developers can upload their code to a GitHub repository, ensuring it is stored and managed centrally. The production server can then retrieve this code using Git commands. This method facilitates the transfer of code, tracks changes, supports rollback capabilities, and encourages teamwork.

In addition to FTP and GitHub, there are other methods for transferring code to a production server. One such method is the **Secure Copy Protocol (SCP)**, which enables secure file transfers between hosts on a network. The Hugging Face platform utilizes GitHub for storing and managing files, making the GitHub method a convenient choice for users. To execute Git commands, you typically use a terminal command console or the official GitHub desktop application.

There are three steps to deploy an application to Hugging Face.

1. Create Hugging Face space
2. Upload requirements and app files
3. Test the app

We start with creating a Hugging Face space.

Create Hugging Face space

To upload any file, we first need to create an account with Hugging Face. The process of creating a Hugging Face account is straightforward, so we will not go through a step-by-step guide. Begin by visiting the link **https://Hugging Face.co/** (note: this is not a **.com** link) and click on the **Sign Up** button. Creating an account is free.

After you sign up and log in, click on the **Spaces** icon at the top of the page, then select the **Create a new Space** button. A screenshot demonstrating how to create a new space is provided as follows:

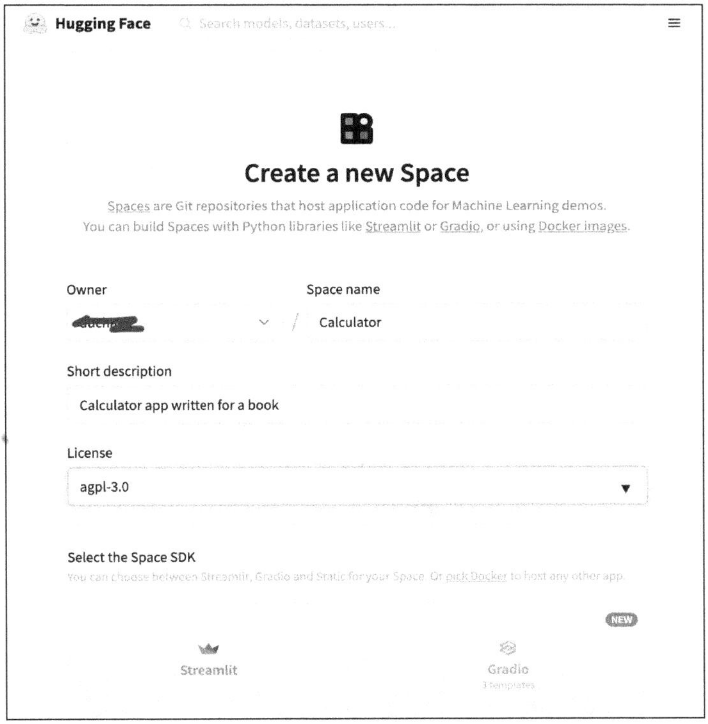

Figure 7.19: Create new space on Hugging Face

Figure 7.19 shows the Hugging Face **Create a new Space** screen. In this form, we entered the space name as **Calculator**, wrote a short description, selected the open-source AGPL-3.0 (GNU) license, and chose Gadio for the SDK. For the space hardware, we opted for the free option, which includes two vCPUs and 16 GB of RAM. Lastly, we clicked the **Create Space** button. Note that the hardware and submit buttons are located below the fold and are not displayed in *Figure 7.19*.

Next is uploading files to Hugging Face.

Upload requirements and app files

After creating your Hugging Face space, upload your **app.py** and **requirements.txt** files. There are two common methods for doing this. The first option is to click on the **Files** icon at the top and then click the **Add File** button to upload the **requirements.txt** file, followed by the **app.py** file.

The second option is to clone your space from Hugging Face. You can use the following Git command to clone: **git clone https://Hugging Face.co/spaces/YOUR_USERNAME/ Calculator**, where **YOUR_NAME** is the username when creating your Hugging Face account. After cloning, use Git commands to add the files, commit your changes, and push them to Hugging Face GitHub.

The last step is to test our calculator app.

Test the app

Once the requirements file and application files are uploaded, the Hugging Face system automatically begins the build process, packaging everything into a containerized environment and deploying the code to a production server.

During this process, we can monitor the build logs in real-time, watching as the system installs dependencies, configures the environment, and prepares the app for deployment. This step ensures that everything is set up correctly. If there are any missing libraries, version conflicts, or errors, we can catch them early before the app goes live.

After a few minutes, the build completes, and the calculator app is officially deployed on Hugging Face. We can test it directly on the platform, verifying that all features work as expected. The final step is perhaps the most satisfying. We now have a live URL that we can share with friends, colleagues, or anyone interested in trying out the app.

What once required extensive manual configuration can now be done in minutes, thanks to the combination of Python, Gradio, and Hugging Face's streamlined deployment system. The image below is of the calculator app on Hugging Face.

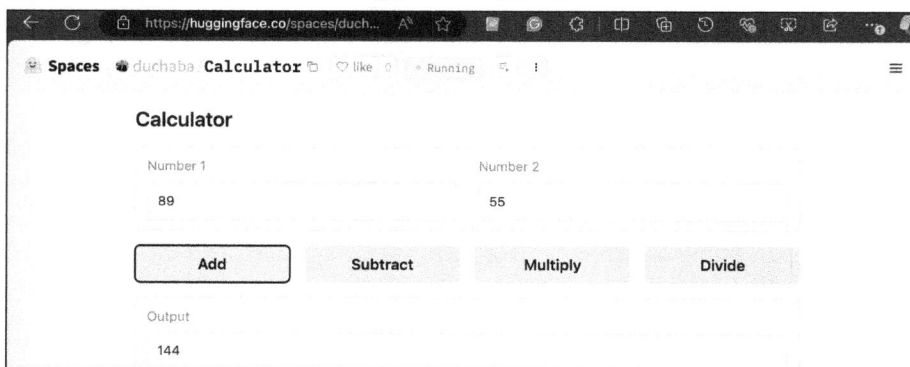

Figure 7.20: Calculator app on Hugging Face

Figure 7.20 displays the calculator app deployed on Hugging Face, now running on a fully functional production server. Visually, it looks identical to the calculator app we built and tested in Jupyter Notebook, and that is precisely how it should be. The logic, user interface, and API calls remain the same, but a lot more is happening behind the scenes.

To get to this point, we have navigated multiple layers of web application deployment. We have learned about client-side interfaces, API communication, server-side processing, Gradio's role in UI generation, containerization, and the transport layer that connects everything. It may seem like a long journey to get the same app running in the cloud, but the true lesson here is scalability.

When building applications, local testing is only the first step. A single user running a script on their laptop is very different from an application handling millions of users simultaneously. The ability to deploy an application to a production server, accessible from any device worldwide, distinguishes personal projects from real-world applications.

We have not just built an app; we have learned the process of making our code accessible, scalable, and shareable. Whether it is a simple calculator, a machine learning model, or a complex AI-powered service, the knowledge gained here applies to any future deployment. So far, we have allowed GPT-4o to choose the suitable Gradio GUI widgets, but next, we will pull back the curtain and examine the Gradio library.

Design with Gradio

Gradio is a Python library designed to simplify user interface development, making it an essential tool for building interactive applications with minimal effort. Throughout this chapter, we have leveraged Gradio to create GUI for our **calculator**, **quick sort,** and **CNN image classification** app. Gradio ability to quickly transform Python functions into fully functional web applications makes it particularly useful for both beginners and experienced developers.

One of Gradio's biggest advantages is its ease of use. With just a few lines of Python code, we can create a web-based interface that allows users to interact with a program, whether sorting numbers, performing calculations, or analyzing snake images. The library abstracts away the complexities of UI development, enabling us to focus on the core application logic rather than worrying about web interfaces.

Gradio supports a variety of input and output formats, making it a versatile tool for building interactive applications. So far, we have relied on GPT-4o to select the most suitable Gradio widgets for our projects, allowing us to focus on functionality rather than manually configuring UI elements.

Gradio provides over 30 built-in components, ranging from basic text boxes, radio buttons, checkboxes, and image uploaders to more advanced elements like audio players and video displays. It even includes an HTML wrapper, which allows for custom HTML integration, giving developers the flexibility to enhance their web interfaces with additional elements beyond the default Gradio components. For more advanced customizations, such as adding custom CSS or JavaScript, Gradio provides options to include these through Blocks or Interface constructors.

The following is an example output showcasing a few Gradio widgets in action:

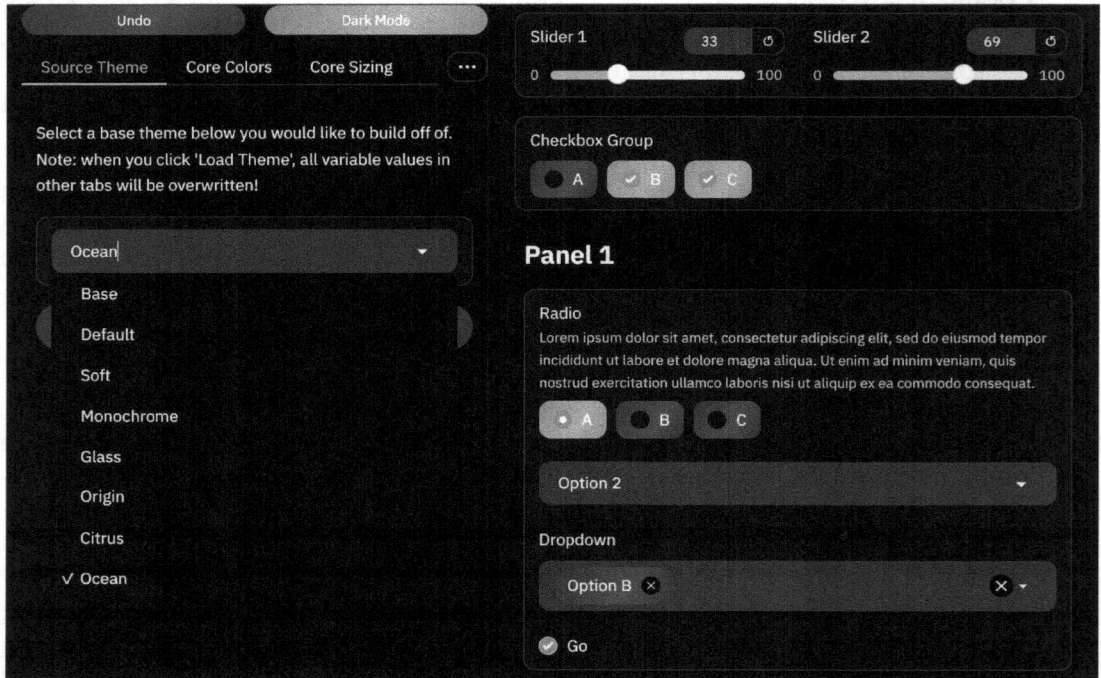

Figure 7.21: Gradio widgets

Figure 7.21 showcases a selection of built-in Gradio widgets, demonstrating the library's versatility. By default, Gradio offers eight themes, starting with Base, the default setting, and extending to more visually distinct options like Ocean, which features a blue and green color scheme. We selected the Ocean theme for our interface, giving the UI a clean and modern look.

The sample interface includes buttons, dropdown lists, tabs, sliders, checkboxes, radio buttons, and panels, each offering different ways for users to interact with a web app. These widgets make it easy to build intuitive and user-friendly interfaces with minimal coding.

Beyond the default settings, Gradio allows extensive customization, offering control over a hundred theme parameters through its built-in theme editor. This flexibility enables developers to fine-tune elements like colors, typography, button styles, and layout spacing, ensuring that the UI aligns with specific branding or design preferences. The following code invokes the theme builder:

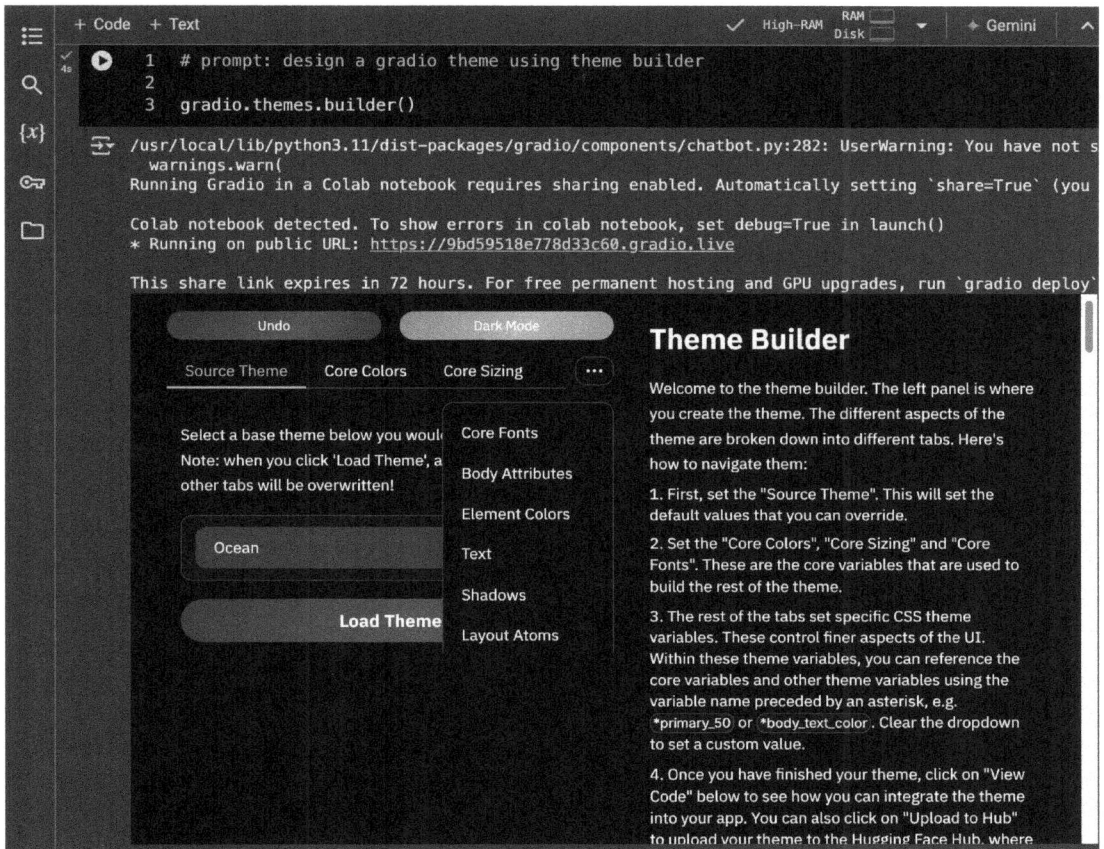

Figure 7.22: *Gradio theme builder*

Figure 7.22 presents the code and output of the Gradio Theme Builder, a comprehensive tool that allows complete UI customization. Line #1 is the GPT-4o prompt, and line #3 activates Gradio's theme builder function using `gradio.theme.builder()`.

The output is a fully interactive theme editor running directly within Jupyter Notebook. With hundreds of customization options, it enables fine-tuning of UI elements such as colors, fonts, buttons, borders, and spacing through a simple graphical interface. This tool is remarkable because it eliminates the need for manual CSS coding. Once satisfied with the changes, the theme settings can be saved and reused across multiple Gradio applications.

One significant advantage of Gradio is its integration with Hugging Face, which enables us to store and manage themes in the cloud. It allows us to apply a custom theme across multiple projects without redefining UI settings each time.

In this chapter, we have discussed various topics, including client-server interactions, API integration, and the deployment of real-world applications. Now, it is time to consolidate our knowledge with a conclusion.

Conclusion

Deploying our code into the real world is one of the most satisfying milestones in learning to program. After investing time in understanding APIs, client-server interactions, and deployment workflows, we have reached a point where our projects are no longer confined to local machines. They are now accessible to friends and colleagues. Seeing something we built live on the web, ready for real-world interaction, is a defining moment that separates learning to code from becoming a developer.

Throughout this Python coding journey, we explored how different parts of an application work together. We learned about APIs, the essential bridges that allow software components to communicate. We examined server-side programming, where the application's core logic runs, and client-side development, which defines the user experience. Understanding these elements has equipped us with the knowledge to deploy functional applications that people can use.

Deploying code is more than just making it work on our machine. It is about hosting it on platforms like Hugging Face, ensuring it runs smoothly on a server, and making it accessible to users worldwide. This process also introduces us to the realities of maintaining live applications, an essential skill in software development.

A key enabler in this journey has been Gradio, a practical Python library that allows us to build web interfaces without needing to master front-end development. With prebuilt widgets such as buttons, sliders, and text boxes, Gradio has simplified the process of making our applications interactive and user-friendly without writing a single line of HTML, CSS, or JavaScript. Whether creating a basic calculator, implementing a quick sort visualization, or deploying a CNN image classifier, Gradio has helped us bridge the gap between Python scripts and real-world usability.

Throughout this process, GPT-4o has been an invaluable tutor and assistant, helping us troubleshoot errors, optimize our code, and even generate UI elements. However, we must not use GPT-4o as a crutch. Learning with AI is about enhancing our understanding, not bypassing critical thinking. The ability to analyze problems, test solutions, and refine code independently remains essential. GPT-4o is an extraordinary tool, but true mastery comes from balancing AI-assisted learning with deep, hands-on problem-solving.

The true joy of deployment comes from watching our work come to life. What started as lines of code in a Jupyter Notebook is now a fully functional application, accessible to anyone with an internet connection. It is not just a milestone in coding. It is a real-world achievement demonstrating our ability to build, deploy, and share technology. It also opens the door to more advanced projects, larger-scale applications, and new opportunities.

As we move forward, it is time to shift gears. The next chapter explores the crucial topic of fairness and bias in programming.

CHAPTER 8

Fairness and Bias

Introduction

In this chapter, we will go over the concept of fairness and bias within GenAI use. Generative AI is rapidly becoming further integrated into everyday life. Although these systems are highly advanced, they are built on data that remains humanmade, which can reflect human prejudice and bias. This chapter explores the relationship between the fairness of content and the use of GenAI, highlighting ethical considerations, unwanted biases, and responsibility as users.

As beginner programmers, we will learn bias and fairness in AI are problems not only for big tech companies to solve. However, the truth is, bias in programming starts at the most basic level, with the choices we make when writing code. Whether designing a new algorithm, building a student recommendation system, or training a CNN model for snake classification, the way we structure our programs, the data we use, and the assumptions we make can all introduce bias without us even realizing it.

Before going further, we will try a simple test. We ask ChatGPT-4o and Gemini to draw a doctor. We have tried it dozens of times, and here is a sample of what we found:

Figure 8.1 *Draw a doctor*

Figure 8.1 shows an image of a male doctor. We tested the same prompt multiple times: **Draw a doctor**, and while each result was different, none of the images ever featured a woman doctor. We did not include anything in our prompt that might skew the results, like: **Draw a doctor, and he is busy in the ER helping a patient**. However, when we adjusted the prompt to: **Draw a doctor, and she is busy in the ER helping a patient**, GPT-4o picked up on the nuance and generated an image of a woman doctor.

According to **PubMed Central (PMC)** and the **Association of American Medical Colleges (AAMC)**, the global percentage of male and female doctors is approximately 60% male and 40% female. That means if we asked GPT-4o to generate 20 images of doctors, we should expect around eight images of women doctors. Yet, that was not the case.

This example is just the tip of the iceberg. Fairness and bias in **Generative AI (GenAI)** go beyond obvious patterns and show up more subtly across all major AI models, including GPT-4o, Claude, Gemini, Copilot, LaMDA, and many others. Understanding these biases is crucial because they shape how AI represents the world, and sometimes, those representations are not as balanced as they should be.

Structure

The following topics will be discussed within this chapter:

- GenAI impacts on humans
- Infiltration of bias
- Fighting for fairness
- Upholding accountability

Objectives

By the end of this chapter, readers will understand the potential for bias in Generative AI, recognize how it affects fairness, and learn strategies to minimize bias in AI development and application. Bias is not always obvious, but it can influence the way AI models generate text, images, and decisions, shaping how people interact with technology in ways that may not always be fair or accurate.

Recognizing bias is the first step in addressing it. AI models are trained on human data, meaning they can inherit and amplify existing biases. Whether it is an AI-generated job recommendation that favors specific demographics, a chatbot that reflects cultural stereotypes, or an image generator that assumes a doctor must be a man, these biases can reinforce real-world inequalities if left unchecked.

Let us start with the first topic: how GenAI impacts humans.

GenAI impacts on humans

There is no doubt that the surge of GenAI has impacted how we function in today's world, from content creation to automatization to ethical considerations. GenAI is not just a social media trend. It is shaping everything from content creation and automation to raising important ethical questions. GenAI is already influencing how we create, communicate, and even operate businesses, and it is only going to grow.

For programmers, even beginners, this is not merely an abstract discussion. GenAI is fundamentally changing how code is written, optimized, and maintained. It is making development more accessible, automating tedious tasks, and accelerating innovation. But it also introduces new challenges: *How do we ensure fairness in AI-driven decision-making? How do we prevent biases from creeping into models that influence millions of people? What happens when AI-generated code becomes so widespread that debugging and accountability become harder?*

Ignoring GenAI is not an option, especially for those just starting in programming. Understanding its capabilities, limitations, and ethical implications will be just as crucial as learning to write efficient code. The programmers who grasp how to use AI and how it affects human lives will be the ones shaping the future.

To understand how GenAI is changing, we will explore the following three major areas that are directly affecting our daily lives:

- Content creation and creativity
- Decision-making and automation
- Employment and skills

We will first take a look at content creation.

Content creation and creativity

GenAI has revolutionized creative industries, enabling faster content production in areas like art, music, and writing. It assists in generating new ideas and automating tasks, making creative processes more efficient. It is no longer just a tool. It is an active collaborator, helping artists generate new ideas, automate tedious tasks, and push creative boundaries in ways that were once impossible. Whether it is assisting with design, composing music, or even writing full articles, GenAI is changing how creative work is made and consumed. However, with these advancements come questions about originality, authenticity, and the role of human creativity in a world where AI can generate content in seconds.

To fully explore GenAI's impact on creativity, we will focus on five key areas where its influence is undeniable:

- Art and design
- Writing and journalism
- Film and entertainment
- Music composition
- Gaming

Art and design are up first.

Art and design

GenAI has significantly transformed the creative landscape, particularly in *visual art* and *graphic design*. Artists and designers now leverage AI to craft unique digital artworks, generate intricate patterns, and experiment with diverse styles, pushing creative boundaries and enabling rapid prototyping of new aesthetics.

In visual art, GenAI enables artists and designers to create unique digital artwork, generate patterns, and experiment with styles. AI-generated art can push creative boundaries, allowing for rapid prototyping and exploration of new aesthetics. For instance, the *Photo Brussels 2025 festival*, in *The Guardian* article, prominently featured AI-generated photography projects, showcasing how artists utilize AI to blend historical contexts with modern themes. For example, *Pascal Sgro's Cherry Airlines* series used AI to create images that merge 1950s air travel with contemporary environmental concerns.

In graphic design, tools like AI-driven design software streamline tasks such as logo creation, layout design, and image editing, making the design process faster and more accessible to non-experts. Platforms like *Canva* have integrated AI technologies to transform data into visuals and provide design inspiration, democratizing design and enabling users without formal training to produce professional-quality graphics, as reported by *Wired* magazine.

Next is how GenAI is impacting writing and journalism.

Writing and journalism

GenAI has significantly transformed content creation and editing, streamlined processes and enhancing efficiency across various domains.

In content creation, GenAI can write articles, blogs, and social media posts based on prompts, freeing up writers for more strategic or creative tasks. Journalists use AI to produce news summaries, reports, or financial updates, speeding up content delivery. For instance, many popular writers on *Substack* have started utilizing AI writing tools to help produce their content. The study from *Wired* magazine revealed that out of the top 100 newsletters on the platform, ten use AI in some capacity, and seven rely heavily on it. This trend is most notable among newsletters focused on investment news and personal finance advice.

In editing, AI-powered tools assist with grammar, style, and structural edits, making the writing process more efficient. They can also suggest improvements based on tone and readability. For example, content creators are increasingly using AI to generate significant monthly incomes by leveraging its powerful video production capabilities. *Synthesia*, a leading company in this space, enables creators to produce lifelike AI video versions of themselves by uploading a short clip, facilitating infinite video creation without expensive setups. As the *New York Post* news website *(NYPost)* reported, influencers can create multilingual videos, expanding their reach globally. *Matt Par*, a YouTuber with over 750,000 subscribers, employs AI for content generation, scripting, editing, and narration, cutting production times from six hours to one and reducing freelancer costs.

These examples illustrate how GenAI is reshaping content creation and editing, offering tools that enhance efficiency and open new avenues for creative expression.

Film and entertainment

GenAI is making significant inroads in the film industry, particularly in scriptwriting and **Visual Effects** (**VFX**), by offering tools that enhance creativity and streamline production processes.

In scriptwriting, GenAI aids in the development of scripts, dialogue, and storylines, offering suggestions that align with specific genres or themes. It helps filmmakers prototype ideas or explore new plot twists more quickly. For instance, the 2024 Swiss film *The Last Screenwriter* was written using ChatGPT 4.0, marking one of the first instances of a feature film script being entirely crafted by AI, as reported in the *Wikipedia*. The film explores a narrative where a human screenwriter confronts an AI scriptwriting system that matches his skills, reflecting the growing intersection of AI and storytelling.

As we pitch the movie to producers, we need an image.

Figure 8.2: *A movie for human writers confronts AI writers*

Figure 8.2 is an image created by DALL-E3 through ChatGPT.

In special effects and animation, AI enhances animation and VFX by automating tedious tasks such as character movements, object rendering, and environmental details, resulting in more dynamic and detailed productions. According to *Synapse Studio*, AI's integration into VFX creation allows for more efficient workflows and the generation of complex visual elements that would be time-consuming to produce manually (in 2024).

These advancements illustrate how GenAI is reshaping the film industry, offering tools that enhance efficiency and open new avenues for creative expression.

Music composition

GenAI is making significant strides in the music industry, transforming both music production and sound design by offering innovative tools that enhance creativity and streamline workflows.

In music production, AI tools assist composers in generating melodies, harmonies, or even entire tracks. Musicians can use AI to create music by providing a genre or mood, blending styles, or remixing existing sounds. For instance, **Artificial Intelligence Virtual Artist (AIVA)** is an AI music generation assistant that allows users to generate new songs in more than 250 different styles within seconds. Whether you are a complete beginner or a seasoned professional, AIVA enables the creation of unique compositions tailored to specific needs.

In sound design, AI-driven platforms help with sound design for films, games, and virtual environments, automating background sounds, effects, or creating immersive audio landscapes. For example, *ElevenLabs* has developed AI technology capable of generating a wide variety of sound effects for various use cases, including film, media, and video games. By simply describing the desired sound effect, users can generate multiple samples to choose from, streamlining the sound design process, as reported by *Y.M. Cinema* magazine.

Gaming

GenAI is transforming the gaming industry by streamlining development and enhancing player experiences.

In game design, GenAI is used to create game environments, characters, and storylines, reducing the workload for developers and enabling more immersive gaming experiences. AI can generate vast, procedurally designed worlds with minimal human input. For instance, *No Man's Sky* utilizes procedural generation to create a universe with billions of unique planets, each featuring its ecosystems, biodiversity, and weather conditions, offering players an expansive and engaging experience, as the *101 Blockchains* website reported.

In adaptive AI opponents, in-game AI is becoming more sophisticated, with AI-generated opponents that adapt to player behavior, creating more dynamic and challenging gameplay experiences. As reported by the *Block Unix* website, AI opponents evolve to mimic real-world player behavior in sports games like *FIFA* and *NBA 2K*, adjusting their strategies based on the player's actions to create more authentic matches.

Let us see if GPT-4o can create a new gaming character for us.

Figure 8.3: *Writer and explorer gamming character*

Figure 8.3 shows a picture of a new gaming character. On weekdays, she is studying to become a writer, and on weekends, she explores ancient ruins. It is difficult to compete with AI when it comes to generating computer gaming characters, as no combination seems too challenging for it. We particularly like her book-size backpack and the ubiquitous writer-hoodie as she searches for rare books in mythical ruins.

These advancements illustrate how GenAI is reshaping the gaming landscape, offering tools that enhance efficiency and open new avenues for creative expression. As we close up on content and creation, we move to GenAI impact on decision-making and automation.

Decision-making and automation

GenAI is dramatically changing how decisions are made and how tasks are automated in a wide range of industries. By offering faster, more accurate data analysis, predictive modeling, and personalized recommendations, GenAI enhances decision-making processes. It also automates repetitive tasks like data processing and report generation, improving operational efficiency and freeing up human resources for more complex, strategic work.

The impact of GenAI goes beyond just making processes faster. It fundamentally shapes how businesses, governments, and individuals interact with data. Organizations no longer need to rely solely on human intuition or past experience to make decisions. AI-driven insights provide a data-backed approach that can predict trends, detect anomalies, and uncover opportunities that might have otherwise gone unnoticed.

We will take a closer look at how GenAI is shaping decision-making and automation by exploring the following topics.

- Enhanced decision making
- Automation of routine tasks
- Personalized decision-making support
- Real-time decision making
- Improved accuracy and precision

Coming up is a closer look at enhancing decision making.

Enhanced decision making

GenAI transforms decision-making and task automation across various industries by processing vast datasets, identifying patterns, and generating insights that inform strategic choices. By analyzing complex information, AI systems enable more informed, evidence-based decisions in fields like finance, healthcare, and marketing.

In data-driven insights, GenAI processes large volumes of data to identify patterns and generate actionable insights. In finance, for instance, AI analyzes market trends and investor behaviors to inform investment strategies. According to the article *7 Unexpected Ways AI Can Transform Your Investment Strategy*, on the *Investopedia* website, over 90% of investment managers are integrating AI into their processes, with 54% already using it to analyze vast amounts of financial and alternative data in real time, enabling more informed decision-making.

In predictive modelling, AI-driven predictive models forecast future outcomes based on historical data. GenAI predicts customer behavior, market trends, and risk factors, enabling proactive strategies. For example, according to the *How AI decision-making improves Business Outcomes* article from the *Lumenalta* website, companies use AI to simulate various business scenarios, allowing decision-makers to test different strategies before implementation. By creating virtual models, businesses can explore potential outcomes without real-world consequences, which is especially valuable in the finance and real estate industries.

In reduced human bias, ideally, AI models offer more objective decisions by relying on data rather than human intuition, which can be influenced by cognitive biases. However, this objectivity depends on the quality of the data and models used, as biased data can still lead to biased outcomes. The article *Shedding Light on AI Bias with real-world* on the *IBM* website highlights that when discriminatory data and algorithms are incorporated into AI models, they can deploy biases at scale, amplifying negative effects.

These examples illustrate how GenAI enhances decision-making and automates tasks across industries, leading to more efficient and informed operations.

Automation of routine tasks

GenAI is revolutionizing how organizations operate by enhancing operational efficiency and automating workflows. By taking over repetitive and time-consuming tasks, GenAI allows human workers to focus on strategic and creative endeavors, thereby driving innovation and productivity.

In operational efficiency, GenAI automates repetitive and time-consuming tasks, such as data entry, report generation, and customer service interactions. This process reduces manual workloads and allows humans to focus on more strategic and creative tasks. For example, consulting firms have adopted AI tools to handle routine tasks, resulting in significant time savings. According to *The Australian* news website, some consultants have reported saving up to 7.5 hours per week by using AI for tasks like email drafting and document summarization.

In workflow automation, AI-driven tools streamline workflows by automating processes like inventory management, scheduling, and document processing. For instance, in HR, AI systems can automatically screen resumes, schedule interviews, and handle onboarding paperwork. Based on reports from the *Business Insider* news website in the article *JPMorgan Generative AI Adoption LLM Suite*, JPMorgan Chase has implemented a GenAI tool known as the **LLM Suite** for its 200,000 employees. This tool enhances efficiency in daily tasks, allowing staff to focus on more complex responsibilities.

These examples illustrate how GenAI is transforming operational workflows, enabling organizations to allocate human resources to more strategic and creative tasks.

Personalized decision-making support

GenAI is transforming how we make decisions by providing personalized recommendations and creating adaptive systems that respond to individual needs and changing conditions. This technology is becoming increasingly prevalent across various sectors, enhancing user experiences and outcomes.

In tailored recommendations, GenAI helps individuals make personalized decisions by generating customized recommendations based on preferences, behaviors, and historical data. This is prevalent in e-commerce (product recommendations), entertainment (movie or music suggestions), and healthcare (personalized treatment plans). For example, in e-commerce, AI analyzes user behavior to offer personalized product recommendations, enhancing the shopping experience and increasing sales. According to *Rapid Innovation's* article *AI-Powered Product Recommendations in Retail E-Commerce*, AI systems can suggest products that are more likely to resonate with individual shoppers by analyzing customer behavior and preferences.

In adaptive systems, AI systems can adapt to changing conditions or inputs, continuously improving their recommendations. For instance, in financial services, AI-powered tools can generate real-time investment advice based on market fluctuations or personal risk tolerance. For instance, Bank of America's virtual assistant, Erica, helps customers make smarter banking decisions by analyzing their financial habits and offering personalized recommendations, as reported in the article *Use Cases and Real Examples of Generative AI in Financial Services* by *WeGile* news website.

These examples illustrate how GenAI enhances decision-making by offering personalized and adaptive solutions across various industries.

Real-time decision-making

GenAI is transforming industries by enabling rapid data analysis and automating complex decision-making processes. In sectors like finance and cybersecurity, where real-time responses are critical, GenAI's capabilities are particularly impactful.

In faster response times, industries like finance or cybersecurity, where real-time decisions are crucial, GenAI can quickly analyze incoming data and generate immediate actions. This innovation can lead to faster responses to market shifts, threats, or emergencies. For instance, in cybersecurity, AI-driven systems can continuously monitor network traffic, detect anomalies, and respond to potential threats in real-time, significantly reducing the window of vulnerability. According to *Palo Alto Networks* article *What Is Generative AI in Cybersecurity* AI is transforming how security professionals predict, detect, and respond to threats by leveraging machine learning models to simulate cyberattacks and defensive strategies.

In automated trading, AI algorithms are used to execute trades at high speeds based on real-time data analysis, removing human emotion from high-stakes decision-making processes. These AI-driven algorithms analyze vast amounts of market data to identify patterns and execute trades with precision. According to the article *7 Unexpected Ways AI Can Transform Your Investment Strategy* reported by the *Investopedia* news website, over 90% of investment managers are integrating AI into their processes, with 54% already using it to analyze vast amounts of financial and alternative data in real-time, enabling more informed decision-making.

These examples illustrate how GenAI enhances operational efficiency and decision-making in critical industries by providing rapid data analysis and automating complex processes.

Improved accuracy and precision

GenAI is transforming industries by enhancing precision and tackling complex challenges. In fields where accuracy is paramount, such as medical diagnostics and manufacturing, GenAI minimizes human error by detecting subtle patterns or anomalies that might be overlooked. Additionally, GenAI excels in modeling intricate systems, simulating scenarios, and proposing solutions to problems that are too complex for human analysis alone, benefiting areas like scientific research, urban planning, and logistics optimization.

In reducing human error, areas where precision is critical, such as medical diagnostics or manufacturing, GenAI enhances decision-making by reducing the likelihood of human error. AI-driven systems can detect subtle patterns or anomalies that humans might overlook. For instance, the article *AI SAY 'Landmark' moment as NHS clinics use AI to 'detect breast cancer cases earlier and faster'* in the *Scottish Sun* news website reported that the NHS is trailing AI technology to screen for breast cancer, aiming to detect abnormalities earlier and faster. This initiative could allow radiologists to identify cancers in their early stages more effectively.

In complex problem solving, GenAI can model complex systems, simulate scenarios, and suggest solutions to problems that may be too intricate for human analysis alone. This process is particularly useful in scientific research, urban planning, and logistics optimization. According to the **Massachusetts Institute of Technology (MIT)** news website article *Scientists use Generative AI to answer complex questions in physics,* AI advancement aids in understanding complex physical systems and accelerates discoveries in material science.

These examples illustrate how GenAI enhances precision and problem-solving capabilities across various sectors, leading to improved outcomes and innovative solutions.

That wraps up the discussion on GenAI's impacts on decision-making and automation. Moving forward, we will analyze employment and skills effects of GenAI.

Employment and skills

The rise of GenAI is dramatically reshaping the employment landscape and the skills needed to thrive in a wide range of industries. As AI takes on routine tasks and automates processes, both opportunities and challenges emerge for workers and organizations alike. The following topics will provide a deeper look into these areas, outlining the key impacts of GenAI on employment and skills development.

The following topics will provide a deeper look into these areas, outlining the key impacts of GenAI on employment and skills development. We will explore how AI creates new career paths, changes traditional job roles, and pushes industries to rethink the most valuable skills. From upskilling initiatives to the rise of AI-assisted professions, understanding these shifts will be essential for anyone looking to stay competitive in a workforce increasingly shaped by AI.

The GenAI impact topics are as follows:

- Automation of routine tasks
- Job displacement and workforce shifts
- Creation of new roles and opportunities
- Changes in required skills

First, we move forward with GenAI impacts automation and routine tasks.

Automation of routine tasks

GenAI is transforming the employment landscape by automating routine tasks and enhancing operational efficiency across various industries. This shift presents both challenges and opportunities for workers and organizations.

In task replacement, GenAI is increasingly automating routine and repetitive tasks across industries such as data entry, report generation, customer service, and even content creation. Jobs that involve these types of tasks are at risk of being replaced, reducing the demand for certain roles in fields like administrative support, manufacturing, and customer service. According to the article *Generative AI for Business Automation: Improving Efficiency & Reducing Cost* from the *Index* news website, McKinsey reports that GenAI could automate up to 70% of tasks, potentially leading to significant changes in the workforce.

In efficiency gains, automating these tasks means increased efficiency and cost savings. GenAI can perform certain functions faster and more accurately than humans, freeing up human workers to focus on more complex, creative, or strategic tasks. A study by *Goldman Sachs* found that companies adopting AI have seen productivity increases of about 25%, highlighting the significant efficiency gains achievable through AI integration; according to the article, *AI is showing "very positive" signs of eventually boosting GDP and productivity* on the *Goldman Sachs* website.

These developments underscore the importance of reskilling and upskilling the workforce to adapt to the evolving demands of the job market in the age of AI.

Job displacement and workforce shifts

GenAI is reshaping the employment landscape, presenting both challenges and opportunities. While automation can lead to job displacement in certain sectors, it also creates demand for new roles that require advanced technical skills.

In job losses in certain sectors, the automation of tasks traditionally performed by humans can lead to job displacement, particularly in industries like manufacturing, logistics, and some service sectors. Workers in roles that are easily automated may face job insecurity as companies adopt AI-driven solutions. A study by *Oxford Economics* predicts that up to 20 million manufacturing jobs worldwide could be replaced by robots by 2030, as reported in the article *How AI is Impacting the U.S. Workforce* by the *Camoin Associates* news website.

In shifts in job demand, as some jobs are displaced, new types of roles are emerging. AI-related jobs, such as AI development, machine learning engineering, and data science, are in high demand. Additionally, roles that require managing and overseeing AI systems, as well as ethical oversight positions, are becoming more important. According to the *U.S. Bureau of Labor Statistics*, careers in artificial intelligence are projected to grow 21% from 2021 to 2031, as reported in the article *Jobs That Are Growing With the Rise of AI* by the *Partner Stack* news website.

These developments underscore the importance of reskilling and upskilling the workforce to adapt to the evolving demands of the job market in the age of AI.

Creation of new roles and opportunities

GenAI is reshaping the professional landscape, creating new opportunities and transforming existing roles across various industries. This evolution is particularly evident in the emergence of specialized AI positions and the development of hybrid roles that blend human expertise with AI capabilities.

In AI development and maintenance, the rise of GenAI has created demand for professionals who can develop, maintain, and improve AI systems. These roles include data scientists, machine learning engineers, and AI ethicists, who ensure that AI systems are accurate, efficient, and aligned with ethical standards. According to *Analytics Vidhya*, careers such as AI engineer, machine learning engineer, and data scientist are among the top in-demand AI jobs for 2025, as reported in the article *Top 10 Most In-Demand AI Jobs for 2025* by the *Analytics Vidhya* news website.

In hybrid roles, AI systems take over routine tasks and many jobs are evolving into hybrid roles that combine human creativity, critical thinking, and oversight with AI-powered tools. For example, in fields like marketing or healthcare, professionals now work alongside AI to analyze data and make more informed decisions, rather than handling all aspects manually. According to the article *Hybrid Roles: An Introductory Guide with Examples* in the *Yarooms* news website, in healthcare, roles such as clinical informatics specialists and health data analysts are emerging, combining medical knowledge with technology and data analysis skills to improve patient care and healthcare operations.

These developments highlight the dynamic nature of the modern workforce, emphasizing the importance of adaptability and continuous learning as AI continues to influence various professions.

We asked GPT-4 to imagine a hybrid role in education. Here is one possible hybrid role for a teacher teaching with AI in the classroom.

Figure 8.4: Future hybrid roles for teachers

Figure 8.4 shows an illustration of a teacher using AI in a kindergarten class. The teacher will remain the principal guide for the students, while AI assists in creating class activities and engaging with students during homework. There may not need to be a physical robot present in the classroom.

Changes in required skills

The integration of GenAI across various sectors is reshaping the skill sets required in the modern workforce. As AI systems become more prevalent, employees are expected to develop technical and soft skills to collaborate effectively with these technologies.

In technical skills, the integration of AI in many sectors requires workers to develop new technical skills. This challenge includes understanding how to interact with AI tools, analyze AI-generated data, and potentially even program or modify AI systems. Employees across industries are being asked to gain proficiency in data analysis, machine learning basics, and AI literacy. According to *HR executive,* as AI becomes more integrated into workplaces, workers need a foundational understanding of AI tools and data literacy, as reported in the article *5 essential skills for thriving in the AI-driven workplace of 2025*. These skills enable effective collaboration with AI systems, enhancing their decision-making processes. Companies should invest in targeted training, like machine learning and data visualization workshops, and encourage hands-on experience through internal AI-driven projects.

In soft skills, GenAI automates technical and repetitive tasks, and there is a growing emphasis on soft skills that cannot be easily replaced by AI, such as creativity, critical thinking, emotional intelligence, and interpersonal communication. Workers who excel in these areas will remain valuable in roles that require human judgment and relationship-building. *Forbes* highlights that soft skills, including communication, adaptability, and critical thinking, are essential for success in the AI era, as reported in the article *5 Soft Skills That Are Critical In The Age Of AI* by the *Forbes* website.

These developments underscore the importance of continuous learning and adaptability in the evolving job market. By enhancing both technical and soft skills, workers can remain competitive and effectively collaborate with AI systems in their respective fields.

Wrapping up the GenAI impacts on humans section, we found that GenAI has reshaped many aspects of daily life, from enhancing creativity and automating routine tasks to changing how decisions are made and how jobs evolve. It brings undeniable benefits in efficiency, personalization, and collaboration, but it also introduces challenges, such as the risk of over-reliance on AI and ethical concerns around transparency and accountability.

GenAI is everywhere, transforming industries and how people interact with technology. AI-generated art pushes creative boundaries, businesses automate workflows, and decision-making is becoming more data-driven. The impact is huge, but it is not without risks. As AI takes on more responsibility, there is a genuine concern about bias creeping into the systems that influence hiring, lending, healthcare, and more.

Just as GenAI can enhance human capabilities, it can also reinforce biases already present in the data it learns from. AI models do not think independently. They reflect patterns in the information they process. If that data contains hidden prejudices, AI can amplify them, making unfair decisions at scale. This is why AI bias is not just a technical issue; it is an ethical one. Fixing it requires diverse datasets, better testing, and constant human oversight to ensure fair AI-driven decisions.

For new programmers, this is not just a problem for senior engineers or AI ethics experts. It is your problem, too. The way AI learns is not magic. It is data-driven, meaning the code you write, the datasets you work with, and the algorithm you design will shape how AI interacts with the world. GenAI is not just about automation or deployment. It is about extending human abilities. However, if we do not actively work to make AI fair and accountable. We are limiting human potential. The best future programmers know how to develop AI effectively and ensure it operates fairly. That is not just good ethics. That is sound engineering.

GenAI is powerful, but it is not perfect. The key is to use it as a tool, not a replacement for human judgment. The real challenge is making AI work and ensuring it works fairly, responsibly, and in ways that genuinely improve human lives.

In the next section, we will explore how bias affects GenAI, the sources of these biases, and the potential consequences for fairness and equality in AI-driven decision-making.

Infiltration of bias

Although GenAI is extremely helpful, there are potential downsides to be aware of as a user of GenAI. Bias is an extremely prevalent issue among GenAI, affecting the accuracy of information and potentially perpetuating stereotypes. Bias is an inherent challenge in any system that relies on data, and GenAI is no exception. As AI becomes more integrated into decision-making, content creation, and automation, the biases present in its training data and algorithms have far-reaching consequences.

For new programmers, bias in AI is not just an abstract issue. It is a problem that can show up in every line of code. AI systems are only as good as the data they are trained on, and biased data leads to biased results. Imagine building an AI-powered hiring system that unknowingly favors specific candidates because the training data comes from a company with a history of biased hiring practices. Or a healthcare AI that misdiagnoses certain patient groups because the training data lacks diversity. These are not small mistakes. They have real consequences that affect real people.

Bias is often invisible until it causes harm. That is why new programmers need to think critically about the data they use and the systems they create. AI is not naturally fair. It reflects the patterns in its training data, good or bad. Every decision made during development, from choosing datasets to defining algorithms, shapes how AI behaves. If fairness is not built in from the start, it will not be there at the end.

These biases can manifest in various ways, from reinforcing harmful stereotypes to producing unfair outcomes in areas like hiring, law enforcement, and healthcare. In this section, we will explore how bias enters AI systems, the different forms it takes, and its impact on the fairness and effectiveness of GenAI applications. Let us take a look at some of the ways bias is shown within GenAI.

We will explore the following topics:

- Training data bias
- Stereotyping
- Bias in decision-making
- Content generation bias
- Bias in recommendations and personalization
- Bias amplification
- Bias in visual and audio generation
- Ethical and social consequences

We begin the discussion with training data bias.

Training data bias

GenAI has become a powerful tool across various sectors, but its effectiveness is closely tied to the quality and diversity of the data it learns from. When this data is imbalanced or carries historical prejudices, the AI systems can inadvertently produce biased or unfair outcomes.

In imbalanced data, if the training data used to develop AI models is imbalanced or lacks diversity, the AI can produce skewed results. For example, if a language model is trained primarily on texts from a specific demographic, it may generate outputs that disproportionately reflect that group's language, culture, or values while underrepresenting others. This imbalance can lead to AI applications that fail to effectively serve a diverse user base.

In historical bias, AI systems can inherit and perpetuate biases present in historical data. Suppose an AI is trained on data that reflects past discriminatory practices, such as hiring data that historically favored certain groups. In that case, it may reinforce these biases when generating new outputs or making predictions. This perpetuation of bias can lead to unfair treatment and decision-making in areas like employment, lending, and law enforcement. According to the *Australian Human Rights Commission* news website article *Historical bias in AI systems*, historical bias arises when the data used to train an AI system no longer accurately reflects the current reality. For example, while the *gender pay gap* is still a problem, historically, the financial inequality faced by women was even worse.

These examples highlight the importance of carefully curating training data and implementing strategies to detect and mitigate bias in AI systems. Developers can create more equitable and effective AI applications by addressing these issues.

Stereotyping

GenAI has made significant strides in various fields, but it is crucial to recognize that these systems can inadvertently perpetuate and amplify societal biases present in their training data. Two notable concerns are the reinforcement of stereotypes and associative bias.

In reinforcing stereotypes, GenAI systems can reinforce societal stereotypes by replicating biased patterns present in the data. For example, AI-generated images, text, or media might depict certain groups in stereotypical roles, such as gendered roles in career contexts, or reinforce harmful cultural assumptions. A study by UNESCO, article *Generative AI: UNESCO Study* reveals alarming evidence of regressive gender stereotypes, revealed that Large Language Models often produce gender biases, with women being described in domestic roles far more often than men and frequently associated with words like home, family, and children, while male names were linked to business, executive, salary, and career.

In associative bias, AI models often make associations based on patterns they detect in the data. Suppose certain words or concepts are frequently paired together in biased ways, such as associating men with leadership roles and women with caregiving. In that case, GenAI might generate outputs that mirror these biased associations. For instance, a language translation system could associate some languages with certain genders or ethnic stereotypes, inadvertently reinforcing harmful biases, as reported in the article *What is AI bias?* from the IBM website.

These examples underscore the importance of carefully curating training data and implementing strategies to detect and mitigate bias in AI systems. Developers can create more equitable and effective AI applications by addressing these issues.

Bias in decision-making

GenAI has become a cornerstone in various sectors, streamlining processes and enhancing decision-making. However, it is crucial to recognize that if not carefully managed, GenAI can inadvertently perpetuate biases, leading to unfair or discriminatory outcomes. Two significant concerns in this context are unfair outcomes and predictive bias.

In unfair outcomes, bias in GenAI can lead to unjust or discriminatory outcomes in decision-making processes. For example, AI-driven hiring tools might disadvantage candidates from certain groups if the model is biased toward qualities more commonly found in the data for successful candidates from historically dominant groups. A study by the *University of Washington*, article *AI tools show biases in ranking job applicants' names according to perceived race and gender*, found that AI tools exhibited significant racial and gender biases when ranking job applicants' names, potentially disadvantaging qualified candidates from underrepresented groups.

In predictive bias, AI may disproportionately favor or penalize specific groups if it has learned biased patterns from training data. This bias can lead to unfair predictions in areas such as credit scoring, law enforcement, and healthcare, where AI is increasingly used for decision-making. Research from *Stanford University's* article *How Flawed Data Aggravates Inequality in Credit*, revealed that credit scores for minority groups are about 5% less accurate in predicting default risk compared to non-minority borrowers, highlighting a significant predictive bias in financial AI systems.

These examples underscore the importance of implementing robust measures to detect and mitigate bias in AI systems. By addressing these issues, developers and organizations can work towards creating more equitable and fair AI applications.

Content generation bias

GenAI has revolutionized content creation, but it is essential to recognize that these systems can inadvertently perpetuate biases present in their training data. Two significant concerns are language and representation biases, and cultural erasure.

In language and representation biases, language models may produce biased or offensive content if the underlying training data contains such biases. This bias can manifest in AI-generated articles, essays, or dialogue that reflect gender, racial, or cultural prejudices. For instance, when generating a product description for beauty products, the model might default to language that emphasizes Eurocentric beauty standards, potentially alienating people with different ethnicities, as reported by the article *How Is AI Biased?* from *Acrolinx* news website.

In cultural erasure, AI models may inadvertently underrepresent or exclude certain cultures, languages, or perspectives if these are not adequately represented in the training data. This issue leads to content biased toward more dominant cultural narratives and ignores marginalized voices. For example, according to the scholarly paper *Cultural Incongruencies in Artificial Intelligence* from *AI Cultures GitHub,* AI systems trained predominantly on Western data may fail to accurately process or generate content relevant to non-Western cultures, resulting in outputs that lack cultural nuance or misrepresent certain traditions.

These examples highlight the importance of diversifying training datasets and implementing robust bias detection mechanisms to ensure that AI-generated content is inclusive and representative of diverse perspectives.

Bias in recommendations and personalization

GenAI has transformed how content is personalized across various platforms, from e-commerce to social media. However, this personalization can inadvertently reinforce existing biases and limit users' exposure to diverse perspectives. Two key issues in this context are personalization bias and selective exposure.

In personalization bias, GenAI systems used for recommendations may reinforce echo chambers or filter bubbles by consistently promoting content aligned with a user's past behavior, potentially excluding diverse viewpoints and reinforcing biased perspectives. For example, social media platforms often use algorithms that prioritize content similar to what users previously engaged with, leading to a narrowed view of information. This bias can isolate users from opposing viewpoints, effectively creating an intellectual bubble, as reported in the article *Filter bubble* from Wikipedia website.

In selective exposure, AI-generated content recommendations can limit users' exposure to varied perspectives or experiences by prioritizing content that aligns with majority trends or commercial interests, thereby contributing to societal biases in media consumption. For instance, recommendation algorithms on streaming services might favor mainstream content, making it less likely for users to discover independent or diverse media. This selective exposure can reinforce existing preferences and limit the diversity of content consumed, as reported in the article *Echo chambers, filter bubbles, and polarization: a literature review* from the *Reuters Institute* news website.

These examples highlight the importance of developing AI systems that promote diverse content exposure and mitigate the risks of reinforcing biases. Developers can create more balanced and inclusive AI-driven recommendation systems by addressing these challenges.

Bias amplification

GenAI has revolutionized various sectors, offering unprecedented capabilities in content creation and decision-making. However, it is crucial to recognize that GenAI can inadvertently perpetuate and even amplify existing biases, leading to significant societal impacts. Two critical concerns in this context are the amplification of existing biases and the formation of feedback loops.

In amplifying existing biases, GenAI can not only replicate biases but also amplify them. Small biases in the training data can become magnified as AI systems generate new content or make decisions at scale, leading to widespread biased outcomes that can have larger societal impacts. For instance, according to the article *Make better business decisions* by *Vogue Business* news website. AI-generated beauty standards have been criticized for promoting hyper-perfectionism and unrealistic ideals, distancing us from natural human beauty and reinforcing unattainable standards.

In feedback loops, AI systems deployed in real-world applications may encounter feedback loops, where biased outputs influence future data inputs. For example, biased search algorithms may promote certain types of content, which become part of the training data for the next iteration, reinforcing the bias over time. A study by UCL found that AI systems tend to take on human biases and amplify them, causing people who use that AI to become more biased themselves, creating a feedback loop that increases the risk of human error, as reported in the article *Bias in AI amplifies our own biases* by the *University College London (UCL)* news website.

These examples underscore the importance of implementing robust measures to detect and mitigate bias in AI systems. By addressing these issues, developers and organizations can work towards creating more equitable and fair AI applications.

Bias in visual and audio generation

GenAI has significantly advanced image and audio generation capabilities, offering innovative solutions across various industries. However, it is crucial to recognize that these systems can inadvertently perpetuate and amplify existing biases present in their training data. Two notable areas where such biases manifest are image generation and voice recognition.

In image generation bias, AI-generated images can reflect bias in terms of race, gender, or appearance. For example, if the training data is skewed toward certain racial or gendered representations, the AI might generate images that predominantly reflect those biases, marginalizing other groups. A study by the *University of Washington's* article *AI image generator Stable Diffusion perpetuates racial and gendered stereotypes*, found that often underrepresenting women and people of color in various professions.

In voice and accent bias, there can be bias related to voice and accent recognition. AI systems may perform poorly on non-dominant accents or languages, resulting in biased outputs in voice assistants or AI-driven transcription services. According to *TechTarget's* article *How AI speech recognition shows a bias toward different accents*, AI speech recognition systems often struggle to understand certain accents and dialects due to insufficient training data, leading to misinterpretations and user frustration.

Using DALL-E3 and GPT-4o, we will demonstrate the biases. At the beginning of this chapter, we showed bias with reference to doctors without gender implied. The AI draws a male doctor, even though the *AAMC* said globally that only 60% of doctors are men. Here is an interesting case.

Figure 8.5: Draw an immigrant

Figure 8.5 depicts the result of using the prompt: **Draw an immigrant**. We did not specify or imply that the drawing should feature a lonely man looking sorrowful, standing in a desolate landscape with a river, gazing longingly into the distance while wearing worn-out clothes. However, that is precisely what is shown in *Figure 8.5*. Even after dozens of attempts, AI consistently produced images depicting desolation or people in bleak situations.

It is essential to note that this is not the AI's fault. It reflects what it learned from data and photos on the internet. News media often share harrowing stories about immigrants and their journeys, contributing to this bias in culture and imagery. Therefore, this representation stems from our societal perceptions rather than from the AI itself.

We have the choice to craft prompts that would yield different representations of immigrants.

Figure 8.6: Image of happy immigrant family

Figure 8.6 shows an image of a happy immigrant family enjoying a meal together: *Draw an immigrant family gathering for a joyful meal, smiling warmly at each other.* We can replace the word *immigrant* from our prompt with the word *American*, and the AI will draw similar images. It is because the proud history of America is a melting pot of immigrants.

These examples underscore the importance of developing and training AI systems with diverse and representative datasets to mitigate biases and ensure inclusivity in AI-generated content.

Ethical and social consequences

GenAI has the potential to revolutionize various sectors, but it is crucial to recognize and address the biases that can lead to significant societal challenges. Two critical areas of concern are discrimination and exclusion, and the resulting loss of trust in AI systems.

In discrimination and exclusion, biased AI systems can perpetuate discrimination and social inequality, particularly when used in high-stakes areas like hiring, law enforcement, and healthcare. These systems may unintentionally exclude or disadvantage marginalized groups, exacerbating existing social divides. For instance, AI-based hiring tools have been found to increase the odds of discrimination in the workplace, potentially disadvantaging candidates from certain groups, as reported in the article *Fight for racial justice* from the **American Civil Liberties Union (ACLU)** website.

In loss of trust, if AI systems consistently produce biased or unfair outcomes, it can lead to a loss of trust in AI technologies, both from individual users and broader society. Ensuring fairness and transparency is critical to maintaining public confidence in AI systems. Building transparency and accountability into AI systems is increasingly being seen as a critical part of developing ethical and responsible AI, as reported in the article *Building Trust In AI: The Case For Transparency* from the *Forbes* website.

These examples underscore the importance of implementing robust measures to detect and mitigate bias in AI systems. By addressing these issues, developers and organizations can work towards creating more equitable and fair AI applications.

To wrap up the *How bias creeps in* section, bias in GenAI is a deep-rooted issue that influences AI systems' fairness, accuracy, and reliability across industries. From the training data AI models learn from to the algorithms that shape their outputs, biases can manifest in ways that reinforce stereotypes, create inequities, and lead to unfair decision-making. These are not just abstract concerns. They affect real people in genuine ways. A hiring algorithm trained on biased data may overlook qualified candidates. A healthcare AI that lacks diverse medical data may misdiagnose patients from underrepresented groups. A law enforcement AI with skewed historical data may unfairly target certain communities.

For beginner programmers, understanding AI bias is not just an ethical consideration. It is a fundamental skill for building reliable, inclusive, and responsible AI. Every flowchart, dataset choice and algorithm tweak shapes how AI interacts with the world. Learning to identify and address bias early on means creating AI that works for everyone, not just a few friends. The consequences of AI bias are not just technical errors. They are social and ethical failures that can deepen existing inequalities.

As AI becomes more embedded in daily life and workplace decisions, the responsibility to address bias falls on those who build, train, and deploy these systems. Recognizing and understanding AI bias is only the first step. The real challenge is actively working to combat it. That means designing fairer algorithms, improving the diversity of training data, and ensuring transparency in AI decision-making. AI should not be a force that reinforces past injustices. It should be a tool that helps create a more equitable future.

Up next, we explore the strategies and frameworks that are being developed to promote fairness in AI. From improving the representation of training data to designing AI models that account for bias, we will break down the practical steps needed to build AI systems that serve everyone, not just the dominant voices.

Fighting for fairness

Fighting for fairness within GenAI involves several key strategies that target both the technical and ethical aspects of AI development. One significant approach is improving the diversity and quality of training data. AI models learn from the data they are exposed to, so ensuring that datasets are representative of various demographics, cultures, and perspectives helps to reduce bias. This process involves curating data that includes underrepresented groups and actively removing harmful biases in historical data. Another method is designing algorithms that are more aware of bias and fairness. Researchers are developing fairness-aware algorithms that detect and correct biased patterns during training, ensuring AI systems produce more equitable outcomes.

Human oversight is also critical in maintaining fairness. Rather than relying solely on automated systems, integrating human judgment can help catch biases or unintended consequences that algorithms might miss. This oversight is particularly important in hiring, legal decisions, or healthcare, where the stakes are high and human context is crucial. Transparency and accountability also play a major role in fighting for fairness. Organizations must be transparent about how their AI systems work, what data they use, and how decisions are made, allowing for public scrutiny and regulatory oversight. Ethical guidelines, laws, and frameworks, such as AI ethics boards and government regulations, are increasingly being adopted to ensure AI is used responsibly and that biases are identified and corrected before they cause harm. In combination, these efforts help mitigate bias and promote fairness, making AI systems more inclusive and equitable for all users.

Fighting for fairness within GenAI is especially crucial in several high-impact areas, where bias can significantly affect people's lives and opportunities. Here are topics in real-life situations where fairness within GenAI is fundamental:

- Hiring and recruitment
- Creative autonomy and integrity
- Recognition and compensation

- Creative competition and market dynamics
- Ethical use of creative data

Starting from the top of the list is hiring and recruitment.

Hiring and recruitment

In automated resume screening, companies are turning to AI-driven systems to screen resumes and rank candidates, making hiring faster and more efficient. However, when AI is trained on biased data, such as past hiring decisions that favored certain genders, ethnicities, or educational backgrounds, it can reinforce those biases, shutting out qualified candidates from underrepresented groups. These hiring systems are only as impartial as the data they learn from, and if that data reflects historical discrimination, the AI will carry those patterns forward.

According to a study by the *University of Washington*, article *AI tools show biases in ranking job applicants' names according to perceived race and gender*, AI hiring tools showed strong racial and gender biases, favoring white-associated names 85% of the time and selecting female-associated names only 11% of the time. Amazon faced a similar issue when it scrapped an AI hiring tool after discovering it was biased against female candidates, ranking resumes with male-associated terms higher, as reported by the article *Shedding light on AI bias with real world examples* from the *IBM* website.

These examples are a wake-up call. AI is not neutral. It reflects the biases in its training data. If hiring algorithms are not carefully designed, they can quietly reinforce discrimination on a massive scale. Developers, recruiters, and companies must take responsibility for building fair AI systems that create opportunities, not barriers.

Creative autonomy and integrity

GenAI is making waves in the creative world, offering tools that assist with tasks like image generation, music composition, and content writing. While these innovations can boost productivity, it is crucial to ensure that the creator's unique voice and vision remain at the forefront without being overshadowed by the AI's inherent biases or tendencies.

In AI-assisted creation, many creatives are now integrating AI tools into their workflows to enhance various aspects of their craft. However, it is essential to maintain control over the artistic direction, ensuring that the AI serves as a supportive tool rather than dictating the creative process. This balance prevents the AI's biases from influencing the final output, preserving the authenticity of the creators' work, as reported in article *AI-assisted works can get copyright with enough human creativity, says US copyright office* from the **Associated Press** (**AP**) news website.

In the preservation of artistic integrity, there is a growing concern that AI-generated works might dilute an artist's unique identity or lead to homogenized outputs, especially if the

AI favors certain trends or styles. Ensuring fairness in AI usage supports diverse creative expressions and prevents the undue promotion of specific aesthetics over others.

According to a study published in the *PNAS Nexus*, article *Generative artificial intelligence, human creativity, and art* by the *Oxford Academic* website, while AI tools can enhance individual creativity by providing novel ideas and streamlining creative processes, their integration must be thoughtful to safeguard the richness and diversity of artistic expression.

The study found that access to GenAI ideas causes stories to be evaluated as more creative, better written, and more enjoyable, especially among less creative writers. However, GenAI-enabled stories are more similar to each other than stories by humans alone, pointing to an increase in individual creativity at the risk of losing collective novelty.

These insights underscore the importance of using AI responsibly in the creative process, ensuring that it enhances rather than diminishes the diversity and integrity of artistic expression.

Recognition and compensation

As GenAI becomes increasingly integrated into creative industries, it is essential to address issues of fairness, particularly concerning attribution and compensation.

In attribution, fairness in AI-generated content necessitates properly crediting original creators whose works, be it images, text, music, or designs, contribute to training AI systems. Without clear attribution, AI-generated works might inadvertently appropriate elements from creators without acknowledging their contributions. This concern is especially pertinent in creative fields where intellectual property and artistic credit are paramount. For instance, Adobe has launched a free web application enabling creators to protect their work, gain attribution, and control AI usage of their content in the digital era, as reported in the article *Adobe Innovates to Address AI Content Attribution Concerns* from the *Technology Magazine* website.

In fair compensation, as AI tools increasingly generate content, questions about compensation arise. Creators whose work contributes to AI training datasets should be fairly compensated, ensuring that AI-generated content does not undercut human creators by offering inexpensive alternatives that devalue original creative labor. A proposed framework suggests compensating copyright owners proportionally to their contributions to AI-generated content, leveraging techniques from cooperative game theory to determine fair distribution, as discussed in the scholarly paper *An Economic Solution to Copyright Challenges of Generative AI* from the *arXiv* website.

Addressing these issues is crucial to maintaining a fair and equitable creative ecosystem in the age of AI.

Creative competition and market dynamics

The emergence of GenAI has sparked significant discussions about its role in creative industries. While AI-generated art, music, and writing offer innovative possibilities, it is crucial to ensure that human creators remain central in the creative process. Fairness in this context means that AI should complement, not replace, human creativity, ensuring that creators are neither marginalized nor undervalued in a market increasingly populated with AI-generated content.

In AI vs. human creativity, the rise of AI-generated art, music, and writing creates new competition between AI-generated and human-made works. Fairness ensures that human creators are not marginalized or undervalued in a marketplace increasingly saturated with AI-generated content. AI should complement rather than replace human creativity. According to a recent article in *The Guardian*: *US Authors Guild to certify books from 'human intellect' rather than AI*, the U.S. Authors Guild has initiated the Human Authored project, allowing writers to certify that their work is created by human intellect, not AI. This move aims to promote transparency and celebrate human storytelling, addressing concerns over the increasing presence of AI-generated books in online marketplaces.

In market visibility and algorithmic bias, many platforms use algorithms to promote creative works, and biased AI can affect which creators get visibility. If AI systems favor popular or mainstream content, less established or marginalized artists may struggle to gain attention. Fair algorithms should give all creators equal opportunities for exposure and recognition regardless of background or style. A report by *Dentsu X*, in the article *Beyond the Screen: Addressing Algorithmic Bias in Advertising*, highlights that biased algorithms might restrict individuals' exposure to job listings, educational opportunities, or housing options based on race, gender, or socioeconomic status, thereby widening existing inequalities.

What if Leonardo da Vinci had access to a GenAI text-to-image model, like DALL-E 3, Stable Diffusion, or Flux? The marriage of AI and creativity might lead to the following figure:

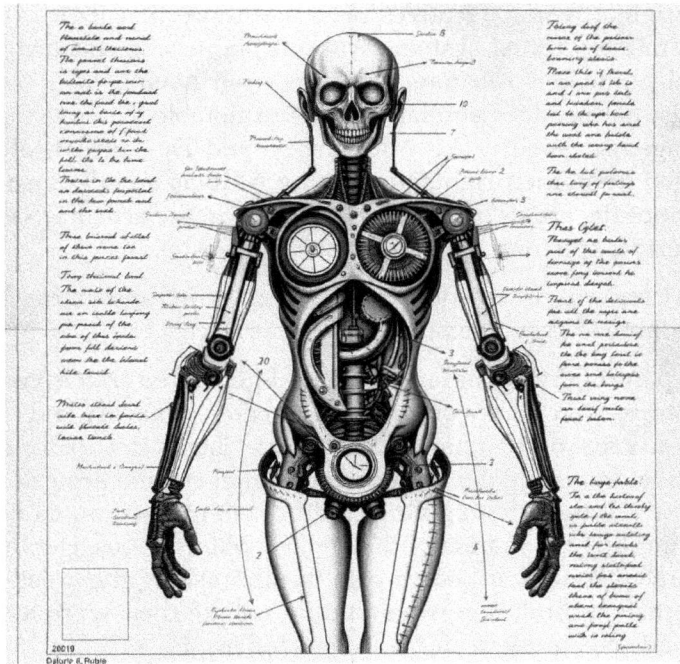

Figure 8.7: *Leonardo da Vinci uses AI*

Figure 8.7 shows an internal drawing of a machine automaton, much like Leonardo da Vinci's classical anatomy study of a human. This fanciful dream exemplifies how AI can complement rather than replace human creativity.

These developments underscore the importance of implementing robust measures to detect and mitigate bias in AI systems. By addressing these issues, developers, and organizations can work towards creating more equitable and fair AI applications.

Ethical use of creative data

As GenAI becomes more prevalent in creative fields, it is crucial to address ethical considerations surrounding data usage and the protection of original works.

In data ethics and consent, AI models used for creative purposes are often trained on vast amounts of existing content. Fairness in AI usage means ensuring that creators whose work is used to train these systems have given consent and are not exploited by AI technologies. Artists, musicians, and writers should have a say in whether and how AI systems use their work. According to *The Guardian*, in the article *The Guardian view on AI and copyright law: big tech must pay*, prominent artists like *Sir Elton John* and *Sir Paul McCartney* advocate for stricter regulations to prevent the unlicensed use of creative works for AI training. A significant petition has garnered support from many artists, demanding transparency, control, and financial compensation.

In protection of original works, creatives need assurance that their original works will not be copied or imitated by AI systems without permission. Ensuring fairness means developing ethical guidelines to protect creators from having their work replicated or diluted by AI tools that produce similar outputs. A notable example is the lawsuit filed by visual artists against Stability AI, Midjourney, and DeviantArt, alleging that these companies infringed upon their rights by training AI tools on billions of images scraped from the web without the artists' consent, as reported in the article *US artists score victory in landmark AI copyright case* from *The Art Newspaper* website.

Addressing these concerns is essential to maintain trust and fairness in the creative industries as AI continues to evolve.

It is time to wrap up the **Fighting for fairness**. As AI-generated art becomes more common, artists may face competition from work that can be created quickly and cheaply, making it difficult to justify the value of their handmade pieces. Clients can opt for these cheaper, AI-generated alternatives, reducing the demand for human-created art. Additionally, AI tools can imitate an artist's style without giving credit or compensation, eroding their creative ownership and saturating the market with similar-looking pieces. Digital platforms often prioritize AI-generated content in search results, diminishing the artist's visibility. These challenges push artists to find new ways to differentiate their work and emphasize the value of human-made creativity in an AI-driven landscape.

Fairness plays a crucial role in the ethical use of GenAI, ensuring that AI systems are inclusive, unbiased, and respectful of the creative and intellectual rights of individuals. By addressing issues such as bias, representation, and equitable access, we can create AI technologies that promote fairness and uphold the integrity of human contributions across various fields. However, achieving fairness in GenAI is not just the responsibility of developers and companies—it also extends to us, the users. In the next section, we will explore our responsibility as users of GenAI, focusing on how we can engage with these tools ethically and thoughtfully, ensuring they are used in ways that respect both creators and broader societal values.

Upholding accountability

In answering the question about your responsibility, let us take a step back and discuss what it means to use GenAI responsibly. AI is an incredible tool. It can streamline workflows, generate creative content, and assist in decision-making, but with great power comes real responsibility. Using GenAI is not just about convenience. It ensures that what we create, share, and apply remains ethical, fair, and transparent. AI does not think, judge, or hold itself accountable. That part is on us.

Understanding these issues early on is not a theoretical exercise for beginner programmers. It is a foundational skill. As a developer, whether we are working on small projects or integrating AI into larger systems, our code will directly shape how AI interacts with the world. Learning about ethical AI use now means that as our skills grow, we build AI-driven solutions that are responsible, fair, and impactful.

First, ethical use means not just taking what AI generates at face value. AI learns from massive datasets, and if that data carries biases, the AI will reflect them. That means AI can unknowingly reinforce stereotypes, marginalize voices, or exclude certain perspectives. When using AI to generate content, be it writing, art, music, or code, we need to be mindful of using existing works without appropriate credit or permission. Intellectual property still matters, even when AI is involved, and understanding how AI training data works will help us make informed decisions.

Bias and fairness are another key concern. AI is only as neutral as the data it is trained on. Hiring algorithms, customer service chatbots, and even recommendations for candidates to be hired can all show bias if not carefully monitored. As a new programmer, you might not be designing large-scale AI models yet, but even when working with AI APIs or datasets, knowing how bias creeps in will help you write better, more responsible code. If a model is making recommendations, reinforcing certain narratives, or consistently favoring one perspective, it is up to us to step in and ensure fairness. The best time to learn how to build bias-aware AI applications is at the beginning of your programming journey—not after bad habits have already set in.

Transparency matters, too. If AI plays a role in creating something, people deserve to know. Whether it is AI-generated text, images, or decision-making in hiring or finance, being upfront about AI's involvement builds trust. AI is imperfect, and pretending it is only sets us up for failure. As a programmer, developing a habit of documenting and explaining how AI decisions are made will set you apart as a responsible developer. Being clear about when AI is used and validating its outputs instead of unquestioningly trusting them will make you a better coder and problem solver.

Privacy is another big one. AI systems thrive on data, but just because data is available does not mean it should be used incautiously. AI that relies on personal data needs to handle that data responsibly. Users should know how AI systems collect, store, and process information. For programmers, this means understanding what data your code interacts with, how it is stored, and how to build AI-driven applications that respect user privacy.

Ethical AI use ensures privacy is protected, data is not misused, and users are not unknowingly feeding AI systems with personal or sensitive information.

Then there is the biggest trap: over-reliance on AI. It is tempting to let AI handle decisions, automate processes, or even guide creativity, but AI is not a replacement for human judgment. AI can assist, suggest, and even inspire, but it should never replace critical thinking. Trust your instincts. As new developers, we will rely on AI for debugging, suggestions, and even learning new skills, but do not let it do all the thinking for you. The best programmers understand how to utilize AI as a tool rather than relying on it as a crutch.

At the end of the day, accountability falls on us, the developers, users, creators, and decision-makers. AI does not take responsibility for its mistakes, but we have to. That means staying informed, questioning outputs, and being mindful of AI's influence. The way we interact with AI shapes how it impacts society. When we program AI, we shape conversations, influence decisions, and define what is considered fair, ethical, and responsible. If we want AI to serve us well, we must guide, challenge, and, most importantly, use it wisely.

Building these habits early will make us better programmers and more thoughtful and responsible contributors to the future of AI. It means ensuring accuracy in how we interact with AI, critically questioning outputs, and applying AI-generated content in ways that respect privacy, inclusivity, and fairness. Ultimately, our responsibility lies in harnessing AI's potential to enhance our creativity, problem-solving, and knowledge while maintaining a commitment to integrity and positive impact, **AI for Good**.

Conclusion

Throughout this chapter, we explored the critical role fairness and bias play in GenAI. AI systems do not operate in isolation. They reflect the data they are trained on, and if that data carries societal inequalities, AI can magnify them. Bias in AI is not just a speculative concern. It has real consequences, from hiring algorithms that favor certain demographics to AI-generated content that subtly reinforces stereotypes. Ignoring these issues allows bias to creep in unnoticed, shaping decisions that disadvantage specific groups while privileging others. That is why addressing fairness in AI is about improving technology and ensuring that AI systems serve everyone equitably rather than reinforcing past injustices.

For beginner programmers, these discussions are not just background noise. They are the foundation for building ethical, responsible AI. Every algorithm you build, every dataset you work with, and every AI system you contribute to will have real-world implications. Learning how to identify and mitigate bias now will prepare you to develop functional and fair AI. Developers, users, and regulators all have a role to play in ensuring transparency, inclusivity, and fairness at every stage of AI development. From choosing diverse training data to designing unbiased algorithms and implementing safeguards against discriminatory outputs, these considerations should be a standard part of AI's evolution, not an afterthought.

By taking these steps, we can work toward AI systems that reflect society as it is and help create a more just and equitable future. AI should be a tool that empowers, not a force that divides. Building AI with fairness in mind and sharing its benefits is called **AI for Good**.

In the next chapter, we will shift gears and focus on asking the pivotal question: *Are you a code walker? In other words, is programming a career that you want to pursue?*

## CHAPTER 9

Your Turn to
Be a Code Walker

Introduction

In this chapter, we reach a pivotal moment in your coding journey. Up to this point, we built a strong foundation, learning Python, developing essential projects, manipulating data, and even getting a taste of machine learning, building GUI, and model deployment. Now, it is time to step back, reflect on how far you come, and look ahead to what is next.

Unlike previous chapters that focused on mastering specific skills or deploying projects, this chapter is about perspective. We will zoom out to see the bigger picture: *What have we learned? How does it apply to real-world challenges? And, most importantly, how do we keep growing beyond what we have already achieved?*

The chapter begins with a review of key concepts and techniques, creating a cohesive understanding of the material learned so far. This foundation sets the stage for exploring practical next steps, such as deepening Python expertise, branching into new programming languages, tackling more complex projects, or engaging with open-source communities to collaborate and grow.

The focus then shifts to the broader career landscape, covering both traditional computer science roles and unconventional fields where coding becomes a transformative skill. Whether the goal is a career in tech or applying coding in innovative ways, this chapter provides a roadmap for planning the next steps. Significant progress has already been made, and now is the time to look ahead and unlock the possibilities that coding offers.

Structure

This chapter covers the following topics:

- Insider view
- Beyond the solo coder
- Career landscape
- Career path

Objectives

By the end of this chapter, we will clearly understand where we stand in our coding journey and what steps to take next. We reflect on and consolidate the critical programming concepts covered so far, reinforcing our foundation before moving forward. From there, we explore practical ways to continue growing, whether learning new programming languages, building real-world projects, or collaborating with others in open-source communities.

Beyond technical skills, this chapter explores the career opportunities available to programmers in traditional tech roles and fields where coding serves as a transformative tool. To bring everything together, the focus shifts to creating a personalized plan for advancing programming expertise and career development. This process includes strategies for continuous learning, networking, and building a strong portfolio.

The chapter's objectives act as a guide, connecting the dots between acquired knowledge and its practical application, enabling informed decisions about the future. By the end, a clear roadmap emerges, tailored to individual goals and complete with actionable steps for education, projects, and professional growth.

Insider view

The previous chapters provide an opportunity to step back and reflect on the concepts and techniques covered. This review goes beyond a simple summary. It solidifies an understanding of foundational Python syntax while connecting it to more advanced topics like machine learning models and AI deployment. More importantly, it highlights the deliberate learning sequence, setting this approach apart from traditional Python learning methods.

Before gradually moving toward practical applications, many beginner Python books focus on syntax and structure, such as loops, functions, and data types. While effective, this approach can often feel disconnected from real-world programming. In contrast, a practical-first or play-first approach prioritizes hands-on learning, building projects, analyzing real-world data, and exploring advanced AI libraries. This method makes coding feel more intuitive and reinforces the purpose behind each concept, making it immediately applicable to solving real-world challenges.

Our journey started in *Chapter 1, Introduction to GenAI*, where we explored **Generative AI (GenAI)**, setting the stage for understanding how modern GenAI helps us write code. Then, in *Chapter 2, Jupyter Notebook*, we introduced the *Jupyter Notebook*. It is a coding platform but a robust interactive environment for writing, testing, and documenting code in a way that mirrors how real data scientists and AI engineers work.

In *Chapter 3, Dissect the Calculator App*, we examined a simple calculator app, moving beyond theoretical concepts to break down actual code and analyzing its structure, logic, and functionality. This hands-on approach made it easier to see how Python syntax is used in everyday applications. Then, in *Chapter 4, Sorting on My Mind*, we shifted gears with *Sorting on My Mind*, exploring classic sorting algorithms, learning to code various sorting algorithms, and understanding problem-solving and algorithm design in a structured way.

With that foundation in place, we explored real-world data processing in *Chapter 5*, aptly named *Pandas, the Data Tamer*. Instead of treating Python as just a programming language, we saw it as a tool for manipulating and analyzing large real-world datasets, a critical skill in data science and AI.

The journey then advanced into more complex AI applications, beginning with *Chapter 6, Decipher CNN App*, which focused on understanding a **Convolutional Neural Network (CNN)** application. This chapter introduced deep learning and image recognition, using a real-world dataset of snake images to train a model capable of identifying poisonous snakes. While CNNs are often considered an advanced topic reserved for graduate-level study, the concepts were simplified with the support of GPT-4, making them accessible and easier to grasp.

This progression naturally led to *Chapter 7, Gradio and Hugging Face Deployment*. The focus shifted to transforming AI models into functional web applications, enabling projects to become interactive and accessible to broader audiences. The journey concluded with *Chapter 8, Fairness and Bias*, delving into the ethical considerations of AI. Understanding GenAI extends beyond building algorithms or machine learning models; it encompasses a responsibility to ensure fairness, address bias, and consider the broader impact of these technologies.

That was a brief overview; now, the following concept will be explored in detail:

- The fundamentals and GPT-4o
- The algorithms and libraries
- The machine learning and deployment
- The ethics

We begin with the fundamental

Fundamentals and GPT-4o

Our philosophy is straightforward: Before we start learning Python programming, being comfortable with using the tools and platforms is necessary. Too many Python books jump into syntax, expecting you to absorb the language passively. While that may work for some, we believe in a more effective, *active learning* approach where you play as you learn. That is why *Chapter 1, Introduction to GenAI* and *Chapter 2, Jupyter Notebook* focuses on explaining what GenAI is, how to set it up, and how to use it effectively. These foundational chapters are not a detour but a deliberate strategy to empower you with the tools needed to explore Python in a hands-on, interactive way.

GenAI, like GPT-4o, is nothing short of a transformative learning companion. It is like having a patient, knowledgeable mentor sitting beside you. Someone who listens to your questions and tailors their explanations to your unique understanding. Need to go fast? It accelerates. Prefer a slower, deeper dive? It adjusts. Struggling with a concept? It rephrases and offers new perspectives until it clicks. This adaptability creates a truly personalized learning experience, empowering you to master coding at your own pace, whether syntax, algorithms, or complex concepts.

Just a few years ago, before 2023, such a tool was unimaginable. No software, book, or lecture came close to this level of intelligence or interactivity. GPT-4o teaches and revolutionizes how we learn, blending guidance, experimentation, and immediate feedback in a way that feels human yet infinitely scalable. To call it a game-changer barely scratches the surface. It represents a fundamental shift in how we approach education, making learning as dynamic and engaging as the challenges we aim to solve.

The concept of *active learning* emphasizes the transformative power of learning by doing. While traditional methods like reading and memorization have value, they often fall short in comparison. A more effective method is to experiment, play, and explore, then refine and improve based on experience. Tools like Jupyter Notebook and GPT-4o facilitate this hands-on approach, allowing immediate feedback on what works, what does not, and, most importantly, why. This interactivity creates a dynamic feedback loop where successes build confidence, and errors become valuable learning opportunities.

Active learning moves beyond rote memorization into exploration, experimentation, and discovery. Writing code, encountering challenges, and solving problems strengthen programming skills and develop critical thinking and problem-solving abilities. It is the hallmark of a great programmer. This approach transforms abstract concepts into practical understanding, turning every trial and error into a step toward mastery. The play-first method is the essence of active learning and the foundation for building a deeper connection to Python programming, which is why we start here.

Algorithms and libraries

The first look at Python code begins in *Chapter 3, Dissect the Calculator App*. Elementary Python concepts such as assignments, loops, if-else statements, functions, and class definitions are introduced, not for rote memorization but as essential tools for building the calculator app. By applying these concepts in a practical project, the insights gained go far deeper than simply learning syntax. These foundational ideas are universal and applicable to all programming languages, whether Python, C++, Java, or JavaScript. Mastery of these building blocks lays the groundwork for tackling more complex problems.

With these basics in place, attention shifts to one of the classical problems in computer science: sorting algorithms. *Chapter 4, Sorting on My Mind*, explores these algorithms, which have been central to programming since the earliest days of computing. Whether it was a BASIC program in the 1960s or Swift in 2024, sorting algorithms continue to power the digital world. The chapter explores algorithms in detail, not just as theoretical exercises but as practical tools for problem-solving. Learning to construct an algorithm is the turning point where coding transforms into programming.

The next step in the journey is learning to leverage libraries, a process akin to standing on the shoulders of giants. Libraries allow programmers to build faster and solve more complex problems without reinventing the wheel. *Chapter 5, Pandas, the Data Tamer,* introduces the Python Pandas library, a powerful tool for manipulating, organizing, merging, and sorting data. For the first time, this chapter connects coding to real-world problems, guiding the use of actual datasets downloaded from the Kaggle website. Analyzing real-world data makes the leap from academic exercises to solving meaningful, tangible subjects.

The progression from foundational concepts to algorithms to real-world libraries represents the evolution of a programmer. It is not just about writing code. It is about understanding how each piece builds on the last to tackle increasingly complex challenges. This journey, however, is made even more remarkable with the help of GPT-4o. Every line of code was generated by GPT-4o, acting as an ever-patient tutor and collaborator, while humans reviewed, tested, and refined the output. This partnership between human creativity and AI assistance has unlocked new levels of learning Python code. Programming is not just a skill. It is a way of thinking, solving, and creating. With tools like GPT-4o, this process becomes efficient and deeply engaging, making even the most complex challenges approachable and manageable.

Machine learning

Machine learning and deep learning represent a transformative shift in computer science. Unlike traditional programming paradigms that follow sequential logic and step-by-step algorithms, machine learning focuses on enabling computers to learn from data and improve their performance without being explicitly programmed for every task. This field serves as the foundation for developing advanced AI systems like GPT-4o, Gemini, CoPilot, and Claude, which are driving the current age of AI. Examples of machine learning's impact can be seen everywhere, from personalized recommendations on streaming platforms and real-time language translation to autonomous vehicles and fraud detection in financial systems.

Machine learning fundamentally differs from traditional programming methods that have dominated computer science for decades. Traditional sequential programming relies on clearly defined rules and logic written by programmers. For example, a sorting algorithm is created to follow specific instructions for comparing and arranging data. At the same time, an iPhone app is designed to execute pre-programmed actions based on user interactions.

In contrast, deep learning operates through artificial neural networks inspired by the human brain. These networks learn to identify patterns and relationships in data independently, enabling them to perform tasks such as recognizing objects in images or understanding human language. However, these challenges are often difficult or impossible to define using explicit rules.

This difference is what makes machine learning so revolutionary. Instead of instructing the computer on every possible scenario, the focus shifts to providing it with vast amounts of data, enabling it to recognize patterns and make predictions independently. For instance, traditional programming could never handle the complexity of understanding a photo of a snake and determining whether it is poisonous. This difference is why *Chapter 6, Decipher CNN App,* is so crucial. It introduces a real-world machine-learning task using a dataset of snake images. By writing a CNN code, the program learns to predict whether a snake is poisonous. What is even more remarkable is its ability to generalize this knowledge to new, unseen photos uploaded by users, showcasing the power of AI to tackle complex, real-world problems.

Machine learning and CNNs are rarely if ever, covered in beginner Python books because they represent the cutting edge of technology, a field only recently integrated into computer science curricula. Yet, AI now powers the global economy, reshaping industries and driving innovation at an unprecedented scale. Introducing these concepts early not only bridges the gap between foundational programming and advanced AI but also equips programmers with the tools to participate in shaping the future of technology.

Chapter 7, Gradio and Hugging Face Deployment, takes this learning journey to the next level by teaching how to build a **Graphical User Interface (GUI)** in Python and deploy applications for public use. This chapter illustrates the complete process of transforming academic projects into real-world tools, making concepts tangible and accessible. Using Gradio, the calculator app, sorting algorithm, and CNN snake prediction model are enhanced with intuitive interfaces that anyone can easily use.

Imagine a friend on a hike who takes out their iPhone to snap a picture of a snake. Instantly, they receive a prediction on whether the snake is poisonous or not. This scenario highlights the potential of combining machine learning with user-friendly deployment. Learning to write GUI and deployment bridges the gap between theoretical concepts and practical applications, demonstrating how Python code can transform into impactful solutions accessible to anyone, anywhere. It takes readers on a complete journey from coding to deployment, turning ideas into tools that can truly make a difference in the world.

Ethics

Ethics in software development and real-world applications is a topic that is often overlooked in beginner Python programming books. However, it is one of the most critical aspects of creating technology that impacts society. *Chapter 8, Fairness and Bias,* directly addresses these ethical considerations. It examines how AI influences content creation, decision-making, employment, and societal norms, providing an honest look at the broader implications of the tools that programmers develop. Each topic is supported by real-world articles, which ground the discussion in current events and make the subject more relatable and actionable.

The chapter discusses how bias can infiltrate AI systems, reinforcing stereotypes and creating skewed results in visual and audio outputs. It also outlines strategies to combat these biases and promote fairness with the same dedication as solving a programming challenge. By referencing real-world examples and research, the chapter highlights the significant impact of these issues and underscores the programmers' responsibility in addressing them.

Programmers play a vital role in shaping the modern world, influencing every sector, such as social media, healthcare, wellness, entertainment, and education. Essentially, the 21st century relies on the innovations created by programmers. With this significant power comes the responsibility to prioritize fairness and ethics in every line of code. These principles should not be postponed until an optional graduate-level philosophy class. Rather, programmers must begin integrating ethical considerations from the first day they write code. By doing so, they can ensure that technology acts as a force for good, helping to build a more inclusive, equitable, and just world. It is named **AI for Good**.

Using DALL-E3, here is a picture of the insider view concept.

Figure 9.1: Programmer insider view

Figure 9.1 shows an image of two programmers peeking through the curtain of their programming journey. DALL-E3 draws the image reimagined in the 1030s Art Deco style.

Beyond the solo coder

Contrary to the stereotypes often portrayed in popular movies or TV shows, programmers are not solitary individuals lurking in dimly lit basements, nor are they outcasts dressed in dark clothing or with questionable hygiene. In reality, programmers work, share, collaborate, and thrive alongside colleagues in offices worldwide, contributing to innovation in every sector.

Take, for example, Apple's headquarters in *Cupertino, California*, commonly known as **The Circle**. Located in the heart of Silicon Valley, it stands as one of the most advanced and stunning office spaces in the world. Designed to foster collaboration and creativity, the building and its surrounding landscape reportedly cost over $2 billion, reflecting the value placed on creating environments where programmers can work and innovate together.

Here are three possible paths to break away from the solitary coder syndrome:

- Mastering multiple languages
- Team projects
- Collaboration

Let us start with multiple languages.

Mastering multiple languages

While Python is incredibly versatile and widely used, limiting expertise to just one language can narrow career opportunities and restrict the ability to tackle diverse challenges. Mastering multiple programming languages allows for greater flexibility, enabling work across a variety of domains and environments. Each language is uniquely suited to a specific task. Some excel in web development, others in performance-critical systems or enterprise applications.

Expanding language skills enhances technical abilities and creates new collaborations and community opportunities. As programmers learn additional languages, they often connect with peers with similar interests, fostering friendships and professional networks that enrich their learning journey. These connections can develop into valuable programming partnerships, where shared challenges and solutions lead to a deeper understanding and greater innovation.

The world of programming offers an incredible diversity of languages, with hundreds to explore, from historical languages like Ada to niche options such as LISP. Popular languages each have their specialties.

C++ is often hailed as a performance powerhouse, making it a go-to choice for systems programming and game development. Its ability to interact closely with hardware and optimize memory usage allows developers to create high-performance applications, from operating systems to real-time 3D games. The language's versatility extends to industries like finance, where speed is critical, and embedded systems, where resource constraints demand precision.

Java, on the other hand, has cemented itself as the backbone of enterprise applications. Known for its portability through the *write once, run anywhere principle*, Java powers large-scale systems across banking, e-commerce, and telecommunications industries. Its robust frameworks, like Spring and Hibernate, simplify complex application development, making Java indispensable for building secure, scalable, and reliable enterprise solutions.

Swift shines within the Apple ecosystem, revolutionizing how iOS and macOS applications are built. Its modern syntax and ease of use have attracted beginners and seasoned developers, enabling the rapid creation of apps that power everything from mobile games to productivity tools. Swift has become the standard for Apple development, designed to be fast and safe, combining the best performance and developer-friendly design.

Golang (Go), created by Google, is built for scalability, making it particularly popular in cloud computing and distributed systems. Its simplicity and efficient concurrency model enable developers to build applications that can handle massive workloads, such as cloud-based services, containerized applications, and microservices architectures. Go's lightweight design makes it ideal for companies building scalable and efficient backend systems.

Rust is a rising star, combining safety and performance like no other language. Designed to prevent common programming errors such as memory leaks and buffer overflows, Rust ensures reliability without sacrificing speed. These features make it particularly valuable in systems programming, where secure code is essential. Rust is increasingly being adopted for developing web browsers, blockchain technology, and other mission-critical software where efficiency and safety are paramount.

Each popular language has carved out a niche, excelling in specific domains while offering unique features that appeal to developers. By mastering multiple languages, programmers can adapt to the demands of different industries, tackling challenges with the best tools for the job.

Mastering these languages expands technical horizons and connects programmers with diverse communities, fostering growth both professionally and personally. The process of learning new languages transforms programming from a solitary skill into a shared journey.

Team projects

Working on projects is one of the most effective ways to strengthen programming skills and gain practical experience. Real-world applications challenge developers to apply concepts, solve problems creatively, and build confidence through hands-on practice. Starting with small, manageable projects is a great way to explore new ideas while honing technical abilities. Inviting friends or a coding buddy to join the project is an excellent way to start. Over time, tackling more complex applications involving multiple components, external libraries, or APIs deepens technical expertise and problem-solving capabilities.

Furthermore, creating a portfolio of completed projects showcases the capability to address real-world challenges independently, an attribute highly sought after by potential employers.

Here are some fun project ideas that can be done using Python code, with a little help from GPT-4:

- **Personal portfolio website:** Develop a portfolio website to highlight skills, projects, and a resume. This project teaches essential web development concepts, while providing a polished platform to showcase your accomplishments.

- **Task management app:** Create a to-do list or task management application. This project covers **Create, Read, Update, Delete (CRUD)** operations, user authentication, and priority settings, offering a solid introduction to building functional applications.

- **Weather app with an API:** Build a weather application that fetches live data from APIs such as **OpenWeatherMap**. This introduces working with external APIs, processing data, and presenting it visually in a user-friendly interface.

- **Blog platform:** Create a simple blogging platform for writing, editing, and publishing posts. Expand by adding features like user authentication, rich-text editing, and comment sections, ideal for learning backend development with frameworks like Python Django or Flask.

- **Chat application:** Develop a real-time chat application using web sockets. This project provides experience in handling real-time data, managing user sessions, and working with technologies for real-time communication.

- **Budget tracker:** Build a personal finance app where users log expenses, categorize spending, and track progress over time. Adding graphs or budgeting goals introduces data visualization and interactive design.

- **E-commerce store:** Create an e-commerce platform where users can browse products, manage a cart, and complete a checkout process. This involves logic for inventory management, payment integration, and user authentication.

- **Movie recommendation system:** Build a system that suggests movies based on user preferences. This project introduces recommendation algorithms like collaborative or content-based filtering and leverages data from sources like *IMDB*.

- **Online quiz application:** Design a quiz platform where users take quizzes, view scores, and access correct answers. This project helps practice state management, front-end logic, and creating intuitive user interfaces.

- **Fitness tracker app:** Develop an app for tracking workouts, exercises, and fitness progress. Features like graphs for performance trends and integration with APIs for daily activity or nutrition monitoring add depth to this project.

Starting with these projects provides hands-on experience in key programming areas, such as web development, API integration, data processing, and user authentication. Over time, scaling these projects or adding advanced features like machine learning, API integration, or mobile app development can take skills to the next level. These projects not only sharpen technical expertise but also create a portfolio that stands out to employers and collaborators, opening doors to new opportunities in the programming field.

Collaboration

Programming is rarely a solitary activity. While personal projects provide an excellent foundation for building technical skills, collaboration takes development to the next level. Working with others on team-based tasks or contributing to open-source projects exposes programmers to diverse coding styles, workflows, and problem-solving approaches. This broader perspective improves technical skills and fosters adaptability by highlighting multiple ways to tackle the same problem.

Collaborating with experienced developers, particularly in open-source environments such as *GitHub, Kaggle, or Hugging Face*, offers invaluable opportunities to learn advanced techniques, refine code quality through peer reviews, and gain hands-on experience with industry-standard tools and practices. Exposure to concepts like version control, code reviews, and continuous integration bridges the gap between smaller personal projects and the complexities of large-scale, real-world systems. Such experiences are essential for understanding how professional software is built, maintained, and scaled.

Collaboration also serves as a gateway to expanding professional networks. Contributing to established projects creates opportunities to connect with other developers, receive mentorship, and potentially unlock career advancements. These relationships often lead to lasting professional partnerships and career growth that are difficult to achieve when working in isolation. Beyond technical development, effective collaboration hones critical soft skills like communication and teamwork, qualities that are increasingly vital in today's distributed and remote work environments. Working with others is more than just a learning opportunity. It is a critical step toward becoming a well-rounded and successful developer.

Using DALL-E3, here is a illustration of the programmer collaboration concept.

Figure 9.2: *Collaborative programmer view*

Figure 9.2 shows an image of programmers collaborating and thriving alongside colleagues in offices all over the world. DALL-E3 draws the image reimagined in the 1030s Art Deco style.

That concludes the discussion on stepping beyond the solo coder. The next focus shifts to exploring the career landscape.

Career landscape

Coding is an essential skill that extends far beyond the realm of traditional computer science. It has become a cornerstone in a vast array of industries, embedding programmers at the heart of sectors that drive modern society. From developing complex algorithms for financial markets to creating life-saving technologies in healthcare, coding fuels innovation and shapes how businesses and industries operate. This section will explore the diverse career paths available to programmers, ranging from established roles in software engineering and data science to unexpected opportunities in fields like entertainment, social media, and education.

Moreover, programmers are the architects of the 21st century, deeply integrated into nearly every market. They design trading algorithms and risk analysis tools in finance that power the global economy. In healthcare, programmers enable breakthroughs in medical imaging, patient data analysis, and even robotic surgeries. Entertainment relies on coding to create immersive experiences, from visually stunning games to cutting-edge visual effects in movies. Social media platforms, connecting billions worldwide, depend entirely on programmers to refine algorithms, enhance user experience, and ensure security. The impact of programming is profound across every sector, from agriculture to education. Broadly speaking, there are two paths to choose from when selecting a career:

- Traditional
- Passion based

Let us start with the traditional category.

Traditional

From the early days of computing to the present, programmers have often been viewed as generalists. The expectation has traditionally been to master technical skills and the syntax of a particular programming language, with the assumption that these core skills would be enough to tackle any project. Once hired, programmers were typically assigned to develop Product X or Service Y, regardless of the industry or specific expertise required.

Over time, however, the field has evolved. Just as doctors specialize in areas like cardiology or orthopedics, programmers now develop targeted skills for specific sectors. This specialization allows for deeper expertise in areas such as web, entertainment, or artificial intelligence, reflecting the growing complexity and demands of these industries. While there are countless specializations in programming today, only a handful can be highlighted here. Popular categories, as frequently seen on job boards, demonstrate programmers' diverse and evolving roles in the modern economy. The popular job listings are as follows:

- Front-end developer
- Backend developer
- Full-stack developer

- Data engineer
- Machine learning scientist

The first topic to be discussed is the front-end developer.

Front-end developer

A front-end developer specializes in creating a website or mobile application's visual and interactive elements. Everything that users see and interact with. This role is essential for crafting user-friendly, responsive, visually appealing interfaces that enhance the user experience. From translating UI/UX design wireframes into functional code to ensuring compatibility across various browsers and devices, front-end developers are at the forefront of web and mobile application design. Their work is not just about aesthetics. It also involves optimizing performance to reduce load times, improve responsiveness, and deliver an exciting user experience.

To succeed in this role, expertise in foundational languages like *HTML* and *CSS* is critical for structuring and styling web pages. *JavaScript*, the backbone of interactivity, enables features like animations, dynamic content, and interactive forms. Familiarity with popular frameworks such as *React, Angular*, or *Vue.js* is often necessary for building modern, dynamic interfaces. For mobile applications, Swift is used for Apple iOS devices, while Kotlin or Java are used for Android devices.

In *Chapter 6, Decipher CNN App*, we use *Python* and the *Gradio* library to build applications such as a calculator, a quick sort, and a CNN-based snake image classification web-app. It highlights that the front-end can be built using programming languages other than the expected ones.

Responsive design skills are also crucial, ensuring websites adapt to different screen sizes, whether on a desktop, tablet, or smartphone. Additionally, front-end developers must collaborate closely with designers and backend developers to integrate design elements with functionality, creating a cohesive and engaging user experience.

Backend developer

A backend developer is responsible for the behind-the-scenes functionality of a website or application, managing the server-side logic, databases, and APIs that make the front-end work efficiently. While the front end focuses on user interaction, the back end ensures data is stored, retrieved, and processed effectively. Server-side code includes tasks such as designing and maintaining databases, implementing secure authentication and authorization protocols, and building the logic that connects the application to its data. Backend development is vital for the scalability and performance of an application, ensuring it can handle increased user demands over time.

In *Chapter 6, Decipher CNN App*, we have learned to develop the server-side code for the calculator, quick sort, and CNN apps and deploy them with a REST API to the Hugging Face production server.

Mastering programming languages such as Python, Node.js, Java, or C# is essential for writing efficient server-side code. It is also crucial to manage databases effectively, whether they are SQL-based like MySQL and PostgreSQL, or NoSQL solutions like MongoDB, to properly store and organize data.

Familiarity with server management technologies like Apache or Nginx and experience with cloud platforms such as AWS or Google Cloud are important for hosting and scaling applications. Additionally, backend developers are responsible for creating and maintaining REST or GraphQL APIs, which serve as the connection between the front-end GUI and the backend server-side code. This allows for smooth and secure data transfer.

Full-stack developer

A full-stack developer is proficient in front-end and backend development, making them uniquely capable of working on all web and mobile application aspects. This versatility allows full-stack developers to contribute to the entire development process, from designing user-friendly interfaces to building server-side logic and managing databases. Their ability to see the project from start to finish makes them highly valuable, as they can bridge the gap between the front-end and backend teams, ensuring a cohesive product.

Full-stack developers possess a wide range of skills, combining expertise in front-end technologies with backend programming languages. They are also adept at managing databases, creating APIs, handling server operations, and leveraging cloud services to deploy and scale applications. In addition, they often work with the software solution architect and DevOps team. Beyond technical expertise, full-stack developers collaborate with designers, domain experts, and other stakeholders throughout the application lifecycle, ensuring the final product is functional and efficient.

Data engineer

A data engineer applies programming, statistics, and machine learning to process and analyze large datasets, transforming raw data into actionable insights. This role is particularly vital in industries like healthcare and finance, where data-driven decision-making directly impacts outcomes. With the rapid rise of AI technologies, data engineering has become one of the most sought-after fields in 2024, bridging the gap between raw data and strategic business intelligence.

Proficiency in programming languages like *Python* and *Jupyter Notebook* is essential, as they provide the foundation for statistical computing and data analysis. Expertise in libraries such as Pandas and NumPy streamlines data processing, while tools like Matplotlib and Seaborn bring data to life through visualization. Knowledge of machine learning frameworks like *sci-kit-learn, TensorFlow, and Fast.ai* enables the application of predictive models, and *SQL* remains indispensable for querying and managing vast databases. Beyond technical skills, a deep understanding of statistical methods ensures accuracy and reliability in uncovering trends, making predictions, and building models for real-world applications such as recommendation engines or fraud detection systems. Data engineers play a critical role in collecting, cleaning, and processing data, ultimately presenting clear insights that guide decision-making and drive innovation.

Machine learning scientist

A machine learning scientist specializes in designing and implementing deep learning models that enable computers to learn and adapt from data. Unlike data engineers, who often focus on analyzing data and conducting research, machine learning scientists concentrate on building and deploying models for production systems. Their work directly powers applications like GPT-4o or Gemini, where advanced models interact with real-world users in dynamic environments.

Strong proficiency in *Python* and *Jupyter Notebook* is essential for coding machine learning algorithms and managing large datasets. Expertise in frameworks such as *TensorFlow, PyTorch, or Fast.ai* provides the tools to build, train, and fine-tune models effectively. A deep understanding of algorithms, including supervised and unsupervised learning, deep learning, CNNs, transformer algorithms, and **Large Language Models (LLMs)**, forms the foundation of their work.

Responsibilities include designing, training, and deploying machine learning models, collaborating closely with data engineers to optimize performance, and monitoring models in production to ensure scalability and reliability. Staying updated with the latest advancements in AI and machine learning is also critical, allowing them to implement cutting-edge solutions that push the boundaries of what technology can achieve.

That concludes the overview of popular programming roles frequently listed on job sites. In reality, there are dozens, if not hundreds, of different job categories for programmers across a wide range of industries. The silver lining is clear: Choosing a career as a programmer opens the door to *millions of job opportunities worldwide*, making it one of the most in-demand professions of the modern era.

Passion based

There has been a noticeable shift in programming, moving away from traditional job categories. Programmers increasingly view coding as a versatile skill that can be applied to various passions and interests, such as cybersecurity, sports, medicine, health, finance, business administration, government, social media, and entertainment, among others.

For instance, a programmer passionate about sports might develop AI models to analyze game strategies. In contrast, someone interested in medicine could work on software for early disease detection. Similarly, a coder focused on social media may concentrate on creating algorithms that enhance user experience and engagement.

At first glance, aligning programming skills with a specific industry may seem to limit job opportunities. While this can be partially true, working in a field that resonates with personal interests often leads to greater job satisfaction and long-term commitment. Programmers are more likely to remain in a role when they feel connected to the purpose of their work. Pursuing a passion makes the work more enjoyable and ensures that each project is personally meaningful. This approach can transform coding from a daytime job into a deeply rewarding journey.

Since 2024, the AI for Good movement has gained significant momentum, moving from niche initiatives to a mainstream focus. At its core, AI for Good leverages artificial intelligence to address some of the world's most pressing challenges, from combating climate change and improving global healthcare to advancing education and reducing inequalities. This movement represents the intersection of technology and purpose, where innovation is about efficiency and creating meaningful social impact.

For young programmers entering the industry, AI for Good offers a unique opportunity to apply technical skills in ways that directly benefit society. It is a chance to work on projects beyond profit-driven goals, contributing to solutions like disease detection in underserved areas, optimizing renewable energy systems, or creating tools that make education accessible to millions. Focusing on this field aligns programming expertise with a greater mission, offering career growth and the satisfaction of knowing that every line of code contributes to a better, more equitable world.

Using DALL-E3, here is a figure of the career landscape concept:

Figure 9.3: *Career landscape*

Figure 9.3 illustrates the vast opportunities available for a career in programming. DALL-E3 draws the image reimagined in the 1030s Art Deco style.

With a glimpse of the career opportunities available for programmers, the next step focuses on building a clear and purposeful career path.

Career path

The journey begins with an insider's look into the chapters of this book, revealing the logical sequence of the content and the pivotal role that programmers play across various industries. Programmers are the backbone of the modern global economy, driving innovation and fostering collaboration, an essential ingredient for success. Today, the job market is filled with opportunities that emphasize how programmers fuel the 21st-century economy and the evolving landscape of AI. It is difficult to envision a world without the contributions of programmers, who shape technology and innovation at every turn.

As the chapter progresses, the emphasis shifts to discovering the career path that best aligns with individual strengths and aspirations. The possibilities are extensive, whether it involves developing cutting-edge AI systems, creating dynamic web applications, working in data science, or engineering solutions in fields such as finance, healthcare, or entertainment. Choosing the right path requires understanding personal passions, exploring sectors that resonate with you, and building the skills needed to meet the demands of those industries. Programming is not just a job. It is a gateway to shaping the future, where every career choice becomes a step toward making a meaningful impact.

For beginner programmers, the two career paths are as follows:

- Academic
- Networking

Let us go back to school.

Academic

Continuing education is essential in a field as fast-paced as technology. Programming constantly evolves, offering a variety of specializations that require ongoing learning to stay competitive. Advanced education expands career opportunities and deepens expertise, ensuring readiness for the latest advancements in the industry.

University degree programs offer comprehensive education covering advanced algorithms and systems architecture. A bachelor's, master's, or Ph.D. in computer science provides profound insights into fields such as machine learning and opens pathways to research, leadership roles, or academia.

Online courses offer high-quality instruction from universities and industry leaders in a flexible, self-paced format. Certificates obtained through these programs enhance resumes and showcase expertise in fields such as cloud computing and data science.

Coding boot camps provide intensive, hands-on training within just a few months. These programs emphasize practical skills and frequently offer career services like portfolio development and interview preparation. This option makes them excellent for individuals looking to transition to new careers or specialize in different fields. However, due to the subject's complexity, boot camps are not an option for focusing on AI.

Self-education with GPT-4o becomes particularly invaluable when formal institutions of education are not available. Besides a college degree, self-education with GPT-4o is a more effective and practical option than boot camps or passive online courses. The flexibility of this approach means learning can happen at any time and pace, making it accessible to individuals in remote areas, those with financial constraints, or anyone unable to attend traditional classes due to work or personal commitments. GPT-4o can generate personalized study plans, simulate real-world coding challenges, and offer hands-on, active learning experiences that rival conventional methods. It also allows for exploring niche topics that standard curriculums might overlook, such as emerging AI technologies or specialized algorithms.

Self-education or continuing with self-education is not just an alternative; it is a powerful and empowering choice for building expertise, gaining confidence, and remaining competitive in the rapidly evolving software and AI industry. With AI-driven tools like GPT-4 or Gemini, education is no longer limited to traditional classrooms. Instead, it becomes a dynamic and personal journey accessible to anyone with the curiosity and drive to learn.

Choosing any of these paths signals a strong commitment to professional growth. More importantly, ongoing education keeps programmers competitive in a constantly changing job market, equipping them with the tools and knowledge to adapt to new challenges and seize future opportunities in AI.

Networking

Programming is rarely an isolated profession, and building a strong professional network is essential for long-term career growth. Beyond the classroom, networking opens doors to new opportunities, provides mentorship, and keeps you connected to the latest industry trends. Collaboration with peers, attending industry events, and engaging in professional communities effectively expand connections, learn from others, and develop skills that support career advancement.

Internships and mentorships bridge the gap between academic learning and professional experience. Internships allow developers to work on real-world projects, gaining hands-on experience and valuable insights into the working culture of tech companies. Often, successful internships lead to full-time roles, but even if they do not, the connections and experience gained remain invaluable. Mentorships, on the other hand, provide personalized guidance from experienced professionals who offer career advice, feedback, and insights. These relationships can emerge through formal programs, professional networks, or reaching out to individuals whose work inspires admiration. Both internships and mentorships build technical expertise and critical soft skills, such as communication and teamwork. In California, internships are required by law to be paid positions. In other words, you learn and get paid for it.

Industry events and conferences are key opportunities for staying informed and connecting with professionals. Smaller local meetups and workshops provide intimate settings to discuss trends and collaborate on ideas, enabling meaningful, lasting connections.

Networking involves forming genuine relationships that can lead to collaborations, mentorships, or job opportunities.

Hackathons are another powerful networking and skill-building platform. These fast-paced events unite programmers, designers, and entrepreneurs to create projects under tight deadlines. Hackathons foster collaborative learning, allowing participants to work in teams, solve real-world challenges, and build tangible portfolio projects. Sponsored by major tech companies, hackathons often introduce participants to recruiters, mentors, and industry leaders, creating pathways to career opportunities. The Kaggle website lists many AI hackathons with a winning price of $50,000 to $100,000 or even a million dollars.

Professional communities offer a wealth of knowledge and opportunities. Platforms like GitHub, Stack Overflow, and Reddit host vibrant developer communities where members share expertise, solve coding problems and collaborate on open-source projects. Engaging with these communities establishes a presence in the industry and connects programmers with like-minded individuals. Social media platforms, like LinkedIn, serve as valuable tools for building networks, sharing projects, and following industry thought leaders.

Career fairs and tech events provide direct access to recruiters and hiring managers from top companies. These events allow developers to showcase their skills, submit resumes, and gain insight into hiring processes. Local networking meetups in specialized areas, such as AI or cybersecurity, create additional opportunities for connections that may lead to job referrals, freelance work, or partnerships on innovative projects.

A strong professional network supports career growth by connecting developers to mentorship, collaboration, and learning opportunities. Whether through internships, hackathons, conferences, or online communities, networking is critical in advancing a tech career. The relationships built through these channels often lead to opportunities and partnerships that help shape the future of programming careers.

Using DALL-E3, here is a figure of the career path concept.

Figure 9.4: *Career path*

Figure 9.4 illustrates the academic and network career path for a programmer. DALL-E3 draws the image reimagined in the 1030s Art Deco style.

Conclusion

This chapter marks a pivotal moment in our programming journey. Each step has added to a growing technical foundation, from learning the fundamentals of Python to building projects like a calculator, implementing sorting algorithms, and training a CNN snake image classification with real-world data. These skills were further expanded with data manipulation in Pandas, tackling real-world datasets, and exploring machine learning and model deployment. This progression built technical expertise and fostered a problem-solving mindset essential for navigating the ever-evolving programming landscape.

This journey, however, is far from over. Coding is a continuous learning process where each new project, language, or challenge adds depth and perspective. The vast coding world offers opportunities to collaborate, contribute to open-source initiatives, and explore new domains such as AI, cybersecurity, or web development. It's a dynamic field where the skills developed so far are stepping stones to even greater growth.

The career paths ahead are equally diverse. Programming skills open doors to traditional roles like software engineering and data science, leading to intersections with healthcare, education, and the arts. Coding is more than a technical ability. It is a tool for solving complex problems, driving innovation, and bridging the gap between technology and human needs. This chapter underscores how coding connects to real-world impact and how the possibilities extend beyond writing code.

As the next phase unfolds, the focus shifts to defining a path forward. Building a portfolio, pursuing certifications, contributing to collaborative platforms like GitHub, and leveraging tools such as GTP-4o are all ways to refine skills and prepare for what's ahead. The next steps will shape future opportunities and determine how this foundation is applied.

The journey of a programmer is always dynamic. It involves continuous reinvention, growth, and exploration. With the GPT-4o and Jupyter Notebook tools, mindset, and foundation now established, the future is full of possibilities. Whether the path leads to software development, machine learning, a unique area of creative coding, or AI for Good, the options are limitless. Ultimately, the decision of where to go next lies entirely with you.

Join our book's Discord space

Join the book's Discord Workspace for Latest updates, Offers, Tech happenings around the world, New Release and Sessions with the Authors:

https://discord.bpbonline.com

Index

C

D

E

www.ingramcontent.com/pod-product-compliance
Lightning Source LLC
Chambersburg PA
CBHW061802210326
41599CB00034B/6853